A MUSING -

Reflections on a wonderful life

by Colin McClatchie

FIRST EDITION

CERTIFICATE OF AUTHENTICITY

COPY 464 of 500

Nevin,

You may recognise some of the cast!

With best wishes,

Col. JB McClatchie

12th December 2019

To Claire, Amanda and Milena.

My biggest stalwarts, heroes and supporters.

A MUSING -

Reflections on a wonderful life

by Colin McClatchie

First published in October 2019

Author: Colin McClatchie

Book title: **A MUSING** - Reflections on a wonderful life
© **2019, Colin McClatchie**
Published by **Prescient, 2019.**
www.colinmcclatchie.com

Designed, printed and bound by:
William Anderson & Sons Limited
34 Loanbank Quadrant
Glasgow
G51 3HZ

www.andersonprinters.com

ISBN 9780956093370

9 780956 093370

INTRODUCTION

"Nor will any man's reputation endure very long, for what men say dies with them and is blotted out with forgetfulness of posterity." Cicero[1]

This book is about people and not just events; a memoir rather than an autobiography. As Oscar Wilde[2] said, "It is personalities not principles that move the age."

I have read many autobiographies and been fascinated by how the authors charted their life. When I first considered writing my own story, I spent some time thinking about how best to present it. As context, my main autobiographical details are presented in Appendix 1.

One of the factors which prompted me to write was how often, while attending funerals, I was astonished by some of the facts that emerged from the eulogies. I learned things about people whom I thought I knew very well, about their achievements, trials, tribulations and the challenges they had faced in their lives, but which had remained almost a secret within their close family and were only being celebrated after their death.

I feel it is important to record for posterity the detail of our lives that we would like future generations to know. I decided the basis for this book quite some time ago. At the very least, I would provide a manuscript for my two daughters Amanda[3] and Milena[4], giving them their family history and what Claire[5] and I have done with our lives. Happily, while working on the book, many people have said they would like a copy, which encouraged me to think about publishing it.

Along the way and with much effort I have been able to construct a family tree going back as far as my great-grandfather and I feel enriched by the knowledge of my family's history. Needless to say, there remain many gaps and unanswered questions.

The male line of the McClatchie family will disappear after the death of my brother's son Iain[6]. I have two daughters and my brother has one son and one daughter. His son has three daughters, hence the eventual end of that line. I stress that the motivation for writing this book is not to record the small part of the McClatchie ancestry our family comprises, but to reflect on a wonderful and fulfilling life. I have enjoyed almost every moment of it and I hope to continue to do so for some time yet. As someone once said, "do not resent growing old, many are denied the privilege."

---

[1] Cicero 106–43 BC, De re publica, written in six books 54–51 BC
[2] Oscar Wilde, 1854-1900, Irish poet and playwright
[3] Amanda Olivia McClatchie, b. 13th December 1983
[4] Milena Kate McClatchie, b. 6th July 1986
[5] Claire Olivia McClatchie (née. McConaghy) my wife.
[6] Iain Richard Tyrone McClatchie, b.1969, m. Martha Kodis, 3d. Anya, Kathleen and Ava, developer High-Resolution Airborne Cameras

I am also extremely grateful that I have lived a rich life full of love, variety, and satisfaction and I have learned a lot along the way. As Muhammad Ali[7] said, "A man who views the world the same at 50 as he did at 20 has just wasted 30 years of his life." Life is the most precious commodity of all and is to be savoured and enjoyed.

I have never been one to look back – the present and, most importantly, the future are much more significant. As a result of meeting the famous Indian business guru and philosopher Jadish Parikh[8] at INSEAD[9] in France in 1994, I subsequently drew up a modus operandi which I have followed ever since. We can have no influence over the past, the present becomes the past in an instant and so the only thing that we can influence in our lives is the future. As Parikh puts it, "Today is the first day of the rest of your life. Yesterday is a dream and tomorrow is a vision. Today well lived, as if it is the only one you have, makes every yesterday a dream of happiness and every tomorrow a vision of hope." Life is about making things happen, where anticipation turns to realisation. In addition, as Benjamin Franklin[10] said, "there are only two things certain in life, death and taxes." Cicero suggested that we accept life as a loan given by nature without a due date and that repayment may be demanded at any time.

When I started writing this book, I decided not to have an index at the back. I wanted to provide some brief biographical details of most of those mentioned. These notes would appear at the bottom of each page, enabling the reader to see them by glancing downwards, rather than having to turn constantly to the back of the book. The second reason I pinched from Piers Morgan[11]. Quoted in The Times about newspaper boss Les Hinton[12] he said, "I told Les that [having no index] is worth a thousand copies, people can't browse in bookshops to see if they're mentioned – they have to buy it."

I have used a number of abbreviations/ acronyms throughout the book. I list them in Appendix 2 to help readers in case they miss them when they first appear.

As I started writing I had three issues. Firstly, I am not famous, so who would buy my book? I only made it into 'Who's Who in Scotland' in 1998 as a result of my own initiative. One of my key tasks at News International was to increase the company's profile in Scotland and one way I could do this was by increasing my own profile, so I submitted a tentative entry to 'Who's Who in Scotland'. It was accepted and I have appeared in it ever since.

The second issue was the vagueness of some of my recollections of my early years. The chapters on my childhood and education are therefore mercifully brief.

The third issue for me was whether I would be able to write and, more importantly, write anything of substance? Fortunately, I have always been a hoarder and from an

---

[7] Muhammad Ali, 1942-2016, a.k.a. Cassius Clay, American boxer and activist
[8] 'Managing Your Self', 1991 Jadish Parikh, Blackwell Press
[9] INSEAD, The European Business School, Fontainebleau, France
[10] Benjamin Franklin, 1706-90, Founding Father of the United States
[11] Piers Morgan, b.1965, British journalist, TV personality, 'celebrity'
[12] Les Hinton, b.1944, Executive Chairman News International 1995-2007

early age kept memorabilia of anything that I had attended or been involved with. After university and at the start of my newspaper career this extended to keeping diaries, programmes of events and even the occasional file note of important occurrences. During my Maxwell and Murdoch years, the collection grew to include seating plans, letters and even more file notes. Before starting the book, I reviewed and sorted everything and ended up with one box, sometimes flimsy, for each year since 1966. It was tremendously helpful in the preparation for starting the book.

As it turned out, I was able almost immediately to find a regime that worked for me and served me well. A lengthy discussion on the subject with Maggie McKernan[13] some time ago was incredibly useful. On her advice I didn't start from the year I was born and work from there. She suggested picking topics, almost at random, starting with those which were perhaps the easiest to recall, rather than writing chronologically.

My regime started before I went to sleep at night, when I reviewed and thought about the topic which I was going to write about the following morning. I did this for no more than ten minutes and would get up at 6:15 am, ready to start writing at 6:30 – just the dog and I with no interruptions. I could write productively, have a coffee and continue until 9:00 am. After that, the newspapers would arrive, the phone would start ringing and I found that I just could not get back into the zone. I wrote by hand and the biggest bonus was that, when I was in the zone, the material flowed. Almost spontaneously I recalled situations that I hadn't remembered until I started writing about them. My guess is that those 10 minutes before going to sleep enabled subliminal thoughts to form throughout the night. Finally, I had my scrawled notes typed up by Jamie Eatock[14], Claire edited them and, somehow, we had our first draft. For those interested in logistics, the exercise eventually accounted for almost 2000 handwritten pages, using over 20 rollerball pens and resulted in twelve separate drafts consuming over 50,000 sheets of paper.

Along the way, many people have helped jog my memory and my thanks go to all of them. They, however, are not responsible for the opinions that I have expressed throughout the book. Finally, any faults, errors, or misjudgements are entirely mine.

---

[13] Maggie McKernan, literary agent and Editor at Large, Head of Zeus Publishing
[14] Jamie Eatock, b. 2000, medical student, The University of St Andrews

Introduction   Page no: **3**

Contents   **6**

Part I: **Childhood and Teens**

    1.   Family History   **9**
    2.   Schooldays   **17**
    3.   Growing Up in Northern Ireland   **25**
    4.   Student Days - Queen's University Belfast   **35**
    5.   Early Travel in the 50s and 60s   **43**

Part II: **The Thomson Regional Newspapers Years 1971-1984**

    6.   TRN Graduate Traineeship 1971-73   **49**
    7.   First Real Job - Belfast Telegraph 1973-78   **57**
    8.   TRN Group Role 1978-79   **69**
    9.   Jingling in Geordieland - Newcastle 1979-81   **73**
    10.   Rocking in Reading 1981-84   **77**
    11.   A Brief Encounter - The Scotsman 16-30th January 1984 **81**

Part III: **The Scottish Daily Record Years 1984-1994**

    12.   Moving to Scotland   **93**
    13.   SDR - The Early Years   **99**
    14.   Introduction to Maxwell   **115**
    15.   Maxwell vs. SDR Unions   **125**
    16.   Dealing with Maxwell   **133**
    17.   Maxwell Free Newspapers 1989-94   **139**
    18.   The Sunday Scot 1991   **145**
    19.   Maxwell - A Final Assessment   **151**
    20.   Administration and Montgomery   **161**
    21.   'Normal' Life at SDR   **167**
    22.   SDR - The Final Chapter 1994   **173**
    23.   INSEAD October 1994   **179**
    24.   Marketing Consultant 1994-95   **181**

Part IV: **The News International Years 1995-2007**

25.   Headhunted 1995   195
26.   Early Days at NI 1995-96   199
27.   Early Battles   203
28.   Kinning Park Refurbishment   207
29.   Industrial Relations at NI   211
30.   Let Battle Commence   215
31.   The Influence of Rupert   221
32.   The Newspaper Press Fund   225
33.   Rupert Murdoch - An Assessment   235
34.   Legal Anecdotes   241
35.   Continuing the Battle   245
36.   Establishing Marketing Leadership   251
37.   Plan B - First Steps in a Non-Executive World   257
38.   NI in Dublin   269
39.   Leaving NI January 2007   277
40.   Decline of the Newspaper Sector   281

Part V: **The Rest of My Life 2001-Present**

41.   Phase 2 - Non-Executive Career   297
42.   Music and Culture   301
43.   Scottish Opera   307
44.   St Columba's School 2007-15   327
45.   The Global Irish Network   229

Part VI: **Sport**
46.   Golf - The Most Beautiful Game   347
47.   The Future of Golf   363
48.   Football   371
49.   Rugby and Piers   381

Part VII: **Family**
50.   Family Life   387
51.   Charity   395
52.   Royalty and the Reptiles   399
53.   Reflections on the Future   411

Acknowledgements   419
Appendix 1 - Autobiographical Details   420
Appendix 2 - Glossary of Acronyms   421

Website and how to order additional copies   422

Chapter 1   FAMILY HISTORY

"It is a curious phenomenon that autobiographers seem to have a detailed recall of their early years, and readers are content to be intrigued by interminable details of idyllic or (you take pot luck) ghastly childhoods. Maybe autobiographers get away with mind-deadening minutiae about their early years because, since they are writing relatively late in life, few people from their formative years are around to contradict them." Giles Gordon[1]

In the climax to 'Les Misérables', Jean Valjean famously asks, "Who am I?" Well, I am Colin James Stewart McClatchie. 'Colin' comes from the Gaelic 'Cailean' meaning Young Wolf and has the following profile, 'Relishes a challenge; he sees life as an adventure to be enjoyed to the full; always the optimist.' As the years progressed, I always felt that this was an accurate description of my persona – the reader can make their own assessment! I am an Ulsterman and also Irish. There are only two kinds of people in the world - the Irish and those who wish they were. At the time of writing, I have spent 28 of my 70 years in Northern Ireland, ten in England, and the remaining 32 in Scotland. I am also British (which may give you a clue to my views on Scottish Independence), but in rugby I will support Ireland to my dying day. I still speak with the same accent (broadish Ulster) as I had in my formative years and, indeed, I am suspicious of people who try to conceal their origins. Someone once described me as being of "mixed ethnicity" and I suspect they meant it slightly disparagingly. If that is what I am, I see it as a virtue, as I am extremely proud of where I come from.

I was born at 7.05am on 1st Jan 1949. My arrival at Johnston House, the maternity wing of the Royal Victoria Hospital in Belfast, was not the first birth of that year according to the local papers, so no early accolade in life for me then. I was the second son of James Richard Graham McClatchie[2] and Kathleen Rose[3] – Jimmy and Kay to their friends. My brother Ted[4], seven years older than me, was also born in Belfast. My father worked throughout his life for the Ulster Bank and in 1949 was based in the Shankill Road branch in Belfast. He had started as a teller at the bank's Belfast head office, where he met my mother. She was the book keeper for her father's nearby business. They were married in 1938. We lived in Castle Avenue in the north of the city, just off the Antrim Road. My recollection of my early childhood in Belfast does not extend beyond recalling being wheeled in my pram. My father was promoted to Senior Cashier in the Portadown, County Armagh branch of the bank and we moved there in 1952.

Academically, my brother Ted was always streets ahead of me. Educated at Portadown College, he emerged as one of their brightest pupils, with the third best

---

[1] Giles Gordon, 1940-2003, literary agent and author, 'Aren't We Due a Royalty Statement?' 1993, Chatto and Windus
[2] James Richard Graham McClatchie, 1907-76, father
[3] Kathleen Rose McClatchie (née. Barr), 1911-88, mother
[4] Dr Edward Alexander McClatchie, b. 1941, brother

set of exam results in Northern Ireland. He studied Physics at Queen's University Belfast (QUB), graduating with first-class honours and completing a PhD in Nuclear Physics at Westfield College, London. He also worked at the Rutherford Laboratory in Harwell, Oxfordshire. He and Adeline[5] were married on 3rd April 1967 and shortly afterwards they set off for California, where they have lived ever since. Adeline worked in the children's hospital in Oakland and Ted became a post-doctoral fellow at the University of California, Berkeley, working at the Lawrence Radiation Laboratory. The University's Physics and Chemistry Faculty was a world-class institution at that time, with 11 Nobel Prize winners on the staff. Ted and Adeline eventually settled in Orinda, about 10 miles east of Berkeley and had two children, Iain and Sharon[6].

At the end of 1969, Ted was enticed into the private sector and joined Andros, a technology company, as a research physicist. Over the next 15+ years, Ted helped Andros become a world leader in the manufacture of infrared gas analysers, primarily used to monitor exhaust emissions and medical anaesthetic levels. Having established a very successful company, he decided to retire in mid-1996, joined the El Cerrito Country Club to play golf and after six months was totally bored. As he said, "There is a limit to the number of days on which you want to play golf." He returned to corporate life, first as an independent consultant and then, shortly afterwards, joined another start-up company Crestline and worked there for the next 18 years, before semi-retiring aged 74 after life-threatening cancer surgery. True to form, he is still working as an independent consultant.

As I was growing up I had little awareness of our family history. Three of my four grandparents were already dead and my maternal grandmother died when I was seven (hers was the first corpse I'd ever seen – and its image stayed in my mind for a long time). Beyond that, I knew very little about my family and I cannot recall any conversation of significance with my parents on the subject.

Until I started researching this book, the only fact I was aware of was that Edward Alexander, my father's oldest brother, had died during the First World War. I was aware of him through a few medals and a telegram from the King notifying his parents of his death. He died aged 20 in 1917, just before the Battle of Passchendaele. My father never mentioned his name or talked about him. My brother, named after him, established that he was buried in the Mendingham War Cemetery in Belgium and had visited his grave some 65 years after his death. I have subsequently researched Edward Alexander extensively. His early death and the impact of it on his family was probably typical of the 979,498 British and Allied casualties of the First World War (or The Great War as it was called – what a terribly insensitive phrase). He enlisted in Belfast, supposedly aged 18. Why Belfast when he lived in Portrush, some 50 miles away? A brief war biographer's note on him suggests, "It was probably something to do with still being a student and deciding to go with a bunch of friends and put on a big show of bravado. The family at home would never

---

[5] Adeline Dorothy McClatchie (née Clingan) LCST, D. Aud., b.1941, speech therapist and audiologist
[6] Sharon Lynn Kerry McClatchie, b.1971, m. Max Beckwith, 1d. Brooke 1s. Blake, Chief Executive Officer, MD Review

have approved it and so it was much easier to go with a crowd of mates, get the job done and admit it afterwards." One suspects the enlisters were not overly fussy on where future cannon fodder came from or, as we shall see later, what age they were. Ted was 5'8" tall, weighed just 10 stones and when he died had just been appointed on a temporary commission as a Second Lieutenant in the 10th Battalion, Royal Inniskillen Fusiliers. He died on the 10th August 1917 and an eye witness account reads, "We had just gone into the trench and were settling down to spend three days in it when a bombardment suddenly started and we all rushed to our posts. While your son was going into the part of the line where his platoon was, a heavy shell landed on the parapet. A piece of the shell hit Edward on the head besides killing eight men and wounding many others. He never regained consciousness."

The 10th Battalion's official war diary from Ypres on 10th August 1917 reads, "Between 4 and 5am, the enemy put up a barrage on our Front Line. Our Artillery retaliated effectively. All day, enemy aircraft were very busy. During the day, two of our aeroplanes were forced to land, one far over the enemy's line and one in No Man's Land, quite convenient to our 'B-Boys HQ'. They were driven down by the enemy. The balloons of each side were raised during the greater part of the day. Our casualties today were; F. Lt. A. Bryan, Sgt. Stuart, Sgt. Sinclair, killed. 2nd Lt. E. A. McClatchie, seriously wounded (he died in hospital 11/8). 2 other ranks (O.R.s) gassed, 10 O.R.s wounded. 10 O.R.s proceeded to UK on leave."

In researching the family history I had an enormous slice of luck very early on. The internet has made the task of establishing family roots so much easier, but there is also the world of professional genealogists, an extremely lucrative business. My good fortune occurred in 2015 when I received a letter from a Bath genealogical company, tracing relatives of a Miss Jean McClatchie. They had been instructed "to identify and locate potential beneficiaries to the estate." Understandably, curiosity led me contacting said firm and established that all they were asking me to do at this stage was to confirm my identity. Almost two years passed and curiosity led me to contact them again. This time I established that the details had been passed on and they provided me with the contact details of a solicitor in Portadown, County Armagh. The solicitor helpfully told me that in Jean McClatchie's will, after all her main instructions had been carried out, there remained a sum of £13,000 to go to her nearest dependants. Establishing who these nearest dependants were, as the will didn't specify them, was the task of the genealogical company. I asked how the £13,000 had been dispersed and was told that the cost of establishing who the beneficiaries were and the solicitor's own fees had accounted for the entire sum and that nothing remained. The solicitor was quite open about this and told me that the bulk of the costs had been incurred by the genealogical company. My good fortune was that the solicitor agreed to send me the detailed findings of their research. They had established the McClatchie family tree going back as far as my great-grandfather. It was a stroke of good fortune in that I now had most of the information that I wanted on the McClatchie family, but it is questionable whether it was such good fortune for the rest of the potential McClatchie beneficiaries. Note to us all - check your will (if you have one; if not make one) and ensure that your instructions as to who benefits from your estate are clear and unambiguous.

I was extremely grateful to have a complete McClatchie family tree. It went back to my great-grandfather James, who married Jane Calvin in 1841. The McClatchies originally came from the townland of Mullalelish, near Richhill in County Armagh. They had eight children - Richard, George, James, Susan, John (my grandfather), Mary-Anne, Joseph and Alexander (father of Jean). Four of them married, two of them to Troughtons. Like the McClatchies, the Troughton family were also from Mullalelish. During the course of my research I established that Mullalelish at one stage had been nicknamed 'Troughtonsville', so predominant was the family there. My grandfather John McClatchie[7] married Mary-Jane Troughton but, unlike other members of the family, they moved away from Richhill. John was a school teacher and he moved to Portrush, County Antrim where he became headmaster of The Kelly Memorial School. Both the 1901 and the 1911 census show him residing at 10 Victoria Street, Portrush, so I can say with reasonable certainty that that was where my father was born in 1907. They later moved to Ardeen, 159 Ballywillan Road and they died in 1944 (Mary-Jane) and 1946 (John) and are buried in Ballywillan Cemetery on the outskirts of Portrush.

Evidence of John's talents is contained in a document that I came across, "Mr. McClatchie was one of the best teachers in the Coleraine District having now won the Carlisle and Blake Premium for the second time, this being the Blue Riband of the teaching profession in the Coleraine District." John and Mary-Jane had four children - Edward Alexander b. 1897 and John William (Jack) b.1905[8], a chemist who eventually ran a pharmacy in Ballywalter, County Down. He married Belinda Armstrong and had one daughter, Diane. The third child was my father, James Richard Graham born 25th April 1907. Finally a daughter, Jeanie Margaret Eileen Annie[9] (a formidable combination of Christian names!) born in 1909, a teacher. She married Jim Crowe and had one son John and a daughter Norah. Edward Alexander was educated at Ballymena Academy, my father at Coleraine Academical Institution (CAI), and Eileen at Coleraine High School. Jack's school is unknown.

One mystery surrounds part of Edward Alexander Senior's life - his date of birth. The family had always understood it to be 12th February 1898, but all Edward's war records indicated that he was born in 1897. This was confirmed by the documents from the Portadown solicitor. It confirmed his date of birth as 12th February 1897. My cousin Diane's husband David Stockham[10] had also done some work on the family history and had secured copies of the 1901 and 1911 censuses. This was recorded in April of each decade and Edward's family had listed him as three and 12 years old respectively, indicating that he was born sometime between April 1897 and April 1898 and so could not have been born on 12th February 1897 as his war records

---

[7] John McClatchie, 1865- 1946, schoolteacher and latterly Headmaster, Kelly Memorial School, Portrush, County Antrim, m. Mary-Jane (née Troughton), 1873-1944

[8] John William (Jack) McClatchie, 1905-65, chemist, m. Belinda (neé Armstrong) 1915-99 1d. Diane

[9] Jeanie Margaret Eileen Annie McClatchie, 1909-87, schoolteacher, m. 1937, Jim Crowe, 1903-92, factory manager, 1s. John 1d. Norah

[10] David Stockham, b.1935, Inspector, Birmingham Police m. Diane (née McClatchie) 1s. Christopher, 1d. Caroline.

showed. His death certificate contradicts this and it was only when I re-examined it that I realised that all the details of those killed in the First World War were registered not by their family as would normally be the case, but by the War Ministry, which of course believed that Edward was born in 1897.

We will never learn why Edward Alexander McClatchie added a year to his age when he joined up. The obvious reason was that he wasn't old enough when he enlisted, or perhaps, as he was only 17, his parents' permission would have been required, especially if he wanted to be considered for a commission. The final twist to the tale was that his gravestone records his true age. One can only assume that his family had been contacted by the Commonwealth War Graves Commission and had clarified the discrepancy of his date of birth.

My mother's side of the family has been more difficult to piece together, but is no less fascinating than my father's in terms of unanswered questions. She was born Kathleen Rose Barr on 17th August 1911, the only daughter of the four children of William Stewart Barr and Rose Edna McKinney. Her parents were from Beragh, County Tyrone and Ballymoney, County Antrim respectively and lived at 354 Lisburn Road in Belfast, where William ran a food wholesaling business at Divis Street. My mother was the second born and her three brothers were John Stewart[11], Harold Orr[12] and William Stewart[13]. Interestingly the name Stewart appears often in not only both my father's and mother's families but also in Claire's family, the McConaghys.

All three boys were educated at Royal Belfast Academical Institution (RBAI) and my mother at Victoria College in Belfast. The Barrs were deeply religious – all were brought up as Plymouth Brethren.

John Stewart studied Medicine at the Royal Society of Surgeons in Dublin and went on to become a GP, firstly in Wakefield in Yorkshire and subsequently in Lakenheath, Suffolk. He had one daughter, Noreen Nicole Stewart[14]. He died in poor health there at the early age of 47. The fourth brother Stewart, like my father, joined the Ulster Bank and served in Belfast, Crumlin and Downpatrick. He had one son Christopher Stewart[15]. My mother worked in the family business, as did Harold for a relatively short period of time.

It seems that for Harold, taking over the family business did not appeal and, whether from a sense of youthful adventure, the increasing likelihood of war, or most likely the possibly questionable future of the business, he chose not to follow in his father's footsteps. Divis Street was on the front line in an already divided Belfast and, even then, would not have been a particularly peaceful billet. Harold wanted no part of it and left Northern Ireland in 1936, never to return. He went to what was then Southern Rhodesia and, at the onset of World War II, signed up in the Southern

---

[11] John Stewart Barr, 1906-53, GP Lakenheath Suffolk
[12] Harold Orr Barr, 1910-90, tobacco farmer, Harare, Zimbabwe
[13] William Stewart Barr, 1912-98, bank manager m. Joan (née Anderson) 1924-2014, 1s. Christopher
[14] Noreen Nicole Stewart (Niki) Barr, b. 5 July 1941, sister
[15] Christopher Stewart Barr, b. 1954, solicitor

Rhodesian army and fought in the Desert campaign in North Africa – interestingly alongside one Ian Smith, later to become Prime Minister of the country. After the war he managed a tobacco farm outside Salisbury, the capital.

Growing up I can remember Harold's letters back home – usually no more than two or three per year. His correspondence was brief and never very informative – no mention of friends, girlfriends or anything like that. There would be some talk about farming, the harvest and, in the run up to independence, comment on the troubled political situation and concern over the future of the newly created Zimbabwe. Over time the letters became less frequent and in the last few years consisted only of a Christmas card inscribed, "With love to all, Harold". They stopped altogether around 1990. By this time my mother had died and my uncle Stewart became increasingly concerned about Harold, particularly as they had taken out a life insurance policy which had now matured and he wanted Harold to have his share.

Harold's niece Niki and her husband Sam Moore[16], who planned to visit South Africa in 1992, agreed to try to solve the mystery by visiting Zimbabwe during their trip. They eventually found his last known address and went there to be greeted by a black woman. They asked if Harold had lived there, and on establishing that he had, asked to see him. They were brought through to the rear of the house and into the back garden where the woman showed them his gravestone.

Sam and Niki were at last able to unravel Harold's history. The lady who had opened the door was his wife Blandina. She was born a Roman Catholic and was of mixed race from the Shona and Matabele tribes. She and Harold met soon after his arrival in Rhodesia, had lived together and had five children - three boys, Edward, Terrence and Shepherd, and two girls, Diane and Norma. At a stroke the McClatchie quota of cousins had significantly increased! Because of Zimbabwe's apartheid system Harold and Blandina had been unable to marry until 1967. Harold had died aged 80 in 1990. Blandina showed Niki and Sam many of his personal effects and correspondence. They were able to discharge their duty and hand over Harold's share of the life insurance policy and Niki and Blandina continued to correspond for many years until the latter's death.

As I suspect with most families, there still remain unanswered questions. Why had Harold never communicated any of this to his family back home? Did he think that having a black, Catholic wife and children born out of wedlock would have been met by disapproval by his family in the Northern Ireland he had left in 1936? Did he not want them to know about his relationship, or indeed was he ashamed of it? Why did he never return with his family to visit his homeland? I found all this perplexing and deeply sad. Were the prejudices and bigotry that existed in Northern Ireland so very different from what he must have encountered in Rhodesia, where black and white were unable to marry until 1967? Whatever the reason, he made a judgement that his family back home would not be told. Curiously we had been visited sometime in the 1980s by two distant cousins David and Colleen Barr, who lived in

---

[16] Sam Moore OBE, b.1932, agricultural engineer, inventor of the Moore Unidrill

Harare. I remember them staying with us for a few days in Portadown and never once did they mention Harold's situation.

The life of my mother's eldest brother John is perhaps the saddest of all, albeit that it eventually had a happy outcome. John was a GP in Lakenheath in Suffolk and in 1940 married a Belgian, Nellie Decock[17]. Her family ran a chicory factory nearby and were originally from Roulers, near Brussels. John and Nellie's daughter Noreen Nicole Stewart was born on 5th July 1941. Niki's first two years were probably the only period of stability in her life until she reached 18. Her father joined the Royal Army Medical Corps and was part of the D-Day invasion in 1944. At the end of the war he was part of the medical team which discovered the Belsen Concentration Camp.

Shortly after he joined up, his wife met another man, took Niki to Belfast, deposited her with her grandparents and went off to live with the other man. Niki never saw her mother again except for two short meetings when she was around 14. My parents realised that living with two by now elderly grandparents was not ideal and so she moved to live with them in 1944. When she reached school age, her father arranged for her to attend boarding school, first in Bury St. Edmund's in Suffolk and then from age ten at Frinton-on-Sea in Essex. After the war she returned to live with her father and his housekeeper during school holidays. His health began to deteriorate and he eventually married his housekeeper Eileen Beaumont in November 1953 but died on 5th March 1954, aged just 47. Niki then stayed with the housekeeper, who remarried and had a child.

At this stage my parents and Niki's grandmother intervened and a battle royal raged between the two families over her future, eventually leading to her being made a Ward of Court. In the short term, she spent her summers with her grandmother in Belgium and Christmas and Easter holidays with my parents in Portadown. One day during a summer in Belgium, her grandmother took her to an apartment in Brussels, which she said belonged to a friend of hers, and whilst there Niki discovered a picture of herself on a bedside table. The apartment belonged to her mother. Her grandmother then suggested that Niki might meet her mother, which she did twice, when she was around 14. As she herself now says, her mother was by then a complete stranger to her, she knew nothing about her and, most importantly, felt nothing for her. She regarded my mother and father as her parents and the love and security that they had given her mattered more than anything else. I remember going with my parents to pick her up from her last term at school at Frinton, packing her trunk in the back of the car and returning to Portadown. In July 1959, this was the start of her life as a fully-fledged member of the McClatchie family. Her own mother, having become involved in yet another relationship, sadly committed suicide in 1958. That autumn Niki enrolled as a student nurse in the Royal Victoria Hospital in Belfast and subsequently qualified as a State Registered Nurse. She

---

[17] Nellie Paul Hélène Rachel Decock, 1922-58

married Sam Moore in December 1962 and had three children, Sammy[18], Karen[19] and Lynnie[20].

What can I say about Niki? If there were ever an example of how a horrendous childhood might have derailed a young girl, she has to be a prime example. Yet she went on to be one of the kindest and most considerate people I have ever met, forever helping those less fortunate than herself. Ted and I wholeheartedly welcomed her into our family and, since she first arrived over 60 years ago, we have regarded her as our sister. More importantly, from that moment our family became five and as tightly knit a unit as it had been when it was four.

---

[18] Sammy Moore, b. 1964, m. Elaine (née. McMaster), 1993, 1d. Elle 1s. Stewart
[19] Karen Nicola Stewart Moore, b.1966, m. Michael Tracey 1999, 2s. Aaron, Paul
[20] Lynda Hélène Moore, b. 1970, m. Kevin Brackfield 2003, 1d. Alex 1s. Isaac

Chapter 2   SCHOOLDAYS

"My school days were the happiest days of my life which should give you some indication of the misery I have endured over the past twenty-five years."
Paul Merton[1]

My first recollection of matters educational was not my first day at school, but rather being surrounded by lots of young school girls - perhaps a forerunner for my everlasting interest in the opposite sex!

My mother used to take me out each afternoon in my pram. When I was just starting to talk we would pass a local girls' primary school, whose pupils wore green uniforms. Some of my first words were "the green girls, the green girls," much to my mother's delight. My reader may be amazed at such early talent.

We moved to Portadown in County Armagh in early 1952 and rented a house called Lylo Villa about two miles outside town. Just under four, I went to a small local school, Bluestone Primary. It had two teachers and classes were divided between two relatively large rooms, with around 25 pupils in each. My only memory there is of a large picnic in a nearby field in June 1953, celebrating the Queen's coronation.

I have little other recollection of that time, except that I walked home each day and had to pass a house with a particularly vicious dog. I was afraid it was going to attack me each time I passed and I suspect that, the more terrified I was, the more the dog sensed it. I don't think it ever bit me, but it would be lying in wait for me each day and growled and barked before chasing me up the road. Fortunately, this early experience did not scar me and in later years as a family we always had a dog. I remained at Bluestone for only two or three years and then moved on to Edenderry Primary School in Portadown.

There was a brief interruption to my primary school education. In late 1956 my mother had a major operation, which necessitated a lengthy recuperation, during which I stayed with my uncle and aunt Jim and Eileen Crowe at Upperlands, County Londonderry. I attended Ampertaine Primary School for 4 - 6 weeks and my cousin Norah[2] remembers getting me word-perfect for a poem that I had to recite to my class.

> You are old Father William, the young man said,
> And your hair has become extremely white,
> And yet you incessantly stand on your head,
> Do you think at your age this is right?
>
> In my youth, said the sage, as he shook his grey locks,
> I kept all my limbs very supple,
> By the use of this ointment, one shilling a box,
> Allow me to sell you a couple?[3]

---

[1] Paul Merton b. 1947, English writer, actor and comedian
[2] Norah Crowe, b. 1942, m. 1968 Jackson Grahame, b. 1940, farmer 2d.
[3] 'Alice's Adventures in Wonderland', Lewis Carroll

I then went to senior school at Portadown College, which my brother Ted also attended. Here I achieved my Junior Certificate at 13. I had completed two terms of O levels when my father was promoted and I had to change school. My experience at Portadown College, unlike that of Ted, was wholly negative. I have very few happy memories of the place and, sadly, little recollection of any of my classmates. I am grateful to Adeline's sister Stella[4] for helping me research some of the details of my time there. She was even able to find an early Limerick contributed by me in my third year there, and published in the school magazine in 1962.

> An enormous policeman from Asuncion,
> Attempted to swallow his truncheon
> When he was asked, "Are you mad?'
> He said, 'No but I have had,
> Not nearly enough food for my luncheon!

Unfortunately, by the time I left Portadown College, almost half way through my secondary education, my future career had already been shaped by my having had to give up several critical subjects. Despite there being an outstanding Principal, Donald Woodman[5], this was the result of the efforts, or rather the lack of them, of several mediocre teachers.

Ted went on to be a brilliant physicist and mathematician. Unfortunately, my interest in the sciences was negated by one teacher. Miss "Peg" Fleming[6] was a Chemistry teacher and had written me off almost from my first day in class. I recently learnt that Ted and Adeline also regarded Peg as one of the worst teachers they had ever had. Another subject in which I had similar treatment was music. Not only did the teacher "Nellie" Knox[7] take an instant dislike to me, but I was frequently forced to stand in the back corner of the classroom, very much the "dunce" of the class. This humiliating treatment, although deeply unpleasant at the time, did not have the intended effect and I have retained a deep love and appreciation of music to this day.

I dropped science from my curriculum for O Level examinations, but fortunately my move to Coleraine Academical Institution (CAI) in County Londonderry meant that I eventually emerged from the secondary school system with nine reasonable O Levels and five A Levels of sufficiently high grades to go on to university. None of the credit for this is due to Portadown College - least of all to Peg or Nellie!

As I mentioned, my father was promoted in 1963 and became Manager of the Ulster Bank in Killyleagh in County Down. He took up his new post just after Easter that year and there was considerable discussion about my future education. It was decided that I should go as a boarder to CAI, my father's old school. He had been a day pupil, as he lived in nearby Portrush.

---

[4] Stella Clingan, b. 1944, schoolteacher, m. Ernie McCann, b. 1944, architect
[5] Donald Woodman BEM BA, Headmaster, Portadown College 1946-73
[6] Miss Margaret 'Peg' Fleming, Chemistry teacher, Portadown College, retired 1974
[7] Miss Eleanor 'Nellie' Knox. Music teacher, Portadown College 1945-82

This would have been a major decision for my parents and, although CAI was a non-fee paying grammar school, the boarding fees would have represented a considerable expense for them. As in many of the decisions they made about their family, my parents always put us first, wanting to give my brother, sister and me the best possible start in life and I am eternally grateful to them for that.

CAI was one of the best schools in Northern Ireland. It was boys only and the school roll was roughly half day pupils and half boarders. About half the boarders were from within Northern Ireland, a quarter from the Irish Republic - principally Donegal - and a quarter from England and overseas, particularly from many parts of what was then still a very significant British Empire. The school had an impressive reputation academically and also a very strong tradition in sport. All was presided over by a formidable headmaster, Dr George "Plug" Humphreys[8] whose son George[9] married Claire's cousin Deirdre Houston.

In contrast with Portadown College, I had an extremely happy time at Coleraine. I quickly adapted to the discipline of boarding school - a much more regimented regime than I'd previously been used to. It was also a far more hierarchical system and the school prefects wielded considerable power, with the right to discipline pupils, including administering physical punishment. A belting on the buttocks with a slipper was the order of the day, with a belief that "a good belting never did anyone any harm." I never received any excessive beltings and a well-placed magazine down the back of the trousers minimised any discomfort.

There was a strict system for leave at CAI. In addition to the half term break, there were three all day Saturday passes per term. Logistically my parents were unable to visit for the day passes, but I was well looked after by my uncle and aunt James and Maud Campbell[10] at Ballyliken Farm, Bushmills. These treasured days, shared with my four cousins John[11], Noel[12], Mary Rose[13] and Alistair[14] are best remembered for their excellent lunches and the restocking of my tuckbox – an essential element of boarding school life. Aunt Maud was a Cordon Bleu cook and had attended the Edinburgh School of Cookery and Domestic Economy, so the quality of the fare at both Ballyliken and in my tuckbox was first class. Food at CAI was adequate but, although wholesome, was pretty dull and ordinary by today's standards. I arrived at CAI a fussy eater, but left able to face most food out of sheer necessity. It took some years for my palate to become more discerning.

James Campbell's brother Jack[15] was also a farmer and he and his wife Tilly lived at Carncullogh, near Dervock. They had two children Shaun[16] and Zara[17]. Zara was an excellent hockey player and had been picked for the Irish squad in early 1963. Sadly, tragedy struck in December 1962 when, aged 18, she was travelling in the back of a car, on someone's knee, when it struck ice and overturned. Zara's neck was broken and she was to spend over a year at Stoke Mandeville Hospital before returning to

[8] Dr George 'Plug' Humphreys 1915-97, Headmaster, CAI 1955-71
[9] George Humphreys b.1944 m. Deirdre (née Houston) b.1945 3s. 2d.
[10] James Campbell 1913-87, farmer m. Maud (nee Connolly) 1907-77
[11] John Campbell, 1940-2011, farmer
[12] Noel Campbell, b. 1942, banker
[13] Mary Rose Campbell, b. 1947, m. Alex Corry, banker
[14] Alistair Campbell, b. 1949, banker, latterly horticulturist
[15] Jack Campbell, 1909-970, farmer (m. Tilly Campbell, née. Haughey, 1912-90)
[16] Shaun Campbell, b. 1940, farmer
[17] Zara Campbell, 1944-2018

Northern Ireland. Until her death in October 2018, Zara was believed to be the UK's longest surviving quadriplegic. During those 56 years, her spirits were remarkable and she never ever complained about what had happened to her. Niki became one of her closest friends and visited her every week for almost 50 years. Zara asked for a message to be read out at her funeral - two sentences from Yeats[18] that she said had been lodged in her heart, her brain, and her soul for countless years;

> Think where man's glory most begins and ends,
> And say my glory was I had such friends.

I must have shown leadership qualities at CAI, as I was appointed a prefect and Head of House for the "Model" Boarding House in my last year. The other House prefects were Rowan Bell[19], Alan Irwin[20] and Derek Torrens[21]. Extra rations were much sought after, often provided by parents or, in most cases, visits to Coleraine on Saturday afternoons. The four of us identified a clear market gap between supply and demand and, using considerable initiative (and despite the high level of risk), we set up an illicit in-house tuck shop. We knew a day boy whose parents had an account at a nearby Cash and Carry and through him we bought stock, anticipating what the 60 or so boarders in our building might like to purchase. Very soon we were operating a thriving little business from our study at evening break time, selling a wide range of sweets, crisps, chocolate, toast, tea and coffee. This was all, of course, was under the noses of the masters, but because it was such a highly acclaimed success, we had a network of intelligence and a well-oiled early warning system of any impending visit from the duty master.

I thrived academically under the boarding regime, encouraged by some wonderful, inspiring teachers. My school reports reflected a middle of the class student, but a vast improvement on my Portadown College days. "Very reasonable ... sound... satisfactory...very satisfactory...very satisfactory work in progress" were repeated phrases. Under some really good teachers, history and geography suddenly became alive to me. Jim "Pop" Edwards[22] and, latterly, John Birch[23] in History and Tom "Paddy" Ryan[24] in Geography transformed these subjects. I had an equally inspiring English teacher – Hugh "The Count" Montgomery[25] - but, despite his efforts and much to my regret in later life, I never mastered the subject and a whole raft of literature was lost to me. Robert "Pop" Riddle[26] managed to get me over the line in Pure and Applied Maths. The Count also introduced me to Drama and in my final year, when he directed the school play, he appointed me Assistant to the Director, which I thoroughly enjoyed.

---

[18] William Butler Yeats 1865-1939, Irish poet and one of the foremost figures of 20th century literature
[19] Rowan Bell b. 1948 engineer.
[20] Alan Irwin b. 1948, retired doctor, Belfast
[21] Derek Torrens b. 1948, naval doctor 1974-80, GP in Norwich 1980-2008
[22] Jim 'Pop' Edwards, History master, CAI 1931-73, latterly Vice-Principal
[23] John Birch, History master, CAI 1964-77, latterly with Inspectorate of Schools
[24] Tom 'Paddy' Ryan, Geography master, CAI 1945-85, latterly Vice-Principal
[25] Hugh 'The Count' Montgomery, English master, CAI 1949-86
[26] Robert 'Pop' Riddle, Maths master, CAI 1956-88

It was also at Coleraine that I developed the first stirrings of what turned out to be a lifetime interest in politics and current affairs, greatly helped by participation in the school debating society. This was stimulated by a growing friendship with Brian Walker[27], who went on to become BBC Northern Ireland's Political Editor. I recently discovered among my many documents the complete results of the 1966 General Election, which I had analysed in some detail. I had also kept, somewhat surprisingly, a copy of Lord Denning's 1963 report into the aftermath of the Profumo Affair.

Although I loved sport, skill and prowess were entirely different propositions. In the first two terms of each year rugby was the sole sport, with compulsory participation. As with my studies, my sporting abilities were average, so I played flanker for the 3rd XV in my last two years. There was occasionally also a 4th XV team, so I wasn't the worst. I scored a single try in a competitive match in my last year, when the 3rd XV won nine out of their first 12 games. On another occasion, when a major flu epidemic wiped out half the school, I played prop forward for the 2nd XV against Foyle College and played against a particularly pugilistic brute, who pummelled me black and blue during every scrum.

Cross country was the preferred sport in summer - no representative honours for me here either. With some others, I usually spent most of the time hiding during the second and third circuits of the practice sessions.

Contact with the outside world was permitted during term time. Most pupils would go into Coleraine town centre on Saturday afternoons. Not necessarily on the School's agenda, there was significant interaction with the girls from Coleraine High School, also a Boarding School. This usually took place during the afternoon matinee at the local picture house and it was the accepted norm that the back rows of stalls were reserved for those with female company. At least once a year there was a School dance attended by pupils from both schools and, although proceedings were very strictly controlled, there were always significant amounts of alcohol consumed (usually vodka). During the evening, couples would frequently disappear. I suspect the masters turned a blind eye to such activities. One of my friends had displayed considerable initiative in having duplicate keys cut for some classrooms. On one occasion I took advantage of this and was locked in with a female companion in a little room just off the Geography department. We then had the terrifying experience of hearing approaching footsteps, the door being opened and someone – presumably a master on patrol – passing within ten feet of us, before exiting and relocking the door. This certainly added an extra frisson to proceedings!

In summer 1966 I obtained my first paid employment at McCormick's, the local garage in Killyleagh, serving petrol (long before the advent of self-service) and selling accessories. For this I was paid the princely sum of £5 per week. By the end of the summer, I had accumulated a small nest egg to help me through my final year at school. I had also started to appreciate the level of sacrifice my parents were making and I resolved to ensure that, from then on, I worked each summer holiday to help with finances.

---

[27] Brian Walker b. 1947, BBC political journalist, Northern Ireland 1970-83, London 1983-2000

I learnt quite a lot from that early work experience and passed on some wisdom to the garage owners, who I'm not sure appreciated my input. My first piece of advice concerned the shop's stock levels, which were minimal to say the least and appallingly displayed. The owners quite snippily told me that, in their opinion, people knew what they needed and would ask for it – actively selling anything was a foreign concept. Their reaction to my second idea of carrying a greater range of stock was similar. I had noticed that people stopping to buy petrol would often ask if we had items such as soft drinks, crisps and chocolate. I suggested that the garage might increase its product range to capitalise on this. This idea was dismissed out of hand with the words: "Sonny, we're running a garage, not a sweetie shop." Unlike my successful tuck shop venture, my second entrepreneurial initiative was swiftly crushed.

In my last year the university application process loomed large. Careers advice at this time was fairly basic. I note that we attended a seminar entitled 'Earning a Living' at Dalriada School in Ballymoney, where we contemplated such riveting topics as:

- What reasons do you have for choosing or rejecting a career in Industry?

- What facts do you consider when choosing a career?

- Do you expect to enjoy earning your livelihood, or will it be sheer purgatory?

- Would you consider a job with very poor prospects and very little money, but which allows you to serve your fellow man? (I see that I had hastily scribbled a "No" to this one!)

How I arrived at my final choice of subject and university remains somewhat of a mystery to me to this day. I eventually opted for Politics, Philosophy and Economics at Durham University, Economics and Political Science at Trinity College Dublin (TCD), and Economics and Politics at The Queen's University Belfast (QUB), and I decided on QUB.

CAI certainly helped me develop strength of character. I look back on my time there with great affection, but a new era in my life was about to begin. CAI continues to be one of the leading schools in Northern Ireland, but sadly now takes only day pupils, having closed its doors to boarders in 1998. I suspect the gradual demise of the British Empire was a factor, with the strong supply pipeline of pupils eventually drying up. In 2015 CAI and Coleraine High School merged to become Coleraine Grammar School.

I recently visited the school for the first time in over 50 years and was shown around by Joe Cassells[28], a former master and co-author of the school's history[29]. He has created a museum in part of the old boarding school, the centrepiece of which is a large board recording the names of all the school's Head Prefects and the Heads of the boarding school houses from 1963 to 1992. The board used to hang in the dining hall and, as Head Prefect of the Model House in 1967, my name was on it. Six new

---

[28] Joe Cassells, b. 1947, master, CAI 1971-2006, curator, CAI Museum
[29] 'Schooldays on the Banks of the Bann - CAI 1860-2010, 2010, Joe Cassells and Len Quigg

House names were created in 1968 with the Model being renamed Dunluce House. I was retrospectively named as the first Head of House of Dunluce.

Joe was also able to show me the Pupil Register from the early 20th Century and I saw my father's name in the register for 1921, when he was 14. As I was leaving, Joe asked me to sign the Visitors' Book. Each visitor is allocated a sequential number and I was the 1149th visitor – an incredible coincidence, as my date of birth is 1st January 1949.

After leaving school I spent the summer of 1967 in King's Lynn in Norfolk as a welder's mate, working for the contractor J & J Laing, who were constructing the first North Sea gas pipeline. To get there I travelled overnight on the Belfast to Liverpool ferry, a horrible, sleepless experience, and then to King's Lynn. King's Lynn is not at the end of the world, but you can see it from there! My net pay was just over 14 shillings per week and the work was extremely tedious. Although at that time I did not know how my life would develop and what my future career would be, I knew that I most definitely did not want to be a manual labourer.

CAI Prefects, 1967 with Dr. George Humphreys, Headmaster.
Rowan Bell, best man front row furthest left,
yours truly front row, furthest right.

Chapter 3   GROWING UP IN NORTHERN IRELAND

"When I told the people of Northern Ireland that I was an atheist, a woman in the audience stood up and said, 'yes but is it the God of the Catholics or the God of the Protestants in whom you don't believe?'"   Quentin Crisp[1]

Northern Ireland is one of the four countries of the United Kingdom (although it is sometimes called a province or a region). It is in the north east of the island of Ireland, although it does not include the most northernly point - that is in the Republic, or the South of Ireland. The 1920 Government of Ireland Act created Northern Ireland on 3rd May 1921. It was formed from six of the nine counties of Ulster - one of Ireland's four provinces. Four counties had unionist majorities and the other two had marginal nationalist majorities. Unionists supported its creation whilst Nationalists were opposed. Confused? Read on!

Living near Portadown from 1952, my brother and I had a comfortable upbringing in what would be termed a conservative middle-class household. My father had very limited culinary tastes and was very much a 'meat and two veg' man. That said, my mother was an excellent baker and we were fortunate that the house also had an orchard and out housing, so my father kept some chickens and grew fresh vegetables. Our cat Nicholas Thomas was extremely adept at keeping rodents away. Ted and I were desperate to have a dog and one day my father surprised us by coming home with a delightful cocker spaniel. We spent a wonderful evening planning the future with our new friend. Sadly, during the night the dog escaped and killed some of the chickens and was swiftly returned to his original owners, leaving much heartache in the McClatchie household.

My father's main interest was golf, whilst my mother was involved in the Women's Institute and the Church. The latter featured prominently in our lives and we regularly attended Seagoe Church of Ireland Parish Church and Sunday School.

I can recall very little from this period of my childhood. I remember a major family discussion about my acquiring some 'interests' and various options were explored: photography, art, philately and numismatics. My parents persuaded me to enter a competition to collect the most differently dated penny coins and for several weeks my father would bring home several sacks of pennies from the bank which I then would sift through. I eventually completed a collection of every penny coin since 1860, which included one of the only two Edward VIII pennies in existence. I duly won the competition and my picture appeared in the Portadown Times, my first claim to fame.

---

[1]Quentin Crisp 1908-99, English writer, raconteur and actor

During this period, I was also a keen Boy Scout. Keen might be slightly overstating my enthusiasm but I attended several annual camps and, although the camaraderie and activities were great fun, I suspect that I enjoyed home comforts too much for life under canvas to be really comfortable. An incident in my early teens finally extinguished my desire for any more camping experiences. A test involved two of us building an overnight billet made from whatever we could find. On a summer evening in the middle of a wood we found a low, reasonably horizontal bough of a large tree and constructed a shelter using wood, sticks, leaves and straw. Our challenge was to sleep in it overnight. We also collected a significant amount of firewood on which to cook our evening meal. Our supervisor then left us, arranging to come back the following morning. Whether such arrangements would be permitted in today's Health and Safety conscious society is open to question. It was now dusk and we had almost prepared our meal when a sudden spell of heavy rain swept in. Within a relatively short period of time it had completely doused our fire and soaked our remaining wood supply. To our horror we also discovered that our newly constructed accommodation was far from water-tight. With the light dwindling and using our torches we carried out emergency repairs and managed to make our den more, but not completely, water-tight. We tried to relight the fire, in the process using all our remaining matches but to no avail. Next our torch batteries expired. Hungry, cold and very wet we crawled into our den in pitch darkness and got into our sleeping bags. It was then I discovered something wasn't quite right with mine. Within a very coarse cover which doubled up as a ground sheet I couldn't find sufficient blankets, indeed they barely covered my torso. The rain continued throughout the night, neither of us slept and I was frozen. The rain at last stopped and at first light it was a beautiful sunny morning. We were by now ravenous and despite finding some dry twigs we were unable to create a flame by rubbing them together as we had seen in the Westerns. We also had no watch, thus no idea of what time it was. Listening to the bells from a nearby church we established that it must be around 9am, abandoned camp and walked home - about three miles away. All the doors were locked and after ringing the bell for an eternity my mother eventually appeared, demanding to know what was going on as it had just turned 6.30am. It transpired that my mother had carefully folded a number of blankets inside the sleeping bag, expecting me to unfold these but in the ensuing darkness I hadn't realised this. That was the end of my pioneering. I didn't sleep under canvas again for the following 55 years, so my children missed out on this experience but didn't seem to object too much. Later I was to buy a caravan but therein lies another story (see Chapter 12).

One consistent factor throughout my upbringing was that it was entirely within the Protestant community. I say with absolute certainty that I only rarely met a Roman Catholic until I went to University in 1967. My parents' social network was exclusively Protestant, as were my school, our Church and all my leisure activities, such as the Cubs and Boy Scouts. Considering that the Catholic population in Northern Ireland at the time was about 40% of the total, this now seems extraordinary.

My parents actively prevented us from mixing with Catholics. Their mindset was that Catholics should be encouraged to stay within their own communities. Despite this I do not believe that my parents were bigots. They simply behaved like the vast majority of the Protestant population at that time, led and encouraged by the Establishment which promulgated the divine order of Ulster Protestantism. A young Ian Paisley[2], later nicknamed the Doctor No of Irish politics, would later perpetuate this myth for a further generation. I remember a very young curate at Seagoe passionately delivering a sermon suggesting that if Jesus Christ were to return, there was absolutely no doubt that he would be a Protestant and not a Roman Catholic. He practically received a standing ovation and it was enthusiastically talked about for months afterwards. When I joined the Belfast Telegraph in 1971 one of my colleagues, then in his sixties, provided me with his personal version of Northern Ireland's history. It concluded with the comment (and he was deadly serious) that, "The only good Catholic is a dead one." This same man was a pillar of the community. I was deeply disturbed with his attitude. Although he held deeply religious views, in my view he lacked any sort of Christianity.

In 1949 one of the province's most famous football clubs Belfast Celtic played their last game. A recent article in The Herald[3] described the situation, "The club's directors decided that they could no longer carry on after the players were attacked in a sectarian riot at the end of the Boxing Day Derby against rivals Linfield at Windsor Park. Striker Jimmy Jones was knocked unconscious and his leg was broken as he tried to leave the pitch. He was lucky to escape with his life, but the police didn't make a single arrest or even draw their batons to protect him. The consequences reverberated far beyond the terraces. Fans say that it effectively told Catholics in Northern Ireland that the state wouldn't protect them or allow them to compete in equal terms – in sport, the workplace, or politics."

Subsequently Northern Ireland was an accident waiting to happen. In my opinion, the political solution that led to the creation of the modern Republic of Ireland in 1921 was a botched one in that it only solved one part of the problem. It delivered the aspirations of Home Rule and nationalism that ran through Irish history for the latter part of the 19th and early part of the 20th centuries. The Republic of Ireland was created from the 26 predominantly Catholic counties. That left the problem of the other six predominantly Protestant counties which didn't want to be part of the Republic of Ireland but did want to remain in the UK. This solution might have worked more effectively if the Westminster Government had managed the transition better and ensured that Northern Ireland maintained the same standards as the rest of the United Kingdom. Instead they left it to the Protestants to manage their own affairs. As Seamus Heaney[4] once remarked, "loyalism or Unionism or Protestantism or whatever you want to call it… in Northern Ireland it operates not as a class system but as a caste system." What followed was 50 years of blatant discrimination against the Catholic community in virtually all aspects of day to day living. For

---

[2] Dr Ian Paisley PC, Baron Bannside 1926 – 2014, Founder, Democratic Unionist Party 1971
[3] 'A Grand Old Team Ready to Rise from the Ashes' Andrew McFadyen, The Herald 18th August 2018
[4] Seamus Heaney 1939-2013, Irish poet and playwright. Winner of the Nobel Prize for Literature 1993

them, life was controlled by the majority - politics, the Civil Service, the judiciary, and the police. The net result was a society of Haves (Protestants) and Have Nots (Catholics). For example, the level of unemployment in the Protestant community at that time was around 5%, but over 40% in the Catholic community. All Northern Ireland's major industries (ship building, heavy engineering etc.) had an almost completely Protestant workforce. When I joined the Belfast Telegraph in 1971, on the 500+ manufacturing side of the business almost every employee was Protestant. There was a highly controlled entry system with the family unit, trade unions, religion, the Orange and the Masonic orders all intertwined in the process.

The extent of the division between the two communities was vast. The Protestant establishment, particularly the Church, continued to demonize Catholics institutionally and to brainwash people about them being second class citizens. There was an example of this division within my own family. On my mother's side of the family, a second cousin Mary, only daughter of James[5] and Ena McKinney, married Dermot Sheehan[6], a Roman Catholic, eventually settling in Wellingborough in Northamptonshire. Her father James completely opposed the union and refused to attend the wedding (which took place in a Roman Catholic church in Belfast) and had no contact with the couple for over seven years. By then Mary and Dermot had three sons, his only grandchildren, so Mary and her family were his only heirs, yet James, on his retirement, sold his farm to a distant relative. Eventually a rapprochement was reached, my mother's brother John having helped broker some form of "deal." The result was that Dermot, Mary and family converted to Anglicanism and relations between them were gradually restored, although those with Dermot took much longer. James McKinney doted on his grandsons and, on his death, Mary inherited the entire estate, with his widow granted only a lifetime tenancy of the family home. My early memories of all this are that members of my family, including my mother, would comment on how well brought up the three boys were - i.e. despite them having been born Roman Catholics.

Dermot and Mary's reconciliation with her parents came at a heavy price. Mary's youngest son John Sheehan[7] recently reflected, "After reconciliation, Grandmother stayed with us for a few weeks every year in Wellingborough. Upon meeting someone new, there would be an immediate inquisition, establishing who the person was, where they came from, or what they did? The first question was always religion. If they were Catholic, regardless of age, whether they were a teacher, a scholar, a neighbour, or a milkman, they were immediately ostracised by Grandmother. Even far from home in England, she would regard a Catholic in the house as akin to a contagious disease. As a result, the family, even in Wellingborough, subconsciously adopted its own religious screening process, and we took the easy option, routinely sidestepping potential new acquaintances, including friends from school, if we found out they were Catholic. The price Mary paid for readmittance into the family fold was readopting much of the prejudice that

---

[5] James McKinney 1881-1964 m. Ena (née Stuart) 1896-1986, farmer
[6] Dermot Sheehan 1916-2006 m. Mary (née McKinney) 1919-97 3s. James, William and John
[7] John Sheehan b.1953 m. Kangphoo Yosying b.1973 1d. 1s., banker, Bangkok

she had been brought up under. When we reached our late teens and started dating English girls, Mary would immediately question their religious background, and would aggressively urge termination of the relationship if the girl was Catholic. It was as if the prospect of a second Catholic marriage within the family, after her suffering and Epiphany, was too much agony to bear again. The burlesque of religious prejudice emanating from Ulster eventually killed off all interest in religious observance within the family. The sons declared religion to be a charade in their teens. Dermot later on confessed that he had only adopted Anglicanism and attended church every week to keep Mary happy. Without support and reinforcement, even Mary's enthusiasm had petered out by the end. After Mary died, she left all her assets to Dermot. He admitted that he had never felt comfortable or 100% safe when in Northern Ireland, and promptly sold everything there."

I suppose it should come as no surprise that after 50 years of discrimination, the Catholic population in Northern Ireland revolted, resulting in a 30-year period of near civil war, now known as 'The Troubles'. There are many accounts of this period, but I regard a book by a distinguished journalist and a teacher of history as perhaps one of the most definitive[8].

I describe in Chapter 4 how the civil rights march in October 1968 was later acknowledged to be the start of 'The Troubles'. It prompted Harold Wilson[9] and his Home Secretary, James Callaghan[10] to take a much tougher line with the Ulster Unionist Government of Terence O'Neill[11], demanding extensive political reform. O'Neill sadly commanded insufficient support within his own party to institute the necessary reforms and his lack of empathy with the Catholic population resulted in 30 years of political disability and civil disorder. O'Neill summed up the situation on leaving office; "It is frightfully hard to explain to Protestants that if you give Roman Catholics a good job and a good house they will live like Protestants, because they will see neighbours with cars and television sets. They will refuse to have 18 children, but if a Roman Catholic is jobless and lives in the most ghastly hovel, he will rear 18 children on National Assistance." This quite astonishing analysis aptly demonstrated the appalling state of affairs in 1968.

In the following chapters I describe in some detail what it was like to work in Northern Ireland during the early years of The Troubles and how eventually the peace process evolved. The Good Friday Agreement of 1998, in the end conducted at great speed, left too many unresolved issues and it was only the St Andrews Agreement in 2006 which ultimately put the process on a much firmer footing.

I spent a short time with Tony Blair[12] during the Press Fund Lunch in Glasgow in April 1999 (see Chapter 34) and asked him about his strategy for Northern Ireland. His plan was to create as wide a centre ground as possible so that those who covertly

[8] 'Making Sense of The Troubles: A History of the Northern Ireland Conflict' David McKittrick and David McVea. Revised edition 2012, Penguin Viking
[9] The Rt. Hon. James Harold, Baron Wilson of Rievaulx, 1916-95 Prime Minister 1964-70, 1974-76
[10] The Rt.Hon. James Callaghan, Baron Callaghan of Cardiff, KG, PC, 1912-2005, Home Secretary 1967-70, Prime Minister 1976-79
[11] The Rt.Hon. Terence O'Neill, Baron O'Neill of the Maine, 1914-90, fourth Prime Minister of Northern Ireland 1963-69
[12] The Rt. Hon. Anthony (Tony) Charles Linton Blair, b. 1953, Prime Minister 1997-2007

but, most importantly, overtly supported the extremists would eventually become isolated. That clearly didn't work. Every time David Trimble[13] nodded in agreement, Ian Paisley was standing behind him shaking his head in disagreement. Ditto Gerry Adams[14] with John Hume[15]. Blair eventually had to abandon that strategy and, as the two sides became even more polarised, Trimble's Ulster Unionists and Hume's SDLP were effectively cast aside, leaving the Democratic Unionists and Sinn Féin to thrash out a solution, having now been forced to work together. I met Ian Paisley several years later in November 2010, during the historic visit of Prince Charles[16] to the Irish Embassy in London. Paisley had come a long way. Indeed, it was unthinkable that he would even have attended such an event until relatively recently. After introducing myself, I said that although I had violently disagreed with his politics for the past 30 years, I congratulated him on his efforts during the latter years of the peace process. I had a thoroughly insightful conversation with him for the next 15 minutes and my parting shot was to remind him of his frequently standing behind Trimble shaking his head whilst Trimble nodded. I asked him how he coped with those at the edge of his own party, now doing exactly the same thing to him. In typical Paisley fashion he replied, bringing down his fist on an adjacent table, "They must be crushed!" I was left to ponder whether the old leopard ever quite changed his spots.

That evening, the Prince of Wales reflected on the changed relationship between the two countries. In an amusing speech he opened by saying, "Ambassador, ladies and gentleman, I must say we have been so incredibly touched that you should have thought of inviting us to come and, as you put it 'put a toe into Irish water' lapping gently at the walls of Buckingham Palace. If I'd known all those years ago that the Irish Embassy was here, I would have been throwing stones to attract attention." (not the most apt line, I thought!). He concluded, "Can I just say before I go that, at the end of the day, I think we should never forget that our acquaintance has been long and we can turn that knowing into something new and creative. We need no longer be victims of our difficult history with one another. Without glossing over the pain and suffering of the past, we can, I believe, integrate our history and memory in order to reap their subtle harvest of possibility. Imagination after all is the mother of possibility. So, I hope we can endeavour to become subjects of our history and not its prisoners."

Bill Clinton[17] said of the Good Friday Agreement, "The path to peace is never easy. They have chosen hope over hate, the promise of the future over the poison of the past." And yet the irony of the Northern Ireland situation was that, of the main parties involved in the negotiations which led to the Good Friday Agreement, Blair, Ahearn[18], and Bill Clinton all agreed what needed to be done. The only people who couldn't agree on anything were the participants from Northern Ireland. An Irish

---

[13] The Rt. Hon. David Trimble PC, Baron Trimble of Lisnagarvey, b. 1944, MP for Upper Bann 1998-2007; First Minister of Northern Ireland 1998-2002
[14] Gerry Adams, b. 1948, President, Sinn Féin since 1983; TD since 2011
[15] John Hume, b. 1937, MP for Foyle 1969-73; Northern Ireland Assembly Member 1973-75; Leader SDLP 1979-2011
[16] Charles Phillip Arthur George, Prince of Wales, b. 1948.
[17] William Jefferson Clinton, b. 1946, 42nd President of the United States 1993-2001
[18] Bertie Ahearn, b. 1951, Fianna Fáil Taoiseach 1997-2008

diplomat, who had served in both Belfast and Tel Aviv, once told me "The Unionists and the Israelis are very similar. In their relations with the Catholics and the Palestinians respectively, they know that one day they will be forced to make massive concessions, so until then, there is no point in them budging one inch." The Northern Ireland Protestants' logic appeared to be based on the assumption that the Catholic population would eventually exceed theirs and that until then they should make no concessions. The result is that both sides vote predominantly on religious grounds, thus the Catholics mostly vote for Sinn Féin. In UK terms Sinn Féin would be viewed as a far left party with extreme socialist policies. Sinn Féin also advocates a united Ireland. For most Catholics there is now only one choice – because since the end of the Troubles, they simply do not trust the various Unionist Governments. They might not necessarily agree with all that Sinn Féin represents, but they have zero trust in the recent administrations of Ian Paisley, Peter Robinson[19] and Arlene Foster[20]. With next to no consensus, it is not surprising that power sharing broke down. Equally, this lack of consensus means that some Protestants find it difficult to accept some of the more extreme demands from Sinn Féin - for example that the Union Jack should not always been flown from public buildings and currently, the teaching of the Irish language in schools.

There is a parallel with the language issue in Scotland: the SNP government has a policy of using both Gaelic and English in all public notices, road signs and public service vehicles. I am utterly opposed to this policy. It panders to a small minority and is a waste of tax payers' money. However, I live in a democracy and accept that, if it is the policy of the government of the day, so be it. It is a pity that more people in Northern Ireland don't have this approach. The outside world still views Northern Ireland politics as one-dimensional, characterised by intolerance and bigotry, but there is an overwhelming hope for the two communities to co-exist in harmony and for the significant progress achieved in the peace process to continue.

I believe that three major external factors helped create a different environment within Northern Ireland and possibly helped facilitate the peace process. Firstly, the onset of cheap package holidays in the 1960s opened up a whole new world to people in Northern Ireland. The fact that the most popular destinations were Spain and the Balearics, predominately Catholic regions, perhaps helped traditional Northern Ireland Protestants to view Catholics in a different light. Second, both the Republic of Ireland and the UK joined the EC in the early 1970s, albeit by slightly different processes. One major consequence was that the border between the two countries became largely irrelevant. For earlier generations, passing through two sets of customs posts only served to underline the separation. Third, the growth of the Celtic Tiger in the 1990s finally dispelled the Protestant myth that the Republic of Ireland had a poverty-stricken, semi-peasant population. Its increased wealth meant that the economic differences were significantly reduced. Even the major recession of

---

[19] The Rt. Hon. Peter Robinson, b. 1948, Leader, Democratic Unionist Party 2008-15; First Minister of Northern Ireland 2008-16
[20] The Rt. Hon. Arlene Foster, b. 1970, Leader, Democratic Unionist Party 2015 - ; First Minister of Northern Ireland 2016 -

2008 and the catastrophic effect it had on the Irish economy thankfully did not allow any of these earlier myths to reappear.

I remain highly optimistic about the future for Northern Ireland. Many people said that the Troubles would prevent normalisation of the two communities for at least a generation. Thankfully that new generation appears infinitely more tolerant and open than the previous one, but there are many, many hurdles still to overcome. Brexit of course remains a major issue. The previous close harmony between the governments of the United Kingdom and the Republic of Ireland, built during The Good Friday and St Andrews Agreements, is currently being severely tested. The Good Friday Agreement itself is intimately bound up with shared EU membership and many fear that a hard border could be a precursor to dark days of terror. The finely tuned nuances of the Agreement bind loyalists and republicans in the status quo. How to regulate the border, the main division between the UK and the EU, will require some imaginative solutions, but I am confident that it will not derail all the positives achieved so far.

On 24th February 2007 I witnessed an incident that well illustrates how both the citizens of Northern Ireland and the Republic of Ireland have grown much more comfortable with one another. Ireland played England in the Six Nations Rugby Championship. Because of the redevelopment of Landsdowne Road, the game took place at Croke Park, the headquarters of the GAA and a bastion of Irish Republicanism. Sinn Féin had tried to organise mass protests. Their argument was that rugby was a 'garrison sport.' Try telling that to the bulk of the Irish population who fervently support their rugby team. A mere 300 protestors turned up and, just before 3pm, the visitors' national anthem was sung. To hear 'God Save the Queen' without a boo or a catcall in a stadium of 82,500 people in Dublin was incredibly moving and a truly historic event. Many Irish people around me were almost moved to tears and it a was clear sign of the remarkable spirit of reconciliation between the two countries. Ireland won by a record score of 43-13. As The Guardian reported, "From the respectful observance of 'God Save the Queen' to the record number of points conceded by an English side in 124 years of championship rugby, this was a day to make modern Ireland proud."

Around that time, I was asked to speak to the Rotary Club of Glasgow and, as the event was on 17th March, it was suggested that I might offer a toast to St Patrick. In my speech I used much of the material in this chapter and, before making the toast, I concluded that St Patrick was probably happier now in his resting place in Downpatrick than he had been at any time over the past century.

The best way I can describe the present situation is thus: in the late 1990s I was approached by a London head-hunter whose brief was to find the next Managing Director of the Belfast Telegraph. I attended an extensive interview in London and got the impression that the head-hunter was impressed by my experience. There was a major stumbling block however. I was not prepared to move my family back to Northern Ireland. We had been away for 20 years and it never occurred to my children to question if their friends were Protestant or Roman Catholic - or anything else. I was not prepared to move back permanently to an environment where religion was still the dominant factor. For me, it would have been one of my proudest achievements to return to head up the newspaper where I had started as a Graduate Trainee over 20 years earlier. My stance, not surprisingly, was a deal-breaker. If I had to make the same decision now, my answer might be 'yes', which shows how far Northern Ireland has progressed.

I make that last statement with some qualifications. In 2019 Northern Ireland is the only place in the United Kingdom where women do not have access to abortion facilities. A recent headline in the Times stated, "Abortion has left us a disunited kingdom and where Northern Ireland is still stuck in the moralistic world of the 1950s and where same sex marriage is not allowed." The same article[21] concluded, "If Westminster abandons the young to a stuffy 1950s moralising politics of shame and blame, why should they not retrain their compass from London to Dublin. For young people, values transcend borders. In the end, it may not be tales of the Easter Rising and memories of hunger strikes that united Ireland but justice for gay couples or sad, pale women boarding southbound trains." Food for thought!

Although the current situation in Northern Ireland may not be the end of the story, it is certainly the end of a dreadful era. Yet as Northern Ireland marks the 21st anniversary of the Good Friday Agreement, the death in 2019 of journalist Lyra McKee[22], shot dead in Derry, reminds us that the relative peace there is fragile. McKee was a remarkably positive young woman calling the city "Legend-derry – avoid that Londonderry/Derry thing - I hate it." but even she acknowledged that fragility, "We were the Good Friday Agreement generation destined to never witness the horrors of war but to reap the spoils of peace. The spoils just never seemed to reach us."

---

[21] Janice Turner, The Times, 16th May 2018
[22] Lyra McKee 1990-2019, journalist and campaigner

Chapter 4

STUDENT DAYS - QUEEN'S UNIVERSITY BELFAST

"The university brings out all capabilities including incapability." Anton Chekhov[1]

I became a student at Queen's University Belfast (QUB) in October 1967, following in the footsteps of my brother. The major difference was that, eight years earlier, Ted had gone there having been awarded a State Exhibition by the Ministry of Education, worth £80 a year, for achieving the third best set of results in Northern Ireland. He was also awarded a Foundation Scholarship by the University – clearly the brains were unevenly distributed in our family!

I elected to study for an Honours degree in Economics and Politics, B.Sc. (Econ). I don't recall any discussion at home about what this could lead to – it was just assumed that a career would follow. Neither of my parents had been to university but I suppose I was part of a middle-class family for whom a university education was now a norm rather than an aspiration.

The Northern Ireland education system at that time meant that student grants were means-tested and I did not qualify for a full student grant. It was agreed that I should live on campus rather than travel from home. I'm extremely grateful to my parents for this as it must have involved a considerable sacrifice on their part.

I suspect that I arrived at QUB a little wet round the ears, but became increasingly streetwise as time went on. In this I was no different from the many hundreds of others enrolling that year. Amanda and Milena would do the same at Edinburgh more than 30 years later, although with much higher academic qualifications.

In my first year I stayed in Hamilton Hall, one of the Queen's Elms halls of residence. It was on the Malone Road, still one of the most affluent areas of Belfast and just under a mile from the university. I shared a room with Derek Torrens, with whom I had been to school and who was now studying medicine. Several other school friends were also at QUB including Rowan Bell (later to be my best man) and Alan Irwin.

The Belfast of 1967, just before the onset of The Troubles, was already a divided city. The University's central location meant its students were sheltered from some of the grim realities of life elsewhere in Belfast. The main campus was in University Avenue, less than a mile from the city centre. The Economics Faculty was centrally located just behind the University library, headed by Professor R.D. Collison Black[2],

---

[1] Anton Chekov 1860-1904, Russian playwright
[2] Prof. R.D. Collison Black, DSC 1922-2008, head of the department of economics, QUB 1962-85

a very distinguished economist. In that first year I also took a semester in Philosophy.

Social life centred around the Students' Union, just across the road from the main building. The two main student pubs, inevitably a crucial part of university life, were the Eglinton Inn (the Egg) and the Botanic Inn (the Bot). Both were conveniently about half way between the Faculty and the Halls of Residence. I particularly remember the Egg because of a very unpleasant early experience with gin!

I wish I could say that I settled into university life with the prime aim of achieving academic success, but that is not quite accurate. A healthy dose of hedonism seemed to run through my time there. I knew that I was expected to acquire a respectable degree at the end of the process, but the aim was also to have as pleasant a time as possible. By the start of the summer term, Alan Irwin, Ed Smyth[3] and I had decided to spend the summer working in New York.

Exams passed, I returned for my second year. With the nest egg accumulated in the summer, I was able to buy my first car. My father knew Jimmy, a second-hand car dealer on the Shankill Road, and I bought an elderly cream and burgundy Triumph Herald for £200. It later transpired that the car consisted of halves from two different Triumph Heralds, both of which had been in major accidents and which Jimmy had welded together. This of course was long before the advent of the MOT certificate and it only became apparent that something wasn't quite right when the car made strange noises on left-hand turns. My father confronted Jimmy, who confessed all and refunded us £100, assuring us that the car would be fine to drive.

In my second year I moved into a Queen's House. QUB had over the years built up an extensive property portfolio. Queen's Houses were buildings adjacent to the main campus, each with a resident warden, who was usually a final year or PHD student, with a fairly undemanding level of responsibility for the day-to-day running of the property. Each house had a cleaner, a communal recreation area, dining and kitchen facilities. I became a resident of 85 Botanic Avenue along with ten others. The location was ideal as it was less than a couple of hundred yards from my lectures.

Having completed my Philosophy semester, I concentrated on my core subjects. I continued to find Economics fascinating, although some of the more obscure economic theory was a little dull. In Politics I continued to be inspired by the venerable Professor Cornelius O'Leary[4], whose tutorials left a lasting impression on me long after I had left QUB.

The political situation in Northern Ireland was starting to deteriorate. On Saturday afternoon, 5th October 1968, a banned civil rights march in Londonderry was broken up by police using batons and water cannons – all in the presence of Labour MPs. The television and newspaper images from this were to put Northern Ireland onto

[3] Ed Smyth b. 1948, psychiatrist, Vancouver BC
[4] Prof. Cornelius O'Leary 1927-2006, Professor of Political Science QUB

the international stage, where it was to stay for the next 25 to 30 years for all the wrong reasons. This event was later acknowledged to have been the start of "The Troubles."

That year I decided to stand for election to the Students' Representative Council (SRC). Within a few days of the march in Derry more than 3,000 QUB students staged a sit-down protest in the city centre. The SRC election was on 22nd October and astonishingly, in view of events, my main platform for election was articulated as "he has strong views on the functions of SRC and is concerned at the recent tendency for SRC becoming a platform for the expression of party political views." I still have a copy of my manifesto. Astonishingly, I was elected!

That year SRC indeed became a hot bed of political debate on civil rights, led by Bernadette Devlin[5], who later became an MP. So much for my reading of the situation leading up to the elections, although, not for the first or last time in my life, I was not put off expressing a minority view.

Although the overall political situation was starting to deteriorate significantly and the University was becoming a centre of political activism, social life continued unabated. That year I also became Business Manager of Qubist, the University magazine. Most importantly this provided me with a Press Pass for the Queen's Festival, staged over three weeks in November. In my two years with Qubist I attended some great events - concerts featuring Julian Bream, Juliette Greco, the Swingle Singers and Jimi Hendrix. In Festival '68 I attended classical concerts with the Ulster Orchestra, opera highlights, a poetry reading by Virginia McKenna, and some great concerts by the Stan Tracey Orchestra, John Dankworth and Cleo Laine, and the Dave Brubeck Quartet. Outwith the Festival I saw Peter, Paul and Mary at the ABC and Spencer Davis, Taste and Pink Floyd at the Whitla Hall.

Student unrest continued in 1969. On 1st January another civil rights march set out from Belfast to Londonderry but was ambushed by Loyalists at Burntullet Bridge. Many of the marchers were injured then and later when they were stoned on arriving in Londonderry. Three cabinet ministers in Terence O'Neill's government were either sacked or resigned, including Bill Craig[6], the Home Secretary. O'Neill himself resigned in April and was succeeded by James Chichester-Clark[7].

Bill Craig was an interesting character. In his obituary The Independent[8] described him: "The extraordinary trajectory of his career saw him lurch – he drank a lot – from a stern pillar of law and order to a dangerous dissident who publicly threatened to assassinate opponents." O'Neill described the latter quotation as "a fatal fluency of speech." Craig was responsible for introducing the breathalyser into Northern Ireland. I remember seeing the first prototype, which was essentially a laboratory in a large caravan which had to be towed around. On one of the first

---

[5] Bernadette McAliskey (née. Devlin), b. 1947, MP for Mid-Ulster 1979-84 and at the time the youngest ever MP, aged 21
[6] William Craig 1924-2011, Ulster Unionist politician
[7] The Rt Hon James Chichester-Clark, Baron Moyola PC DL 1923-2002; penultimate Prime Minister of Northern Ireland; leader of the Ulster Unionists 1969-71
[8] Desmond McKittrick. The Independent 7th May 2011

weekends it was introduced, it was parked near Balloo House, a very fashionable restaurant near my parents' home, about 20 miles south of Belfast. Rumour has it that at least two judges were breathalysed that night and Bill Craig allegedly received a furious phone call on the Monday morning, telling him never to place his caravan and circus near Balloo House again.

One Saturday evening some of us travelled to Bangor, ending up in Caproni's Ballroom. These evenings were always accompanied by the taking of some serious refreshment. Later that evening our driver, who shall remain anonymous, was stopped by the police on the Holywood bypass and, under suspicion, instructed to join a long queue on the hard shoulder, waiting to be processed in the breathalyser unit in the now infamous caravan. Our driver was extremely concerned that he might not pass muster, but his skin was saved when one clearly inebriated driver ploughed into the last vehicle at the end of the queue. The police immediately ran to the incident, whereupon the entire queue drove off at some speed, except the poor sod whose car had been rear ended.

A permanent feature of student life was a shortage of money. Although a trip to New York had provided me with extra cash, the car and its running costs meant that my allowance always seemed to run out towards the end of the month. During this time, although I usually had lunch in the Students' Union, I was starting to acquire some basic culinary skills, although the kitchen at No. 85 was the site of some quite gruesome experiments. My skills always seemed inferior to the others, one of whom even baked his own bread.

An unexpected bonus occurred just after April, when the student travel company told us that we would be able to claim back Federal Income Tax from our work the previous summer. After some correspondence with the IRS, a most welcome cheque arrived. Alan, Ed and I decided that we would go back to New York that summer, with our IRS cheques financing the trip. On my return I upgraded my car to what was to be my pride and joy, a bright red, soft top MG Midget.

The academic pressure was of course continuing to build, but third year still allowed for plenty of extra-curricular activities. Rowan Bell had become very interested in rallying and was determined to compete in the following year's Circuit of Ireland International Rally, which took place over Easter weekend. It was a five-day event over 1500 miles around Ireland. Rowan was keen that I should be his navigator and co-driver. I needed to acquire map reading skills and for this I was to have an excellent tutor - Terry Harriman[9], who had won the Monte Carlo rally with Paddy Hopkirk[10]. Through a friend I was introduced to Terry, who readily agreed to teach me the necessary skills and was incredibly generous with his time.

It was a gruelling event involving navigating between a series of special speed stages, which were held on closed roads or forestry tracks. The rally started on Friday evening and continued throughout the night and all the following day,

---

[9] Terry Harriman, co-driver for Paddy Hopkirk, Ari Vatenan and others
[10] Paddy Hopkirk MBE, b. 1933, winner Monte Carlo Rally 1964.

ending up in Killarney, County Kerry. Sunday involved a series of stages around the Ring of Kerry. Restarting on Monday morning and again driving throughout the day and night, the Rally ended in Larne on Tuesday morning.

The 1970 Rally started on Good Friday, 26th March with over 150 competitors, only 67 of whom finished. It was won by Roger Clark[11], representing the Ford Works Team and driving a Ford RS 1600. We were very proud to finish in 60th place, having experienced many hairy moments. I also competed in the 1971 event, this time with Dessie Nutt, a university friend from Limavady, whose father also owned a garage – an essential requirement for competing in these events. Dessie was to achieve further fame and became British Historic Rally Champion on more than one occasion.

Throughout 1969 the political situation continued to deteriorate. Between July and August ten people had been killed and hundreds wounded in rioting, mostly in Belfast and Londonderry. Chichester-Clark eventually requested assistance and the first British troops arrived on 14th August. This was followed by a honeymoon period and, although the level of violence temporarily diminished, political activism continued and in late December a split in the IRA led to the formation of the Provisional IRA. A leader in the Belfast Telegraph on the last day of the year summed up the situation: "Every man is born equal. If that simple axiom is ignored, as it has been too often in the Ulster you leave behind this New Year's Eve, then the wrath of 1969 will go on re-occurring."[12]

Ironically, in view of what was to happen later, 1970 was something of a calm before the storm. Although 25 people died as a result of the Troubles, this was to be the lowest figure for any year in the 1970s, but the number of deaths was to be seven times higher in 1971, when Internment was introduced.

This seemed a long way away from life at QUB although much of it was taking place less than a mile away from the campus. I was careful where I went, but I had one frightening experience early in 1970. After a late card session, someone had run out of cigarettes and I offered to drive him to an all-night convenience store in the Markets area. Emerging from the store, we found my car boxed in by two vehicles and a group of vigilantes closely interrogated us on who we were and why we were there. They let us go but told us never to return to the area again.

Returning to QUB in October for my final year I was appointed Warden of 42 Mount Charles, another University house, smaller than No. 85 Botanic Avenue with just seven other residents. We had a fantastic cleaner called June, who would sometimes stumble across a female first thing in the morning and express outrage, calling my charges "brutes" - or worse!

Academic reality hit me and this was to be a year of intensive study. I hadn't exactly over-extended myself during those first three years so I had to catch up fast. Social activities were curtailed. I also had to find a job after graduating. I recently came

---

[11] Roger Clark MBE 1939-1998. First British rally driver to win a World Rally Championship event
[12] Belfast Telegraph, 31st December 1969

across my 5000-word Politics dissertation entitled, "How great is the influence of television and press on public opinion and voting behaviour?" Given my future career it was an apt subject. I note a great line: "The danger of the 1960s is not that electors will be drowned in a torrent of gin and beer (to quote Gladstone) but that they will be suffocated by a surfeit of posters and newsprint". Cornelius O'Leary was sufficiently impressed to describe it as "a good essay" and awarded a B++. He also observed that it was "a little long-winded" – a prescient remark. 50 years later the first draft of this book ran to 225,000 words, 75,000 more than required. This can be the only trait I share with the great Hugh McIlvanney[13], who famously described anything less than 1,500 words as "a mere vignette."

I still had no real idea what career I wanted to pursue. My brother by this stage had a First-Class Honours degree in Maths and Physics and had completed his PhD in Nuclear Physics. I wouldn't be going down that particular route but worryingly I didn't actually have any route in mind and there was some pressure from home. My parents were becoming increasingly concerned at the total absence of any road map for my future ahead. I was also feeling a different type of pressure in the knowledge that I would have to start applying for jobs early in the second term, as the annual 'milk round' of visiting employers would start.

Inspiration finally came from what at first seemed an unlikely source, The Times. As part of its marketing strategy the paper was offering free copies for final year students so I picked up a daily copy at the Students Union. I found myself drawn to the business pages of the paper and increasingly attracted to the world of Sales and Marketing. I started to convince myself that I had a natural sales talent, with running the illicit tuck shop at school early evidence of it. Some of my university course modules had covered Marketing Theory and I reread several textbooks with renewed interest. Between September and December 1970, I started to form some ideas on what I wanted to do. I had already decided that academia was not for me (my 2.2 Honours degree subsequently confirmed that!). A gradual narrowing down of options led me to consider a career in marketing in the private sector. This was still a pretty wide canvass but I was infinitely more focused than I had been three months earlier.

I sent off eight applications and, from those, secured interviews with four companies, Esso Petroleum, the Ford Motor Company, J. Walter Thomson Advertising and Thomson Regional Newspapers (TRN). All four held their initial interviews in Belfast and by February I had been offered second interviews with Esso and TRN, both in London. I was offered graduate traineeships by both. To accept either I would have to leave Northern Ireland, immediately in the case of Esso.

TRN offered me the job first. Esso's offer came two and a half weeks later, by which time I had virtually made up my mind to accept the Thomson offer. I liked the people I had met there. I was initially interviewed by Ron Wallace[14] in Belfast and in

---

[13] Hugh McIlvanney OBE, 1934-2019, sports writer.
[14] Ron Wallace Personnel Manager Belfast Telegraph

London by Tudor Hopkins[15] (our paths were to cross again many years later). I particularly liked the format of TRN's graduate recruitment scheme but there was one initial downside. TRN did not recruit graduates directly into Marketing and all entrants had to go through Sales first. I almost discounted TRN when they first told me this, but the more I learned about the company, the less it mattered. Ironically it would be almost 15 years before marketing became part of my responsibilities, not with TRN but with the Scottish Daily Record and Sunday Mail Ltd. (SDR).

The TRN Graduate Trainee Scheme lasted 18 months. At that time the company had nine different publishing centres throughout the UK and graduate trainees spent six months in each of the main sales departments, Classified Advertising, Display Advertising and Newspaper Sales (Circulation). Each module could be in a different publishing centre and after 18 months there was a formal appraisal process with successful candidates offered a full-time position. My graduate traineeship with the Belfast Telegraph Newspapers Ltd. (BT) would start in September. I now needed to concentrate on passing my finals!

Between 31st May and 9th June 1971, I sat my final exams in subjects including Principles, Monetary Problems and Industrial Fluctuations, Structure and Problems of Modern Industry and Trade, Political Theory, Corporate Government and British Government. Re-examining the questions now, the mind boggles:

- Examine Edgeworth's contention that price in bi-lateral monopoly is indeterminate.

- Show that the equilibrium in the Parkinson Aggregative Model is stable.

- How far can workable competition provide a theoretical basis for Anti-Trust Policy?

- Is there a connection between Philosophical Idealism and Conservatism?

- What do you consider to be the most epoch-making decisions of the US Supreme Court since 1937?

- Is social class a dependent or independent variable in influencing voting behaviour? (Thank God for a yes/no answer!)

To say that I found the whole experience tough is a gross understatement, but I managed to get through and nervously awaited the results. My 2:2 Honours Degree in Economics and Politics was probably a fair reflection of my time and effort at university but it was sufficient for the first step on my career ladder.

I graduated on Monday 5th July 1971 in the presence of two extremely proud, happy and probably very relieved parents and the next phase of my life was about to begin.

Footnote: 30 years after graduating I was extremely proud to become the first President of The Queen's University Association Scotland (QUAS). I had been

---

[15] Tudor Hopkins, 1937-2003. Personnel Director, TRN, and latterly Personnel Director, News International

contacted by the Alumni Office in Belfast to help form an association in Scotland. Gerry Power[16], still there, visited Mike Graham[17] and me and together we established a Scottish committee who in turn contacted the 900+ Queens graduates supposedly living in Scotland. The association was established in 2003. I chaired the first annual dinner at the Royal College of Surgeons, Edinburgh where our principal guest was Sir George Bain[18], then Vice Chancellor.

The Graduate

---

[16] Gerry Power b.1959, Communications Officer, Development and Alumni Relations. QUB
[17] Mike Graham b.1944, Director of Business Law, MacRoberts 1999-2016, m. Christina (neé Sinclair) b.1945
[18] Sir George Bain b.1939, 10th President and Vice Chancellor of QUB 1998-2004

Chapter 5   EARLY TRAVEL, 1950s and 1960s

"One's destination is never a place but a new way of seeing things."   *Henry Miller*[1]

Up to the age of 15, my travelling experiences were fairly modest. Holidays were limited to a rented house in Portrush, with early memories of sunny days on the beach and the sea being freezing. Portrush was on the North Atlantic coast of Northern Ireland and, after that, I rarely swam in British coastal waters again. We ventured outside the borders of Northern Ireland on a few occasions with caravan holidays in Roundstone in Connemara and Portnoo in Donegal.

Roundstone is where I recall the only time I ever heard of my father overindulging. Whether or not he had actually done so is a moot point, but my mother firmly believed it. Returning late from the local pub, where I suspect she automatically assumed he'd had one Guinness too many, she vented her fury on him, much to the amazement of my brother and me. Next morning, Dad told us that the whole affair had been totally exaggerated, but with a mischievous wink behind my mother's back. I suppose, bearing in mind her brother's fondness for alcohol, and with her own very strict upbringing, my mother's reaction was understandable.

30 years, a wife and two children later, I was to return to Portnoo when we rented a house there for several summer holidays. Amanda and Milena have many happy memories of them. We felt it was completely safe for young children and they were first allowed to walk by themselves from the beach to Inan Morgan's shop for ice cream.

Although I don't recall my parents having any particular interest in racing, we went to Fairyhouse racecourse near Drogheda in County Meath for the Irish Grand National Meeting on Easter Monday several times and I saw the great Arkle win the main race there in 1964.

My first trip outside Ireland also took place that year, when I visited my brother in London. I flew for the very first time from Aldergrove to Heathrow in a fairly elderly British European Airways Viscount. Apart from the flight, the highlight of the trip was a visit to the motor racing circuit in Snetterton in Norfolk. My other memory is of the huge traffic jam on the way back to London. Norfolk's roads then were apparently no better than they are now.

At university, Alan Irwin, another medical student Ed Smyth and I had started to think of going somewhere abroad to work for the summer of 1968. The students' travel company USIT was offering an incredibly attractive package to New York – a return flight from Dublin to New York, five nights' accommodation in a Manhattan hotel and a J1 visa enabling the holder to work in the United States for up to six months, all for £55. At Easter, Alan and Ed had hitchhiked to Dublin and were given

---

[1] Henry Miller 1891-1980, American writer

a lift by an elderly American couple from New York, Tom and Kay Corcoran. Both of Irish descent, Tom was a retired ex-New York Policeman and now Head of Security at British Overseas Airways Cooperation at Kennedy Airport (JFK) in New York. Alan and Ed told the Corcorans of our plans to go to New York that summer and Tom volunteered to make some contacts for us that might help us find work at the airport. Within a fortnight of returning home, he was in touch to tell us that he was pretty certain he could find us jobs with a service company at the airport called Allied Aviation International. In late June 1968, we flew into JFK. Tom took us to our hotel, the Penn Central on 7th Avenue /31st Street, just beside Madison Square Garden. The next five days was a time of intense activity. On the first day we took the subway and bus to the airport and met up with Tom, who took us to meet our prospective employer. All went swimmingly well; we would be employed immediately as part of a large team of aircraft cleaners. At the very end of the conversation they dropped the bombshell that we would require social security numbers and US driving licences. Tom clearly had not realised this but immediately set out to find out what was required. He was an absolute Colossus and within two days we had obtained social security cards, taken a driving test and had US driving licences.

The final part of the equation was to find reasonable accommodation and this we did ourselves. We found what can only be described as a 'hellhole' in the Jamaica district of the Borough of Queens. It was a concrete floored basement with three camp beds and very basic bathroom facilities. For this the landlords (the Rachmans as we called them) charged us $75 a week. There was no air conditioning and we had to plead for a small fan in what felt like a furnace during that particularly hot summer. Jamaica was a pretty tough area of Queens and even Tom was slightly concerned about us staying there. If our parents had had any idea of our situation, I suspect we would have been on the first flight home. Finances were inevitably tight, we didn't know exactly when we would be paid, and needless to say the Rachmans had demanded cash in advance. We discovered and became regular customers of Tad's Steak Bar, where for $1.29 you could get a 16oz New York strip steak, a giant Idaho baked potato with butter, corn on the cob and a cup of coffee.

On the sixth day we started work at midday, working a 2-10pm shift. We quickly learned that staffing levels were a contentious issue at Allied, a highly unionised set up. The company managed on the principle of core staffing levels backed up by overtime at either time-and-a-half or double time depending on the circumstances. In 1968 Allied's solution to their fluctuating staff requirements was that they would employ temporary workers in the peak summer season and integrate them into their permanent shift patterns. The unions didn't like this solution and, being part of the first tranche of temporary employees, Alan, Ed and I were not well received by our fellow workers.

That first day we were allocated to our teams and it became clear that jobs were on a two-tier system, the prime jobs being in baggage handling, apparently due to the opportunities presented of supplementing income by theft. Fortunately, we were in the cleaning section and our workmates were a motley assortment, clearly not savvy enough to be baggage handlers.

All rubbish had to be removed from the aircraft. One of the principles laid down to us by the team leader was that anything of value found on board was to be turned over to him to be returned to the airlines' representatives. We quickly learned that, to a man, our teammates were – almost without exception – a bunch of petty criminals and that the Team Leader shared out all the spoils with his friends. There was even a pecking order, with the Team Leader always cleaning out the First-Class section and his deputy Business Class. It was not an exacting job but the main pressure on us was time, with around 45 minutes allocated per flight. Late arrivals meant even more pressure. Turning an aircraft around on time required a high level of coordination and I quickly learnt the values of team working and organisation.

That first summer was difficult. Getting to work from our cauldron in Jamaica took well over an hour and at night on the return journey we wisely decided to go together, which meant waiting until all three of us had finished our shifts. Travelling at that time and walking through Jamaica was rather scary, although none of us would admit it. Because of union rules overtime was inevitably given to the regular employees, but we got the odd hour here and there if a job ran over. As we gradually got to know the rest of the team and they us, they realised that we were not a threat but just three young students trying to earn an honest crust and that we would be gone by the end of the summer. Some were more affable than others but I certainly wouldn't have trusted any of them. However, I did learn about relationships, people working together and how to interact with others. You don't have to like people to cooperate and work with them. All this would serve me in good stead in later years.

New York was a great place to be in 1968. On our days off we would go sightseeing. Tom Corcoran would sometimes meet us and show us around, or take us for a barbeque at his home in New Rochelle, Westchester County. We would sit in his yard and he and Kay would regale us with tales of their life together, his time in the New York Police Department and their great shared love of Ireland. That summer was extremely hot. It could be extremely humid at times and it never seemed to rain. Tom drove us around many other parts of the city and I particularly remember one night when he drove us back home through Harlem, where in over 30 blocks we never once saw a white face.

Politically, it was fascinating being there in a Presidential election year. The previous three months had seen violence, unrest and riots in over 100 US cities following the assassination of Martin Luther King[2] on 4th April and of Senator Bobby Kennedy[3] on 5th June. Senators Kennedy and Eugene McCarthy[4] had been running for the Democratic nomination and, after Kennedy's death, New York switched its support to McCarthy. We visited McCarthy's campaign headquarters, where hundreds of

[2] Martin Luther King 1929-68, American Baptist Minister and activist. Leader of the Civil Rights Movement 1955-68
[3] Senator Robert F Kennedy 1925-68, American politician and lawyer. US attorney 1961-64
[4] Senator Eugene McCarthy 1916-2005, American politician and poet. Senator for Minnesota 1959-71

young people were running around enthusiastically. Quite what they were doing was something of a mystery!

 I had planned to visit Ted and Adeline in California, so I only worked until the end of August. That summer I earned $1,518 and paid $272 in income tax. We later found out that our J1 visa status meant that we shouldn't have had income tax deducted and were able to reclaim it from the IRS at the end of the tax year.

I booked the cheapest flight from JFK to San Francisco and visited Ted and Adeline in their first home in Miller Avenue in the hills above Berkeley, with a panoramic view west over the Golden Gate Bridge. Adeline was expecting their first child, Iain. I stayed with them for two weeks, the first of my many visits. It was also a great time to be in San Francisco - during the hippy period and in the final lead up to the election.

My taste buds were considerably enhanced as Ted and Adeline were developing the culinary skills that made both of them outstanding chefs. The highlight of this trip was dinner at the world-famous Exposition Fish Grotto at Fisherman's Wharf in San Francisco. Here I had my first ever Lobster Thermidor, priced at $4.25, which seemed extortionate at that time. Sadly, the lobster and I parted company during the night and, after sampling shellfish on one more occasion during the visit, it was to be 20 years before I risked it again.

During the following year, Tom managed to arrange a start date at Allied for us. We unanimously decided to give Jamaica a miss and move somewhere slightly more upscale - i.e. safer.

Our initial five days at Penn Central enabled us to hit the streets of Long Island looking for accommodation and within a couple days we had rented another basement - indeed this one could almost be described as an apartment. There was even a swimming pool in the back yard and it almost proved our undoing. One night after work we had repaired to a late opening bar, consumed a few beers, acquired some female company and indulged in a bit of skinny dipping in the pool at around 4am. The result was that next evening we returned from work to meet very stern landlords creating hell and threatening to evict us on the spot. Some nosy neighbour had apparently observed part of the proceedings and the day was only saved when I was able to produce a pair of pale fawn swimming trunks. As they were practically flesh coloured, said neighbour must have been mistaken in thinking that I was naked. How prudish the Americans are!

That summer, working at JFK was much less stressful and much more enjoyable. We established a relationship with a group of Aer Lingus stewardesses. Their rota included one overnight stay at their New York base, The Statler Hilton Hotel in Manhattan. When they were in town, we finished our shift sharp at 10pm and got into Manhattan as soon as possible as some of their parties there were legendary! (For those who love irrelevant information, the hotel's phone number was PE6500 as in the famous Glen Miller song.)

The summer was also much more lucrative. The practice of 'temporary labour' had been established the previous summer and we were, if not quite welcomed back, no longer seen as a threat. The overtime potential, which had been covertly blocked the previous year, was now freely available and my IRS return for 1969 shows earnings of $2,731 and income tax of $584, which I was again able to claim back the following year.

In summer 1970 we headed back to New York, this time with a different plan. After five very pleasant days in Manhattan, we headed to the Pocono mountain resorts in Pennsylvania, looking for hotel, waiting, and bar work. We spent two fruitless days, didn't really like the look of the area and, within 48 hours, were back working at JFK. Through good fortune we had also stumbled on a house in Queens occupied by a trainee Irish priest Sean, who was looking after it for the owners who were in Ireland for the summer. What followed was an eventful summer, with Sean eagerly participating in every activity alongside us, drinking, clubbing, women et al.

That year I only stayed for ten weeks, returning for a six-week tour of Europe with Rowan Bell and Finlay Orr. I flew to Dublin overnight. My parents delivered me immediately to Rowan's house in Craigavad and we set off in an elderly Humber Super Snipe on that evening's Larne-Stranraer ferry and drove overnight to Dover. Exhausted, the following morning we stopped in Deauville and I immediately fell asleep on the beach, awakening with severe sunburn. We travelled through France and Switzerland and into Italy via the Bremner Pass where the car's brakes burned fiercely on the way down and almost ran out during the final descent. We attended the Italian Grand Prix in Monza, a mix up over tickets sorted out by Rowan's father's old friend, the famous Count 'Johnnie' Lurani[5]. The meeting was marred by the death of Jochen Rindt[6] in practice on 5th September. We travelled extensively through Italy, retraced our steps and returned home, our entire six-week trip costing us £77 each.

[5] Giovanni 'Johnnie' Lurani, VIII Count of Calvenzano, 1905-95, automobile engineer; racing car driver and journalist
[6] Jochen Rindt, 1942-1970, Austrian-German racing driver; Formula 1 World Champion 1970, the only racing driver to be awarded the title posthumously

Circuit of Ireland Rally 1970, with Rowan Bell

Circuit of Ireland Rally 1971, with Dessie Nutt

CHAPTER 6   TRN GRADUATE TRAINEESHIP 1971-73

"God, grant me the serenity to accept the things I cannot change
Courage to change the things I can,
And wisdom to know the difference."   Reinhold Niebuhr[1]

In Spring 1971 I signed a contract with TRN, then one of the largest regional newspaper groups in the UK and owned by Roy Thomson. The Canadian Thomson[2] had come to the UK in 1952 and, according to Harry Reid[3], bought The Scotsman for 'peanuts'. Thomson went on to be a press baron like his fellow countryman Lord Beaverbrook, but Reid finds few similarities between them. "Beaverbrook was not motivated by financial considerations; he was essentially a megalomaniac journalist and he was prepared to throw money at his newspapers in defiance of all commercial convention. Thomson on the other hand was utterly uninterested in editorial matters and wanted to use his newspapers to make money."[4] He famously described editorial as "the bits between the advertisements". In 1959 he purchased the Kemsley Group of newspapers, which included The Sunday Times. He added The Times in 1966 and presided over a media empire of more than 200 newspapers in Canada, the United States, and the UK. The Thomson Organisation eventually became a multi-million-dollar corporation, with interests in publishing, printing, television, travel and North Sea oil. In his takeover of Scottish Television, he also famously described the company as "a permit to print money" (often misquoted as 'a licence to print money').

His purchase of the Belfast Telegraph (BT) was marred by controversy. The paper's owner Bobby Baird[5] had died in a motor racing crash in Snetterton in 1953. Several potential buyers, including Roy Thomson, began courting the trustees from early 1960 and a messy takeover battle ensued, eventually ending up in the courts and dragging on for over a year. It was not until September 1961 that a High Court Ruling enabled Thomson to buy the company.

He was deeply hurt by his experience and in 'Abuse of an Innocent Tycoon,' a chapter in his autobiography[6], he wrote, "Such imputations on my integrity and honour as were made in Belfast, have never been made in any other court or, as far as I know, in any other place. Though I own its main newspaper, and though I was invited on one occasion by the Governor General, and again by the Prime Minister, I have never gone back to that tragic city and I never will. This whole affair left me with a great feeling of unhappiness and a deep sense of injustice. The accusations they hurled at me, though later rescinded, were the one blot on my business career." Interestingly he also made some prescient observations on the political situation in

[1] Reinhold Niebuhr 1892-1971, The Serenity Prayer
[2] The Rt. Hon. Roy Herbert Thomson, 1st Baron Thomson of Fleet, 1894-1976
[3] Harry Reid b.1947, Editor of The Herald 1997-2000
[4] 'Deadline: The Story of the Scottish Press', Harry Reid, 2006, St Andrew Press, Edinburgh
[5] Bobby Baird, 1912-53, newspaper proprietor; racing driver
[6] 'After I Was Sixty', Lord Thomson of Fleet, 1975, Hamish Hamilton London

Northern Ireland, "For the record, I should add that, even under the editorship of JE Sayers[7], whom we kept in office, and to a more substantial degree under that of Eugene Wason[8], who succeeded him, the Belfast Telegraph became a more liberal and fairer and a much better paper. Maybe this advance of liberalisation in the paper was really what had been fought in that court and it was one of the changes that came too late to stop the Ulster tragedy." True to his word, Roy Thomson never did return to Belfast, but there is no doubt that he regarded BT as the jewel in his crown.

In actual fact, Sayers was to make a major contribution to promoting the ideals of tolerance, justice and peace in Northern Ireland. A number of his editorials in the immediate lead up to The Troubles got to the heart of the matter but sadly the bulk of the Unionist population were not in the mood to listen.

"The enemies of Northern Ireland are a very small body of extremists of one kind or another; the great majority of the population are responsible citizens, all of whom have a contribution to make and all of whom must have equal rights. The changes that will be entailed in some areas, Derry among them, may be painful to some traditionalists. But they will be less painful than periodic outbreaks of disorder that will keep the political pot boiling and Northern Ireland under a perpetual cloud." (8th October 1968)

"Half a century is certainly none too short a period for any ruling party to have undertaken the adjustment that is now inescapable. The greatest regret today is that it was not begun 15 instead of five years ago." (25th October 1968)

"The threat to Northern Ireland's future…comes from Protestant Ulstermen who will not allow themselves to be liberated from the delusion that every Roman Catholic is their enemy." (5th November 1968)

Thomson was eventually succeeded by his son Kenneth[9]. I met Kenneth Thomson when he visited BT shortly after his father's death. He was a very different character to his father and spent an increasing part of his life amassing a significant art collection. Strangely, he never used his title in Canada, "In London, I'm Lord Thomson, in Toronto, I'm Ken. I have two sets of Christmas cards, and two sets of stationery. You might say I'm having my cake and eating it too. I'm honouring a promise to my father by being Lord Thomson and, at the same time, I can be just Ken."[10] When he died, Forbes listed him as the richest person in Canada, worth $19.6 billion.

In September 1971 I started at BT as a graduate trainee, with an annual salary of £1,100. I was initially assigned to the Classified Advertising Department and spent four months in the Field Sales team and two in the Tele-Ad section.

Living at home and suitably suited and booted, having passed muster from my mother (who had very strong views on how one should dress), I set out for Belfast

[7] Jack Sayers, Editor BT 1953-69
[8] Eugene Wason, Editor BT 1969-74.
[9] Kenneth Roy Thomson, 2nd Baron Thomson of Fleet, 1923-2006
[10] Interview in Saturday Night magazine, 1980

on Monday 6th September. Taking around 30 minutes, it was not a particularly arduous commute. The Classified Advertising department was on the ground floor of 124 Royal Avenue, BT's impressive building. The Classified operation was a huge revenue contributor and the department was headed by Paul Jellett[11], who had joined the company in 1963 as a sales representative and had a meteoric rise before being appointed manager in 1968. Under Paul, the Tele-Ad team of some 30 people was headed by the formidable Margaret Clarke[12] (later to become Deputy Managing Director) and Field Sales, a team of six, was headed by Terry McCaughey[13].

It turned out I was the first ever graduate trainee at BT. The problem with being the first was that there was no established norm, so my role was subject to interpretation every step of the way. Terry introduced me to his team and, although they were friendly enough, there was no great enthusiasm for my arrival. In some ways I was seen as a threat but they weren't quite sure what the threat was. On top of this, the Classified Sales representatives had an inbuilt inferiority complex compared to their counterparts in Display Advertising. From the start what impressed me was the standard of training. One of Roy Thomson's shrewdest moves was importing two advertising 'gurus' from North America – Jim Alexander in Display and George Pappas in Classified. They were responsible for creating the training programmes which later made TRN the envy of the sector. Even almost 50 years later I can still remember Pappas's four stages of salesmanship, AIDA – Attention, Interest, Desire, Action.

As I had no company car, I was given a rather loosely defined area of the city centre to explore for new leads but, since that inevitably resulted in treading on someone else's toes, there was always a level of tension. What my new colleagues failed to realise was that, as I was only there for four months, any significant leads I developed would be handed to them when I left.

Politically and logistically, it was not the best time to be operating in Belfast city centre. Internment had been introduced by the Faulkner Government[14] in August 1971 and it led to increased shootings, bombings and attacks on the security forces. Between August and September there were 140 deaths, with the worst attack very close to the office at McGurk's Bar in North Queen Street, in which 15 people died. I had two frightening experiences. The first was crossing a busy street near Unity Flats and hearing shots fired nearby. The natural reaction was to take cover and half a dozen of us piled into the nearest shop doorway, crouching there for almost an hour before the area was cleared. The second incident took place in the office itself which was to come under attack several times during the Troubles. The Classified Department was on the ground floor and its windows, which faced Royal Avenue, were bomb proof. One morning, a bomb exploded just across the street and, as I looked out of the window, I saw a woman literally lifted into the air by the force of

[11] Paul Jellett, Belfast Telegraph 1963-84, Classified Manager 1968-77
[12] Margaret Clarke b. 1936, Belfast Telegraph 1963-96, Tele-Ad Manager 1969-78
[13] Terry McCaughey b. 1942, Belfast Telegraph 1966-2006, Classified Field Sales Supervisor 1969-78
[14] The Rt. Hon. Brian, Baron Faulkner of Downpatrick 1921-77. Sixth and last Prime Minister of Northern Ireland

the blast. Miraculously, she got up, dusted herself down and carried on - a normal day in Belfast.

A BT editorial in early 1972 did not envisage an imminent bright future, "If it is true that the darkest hour precedes the dawn, then Northern Ireland may hope for streaks of light in the sky in 1972. The year past could hardly seem worse. The turning point must come soon."

I had two major successes during my time in Field Sales. I was responsible for the first advertisement in Northern Ireland for a massage parlour/sauna. I had identified a new business registered in Glengormley in the north of the city and secured an appointment. After giving proof of my identity, I was admitted (the door was initially locked) to a small suite of offices above a shop and made my pitch to an extremely attractive lady. I presented a series of small ads on postcards, which she could peruse at her leisure. My initial suggestion for this business was, "Enjoy a deep massage by one of our attractive assistants." She loved this approach and I left having secured a six-month contract and came back to the office a hero. Subsequent visits always had the same pattern: locked door, very attractive female staff, and each time they increased the size of their advertisement. Business was clearly booming. Shortly after I left BT, they were raided by the police and closed down, allegedly for running a brothel.

Sadly, my other claim to fame was as a result of the Troubles. A large bomb had exploded in North Street Arcade, again quite close to our office. A warning had been given, so fortunately there were no casualties but about 20 small businesses were almost completely destroyed. Despite this, a fantastic spirit emerged from the people affected and they worked for the next 72 hours to get back on their feet. One of them, a jeweller, was one of my customers and when I heard what had happened, I asked our Art Studio to mock up a full-page advertisement. "Business as Usual" occupied the top third of the page, with the bottom two-thirds divided into 18 small spaces, one for each business in the Arcade. The following morning, I met the jeweller at a nearby coffee shop. I had prepared a lengthy sales pitch, but as soon as I met him, he was transfixed on my brown paper parcel containing the made up ad. "What's in there?" he kept asking as I made my pitch. The second I finished he ripped off the paper. Not only did I secure an instant sale, he was so impressed that he helped me persuade the other 17 businesses to do the same. The resulting full-page ad appeared in the paper the evening before the Arcade reopened. The result was major kudos for me within the Classified Department and a major kick up the backside for the Display Department for not having come up with the idea themselves. It's difficult to describe accurately what life was like in Belfast then. I had great admiration for the city's retailers, who existed on a perilous basis, their premises bombed on a fairly regular basis, sometimes without any warning being given. It was a grim state of affairs, but life went on.

During that Christmas season in the Classified Department there seemed to be an endless series of parties. Margaret Clarke's Tele-Ad team (exclusively female in those days) was as hardnosed a bunch of salespeople as you will ever encounter, operating in a highly competitive environment, but they also knew how to let their hair down. Office parties were mind blowing.

In early 1972 I moved into the Tele-Ads Section for eight weeks to complete the first phase of my traineeship. Margaret Clarke was one of the best managers of people I have ever worked with. Although the staff were from both sides of the community, there was an enormous sense of inclusiveness and Margaret's belief that the workplace should be fun shone through.

Part of my training involved answering incoming calls and on my first day I spoke to an elderly lady, who wanted to place an ad for her lost dog. My proposal didn't quite match the famous classified advertisement that was mentioned in Tom Shields' Diary in The Herald many years later; "Lost - black and white dog. Half of tail missing. Torn ear, blind in one eye, limps a bit. Answers to the name Lucky." This lady was deeply upset about her loss and dithered over the numerous suggestions I presented to her. After about 15 minutes I glanced up to see everyone in the room rolling around in fits of laughter. The call had been made by one of them and everyone was listening in. My initiation ceremony completed, I was given a huge round of applause. Happy days.

In March I was advised that the next part of my traineeship would be in Newcastle-upon-Tyne, as part of the Display Advertising team on The Journal, the north-east of England's morning newspaper.

By this stage my MG Midget had seen better days, not helped by an incident in late March. On a beautiful sunny day, I was driving down the Shankill Road when my attention was drawn to an attractive blonde. So transfixed was I that, when the traffic stopped, I didn't and my car was impaled on the towing hook of the enormous lorry in front. Luckily there was not a mark on the lorry, but the front of my car looked very much the worse for wear. (Note to self: keep eyes on road at all times and do not get distracted by blondes with long legs and short skirts).

I arrived at the Newcastle Chronicle and Journal Ltd. (NCJ) in early April. I responded to a Classified ad to join three other professionals renting a house in Jesmond and passed the 'interview'. One of the major challenges was that each occupant was expected to produce an evening meal and I was allocated the following Thursday. That day I went shopping during my lunch break and bought what turned out to be the toughest steaks I have ever tasted. I was informed by my companions that the standard would need to improve by the following week, so I purchased the first of many cookbooks and started to take cooking a little more seriously.

NCJ was very different to Belfast. It was a much bigger operation, publishing three newspapers - The Journal, The Evening Chronicle, and The Sunday Sun. It was in the Groat Market, with more than 20 pubs and restaurants within two minutes of the front door. The Bigg Market, just 50 yards up the street, was one of the city's major centres of nightlife.

I was not the first Graduate Trainee there, so had a better-defined role. My boss was Joe Logan, an Aberdonian, whom I was to encounter again many years later during my brief sojourn at The Scotsman. The Field Sales Manager was Stuart Robertson[15], a tall, lean Scot with a great sense of humour. Stuart took me under his wing and I spent a lot of time with his team socially, not always with the approval of his relatively new wife Moira. Stuart and Moira were both from Edinburgh and he eventually returned there to launch Robertson Advertising. Joe was demanding but fair. He held a daily 9am team meeting and operated a rigid system of time keeping so woe betide anyone who was late. Daily sales figures were produced and recorded by Stuart – my introduction to instant accountability.

As in Belfast, Sales Reps were assigned specific territories. I was assigned the 'graveyard territory', consisting of anything west of Hexham, including Carlisle (less than 2% of the total Journal sales) and the rump of the South Durham coalfield towns of Consett, Stanley and Beamish – not exactly dominant Journal country. I had to forage for whatever pickings were available, which involved a significant amount of cold calling. I had some success, including a full-page ad for a new hotel in the Allenheads area and some modest advertisements from retailers in Carlisle.

As throughout my career with TRN, the training in Newcastle was first-class. Advertising then was very different to today and a list of the standards in the 1982 British Code of Advertising Practice makes interesting reading. Breath Testing Devices and related products, Artificial Sweeteners, Betting Tipsters, Smoking Deterrents, and Self-Defence Courses were all banned. There were specific, very detailed appendices for advertising in the following categories: Slimming (five pages), Consumer Credit, Hair and Scalp Products, and "Diseases to which no reference or only limited reference may be made." This was accompanied by a list of 82 such diseases which included; Barber's Rash, Breast Diseases or the development of same, Carbuncles, The Itch (See Scabies), Sexual Weaknesses, and Varicose Veins except where the reference is confined to relief by plastic stockings." It was fascinating but a huge amount of information for a trainee salesman to adsorb.

I seemed to have mastered the techniques of selling display advertising and received an excellent review from Joe, before moving to the Circulation Department for the final part of my training. Life within Circulation was perhaps not as sophisticated as Advertising, certainly in the eyes of the Display team. I nonetheless made many new friends during this period.

Social life in Newcastle was fantastic, especially for a young single man. It was an endless succession of evenings and weekends in pubs, nightclubs, restaurants, casinos and the like. It was also the start of my lifelong love of Newcastle United Football Club and many visits to St. James' Park. In early March I had my final review with Tudor Hopkins. It was very positive with excellent feedback, resulting

---

[15] Stuart Robertson b.1950 m. Moira 1s. 1d., Field Sales Supervisor, The Journal 1971-73, Founder, Robertson Advertising 1978, Marketing Advantage 1989

in the offer of a permanent role within the organisation as Assistant to the Circulation Manager at the Belfast Telegraph.

One of the most important things that I learned during my traineeship was the importance of presentation. 20 years later Tony Blair and his gang of five were to make it one of the cornerstones of New Labour. A great illustration of presentation is a story from the Milne brothers, all Scottish rugby internationals. Iain Milne[16] tells of how he was capped 44 times for Scotland, his brother Kenny 39 times whilst brother David managed only 1 cap "or as he likes to put it, he is one of the three Milne brothers who between them have played 84 times for Scotland."

---

[16] Iain 'The Bear' Milne b.1958, speaking recently at a Dollar Academy dinner

Early colleagues in Belfast, l-r:
John Refausse, CMcC, Philip Graf and Ken Simpson

Chapter 7

FIRST REAL JOB - BELFAST TELEGRAPH 1973 - 78

"If you aim for the sky, you'll reach the ceiling. If you aim for the ceiling, you'll stay on the floor." Bill Shankley[1]

I started my first "real" job in the BT on a cold and dreary 2nd April 1973. Neither the newspaper nor the political situation in Northern Ireland had changed. I was in a new department and working with a team largely new to me. The Circulation Department was headed by Lynn Kearney[2], a highly intelligent newspaper veteran and a bon viveur (to put it mildly). Lynn's team comprised Roy Lyttle[3], (who was to become a lifelong friend); Raymond Connor[4], Joe Adams[5], and John Allen[6]. My relationship with John was marred by my two major skirmishes in company cars during my time there – never a great way to endear oneself.

My role as Assistant to the Circulation Manager was a newly created one. The team had all come through the ranks locally and might have been regarded as slightly insular by people in London. Since Roy Thomson had acquired the BT in 1961 there had been permanent tension between the parent company in London and its various subsidiaries, including Belfast. I was to encounter similar situations frequently during my later spells at Mirror Group and News International. I suspect that Tudor Hopkins was following a well-oiled strategy of installing an outsider in one of the publishing companies. He would have hoped that my being from Belfast might make the situation easier. Lynn's reputation would have caused some concern in London and strengthening the Belfast management team was prudent. I am sure that Lynn sensed the motive behind my appointment, but he always treated me with unfailing courtesy and helped enormously in my integration into the team. Also, BT operated in a marketplace considerably more dangerous than any other TRN centre. The group was therefore determined to give its management all the help and support they needed.

From April 1973 until September 1978 I had a variety of roles within the Circulation Department, eventually becoming Deputy Circulation Manager under Lynn's successor, Roger Roach[7]. I remained with the Group until 1984 and, during that time, the level of training and personal development I received was impressive. TRN invested heavily in staff development. I attended internal training courses, usually a week long, on Managing People, Communication Skills and Management

---

[1] Bill Shankley OBE 1913-81, Manager Liverpool FC 1959-74
[2] Lynn Kearney, Circulation Manager BT
[3] Roy Lyttle, b.1947, Field Sales Supervisor BT 1972-80, Circulation Manager, latterly Circulation Director
[4] Raymond Connor, Van Sales Supervisor BT
[5] Joe Adams, Direct Delivery Supervisor BT
[6] John Allen, Transport Manager BT
[7] Roger Roach, Circulation Manager BT

Techniques and I also attended an external Management Techniques course at Ashridge Management College. I had my first formal training in Marketing with two modules, one with MDS Belfast and the other with the Irish Management Institute and I also attended an Industrial Relations course at Linden Hall, Oxford. Here I met the trade unionist Joe Wade[8] over dinner one evening – organised, I suppose, to give us all some impression of life on the other side. Joe consumed copious amounts of alcohol, especially during the after-dinner discussion and, when he became incoherent, was wheeled off to bed.

1972 was by far the worst year of the Troubles to date, with 467 dead, 10,628 shootings and 1,382 bombs. Government was by now by Direct Rule from Westminster, the Northern Ireland Parliament at Stormont having been suspended in March 1977. Willie Whitelaw[9] was the first of many Secretaries of State for Northern Ireland.

BT had a very strong management team; Tim Willis[10] was MD, Bob Crane[11] his assistant and Eugene Wason, Editor. The legendary Malcolm Brodie[12] was the BT's Sports Editor and Editor of Ireland's Saturday Night. Years later Malcolm wrote the excellent official history of the Belfast Telegraph[13]: He was a great friend to both Claire and me and I was delighted to invite him to Glasgow when I was Chairman of the Newspaper Press Fund. He was a sports journalist of international reputation and had covered every football World Cup since 1958. He was a great raconteur and often told the story of covering a game in deepest Russia in the early 1960s when he had great difficulty in filing his copy. After many attempts he eventually got through to BT's switchboard and had just got out the words "Malcolm Brodie" when the switchboard operator interrupted and said, "sorry, he's in Russia" and cut him off. Claire is mentioned in Malcolm's book (I don't feature!) but he credits her as being part of the Promotions team which ran a terrific fund-raising campaign in celebration of Mary Peters'[14] 1972 gold medal at the Munich Olympics. Claire actually joined BT in October 1973, but never let the facts get in the way of a good story!

The other members of the BT management team were Mike McCann (Display Advertising Manager), Jay Oliver Jnr (Promotions Manager), Jim Craft (Production Manager) and Roy Shaw (Accounts Manager). In turn Roy Lilley[15] took over as Editor, with Ed Curran[16] as his Deputy. Ken Simpson[17] succeeded Roy Shaw and Philip Graf[18] succeeded Jay Oliver Jr.

[8] Joe Wade 1919-2004. General Secretary National Graphical Association 1976-84
[9] The Rt Hon The Viscount Whitelaw, William Whitelaw 1918-99. Conservative politician, latterly de facto Deputy Prime Minister
[10] Tim Willis BT Managing Director 1970-77
[11] Bob Crane BT Managing Director 1979-95
[12] Malcolm Brodie MBE 1926-2013. Scottish born sports journalist
[13] 'The Tele, A History of the Belfast Telegraph' Malcolm Brodie, The Blackstaff Press, 1995
[14] Dame Mary Peters DBE CBE, b.1939, Gold Medal winner, Pentathlon, Munich Olympics 1972
[15] Roy Lilley OBE b.1938, Editor Belfast Telegraph 1974-92, only UK journalist to receive the World Association of Newspaper's Golden Pen of Freedom Award 1977
[16] Ed Curran Deputy Editor, then Editor of the BT 1993-2005
[17] Ken Simpson latterly Accounts Manager BT
[18] Philip Graf, Promotions Manager BT, subsequently Liverpool Post and Echo and eventually CEO, Trinity Mirror plc

What was quite remarkable about Belfast was its ability to produce its own talent. Within TRN as a whole, bright and promising people could forge careers by regularly moving between the various publishing centres. After leaving Belfast I spent a year working for the Group in London, followed by three years in Newcastle-Upon-Tyne and three years in Reading, before moving briefly to The Scotsman in Edinburgh. Not surprisingly, people were reluctant to move to Northern Ireland at the time. BT therefore had to produce much of its own talent in-house. Bob Crane, after a brief spell in Chester, returned as Managing Director. Production Manager Derek Carvell eventually rose to the same position. Margaret Clarke became Assistant Managing Director and my old friend Roy Lyttle Circulation Director. Many also went on to greater things elsewhere. Early trail blazers were Tom Lennon[19] (head of Thomson Publications in South Africa) and Ambrose Turnbull[20] (MD, Thomson Magazines, London). Former MD David Sneddon[21] went on to be TRN's Joint Managing Director and subsequently CEO and Chairman of Liverpool Post and Echo plc. Philip Graf became CEO of Trinity Mirror plc. There were many others and I attribute any later career success of my own to having been shaped, prepared and made ready to join the talent line by my time in Belfast.

On my return to Belfast I had responded to an advertisement in the paper to share part of a rather impressive house in Holywood, County Down, about six miles from Belfast. The elderly owners had decanted to the ground floor and converted the rest of the large, three storey building into an impressive four bedroom flat. An ability to cook to a required standard was again a prerequisite. I was soon joined by Jim Paul,[22] a Mancunian working for the Northern Ireland Tourist Board. Jim would become my partner in crime for many hair-raising episodes during our time there.

It's hard to convey what it was like living in Northern Ireland at the height of The Troubles. On one extreme was a daily menu of violence, bombing, shooting and civil disorder and on the other an attempt to maintain some form of normality on a day to day basis. Bombs regularly went off in the area around BT at the time, so I suppose it was inevitable that there would be a major incident in the plant itself. I was not in the building on Wednesday 19th September 1976 when a large bomb was driven into the loading bay. After the bombers shot their way out, it exploded without any warning being given. Tragically, one employee died and 14 others were wounded. It was miraculous that the casualties weren't higher, with 800 staff in the building. The building was badly damaged, with three of the four presses taken out of commission, but a four-page paper was produced the following afternoon.

BT's branch offices were also regularly targeted and on Saturday 10th October 1976 two delivery drivers were shot dead as they distributed the sports paper on the Crumlin Road. During the Troubles, well over 100 BT delivery vans were hijacked or

---

[19] Tom Lennon Managing Director of Thomson Publications, South Africa
[20] Ambrose Turnbull Managing Director, Thomson Magazines, London
[21] David Sneddon 1933-2017. BT Managing Director 1967-70, CEO and latterly Chairman Liverpool Post and Echo plc and subsequently Trinity International plc
[22] Jim Paul b.1951, General Manager Northern Ireland Tourist Board, latterly Tourism Ireland's Head of Australia and emerging markets

destroyed and the company operated a contingency plan for such occasions. When a delivery van was hijacked, the driver would phone in the details of the incident and someone would drive to a pre-agreed rendezvous with a new van and supply of papers. The traumatised driver would then complete his run. Newsagents' premises also suffered a high rate of attrition, hence the slogan, 'Buy now whilst shops last'.

Despite this, life continued and it certainly wasn't an easy time, but I believe that the odds of being killed or maimed during The Troubles were around the same as being in a serious road accident, so you simply hoped that the chances of anything happening to you were fairly slim. These odds further increased if you took an element of care in day to day living, avoided known trouble spots and were always on the outlook for anything unusual. However, as I left the office late one night, a bomb went off nearby outside a bar just beyond our carpark. I ran to the scene to see if I could help. Several people were injured and the army and medical teams arrived very quickly. I was just leaving when I stepped on something. To my horror, I discovered it was a body lying in some rubble – a torso actually, with no limbs. The memory of that remains with me still. A huge number of people left Northern Ireland in this period, fearing for their safety. The rest of us just made the best of it, and, believe me, it was possible to do just that, surprising as it may seem.

BT had its own established pub – in fact it had two: McGlade's and the Brown Horse. The first was my favourite. It was owned by Frank McGlade, a great host, always immaculately turned out, with a fresh rose in his lapel every day. Owning a pub in Belfast then was extremely risky and McGlade's experienced its fair share of terrorist attacks. I (and subsequently Claire) have many happy memories of the pub. Indeed, Frank presented us with a beautiful oil painting of Muckish Mountain in Donegal as a wedding present and it hangs in our home to this day. To many in BT, McGlade's was an institution and very much part of our day to day life. My colleagues and I lunched there frequently and often also repaired there after work. On Saturdays, which I worked once a month, it was the lunch and pre-match drinking den for the football writers - apart from Malcolm Brodie, who was a Brown Horse man. The hacks would assemble at midday and swap stories and anecdotes until around 2.15pm, when cars would pick them up and take them to whatever game they were covering. I particularly remember Paddy Toner from the Sunday Mirror. He was capable of having five or six pints during lunch before being poured into a car, and I often wondered how he could actually see and remember what took place during the game that he reported on.

I now had an increasing circle of friends outside work. Rowan Bell and Finlay Orr from University days had been joined by David Wilson, an estate agent, Billy Johnson, a toy wholesaler and Bobby Gilmore, who was in the construction industry. Life revolved more around organised events like parties and barbecues, rather than going out on the town. Golf was now very much part of my life and I had joined Holywood Golf Club, from which Rory McIroy[23] was to emerge years later. A very

---

[23] Rory McIlroy MBE, b. 1989, World No. 1 Ranking for 95 Weeks, US Open Champion, Congressional 2011, PGA Champion, Kaiwah 2012, PGA Champion, Valhalla 2014, Open Champion, Royal Liverpool 2014

young David Feherty[24] had just joined as a Junior Assistant Professional. At the end of a lesson with a senior lady member she asked him how he thought she was getting on. He replied, "Madam, if I were you, I would give up the game."

Feherty of course went on to play successfully on the European Tour and became a leading broadcaster in the US. Over the years he found unique, colourful and uninhibited ways of describing what he saw. Amongst his gems are;

"It would be easier to pick a broken nose, than a winner in that group."

"That ball is so far left Lassie couldn't find it even if it was wrapped in bacon."

"I'm sorry Nick Faldo[25] couldn't be here this week. He is attending the birth of his next wife."

"Jim Furyk's[26] swing looks like an octopus falling out of a tree."

"That's a great shot - with that swing."

"That was a great shot, if they had put the pin there today."

"That green appears smaller than a pygmy's nipple"

In October 1973, I heard there was a new member of staff in the Promotions department, Claire McConaghy. I'd caught a glimpse of her in the staff canteen on the day she joined and immediately found an excuse to visit her department that afternoon. We were introduced by Mollie McKelvie, one of the Promotions executives, and, as they say, the rest is history! During her induction Claire visited the Circulation department, where we never needed much of an excuse to organise a good lunch. Raymond Connor had arranged for us to go to Corr's Corner, then a fashionable restaurant in Glengormley. We all had a most agreeable lunch with a few glasses of wine and I became increasingly taken with Claire.

It was not long before I asked Claire out. Gradually we discovered a great ease in each other's company and started seeing a lot of each other, sometimes going to McGlade's after work. She had a boyfriend but I'm delighted to report that he didn't last long! In 1974, Claire's photograph appeared in the paper. According to my sister Niki (I have no recollection of this) I phoned her and told her to buy the paper that day as there was a picture in it of the girl I was going to marry. I clearly had a well-developed sense of prescience. "Claire" comes from the Latin 'clara,' meaning

---

[24] David Feherty b.1958, former professional golfer CBS TV golf commentator 2007-15
[25] Sir Nick Faldo, b. 1952, winner of six Major Championships, The Masters 1989, 1990, 1996 Augusta, The Open 1987 Muirfield, 1990 St. Andrews, 1992 St Andrews
[26] Jim Furyk b.1970, winner US Open 2003, Olympia Fields Illinois. Record lowest score in PGA tour history 58, 2016 Travelers Championship.

'bright and clear'. Other qualities include 'ladylike, caring, blessed with many feminine virtues.' I couldn't agree more!

Our relationship developed rapidly and I was soon introduced to Claire's parents Stewart[27] and Olive[28]. Stewart lectured at the Department of Agriculture at QUB where one of his students had been my brother-in-law Sam Moore. Claire had also attended QUB, graduating in Honours in English in 1972, a year after me, but our paths had never crossed. Claire met my parents and, despite my anxiety, all went well. Mum and Dad were instantly charmed by her. It still deeply saddens me that she only met my father three times before he suffered the massive stroke which was to partly paralyse him for the last three years of his life.

Claire loved the theatre. She was part of Format drama group and appeared in several of their plays. My appreciation of drama and theatre was relatively under-developed but I quickly grew to love it and over the years Claire and I have been incredibly lucky to see some of the world's greatest actors perform – Dustin Hoffman, Paul Scofield, Kenneth Branagh, Emma Thompson, Shirley Maclaine, Judi Dench, Maggie Smith, Derek Jacobi and Ian McKellen to name a few. Claire's own acting career was put on hold as we moved around the UK for the next 15 years but in 1994 she joined the Kilmacolm Dramatic Society and has appeared in many plays, including memorable performances in Calendar Girls and Quartet. Claire's final performance in Belfast was in a play called Albert's Bridge, in which I made my acting debut. It involved me and several others (in non-speaking parts) parading round and round the aforesaid Albert's Bridge. It was also my final role - not much of a loss to the acting profession, I can assure you. Together we developed an interest in classical music and from 1974 became regular attendees of the Ulster Orchestra, initially under Alun Francis[29] and latterly Bryden Thomson.[30]

Claire's experiences of The Troubles were far more dramatic than mine. In late 1974, she had just got into her car in a company car park when the door was wrenched open and an extremely agitated man pressed a knife to her stomach, demanding that she drive him to where he wanted to go, or she would be dead. As it was a two-door car, he wanted Claire to get out so that he could sit behind her in the back seat. Claire, unbelievably calm under the circumstances, said that she would take him wherever he wanted but that, as the back of the car was full of promotional material, he should go around and sit in the front passenger seat. As he did, she closed her door, slammed the car into reverse and shot out of the extremely narrow and tricky parking area onto the main street, with him chasing her with the knife. In a state of complete shock, she drove the seven miles to her parents' Holywood home, without stopping at a traffic light. When the police arrived, they told her that the man had stabbed someone in a nearby carpark just before the incident, hence his agitation.

---

[27] Dr Stewart McConaghy BSc, DSc, FRSC, 1919-2001, Soil Scientist, latterly visiting Professor University of the West Indies and University of Mexico City
[28] Olivia Cora McConaghy (neé Davidson) 1921-2009 2d. Claire, Joan 1s. Neil
[29] Alun Francis b.1943. Welsh conductor, Principal Conductor Ulster Orchestra 1966-76
[30] Bryden Thomson 1928-91. Scottish conductor, Principal Conductor Ulster Orchestra 1977-85

Claire was naturally very badly shaken by the whole affair so it was timely that shortly afterwards in November 1974 we had planned a holiday in the West Indies. Her father Stewart had been Professor of Soil Science at the University of the West Indies and the family had lived in Trinidad between 1968-71. Claire had done the first year of her university course in Trinidad, before returning to QUB for the remaining three years of her degree. For the holiday we saved up all our annual leave to spend four weeks in Trinidad, Tobago and Barbados. One of Stewart's colleagues had a holiday home in Barbados, where we stayed for more than two weeks. The house in Bathsheba had stunning views over the ocean on the east coast near where the Harry Belafonte movie Island in the Sun was filmed.

Roy Lilley succeeded Eugene Wason as Editor in early 1974 and built a strong team who performed admirably in difficult circumstances. I had the upmost respect for them all – Roy, Ed Curran, Norman Jenkinson,[31] Des McMullan,[32] Tom Carson[33] and Jim Gray.[34] The Troubles had now spread beyond Northern Ireland, with bombings and casualties in Birmingham, Guildford, Dublin and Monaghan. Invariably the front pages of the paper were dominated by the latest atrocities. Many people thought that this presented the Circulation Department with great opportunities for building sales. In fact, the events themselves and the mayhem they caused often led to lost sales as a result of evacuations and traffic chaos.

The first attempt at power sharing in Northern Ireland took place with elections for a new Assembly based at Stormont, the Parliament building on the East side of Belfast. The Assembly started in 1974 but only lasted five months in the face of violent opposition of many loyalists, who were opposed to the concept of power sharing. The end came after a loyalist workers' strike which virtually shut down the province. The BT was published throughout it and I had to negotiate several road blocks to get to work. This often led to an angry confrontation, depending on the participant's views of the BT itself. The newspaper's stance at that time was that power sharing was still the only basis upon which Northern Ireland could have a measure of self-government. On one particular day during the strike I feared my car was about to be torched by a belligerent crowd of protestors, until I heard a voice shout out, "He's OK, let him through". The voice belonged to a BT van driver.

It was during this time that I began to give some thoughts to proposing to Claire. Another event was also to nudge me in that direction. At the very end of 1974 one of our BT Display Advertising Representatives Arthur Raine appeared in the office. Arthur and his wife were emigrating to Johannesburg in South Africa (thoughts of out of the frying pan and into the fire did go through my mind at the time!). Arthur was selling his house and contents and, with their departure date growing closer, the sale had fallen through. He said to me, "I don't suppose you fancy buying a house?" A week later, now in even more debt, I was the proud owner of 32 Christine Drive, a three-bedroomed semi-detached bungalow with a small garden in Carnmoney,

[31] Norman Jenkinson, BT News Editor
[32] Des McMullan, BT Production Editor
[33] Tom Carson, Features Editor
[34] Jim Gray, Assistant Editor

North Belfast. I also purchased all of Arthur's remaining furniture, so I was able to move in almost overnight to my first house, which cost £6,200. More importantly, it was somewhere Claire and I could live if she agreed to marry me.

I proposed in July, over a romantic dinner at the Pepper Mill in Holywood, one of Northern Ireland's best restaurants at the time. Our engagement was a very short one (just over six weeks), because Ted, Adeline and their children were due back from California for a holiday the next month. Finding a venue for our August reception provided a much sterner challenge. Our enquiries provoked the response "August in which year?" Most venues were completely taken aback by the answer – "next month.". Nevertheless, we eventually secured a slot at the Dunadry Inn, a beautiful location north of Belfast, and we were married just after 5pm in Ballymacarrett Church on Friday 15th August 1975. My best man was Rowan Bell and Claire's sister Joan[35] was her bridesmaid. I am more than a little biased when I say that it was the best day of my life.

Claire and I stayed at the Dunadry Inn that night, leaving the next morning for a short honeymoon in Donegal. Leaving was something of a challenge because, as we went to drive off, we discovered the rear wheels of my car had been bricked up and were an inch off the ground. We spent our honeymoon at the Rosapenna Hotel in Downings, County Donegal, a wonderful place still going strong under the stewardship of Frank and Hilary Casey. We celebrated our 40th wedding anniversary there in 2015 with Amanda, Milena, her husband Kumar[36] and Niki and Sam, who entertained us all regally, having been regular visitors at Rosapenna for almost 50 years.

I was at this stage going through what Claire described as my 'picante' phase and had become adept at producing excellent curries. Claire's brother Neil[37] reported to his parents that it was a full six months before he was served potatoes in our house! Sometimes I spiced up some of Claire's culinary efforts. On one occasion she had prepared a casserole for a party. I decided it was too bland and added cayenne pepper just minutes before Claire put her finishing touches to the dish by adding, yes, more cayenne pepper! Result - many guests clutching their throats.

By the end of the year we were on the move again. We wanted something a little bigger and realised that our hearts lay in County Down. In early December we moved into Bryansford Meadow on the outskirts of Bangor, where were to stay for just over three years. Bangor was a lovely seaside town and we felt very much at home there. We sold our house in Christine Drive almost immediately. One thing I remember was that our house had tiny front and back gardens and no garage. Unbelievably one potential buyer, as he was viewing the house, confided that he was thinking of building a stable as he intended to keep a horse there. It was in Bangor that we acquired our first dog Paddy, a golden Labrador, from Claire's parents. Stewart had decided to take up a post in Mexico as Professor of Soil Science

---

[35] Joan Goodwin (neé McConaghy) b. 1953, Company Secretary GBC, m. Mick Goodwin, 1d Sarah Stewart
[36] Dr Kumar Cameron Chetty, GP, Glasgow, b. 1983, m. Milena 2014, 1d. Tarryn Olivia
[37] Stewart Neil Marshall McConaghy, b. 1958, oil industry Consultant, m. Anne (née) McKenzie, 1s. Jack

at the University of Mexico City (a joint Mexico/UK government project). They lived there for the following four years. Although they had lived abroad in Trinidad in the late 1960s, the move to Mexico was a daunting prospect for a couple in their late fifties, neither of whom spoke Spanish. For the whole family the move presented logistical challenges. Claire and I were newly married, Joan was working in Birmingham and Neil was boarding at my old school CAI. We were to have virtually no day-to-day contact with Stewart and Olive in those four years. Telephone contact was notoriously unreliable and also extremely expensive, so only used in cases of extreme emergency. Stewart and Olive spent January in London on an intensive Spanish language course and left for Mexico shortly afterwards. Claire and I visited them three times while they were there.

Our first impressions of Mexico City were the sheer scale of it and how long it took to get anywhere. There was a perpetual 24-hour traffic jam, with a permanent haze of smog hanging over the city. The city authorities had come up with an ingenious scheme to reduce traffic and pollution levels. Drivers would only be allowed to use their cars on alternate days, the last odd or even number on the licence plate determining on which days the car could be used. Fairly quickly it became apparent that the scheme did not work. Many rich drivers simply bought a second car, having paid a 'consideration' to the relevant authority to ensure an alternative number plate. Consequently, there were actually many more vehicles in existence, with pollution levels increasing substantially.

Mexico was a country of Haves and Have Nots, with corruption from top to bottom. We saw many examples. Stewart and Olive had to have Mexican driving licences and also sit a driving test. When they arrived at the test centre, there were several other people there for the same purpose. The officials simply selected one individual to do the test on behalf of the group and from the others collected a 'fee' which ensured they passed. Needless to say, no one ever failed, which perhaps contributed to very poor standards of road safety and a high level of road accidents. The police seemed to operate in much the same capacity. Any minor discretion could only be sorted out by the payment of a roadside 'fine' – always in cash.

Through Stewart and Olive, we met and were entertained by many Mexicans. Mexico was a stunning country with both Aztec and Mayan cultures and we travelled extensively through central Mexico. We visited Acapulco, playground of the rich and famous at that time, and dined at the Acapulco Princess, where the eccentric Howard Hughes[38] spent his last years occupying the entire top floor. I suspect that Mexico today, with its high level of crime and drugs, is very different from the one we experienced in the late 1970s.

Claire and I were extremely lucky in our various moves over the years, particularly in the early years when they were helpfully part-financed by TRN and, subsequently, SDR. We had decided to mortgage ourselves to the maximum and as a result of a rising housing market during most of our working lifetime, we have been

---

[38] Howard Hughes 1905-76. American business magnate, pilot, film director and philanthropist, known for his eccentricities and reclusive lifestyle.

very fortunate. The downside was of course that we were usually financially stretched.

The Bryansford Meadow house was not in particularly good condition and needed considerable work. I quickly established that my DIY skills were extremely limited. Even hanging a picture often resulted in several holes in the wall. Fortunately, Claire emerged triumphant in that area and assumed the role of clerk of works and master tradesman, with me very much the apprentice. There was nothing she couldn't turn her hand to - painting, wall papering etc. Over the years I had only to utter my stock phrase on very rare occasions, "Look this is not my area of skill. If you wanted someone to do this you should have married a tradesman."

Sadly, my father died on 17th December 1976. He had retired from the bank in April 1970. He and my mother settled very well into retirement life in an ideal setting on the shores of Strangford Loch. He suffered a massive stroke just three years into his retirement and was lucky to survive, albeit with severely reduced mobility. In many ways, I think Ted and I inherited a lot of our father's personality and eccentricities. He was very outgoing and gregarious and the life and soul of any party, whereas my mother was much quieter and more reserved. Nevertheless, they were an extremely happy couple and Ted, Niki and I enjoyed loving and fulfilling childhoods. I miss them both terribly. There is so much more I would like to have known about them, hence this book.

The situation in Northern Ireland was starting to cause massive operational problems for BT. In Circulation we could no longer ask our Sales representatives to go into areas where their religion could potentially expose them to great personal danger. One member of the team, who was working temporarily in Londonderry, unwittingly found himself in the wrong area and was interrogated at gunpoint. As in my experience at QUB, he was warned never to set foot in the area again. The incident resulted in our re-evaluating our policy. The Troubles were now imposing directly on our business. We could not operate an employment policy based on religious discrimination, but the reality was that no Protestant could go into the Catholic enclaves - it would have been be suicide to do so. Equally, we could not expect a Catholic to operate in parts of East Belfast or the Shankill Road. Indeed, as things got worse throughout the 1970s, we realised we could not allow our Sales Force to venture into some of the more extreme areas at all, even if they were of the same religion. To the outside world, this may seem implausible. The rule of law operated in Northern Ireland, but enforcing it was sometimes an entirely different matter.

In early 1976 I started thinking about how to get around the problem. I realised that, if we felt we were losing touch with our retailers, they themselves also must be feeling cut off and isolated. This led to my recommending the creation of a Tele-Sales Unit (TSU) within the Circulation Department. Agreed in early 1977, the concept was based on us adding another layer to our communication process with retailers. In addition to our van drivers and Sales representatives, we would introduce a TSU to improve our communication with retailers. In creating the TSU, I had to be extremely careful not to upset the Sales Reps, who were doing sterling work. I didn't want them to see the TSU as a threat. It was important that both teams should work together. Roy Lyttle, who was in charge of the Sales reps, supported the plan from the outset and we appointed Senior Sales Representative Conor Boyle to head the unit of four people. Their objective was to cultivate long-term relationships with retailers and to empathise with the large number of day-to-day issues which those retailers inevitably had by dint of operating in that sector in the Northern Ireland of the late 1970s. The original team typified that objective and they became a highly successful addition to the Circulation Department. Encouragingly, our research at the time showed that our retailers regarded the team as very helpful partners.

The TSU's success in part led to my next career move. David Yarrow, the Group Circulation Director, asked me to London for a chat, resulting in my being appointed Group Circulation Executive (another new role!) in October 1978. I left BT at the end of August and Claire and I spent September in Mexico. I still look back at my five years at BT with great affection. I made many friends there; it was my first management role and I still regard the company as my alma mater.

Early Belfast Telegraph days - with Bob Crane,
Assistant Managing Director, 1977

Chapter 8   TRN GROUP ROLE 1978-79

"Whether you think you can, or you think you can't, you're probably right."
Henry Ford[1]

Claire continued to live in Bangor but, in my new Group role, I became a nomad, only returning home on each, but not every, weekend. Claire was spending an increasing amount of time abroad, as she set up a new Reader Travel initiative, which involved making inspection visits and accompanying some readers' trips. It was considered to be a good public relations exercise, but also opened up an entirely new revenue stream and most newspapers, national and local, still operate such schemes.

The TRN Group had nine publishing centres, with its headquarters in Greater London House at Mornington Crescent in London. David Yarrow had been impressed with what I had done in Belfast and wanted me to set up Tele Sales units throughout the Group.

I wasn't prepared for the politics between the Group's HQ and the individual operating companies. The publishing centres were very powerful fiefdoms and considered themselves independent. They certainly didn't see themselves as subsidiary companies of the type with which I would later work in both Mirror Group and News International. HQ had the ultimate sanction of hiring and firing, but this was a nuclear option to be used sparingly. It didn't help that the group HQ was a large organisation in its own right, with more than 400 people based there. It also came under the control of the London Central branches of the trade unions and conditions of employment were far more distorted than in the publishing centres. For example, all HQ clerical staff worked a nine-day fortnight and had six weeks' sickness entitlement, which was regarded as six weeks' additional holiday on top of normal entitlement. It was yet another example of trade union abuse of the system. TRN eventually closed the entire HQ and moved to Shire Hall, outside Reading, in a union free environment.

Although David Yarrow wanted a Tele-Sales unit in every centre, the decision was up to the individual publishing centres. My task was not helped by the fact that Yarrow did not have a particularly good relationship with several of the regional Managing Directors and crossed swords with them quite regularly. We finally thrashed out the best way to achieve it. Yarrow would 'warm up' the publishing centres before I visited them to extol the virtues of the Tele-Sales concept. We would pick the low hanging fruit first – in this case, Cardiff, which bought into the idea with great enthusiasm. Elsewhere there were varying degrees of enthusiasm. Newcastle was particularly resistant because of personal animosity between Yarrow and Len Harton, the managing director. Some of the smaller newspapers were not

---

[1] Henry Ford 1863-1947, American business magnate and Founder of The Ford Motor Company

big enough to justify the concept, but I was able to reorganise those circulation areas to accommodate the principles of the operation without having to employ any additional staff.

Cardiff was the headquarters of the Western Mail and South Wales Echo Ltd., one of the largest in TRN. Alex Davidson[2] was my main supporter there and I spent almost three months there on the project. I had never been to Wales, but I was able to travel extensively throughout the Principality. Socially Cardiff was a great place and I became particularly friendly with Colin Champ, one of the Advertising Managers. We visited many of the town's hostelries, including the then famous Key Club in the shadow of the old Arms Park.

David Yarrow would ask to see me on a Friday in London roughly every six weeks. We would meet at midday, with me bringing him up to date on how things were going and him telling me of any relevant developments in the Group. He would then go through my expenses in minute detail, often querying the smallest items. It turned out to be extremely useful training for the future – overstating a couple of trivial items would form the basis of a major discussion and result in a couple of concessions, enabling him to feel that he was saving the company from profligacy. It also kept him away from some of the more embarrassing expenditure which, more than likely, would have occurred in the company of the said Colin Champ.

Yarrow would then take me to lunch. This is a bit of an exaggeration, as lunch consisted of a round of tiny sandwiches and five pints of beer. I would then reel onto the Tube to Heathrow for an early evening flight. Whether Yarrow did this every day or just liked to wind down on Fridays I never did find out.

In early autumn, he asked me to go to Middlesbrough for a project. In the interim period, Alex Davidson had been appointed Managing Director of the Evening Gazette in Teesside. He had inherited a totally out of date distribution system and asked Yarrow to release me for a couple of months to work on it. He wanted both external leadership and for the project to be offsite, so had organised a suite of rooms for me at a local hotel. Initially, Alex spent a couple of days driving me around the area. My brief was to start with a blank sheet of paper, with no existing assumptions or obstacles. The present edition structure of the paper had been unchanged for decades and I could alter it as I saw fit.

The Teesside of the late 1970s was utterly depressing - a heavily industrialised area dependent on two declining industries, steel and chemicals. Alex and his wife Pam[3] had decided to live in North Yorkshire, sensibly putting a range of hills between themselves and Middlesbrough. Their home was a beautiful farmhouse in the village of Moorsholm and I had dinner with them there several times.

The Distribution Project was proceeding smoothly until I got a call from David Yarrow instructing me to attend an interview in Newcastle upon Tyne for the

---

[2] Alex Davidson, former Managing Director Northcliff Newspapers Ltd.
[3] Pam Davidson b.1948, professional sales trainer with organisations including TRN and Oxford Training Group

position of Circulation Manager of The Journal, the northeast's regional morning newspaper. I was interviewed by Geoff Clark, who offered the job there and then. They wanted me to start immediately and yet another battle commenced between Yarrow and Len Harton, this time over the start date. In the end, I had to hot-foot it back to Teesside and work virtually night and day to complete the project there in two, rather than four, weeks. Alex accepted my recommendations and the new distribution system was launched almost immediately. Sadly, I wasn't there to see it, having now embarked on the next part of my TRN journey.

Claire's BT leaving presentation 1979
Front row l-r:
Mollie McKelvie (who introduced us),
Peter McCartney, Len Tweedie and Claire

Early business card

CHAPTER 9   JINGLING IN GEORDIELAND - NEWCASTLE 1979 – 1981

"It doesn't matter who you are, where you come from. The ability to triumph comes from you. Always." Oprah Winfrey[1]

The Newcastle move was a game changer for both of us. It was our second move, we had a house to buy and a house to sell and it meant Claire leaving her job at BT, where she had worked for more than six years. Unlike some of our later moves, this one went smoothly and the transition was relatively short, although my weekly commute via the Larne-Stranraer ferry was not particularly easy, especially in winter.

Claire would collect me from the ferry on Friday evenings. On one occasion, as she approached her car, she realised that two men were standing beside it and another was actually in it. Furious, she ran towards them waving her umbrella and shouting "Get away from my car!" Remarkably, they did, but she earned a rebuke from the company for being reckless with her own safety – but she picked me up on time.

As I was already familiar with Newcastle, it didn't take too long to find another property. We took out the maximum mortgage we could afford and bought a three bedroomed, detached house less than 1½ miles from the city centre, on the road to Hexham. It was on the route of Hadrian's Wall and we liked to think that some of the distinctively marked stones in the garden were from the actual Wall. We moved in early in January. Claire's introduction to Geordieland was making tea for our removal men and being virtually unable to understand a word of their conversation. She settled quickly in Newcastle, helped enormously by the fact that she started a new job almost immediately. At BT she had worked with TTS Tours, a Newcastle based company which specialised in group and newspaper readers' holidays. On learning that she was moving to Newcastle, they asked her to join them to help run the newspaper side of the business. One huge bonus of her new job was that I was able to accompany her on two cruises. The first was a week-long cruise to Bergen, Helsinki, Gothenburg, Copenhagen, Amsterdam and Hamburg. The second was an inspection cruise to Madeira, Lanzarote, Gran Canaria, Tenerife and Gibraltar and we travelled in style, with one of the best cabins and seats at the Captain's table.

The Newcastle Chronicle and Journal Ltd. (NC&J) under its long serving Managing Director Len Harton regarded itself as the jewel in the crown of the Thomson empire. It was an extremely powerful fiefdom with three newspapers, the largest staff numbers, turnover, newspaper sales, and advertising revenues in the entire Group. I reported directly to the General Circulation Manager Geoff Clark, a small, well-groomed man, very much old-school, and intensely political. His political

[1] Oprah Winfrey b.1954 American media executive, actress, talk show host and philanthropist

73

instincts were enshrined in the old saying "Success has many fathers but failure is a complete bastard"[2] Thus his modus operandi was that all good things within the Department were directly down to him, but all examples of poor management were directly attributable to his Circulation Managers, in whom he had vested complete autonomy (for the poor management cases only). He was immensely private and I can't say I even remotely got to know him. I received virtually no guidance or management development under his tutelage during my two years there. It was my first real management role. I had my own team and a level of autonomy which enabled me to pursue my own ideas.

The Journal was one of a handful of UK regional morning newspapers and circulated throughout the North East, with an upmarket readership, primarily in the business and agricultural sectors. My first major challenge was the paper's availability. Unlike The Evening Chronicle, which was distributed directly to retailers, The Journal was distributed through a wholesaler. With a huge circulation area and operating full sale or return, maintaining maximum availability was a real headache. I was forever being berated by Clark for operating the high returns levels needed to achieve satisfactory availability. I also received a bollocking every time any of his Saturday fourball at Ponteland Golf Club was unable to buy a copy. It became a frequent Monday morning occurrence – a great way to start the week.

The other major challenge was maximising the market opportunity when competitors failed to appear. This coincided with the Fleet Street Trade Unions being at their most powerful. Disrupted print runs were commonplace and early, accurate intelligence was vital. The Journal had its own Night Circulation representative, who was supposed to manage events by increasing the print order to ensure that opportunities were exploited. He took a perverse pleasure in calling me in the middle of the night to discuss things when a major story broke. He would phone me at least twice a week and often I would have to go into the office as a result.

Once, attempting to exploit a significant sales opportunity, I sizeably upped the print figure so much that it led to detailed negotiations between senior production managers and the print unions. The following morning I received a severe dressing down from Geoff Clark and Len Harton about my lack of consultation and not realising the consequences of my actions. I was absolutely furious. Clark had clearly been taken to task by Len Harton and, instead of defending my actions, had passed the blame directly onto me. I challenged him on it and asked him if he wanted to be called at 3am every time we wanted to increase the print figure. What made me even angrier was that at no stage did anyone consider whether my decision to increase the print figure was justified. I did mention this to Len Harton during the conversation but he seemed to consider it irrelevant. When I established the significant sales

---

[2] This may have originated as "Victory has one hundred fathers but defeat is an orphan" It was popularised by John F. Kennedy but originated by an Italian diplomat Count Galeazzo Ciano, 1903-1944, son-in-law of Benito Mussolini

increase some days later, I at least had the satisfaction of knowing that my judgement had been correct.

What I had been caught up in that night was not just management by appeasement, but total capitulation. I was becoming increasingly aware of the immense power of the print unions and their greed in exploiting every situation to their personal benefit. What I was also witnessing was weak management. Although publishers wanted additional sales, they equally wanted continual production with no hassle from the unions. The latter exploited every situation - for example, by demanding more unnecessary overtime. Principles were apparently irrelevant and it seemed that successive managements had conceded that they were not worth fighting for.

I found the NC&J very similar to Belfast in that it had a male-dominated, heavy drinking culture. There were 29 pubs and restaurants dotted around the Bigg Market, each patronised by a particular section of the company. Many colleagues spent every lunchtime in them, consuming three or four pints of beer before returning to the office. At close of play, the same people would then repair to other hostelries for a few sharpeners before going home. The Printer's Pie was the official office pub, ironically conveniently situated between the staff entrance and the company's garage (and car park!).

Claire and I thoroughly enjoyed Newcastle. The climate was bracing to say the least. Unbelievably when we came to sell our house, one potential viewer queried in some detail whether the back garden was completely private. He eventually confided that he and his wife were naturists – clearly very hardy ones.

There was a fantastic heartbeat to the city. We went to the Theatre Royal fairly regularly and saw many great productions, including Terry Scott in A Bed Full of Foreigners, Dora Bryan, Carol Drinkwater and Christopher Timothy in The Curse of Love, and a memorable Private Lives with Joanna Lumley and Simon Cadell.

Our early experiences with opera were enlivened by attending Scottish Opera's productions at the theatre, a regular feature in those days. We also made our first trip to the Royal Shakespeare Company in Stratford-upon-Avon for a great performance by Sinead Cusack as Rosalind in As You Like It. Football and golf also featured prominently. I continued actively supporting Newcastle United and became a member of Tyneside Golf Club in Ryton.

Another memorable occasion was attending The Northumberland Plate Race Meeting at Gosforth Park on 28th June 1980. I had played golf at Tyneside that morning and picked up a tip - a horse called Mons Beau. I discovered that it was in the feature race at odds of 33/1, but, thinking myself a betting expert, I decided it was a no-hoper and ignored it for a more favoured horse. Luckily, I had told Claire about the tip and she waged £1 on Mons Beau. She was thrilled when it romped home, resulting in a very happy McClatchie household that evening. For us, the most impressive part of the North East was rural Northumberland and we spent many weekends exploring. The restoration work on Hadrian's Wall was incredibly impressive and the Roman forts, such as Chesters at Chollerford, were fascinating.

We spent Christmas and New Year 1980 in Holywood, but no sooner was I back in the office than another move was in the offing. Shortly afterwards I was appointed Circulation Manager of Thames Valley Newspapers (TVN) in Reading. The contractual details took a little longer to sort out this time as it involved my moving from the North East, with its lower than average housing costs, to the Thames Valley, one of the highest priced areas outside London. TRN had an ingenious solution to this problem. If we purchased a similar house in Reading, the company would give me half the difference in price between it and our Newcastle property in the form of an interest free loan. This was fair for both parties but, in a rising housing market, was an extremely good deal for us, in that the company was putting in equity, but any subsequent profit went to me. While this was being sorted out, Len Harton tried to put a spanner in the works. He was furious that TRN was moving a member of 'his' staff, who had been there for just over two years, and he tried to block the appointment. However, common sense prevailed and in early February 1981 I set off for Reading, for what was to be the penultimate stage of the TRN journey.

Chapter 10   ROCKING IN READING 1981-1984

"Our attitude towards ourselves can keep us imprisoned in limitation or set us free with possibility."   Unknown

Thames Valley Newspapers Ltd. (TVN) in Reading published The Evening Post and The Wokingham, Bracknell and Crowthorne Times, a group of weekly newspapers. Its Managing Director was a Scot, Ian Richard[1], and the company was based in an industrial estate alongside the Thames. I reported directly to one of the Assistant Managing Directors, Vic Morea, an accountant. This was my first experience of working directly for an accountant and, although I learned a great deal from Vic, it was at times frustrating. The old adage of "accountants being the contraceptive on the prick of progress" comes to mind here, as Vic could not have been described as a man of vision. My weekly commute by road was long - 300 miles on some of Britain's busiest motorways, but I had inherited my predecessor's company car, a three-litre Ford Capri, and this powerful beast eased the journey.

Our move did not go smoothly, as our house took some time to sell. The eventual buyer showed up in a black and white checkered Rolls Royce, said very little, but the same evening offered the asking price. We never saw or heard from him again, but our solicitor worked towards completion. Late in the morning on the day we moved out, with the removal van partly loaded with much of our possessions, our solicitor phoned to say that the money had not been transferred and that the purchaser's solicitor had been unable to contact his client. Much panic. I phoned Vic Morea in Reading. His first suggestion was that we stop everything and unload the van until things were sorted out. Needless to say, neither Claire nor I thought this a particularly good idea. After much negotiation, it was agreed the company would bridge us over the weekend. By sheer coincidence Claire discovered that the mother of our next door neighbour Anne was a friend of our buyer's mother. A few phone calls resulted in contact being made with our buyer who completed the sale on the Monday. He paid the financial penalties for delayed completion without complaint.

Claire was again successful in finding a new job. Philip Graf, her former boss in Belfast, now worked at TRN headquarters in London. He and Jim Brown,[2] the Group's Circulation and Promotions Controller, interviewed her in London and offered her a position as Promotions Consultant at Greater London House. She now experienced life as a London commuter – train to Paddington then two tubes to Mornington Crescent. Her commuting experiences influenced me in my later career at both Mirror Group and News International in Glasgow, when I strongly resisted overtures to move to London.

We settled into a weekday routine. I would drive Claire to the station for her 7.45am train. We lived in Caversham, north of the Thames, and although the journey was less than three miles, we had to allow at least half an hour for the journey to the

---

[1] Ian Richard Managing Director TVN and latterly at the Cambridge News
[2] Jim Brown, CBE, b. 1939, Chairman Newsquest 1996-2006

station. I would pick her up at around 6.30pm, but there could be a variation of up to 20-30 minutes in her arrival time. A huge positive was that we could almost guarantee that we could be sitting in the back garden with a glass of wine when the 7.15pm Concorde flight for New York thundered overhead. The difference in climate between Newcastle and the Thames Valley was huge. In Newcastle we could rarely sit outside in the evenings, while in Reading we would still be there as darkness fell and our resident hedgehog shuffled across the lawn. We lived close to the South Oxfordshire border and most Sundays we would take long walks through the beautiful surrounding woods and end up having lunch at the Pack Horse or the Pack Saddle (then both Brakspear pubs), or the King Charles' Head. London was easily accessible and we went there fairly frequently.

TVN had been launched in the 1960s and was part of a grand plan by TRN to ring London with a series of evening newspapers. The model was to be based on the typical American small-town newspaper, the main point of difference being that most readers would have their copy directly delivered by the company. The Direct Delivery Network was well-established in the USA and various executives had gone there to research it. In later years, I attended several international newspaper conferences in the US and visited more than a dozen newspapers of varying sizes.

Unfortunately, the UK model simply didn't work. TRN launched only three evening newspapers - in Reading, Slough and in Hemel Hempstead - and realised that the model was unsustainable. The concept failed for two reasons. First, there was no established home delivery subscription model involving payment in advance. Reading operated a hybrid system with payment in arrears, which inevitably produced a high level of bad debt, particularly in a transient area like the Thames Valley. Second, the concept of retailers/newsagents was almost unknown in the US, with non-delivered copies usually accounting for only 10-15% of total sales. These copies were sold almost entirely through newsstands or vending machines. In the UK there was a network of over 40,000 retailers, many of whom also operated a home delivery service. When TRN pitched into Reading, the area very quickly became a battleground between the Evening Post and the area's retailers, further intensified by the need for the paper to refresh its home delivery subscribers constantly. The inevitable result was a huge level of subscriber 'churn'. Creating a customer database was still some time away, so the newspaper simply cold-called every household in the area phone directory. With such an unsophisticated operation, it was inevitable that the newspaper would regularly canvass newsagents' existing customers, hence the ongoing warfare with the news trade.

My time in Reading was not the most stimulating experience – indeed I felt on a perpetual treadmill. I did not get a great deal of personal development from Ian Richard. Although I liked him enormously, his management style was 'paralysis by analysis'. As Jack Welsh said, "It's better to act too quickly than wait too long."

Socially, we enjoyed Reading. I regularly watched England and Tottenham Hotspur in north London, played golf at Wentworth, Sunningdale and the Berkshire courses and Claire and I attended our first Royal Ascot meeting in 1982. The evening before

Prince Charles' wedding, we drove to London to soak up the atmosphere. It was extraordinary, with the Mall at midnight already lined six or seven deep with people determined to get the best vantage points for the big event. One group was dining regally, drinking champagne, seated round a table in full evening dress. We were stuck in a traffic jam around Trafalgar Square at 2.30am.

We indulged our love of the theatre and opera, both in the West End and Stratford-upon-Avon. We saw fantastic productions of The Winter's Tale, with Patrick Stewart, Gemma Jones and Sheila Hancock; The Taming of the Shrew, with Mark Rylance and Sinead Cusack; and a memorable production of Shaw's Heartbreak House starring Rex Harrison, Diana Rigg, Frank Middlemass and Rosemary Harris. In the West End we went to a production of The Mouse Trap, then in its 30th year.

Sadly, we had to have our dog Paddy put down in 1983. At 13 she had had a good innings but it still felt like a death in the family. We were expecting our first baby in December 1983 and life was about to change dramatically. Around that time, I was headhunted by Northcliffe Newspapers, who wanted me to take up a position with the Western Morning News in Plymouth. Claire and I spent a very agreeable autumn weekend there with Bob Tyldsley[3]. Although impressed by the company, the role wouldn't have presented much more of a challenge than my current one. Plymouth was also extremely far from Northern Ireland and, with the imminent arrival of our baby, we realised that we didn't want to be so far away from our parents in Northern Ireland which was still 'home.'

I turned the job down. Amanda was born on 13th December and within a month TRN had offered me a significant promotion to the role of General Circulation Manager at the Scotsman Publications Ltd. in Edinburgh. The final - and brief - chapter of my time at TRN was about to begin.

---

[3] Bob Tyldsley MBE, Managing Director Northcliff Newspapers in Leicester, Plymouth and Cardiff

Early sketch of yours truly by Claire c 1980

Chapter 11   A BRIEF ENCOUNTER –

THE SCOTSMAN 16- 30TH JANUARY 1984

"You'll never find a rainbow if you're looking down."   *Charlie Chaplin* [1]

On 16th January 1984 I stepped off the red-eye from Heathrow into several inches of slushy snow at Edinburgh Airport. My fine Italian shoes instantly took in a lot of water. This was my first day as General Circulation Manager of The Scotsman Publications Ltd (SPL). Exactly two weeks later I resigned. I think I hold the record for the shortest stint of anyone in their senior management team.

Weatherwise, that first day didn't improve. My walk to lunch with David McKay[2] at the George Hotel involved walking through wet snow in my already ruined shoes. After a convivial lunch I went straight to Jenners department store and purchased a pair of stout brogues, a tweed hat and a pair of socks. Back in the office, my ruined shoes were consigned to the bin.

What was to shape my life for the next decade took place at the end of that first day. At 6 pm Murdoch MacLennan,[3] Production Director at the Scottish Daily Record and Sunday Mail Ltd. (SDR), Scotland's largest publisher and part of Mirror Group, called and asked if I would meet Liam Kane,[4] the Deputy Managing Director. Although not specifically mentioned, it was clear that this was to talk about a job. Later that week I caught a train to Glasgow and met Liam for dinner at a restaurant in Byers Road.

I only knew Murdoch vaguely and had never met Liam - the conduit turned out to be Adam McKinlay,[5] the wily ex-Fleet Street veteran, then Editor of TRN's Wokingham Times, based in Reading. While there, Adam and I had become close friends, regularly playing golf at East Berks Golf Club and Claire and I had gone to Ladies' Day at Royal Ascot the previous year with him and his wife Dot. Adam was aware of developments at SDR and had recommended me to his old friend Murdoch. I recalled Adam asking me on the golf course if I knew much about the Scottish company. Never having lived in Scotland, I didn't, but had been sufficiently curious to research the company.

Over dinner Liam told me about SDR. Part of Mirror Group Newspapers, then owned by Reed International, it dominated the tabloid market in Scotland and was enormously profitable, but there was an uneasy relationship between the two companies. The Scottish company made most of the group's profit, but was regarded as a very junior partner by the parent company.

---

[1] Charlie Chaplin 1899-1976, English comic actor who rose to fame in the era of the silent screen
[2] David McKay, b. 1943, John Menzies Plc. 1964-2003; latterly CEO
[3] Murdoch MacLennan, b. 1949, then Production Director of Scottish Daily Record and Sunday Mail 1982-84, currently Chairman The Press Association, Independent News and Media, Scottish Professional Football League
[4] Liam Kane MBE 1950 - 2019, SDR Deputy Managing Director 1978-84
[5] Adam McKinlay, former Fleet Street veteran, latterly Editor Wokingham Times Series

In Glasgow SDR had a separate board chaired by Derek Webster[6], with Vic Horwood[7] as Managing Director. All commercial areas reported directly to Liam. The Circulation Director had just retired. Liam felt that none of the current and long-standing team fitted the bill, so wanted an external appointment. He was nervous at the possible impact of this on the existing team. He had considered approaching me the previous summer, but was apprehensive, given the team's rather parochial attitudes. As I was now based in Scotland, this presented less of a problem.

Liam and I got on extremely well. I liked him and he was sufficiently impressed by me to pursue the matter further. We agreed I would have dinner with Derek Webster and Vic Horwood the following week and, if all went well, we would commence negotiations on a contract.

The following week's dinner with the short, cunning and highly political Webster (an ex editor of the Daily Record) and the lanky, polite, lugubrious Horwood was a very different occasion. I remember nothing of the restaurant or the food, as I was concentrating so hard on the discussion. Liam rang the next morning to report that it had gone well and a draft contract would be delivered to me that evening.

As I read it, what struck me was the huge contrast between the terms being offered by a national newspaper compared to the regionals with which I had been working for the previous 13 years. The only contentious issue was that I was being offered the position of Deputy Circulation Director, with a review in six months which, if successful, would result in my being appointed Circulation Director with a seat on the Board. Liam was covering his options. Otherwise the offer was excellent. I had every confidence in myself and, although I didn't know much about the company, its people and culture, Liam and I were both convinced I would fit in and be successful. In his view, the risk of my failure was minimal. Financially it also meant that Claire didn't have to work.

I flew back to London on Friday with a lot to talk to Claire about over the weekend. Not one to hang about, Murdoch MacLellan flew down on the Sunday to have dinner with us. We had an excellent evening at The French Horn in Sonning, the contract was signed and the rest is history!

On Monday 20th January I flew back to Edinburgh and handed in my resignation to my stunned boss Ian McAuley. We agreed that I should depart immediately and I flew back to Heathrow that afternoon – my 13 years with TRN now over.

SPL publishes The Scotsman, the Edinburgh Evening News, Scotland on Sunday, and The Herald and Post series of free newspapers in Edinburgh, Fife and West Lothian. In 1984, The Scotsman sold 94,000 copies daily and The Evening News 117,000. At the time of writing they sell just over 16,000 copies each - sales declines of 77% and 86% respectively. Sales of The Times in Scotland have long since exceeded that of The Scotsman.

---

[6] Derek Webster CBE, 1927-2013, Chairman, SDR 1971-84
[7] Vic Horwood, b. 1937, Managing Director, SDR 1978-91; Joint Managing Director, MGN 1991-92

During my brief time there I met The Scotsman's editor, Eric MacKay[8] who was coming to the end of his 13-year tenure. He had worked for The Scotsman for almost all his working life and was the archetypal image of an editor – jacketless, shirt collar undone, sleeves rolled up, spectacles on top of his head. My recollection is that he talked mainly of the past – how the paper had almost reached the pinnacle of 100,000 sales and how close the dreams of devolution and Scottish independence had been – and very little of the challenges ahead.

When Eric MacKay retired in 1985, he was the eleventh editor of The Scotsman since 1817. Since his departure, The Scotsman has had 13 editors, which is well illustrated in a room of what is now The Scotsman Hotel in North Bridge. On the cornice are recorded the names of all the editors of The Scotsman. Three of the four walls record the editors from its first 168 years; the fourth wall those of the last ten.

Interestingly, The (Glasgow) Herald has had 26 editors since 1783. Changing editors with such frequency comes with high risk. Every piece of newspaper research I have seen in my 40-year career has had a common theme – newspaper readers are conservative and like familiarity and consistency in their paper, even more so if they are regular readers. Change needs to be introduced carefully and slowly. Sir Harold Evans[9] echoed the same sentiment when he said that changing a newspaper should be like surgery, in that the patient should feel no pain. In contrast, a new editor wants to make an immediate, personal impact on the paper, to stamp their own mark. Very often the reader is the casualty rather than the beneficiary.

In late 2003, I sat on a Committee of The Royal Society of Edinburgh (RSE) chaired by Sir Charles Fraser[10] and charged with organising a media seminar to discuss and debate the issues of the day, particularly in relation to the Scottish newspaper industry. I would describe most of the committee as core Scotsman readers and, over several meetings, I heard considerable disillusionment and concern about "their" paper. When the seminar took place in March 2004 similar views were in abundance among the 100 or so participants. There was a consensus that the paper had lost its way under the stewardship of Andrew Neil[11], then Chief Executive of SPL. Amusingly, unsaid but obviously present, was an element of Edinburgh snobbery, "To have Andrew Neil, an ex-pupil of Paisley Grammar School, running our paper is simply intolerable." I suspect similar comments were expressed when Fred Goodwin[12] became Chief Executive of the Royal Bank of Scotland.

Around the same time, I became aware of a consortium being formed to try to buy SPL. Like many others, the consortium members were unhappy with how the company was run. Peter Jones[13] had been approached to be editor of The Scotsman and I was informally sounded out to be Chief Executive. My response was very

[8] Eric MacKay 1922-2006. Editor The Scotsman 1972-85.
[9] Sir Harold Evans, b.1928, British-American journalist; Editor, Sunday Times 1967-81
[10] Sir Charles Fraser FRSE, b. 1928, Partner WNJ Burness; Senior Non-Executive Director, Scottish Media Group, Scottish Widows Fund, and Stakis Plc.
[11] Andrew Neil, b. 1949, British journalist and broadcaster; Editor, The Sunday Times 1983-94
[12] (Sir) Fred Goodwin, b. 1958, Chief Executive Officer, Royal Bank of Scotland 2001-09; Knighted 2004, annulled 2012.
[13] Peter Jones b.1953. m. Rhona Brankin MSP 1999-2011 Scotland and Northeast England correspondent The Economist 1995-2005. Freelance economics and business journalist 2005-18

clear: I was contracted to News International, but if someone were to make me a formal offer, I would listen, but not until then. No offer was made and I believe the plans never came to fruition.

There have been three changes of ownership of SPL since 1984. The Barclay brothers bought it for £85 million in 1985 and sold it to Johnston Press (JP) for £160 million in 2005. After that JP embarked on a major acquisition trail, which resulted in it becoming a major player in the media sector, with a market capitalisation of more than £1 billion (albeit with debt which peaked at £750m). I suspect that many of that disaffected group at the RSE Seminar must now shake their heads in disbelief at its subsequent downfall. It was a classic example of management hubris followed by a market downturn of unparalleled ferocity, mainly caused by the impact of the internet. It was also a case of buying at the very top end of the market and being unable to service the debt in the downturn. No wonder the consortium did not go ahead with its proposed buyout in 2004. In October 2018 JP announced that the entire group was for sale. With a market capitalisation of £3m and debts of £220m, its position was perilous and there were no buyers. JP went into administration, with its shares said to be worthless. As part of a pre-packaged deal, control of its assets - including SPL - was transferred to JPI Media Ltd, a special purpose vehicle owned by the creditors. Ownership passed to a consortium of lenders.

What happened at SPL has subsequently been mirrored across the newspaper industry as a whole with the internet the prime reason for its downfall. In Chapter 40 I detail the catastrophic decline of the sector as a whole.

TRN Circulation Managers' Conference 1983

Back row l-r: ?, Andrew Harton, CMcC, Bob Hughes,
John Thomas, Geoff Hoyle, Ian Lovatt, Ian Moore, ?,
David Perry, Roy Lyttle

Front row l-r: Tony Ostler, Philip Graf, Jim Brown, Barbara Elton,
Roger Nicholson, Claire, Norman Anderson, Stephen Parker

DRAMATIS PERSONAE

My grandparents, John and Mary-Jane McClatchie c. 1935.

Edward Alexander McClatchie 1898-1917 (note his correct age on the grave)

The McClatchie Family c. 1935, l-r : Mary-Jane, John, Jack, Belinda,
my parents Kay and Jimmy, Eileen and Jim Crowe

Jack, John and Jimmy c. 1936

An early picture of my mother and father c. 1936

Their wedding in 1938

The Barr Family, l-r: Kay (my mother), grandparents (William and Edna) and Stewart
c. 1930

Youngest photographic evidence of yours truly c. 1956

My brother Ted and I at Niki's wedding, December 1962

"I graduated on 5th July 1971 in the presence of two extremely proud, happy and probably very relieved parents."

Our wedding day, 15th August 1975
Claire's parents in the background

Looking happy 25 years later, Donegal August 2000...

...and still looking happy 45 years later, Tenerife June 2019

Chapter 12   MOVING TO SCOTLAND 1984

"The first time I came to Scotland I was twenty-one. When I got off the train, the streets were full of people laughing, drinking and puking. I thought this place was incredible… and it's only Thursday. Then I learned that there was a rugby game between Scotland and Ireland." Steve Martin[1]

After nearly 35 years, most of them spent in Northern Ireland, we moved to the west of Scotland. Neither Claire nor I realised that we would spend the rest of our lives there - to date.

We put our house in Caversham on the market in January 1984. What we had not anticipated was the first housing slump in the South East for many years, resulting in a very frustrating situation. We agreed a sale twice only for it to collapse. It took us until October to complete the sale. Until then I was based in Scotland, while Claire was in Caversham with Amanda, but Liam was very patient and supportive.

I had only ever spent two days in Glasgow and found the task of starting to look for somewhere to live extremely daunting. The upside to taking so long to sell was that it gave me time to look at property throughout the west of Scotland. I viewed more than 60 properties within a 20-mile radius of the city centre, including some turkeys. I quickly learned to spend no more than five minutes in any unsuitable property before saying, "I don't want to waste your time - this just isn't what I'm looking for." Most people found this satisfactory, although some sellers (usually in a property that had been on the market for some time) would interrogate me about exactly what was wrong with it.

Fairly quickly I narrowed down the search to Renfrewshire. On a beautiful evening in early May I viewed a house in the village of Kilmacolm, an area which I had initially ruled out, thinking it was too far out of Glasgow. However, driving into the village, I caught my first sight of the beautiful Knapps Loch. I didn't like the house, but was sufficiently impressed to drive around the rest of the village. I returned early the next morning to test rush hour traffic into Glasgow. I left Kilmacolm at 7.45am and was at my desk at Anderston Quay at 8.25am, despite a lengthy queue at what is now the St James Interchange.

By August I had viewed just about every house for sale in Kilmacolm, Bridge of Weir and the surrounding area, so Claire came up to make what I hoped would be our final choice. We settled on a house on Barclaven Road in Kilmacolm, but the next morning the estate agent phoned to tell us that another property on the same road had just come on the market. By that evening we had agreed with the sellers the purchase of the house which was called Tandlehill. We were thrilled, Liam was much relieved and we were to spend 12 very happy years there.

[1] Steve Martin b.1945, American comedian and actor

Claire had already visited Kilmacolm: first in the 70s, when she stayed with family friends Edith and Oliver Birch who had moved there - their son John was my history teacher at CAI. Later Claire was part of the TRN launch team for the proposed Clyde Post, one of their early forays into the free newspaper market. She accompanied Joe Logan the MD on a reconnaissance drive around the village. Sadly, the Clyde Post was never launched, as the trade unions managed to scupper the plans – an early introduction for me into the world of newspapers in Scotland.

Our next-door neighbours at Tandlehill were, on one side Alastair and Jane Wilson [2] and, on the other, a retired Royal Naval Surgeon Commander, who occasionally threw his empty gin bottles over the wall into our garden, but who was otherwise delightful. Within a short time, the Wilsons introduced us to a wide circle of their friends, including John and Liz Hunter[3]. By Christmas John had proposed me for membership of Kilmacolm Golf Club. Amongst many others we became friendly with Peter and Louise Eadie, Robert and Ruth Dickinson and Brian and Dru Hunt. By Christmas we felt absolutely at home. The only downside was that, during that first month, it rained almost every day and Claire was beginning to wonder if this was a permanent feature of Kilmacolm – it pretty much is! By January I had joined Kilmacolm Golf Club, after an interview with the committee.

Milena's arrival on 6th July 1986 was certainly not a textbook one. In the early hours of the morning, Claire started having contractions and we phoned our doctor Iain McLellan[4] who was on call. Iain lived just a short distance away and, most impressively, arrived almost immediately. The now regular contractions suggested that the baby's arrival was imminent and Iain, just as in the films, called for towels and hot water. Shortly afterwards, the contractions slowed and Iain phoned an ambulance which took us at breakneck speed to the Royal Alexandra Hospital in Paisley instead of the planned Queen Mother's in Glasgow. Again, as happens in the movies, a crew were waiting for us at the door of A&E and Claire was whisked away on a trolley. Milena, never one to hang about, was born less than 30 minutes later.

I have since reflected on what it was that attracted us to Kilmacolm in the first place. In those first few months, as we saw more of the west of Scotland, we had decided that we wanted to live in the country and be part of village life, rather than being in a major conurbation, particularly as we had a young daughter, and Kilmacolm fitted the bill perfectly. Another attraction was its relative isolation. Logistically, unless you lived there, you did not pass through the village en route for anywhere else which was most appealing.

Kilmacolm had two other main advantages which became very important in later years, but did not play a part in our original choice. The first was proximity to Glasgow Airport. In my subsequent business life, air travel was increasingly frequent. Its second advantage was schooling. Naively, Claire and I had given absolutely no thought to education when we decided to move there. Luckily

[2] Alastair Wilson, b.1949 m. Jane (née Ogg), distribution manager The Glaswegian 1989-92, latterly founder Osprey Engineering
[3] John Hunter b.1950, m.Liz (née Ogel) Partner McLay, McAlister and McGibbon 1981-2015
[4] Dr Iain McLellan MBChB b.1946 GP Dorema practice Kilmacolm 1980-2008

Kilmacolm had an excellent nursery school and one of the best independent schools in Scotland.

We found Kilmacolm very friendly and welcoming and quickly experienced a sense of community. We had a copy of the local directory for 1984[5] which helpfully listed 43 various clubs and societies in the village. Sport was well catered for, with bowling, cricket, curling, football, golf, rugby, squash and tennis. There were agricultural and horticultural societies, a Civic Trust, a Community Council, dramatic, choral and light opera societies, along with many youth organisations. The village also had playgroups, a nursery school, an art class and even a Masonic Lodge. The Guide listed over 60 businesses within the village.

The property market was in a very healthy state, as we knew from our personal experience. In our time in the village the property market has fluctuated, mostly upwards, although it peaked in 2008. In 1984 houses sold very quickly. Several estate agents confirmed that properties usually sold without being advertised, as was our experience with Tandlehill. We bought our next house in almost the same way in 1996. We had been tipped off that it might be coming onto the market, viewed it on a Sunday afternoon and agreed the sale within 24 hours.

Looking at the businesses listed in the 1984 directory, many still remain – Colin Love, Pieri's café (albeit in several guises), Francis Perry, the Cross Café and Blackwoods, the butcher. Others have long since gone and many new ventures now exist. The overall mix of business has also changed dramatically. In 1984 there were two chemists, two butchers, two fish, fruit and vegetable shops, two newsagents, two dress shops and two garages. Now we have one of each, but sadly no garage or dress shop. Indeed, the garage in nearby Bridge of Weir has also closed. The present mix now includes seven coffee shops and restaurants.

The challenges for retailing today are enormous and many of our local businesses struggle to survive. We have always made a point of supporting village businesses and, if Kilmacolm wants to enjoy the sense of community which a local High Street provides, then everyone must support it. Local fishmonger and greengrocer Colin Love is a classic example. Colin will never be able to compete with the major supermarkets in price or product range, yet he goes to the Glasgow markets six days a week, long before most of us are even up. Colin's business is no different to Blackwoods, the Cross Café, or a host of others – they all need local support to survive.

The other major strategic issue is the future growth of the village. How much bigger can the village become before it loses its character and becomes something entirely different? One positive factor is that there have been only two major housing developments during the last 30 years. The odd cluster of houses has also appeared here and there, but limited growth has been the norm.

---

[5] The 1984 Guide to Kilmacolm, JLP Ltd., Quarriers Village 1984

By and large the will of the village in the same period has been actively against any major housing development. The local laird, Lord Maclay[6], has tried to develop housing in Duchal Woods throughout this period, but unsuccessfully. The will of the residents is formally expressed through the Community Council, the Civic Trust, or personal objection to planning applications.

There is also, inevitably of course, a degree of NIMBYism: "We live here, but we don't want anyone else to." This has resulted in a well-oiled machine ready to be trotted out every time a major (or minor) developer appears with plans for additional houses. This does not seem entirely right. As our population increases, Kilmacolm simply cannot pull up the drawbridge and ignore what is going on around it. There needs to be a more coordinated local plan that tries to achieve some consensus. The least intrusive solution might be for Lord Maclay to develop part of his extensive land in the middle of Duchal Woods. Development of course is only one part of the equation. The infrastructure required to support even another 100-200 houses would be significant. The tragedy in all of this is that the local authority does not appear to be on the same wavelength as many of the residents of Kilmacolm and perhaps both sides need to recognise that fact.

Another issue is that many of the residents in impressive large villas in the village are now of an age where they wish to downsize, but want to remain in the village where they have spent their lifetime. There are very few properties available for them – high quality flats, with managed gardens, within walking distance of the village – so the solution may well be to demolish some of the larger sites, or adapt them. Either way the challenge will be to do this without sacrificing the character of the area and to maintain the charm of Kilmacolm, which the Local Guide, some 30+ years ago, described as follows: "Few villages in Renfrewshire have grown as gracefully over the years as Kilmacolm and retained the douce charm which made it so attractive to Victorian and Edwardian businessmen who chose to build their houses away from the great industrial centres and enjoy rural life in a most pleasant setting."

In early 1987, against my better judgement I purchased a small second-hand caravan for the family. We were determined to see as much of the country as possible and, with two young children, what better way to do this than in a caravan – or so the theory went. The first major difficulty occurred when I discovered how extremely narrow our entrance was. I should say that I only discovered this <u>after</u> I had driven in with the caravan on a Friday evening, removing the top of the gate post and smashing one of the caravan's windows. We had planned to set off on our first journey to Mull on Saturday and that morning I encountered the second major difficulty. The caravan wouldn't operate in reverse. During the course of the day an increasing number of neighbours helped me manoeuvre it so I could drive it out again. I then encountered the same problem again as it was of course just as difficult to get it out of the driveway as it had been to get in. Somehow we managed it without damaging another gatepost or window. Having blocked the entire road for

---

[6] Baron Joseph Maclay, (third Baron) DL b. 1942

hours we eventually set off on our journey the next day to a huge cheer from our neighbours, who were no doubt hoping to never see this wretched thing again! Their wishes were granted. I was extremely fortunate that our friend Charlotte Williams had space in a large garage and we stored the caravan there for several years.

That summer we set off to the explore the Western Isles and on a fantastic three-week trip we visited Lewis, Harris, North and South Uist, Benbecula and Skye. The weather was mixed and the midges ferocious, but the scenery was spectacular. We of course always had to park where we could drive out without reversing which meant odd manoeuvres in some towns. One Saturday afternoon we parked on the main street in Stornoway outside a hat shop. We couldn't remember the last time we'd seen one and wondered how on earth it could survive in a small place like this. Driving around Lewis on Sunday provided the answer – everyone wore hats walking to church. Sunday afternoon was a complete contrast – everywhere was deserted, with children enviously looking out the window of their house as we drove past, not allowed out to play outside on the Sabbath. Fortunately, we had been pre-warned that no shops would be open on Sunday but it was nevertheless strange buying the Sunday newspapers on Monday morning. All in all it reminded me of my own childhood growing up in Northern Ireland some 30 years previously. We felt as if we were in a time warp throughout our visit.

Sadly, my mother died in February 1988 but she had been able to see us safely settled in Scotland and enjoy the early lives of our children. She had stayed with us during Christmas and, although in apparently good health, she was increasingly concerned about living on her own so far away from all the family. There had been some discussion about her moving to Ballymoney to be nearer Niki, but she was reluctant to move from her beautiful bungalow on the shores of Strangford Lough. In early February she had a stroke and spent the last three weeks of her life in Downpatrick hospital. At her funeral as the hearse drove from her house, Ted, Niki and I concluded that she would have been very happy never having had to leave such a lovely place.

Chapter 13   SDR – THE EARLY YEARS

"Have the courage to follow your heart and intuition. They somehow know what you truly want to become." Steve Jobs[1]

Exactly seven weeks after I had joined the Scotsman, I moved to the Scottish Daily Record and Sunday Mail Ltd. (SDR). No early flight this time - I had driven to Glasgow on Saturday 5th March 1984. Thankfully no snow either, thus no new shoes or hat. A new chapter in my life was about to begin. SDR was part of Mirror Group Newspapers (MGN) with two titles - the Daily Record and the Sunday Mail - dominating the Scottish newspaper market. It occupied a most impressive nine storey building at Anderston Quay on the banks of the Clyde.

On my first morning Liam Kane and I set off on an impromptu tour of the building. One encounter on the editorial floor stands out. After moving through the vast Daily Record area, we entered a small office set in the corner. Two men sat at a meeting table strewn with dozens of small pieces of paper, almost as if they were trying to complete a jigsaw puzzle. This was my first introduction to Jim "Jolly" Rodger[2] and Jimmy "Solly" Sanderson[3], sports writers from the Daily Mirror and Sunday Mirror. Liam remarked dryly: "I see, gentlemen, that as usual you are using your time productively. I assume there was a big match abroad last week?" Indeed, there had been, and Rodger and Sanderson were, as Liam described afterwards, "cobbling together their expenses, no doubt as elaborate a piece of deception as you will ever encounter!"

At the end of the tour Liam brought me to my office on the 8th floor. It was a huge space with panoramic views of the Clyde. There were two doors: a private one and one to my secretary's office, which alone was bigger than many of the offices I had occupied in other companies. I was introduced to my secretary. She and I were not to have an easy relationship. Probably in her late 50s, she had been there for some time. She had previously worked for a number of Directors and had fallen out with most of them. Sadly, she operated at one pace only - very slow! Quite how she had survived in this fast-paced environment for so long was something of a mystery to me. However, as I was going to learn quickly, in the heavily unionised environment of SDR, getting rid of someone who wasn't up to the job was a tall order. Our relationship would be best described as tolerating each other. She was somewhat inflexible and worked to the absolute minimum standards, careful to work her required hours and not one second more.

I met with the recently retired Circulation Director Frank Gault, who now acted as a consultant for the company. Liam had been looking for a replacement for Frank for some time and had concluded that there was no obvious internal candidate. By recruiting me as Deputy Director he was keeping his options open. In the worst-case scenario, if I wasn't up to the job, he could get rid of me (or keep me and arrange

[1] Steve Jobs, 1955-2011,Chairman CEO and co-founder of Apple Inc.
[2] Jim 'Jolly' Rodger, OBE 1923-1997, sports journalist
[3] Jimmy 'Solly' Sanderson, 1929-1986, sports journalist and part of Radio Clyde's first football phone-in

early retirement for Tommy Mansbridge, number two in the department). The best scenario of course was that I would become Director within six months, as we had discussed. Brilliant strategist that he was, Liam wanted to keep track of what I was up to and how I was getting on with my team. What better way to do this than retain the services of the retiring incumbent as a consultant until he was sure the new man had totally settled in?

I was quite happy with this arrangement. I listened carefully to Frank's views on both the marketplace and the department and on how things had been done on his watch. We agreed on how we could make the arrangement with Liam work best. Frank would be my eyes and ears on the ground. He worked half a day a week and would visit different areas and continue to talk to his old friends in the trade, thus providing me with intelligence on what was happening in the marketplace. The arrangement worked well. Six months later I became Circulation Director and I made sure the consultancy ended soon afterwards.

On the Friday morning the entire department flew to Majorca for its annual Sales Conference. Although predominately a "jolly" it was also an excellent opportunity for team building. That year it also provided Liam with an ideal platform to introduce me to the entire team, who were spread throughout Scotland. In addition, several others were in the party including Jim Wilson (Deputy Editor, Daily Record), Bob Joyner (Promotions Manager), Jim Frew (accountant) and Harry Scott[4]. There was a serious side to the proceedings. On the Saturday morning there was a formal session with sales and marketing reviews and a discussion on future strategy. Liam and I had agreed in advance that, as I had just arrived, he would chair the proceedings, giving me an excellent opportunity to observe the event closely, see who contributed and who didn't and start forming an opinion on the resources I had inherited. It was also a great opportunity to meet everyone socially. We all flew back to Glasgow on the Monday with the alcohol stocks in that part of Majorca in severe need of replenishment.

Once back I settled into getting to grips with my new job. The Scottish Daily Record and Sunday Mail Ltd (SDR) was a wholly owned subsidiary of MGN. It traded as a separate company with its own Board of Directors, but was very much the junior partner in the eyes of senior management in London. MGN was owned by Reed International and newspapers were not a natural fit within a conglomerate whose interests included wallpaper, paint, paper and a whole host of other businesses. The relationship between MGN and SDR was extremely toxic. Part of Reed's frustration was that MGN made a derisory profit on a very considerable turnover. The major contributor to the profit was SDR. MGN's stable of newspapers comprised the Daily Mirror, the Sunday Mirror, and The People. Market domination had long been conceded to the News International tabloid titles The Sun and the News of the World. In Scotland the opposite was true. The Daily Record dominated its market, read by two out of every three adults in Scotland, and the Sunday Mail was swiftly closing in on the Sunday Post for dominance of the Sunday market. Sales of Mirror

---

[4] Harry Scott 1942-2017, m. Irene 1s. Barry 1d. Gillian. Co-founder Scott Stern 1972

titles in Scotland were a fraction of anywhere else in the UK. That market dominance more than anything else contributed to the dreadful relationship between the two companies, with jealousy and, worse still, almost grievance on the part of the MGN team. A contributory factor to the jealousy was that, under Derek Webster and Vic Horwood's stewardship, SDR was an exceptionally well-run company. In my ten years there I was part of a team which extended that market dominance even further, while MGN continued to decline.

Reed had decided to exit newspapers and Clive Thornton[5] had been brought in as Chief Executive to handle the sale. Sadly, Thornton had lost part of one leg and with cruel humour, his stewardship was referred to as "In the land of the legless the one-legged man is king". In reality this was more a reflection of the MGN Board's alcohol consumption and the ineffectiveness of their stewardship of the company, particularly in relation to its profit level.

Under Webster and Horwood there was a formidable team comprising Liam Kane, Bernard Vickers[6], Endell Laird[7], Derick Henry[8] and Murdoch McLennan. In March 1984 there were no Advertising or Circulation Directors. Gordon Terris and I were appointed to those positions in October 1984, whilst rather strangely there was no Marketing Director. There were also no Non-Executive Directors, perhaps reflecting Reed's view that this was not a 'real' Board, but more of a subsidiary company.

Subsidiary or not, the SDR very much reflected the lifestyle of the parent company and therein lay part of its problem. It had the same cost base as its parent. It was also what would now be regarded as a rather old-fashioned company with a well-defined hierarchical structure. For example, in the 9th Floor Executive Suite there was a boardroom where the Directors would dine after Board Meetings and with visitors, with a full waitress service from the 'Executive Kitchen'. Next door was the Senior Executive Dining Room where the top tier of editorial and commercial management dined, either by themselves or with visitors, with the same waitress service. There was a full bar service and an extensive wine list, all free of charge. The justification for this, as Liam explained, pragmatic as ever, was that it was much more efficient to have the executives entertain on their own premises at significantly less cost than if they were doing so at restaurants. Nonetheless it was a most impressive executive 'canteen' and was famous throughout Glasgow.

SDR also had a staff canteen. In Chapter 5, I describe discovering Tad's Steak Bar in New York City, where in 1968 $1.29 would buy you a 16oz New York strip steak, an Idaho baked potato with butter, corn on the cob, and a cup of coffee. 16 years later, you could almost buy much the same meal for the same price in the SDR staff canteen. The operation was heavily subsidised by around £200k a year. Every move to increase price levels met with huge resistance from the trade unions, who felt they had a divine right to eat high quality food at ridiculously low prices.

[5] Clive Thornton, b 1929, Chief Executive, Abbey National BS, 1978-83, Chairman MGM 1984
[6] Bernard Vickers, 1932-2014, Editor Daily Record 1973-88
[7] Endell Laird, 1933-2015, Editor, Sunday Mail 1981-88, Daily Record 1988-94
[8] Derick Henry, b 1948, Finance Director SDR

Like the Senior Executive dining room, the staff canteen was also famous throughout Glasgow. As we were to find out, it was far more famous than we realised! About to go into yet another series of negotiations about pricing, Vic asked me to liaise with Pat Kennedy (Head of Security) to get a feel for the canteen's utilisation levels, particularly in mid to late evening. An ex-Strathclyde policeman, Pat (or Inspector Knacker as he was known) embraced the project enthusiastically, indeed rather more enthusiastically than I would have liked. One evening, with several colleagues, he swooped on the canteen, sealed the entrances, and checked the identities of everyone inside. To our horror, as well as our own staff we discovered 15 taxi drivers, 12 contractors, six unknown individuals with no connection to the company whatsoever, and two vagrants from a nearby lodging house. No wonder the subsidy was costing us so much – we were feeding half of Glasgow! Vic was delighted with the outcome. The company took measures to ensure that, in future, only our staff ate there and also managed to achieve a significant hike in prices that year.

And then there was alcohol. To say that there was a heavy drinking culture running throughout SDR is probably an understatement, although it was no different to Fleet Street, on which it was modelled. Of course, not everyone was embedded in this culture or, if they were, they participated to varying degrees, but nevertheless it existed and permeated throughout the organisation. Even in a newspaper world pickled in alcohol, SDR was in a class of its own.

One example was on my first day as a Director. A gentleman arrived in my office with a trolley and began stocking my 'drinks cabinet'. I had previously seen this cupboard with its own key, and concluded that it was perhaps a safe, but I now learnt that all Board members had drinks cabinets for internal and external entertaining. Regularly, the same gentleman would come around and top up the cabinet's impressive contents. Very often in the interim, my PA might have a visit from Bernard Vickers' PA, temporarily borrowing this or that - usually bottles of gin.

Bernard was a fascinating man. Originally from the north of England and affectionately known as 'T'editor', he was very much in the Fleet Street tradition. A convivial man with a ruddy complexion, he was 'a legend in his own lunchtime', with a particular penchant for gin and tonic and Sicilian Corvo white wine. Like William McIlvanney[9], he commanded his own table at La Lanterna in Hope Street. On arrival he always held several fingers in the air to indicate the number of bottles of wine to be chilled. Colin Dunn, who worked for SDR in London, describes him thus, "Bernard excited admiration and occasionally astonishment for his drinking capacity. He was an extraordinary man and with his slanting florid face, flattened hair and large glasses, he looked like a Japanese general." Bernard certainly drove his troops hard, patrolling the editorial floor, biro in hand like a conductor's baton. Frequently, after a long day, many a senior executive, not quite understanding the Editor's instructions, would be curtly told, "You're fired." If the transgression was

---

[9] William McIlvanney 1936-2015, Scottish novelist and poet

really significant, Bernard might phone a short time later to tell them, "You're fooking fired" but by next morning all would be forgotten and forgiven.

There were many other memorable stories about Bernard's drinking. A copy boy was summoned to his office and sent in search of a corkscrew. Unable to find one, he used his initiative and obtained one from The Copy Cat (one of the two Daily Record local pubs, the other one being the Off the Record). The Copy Cat's barman instructed the boy to return it immediately afterwards on hearing that it was required for Bernard. Conveying this news to Bernard on his return, Bernard's reply was, "That's not a problem, dear boy." and promptly opened five bottles of his Sicilian Corvo. Bob Joyner also talks of an embarrassing occasion when a case of very expensive white wine was the first prize in a reader competition. The prize was securely locked up in his office but, to his horror, starting work the following morning, he discovered six bottles were missing. He established that Bernard had ordered the security staff the previous evening to break into his office and obtain some of the excellent wine.

Despite all this, Bernard Vickers was universally admired by his staff. He had assembled probably the most talented bunch of journalists in Scotland at that time. Someone described a good editor as like tinsel on a Christmas tree – they add the perfect amount of sparkle without being gaudy. Bernard fitted that bill. He was also one of the first to recognise the increasing importance of television in people's lives and had noted that soap operas were regularly at the very top of viewing figures. Although not everyone agreed with his policy of 'splashing' (the front-page lead story) on story lines from Dallas and Coronation Street, it was hard to argue with the Daily Record's sales performance during the Vickers' era. He described it as "froth and pap" but, whilst his paper was a bright and brash tabloid, the Daily Record also had a serious side and he worked hard on balancing the overall offering.

Vickers was also extremely shrewd in his dealings with 'Management'. Maxwell was later to coin the phrase, "Editorial on top, Management on tap". Bernard, however, was years ahead of him in describing his relationship with Vic Horwood, "Vic and I walk hand in hand, with him a respectful half step behind me." Bernard was later to fall out with Maxwell. He was appalled at Maxwell's attempts to intimidate 'his' journalists, which effectively meant the end of their four-day week. I suspect, in his heart of hearts, he knew it was the end of an era for him personally when Maxwell moved him to London in 1986 as Assistant Publisher. For the Daily Record it marked a significant change. Vickers had been an extremely successful Editor, but the paper was becoming tired, and an increasingly sophisticated readership wanted more from their newspapers than just the latest developments in soap operas. Endell Laird, Editor of the Sunday Mail, was appointed to replace Bernard and he and I were to work closely together in countering the increasing threat of The Sun, now printing in Scotland from January 1986.

The absence of a Marketing Director was more of a reflection on creative tensions within the company at that time. Marketing had traditionally been the preserve of Editorial and was chiefly concerned with promoting content rather than the brand itself. Liam had been acutely aware of this and recognised that, if the titles were to continue to grow, he needed to build a brand and market presence for them. Furthermore, the onset of newspaper bingo and other significant promotional games was just beginning and SDR needed to lead this in Scotland. Finally, he felt that SDR's traditional advertising agencies were simply not up to the job. His solution was to identify one of the most creative and innovative promotional companies in Scotland at that time - Scott Stern, headed by Harry Scott and Raymond Stern[10].

By the time I arrived in 1984 Liam had managed to wrestle the promotions side of the business away from editorial and had split marketing into above and below the line categories[11], with separate budgets and agencies. Scott Stern now became responsible for all below the line advertising. They were predominately a design and packaging company whose clients included Scottish Power, the Gas Board and Whyte and McKay. They quickly grasped the SDR brief and gradually updated the brand. 'Your Papers Made in Scotland' became the brand slogan and an integral part of all advertising material. They also understood the whole mechanism of sales promotion better than anyone else. Newspaper bingo and other promotional sales drivers had been around for some time, but a new breed of tools - scratch cards, number derivatives and all the other tricks of the trade- were either invented, or in some cases, recycled better by Scott Stern than by anyone else. One principle which I learnt from Liam then, I was to replicate for the rest of my business life. Be the first to identify new trends and the new kids on the block who are faster and more fleet of foot than anyone else.

Harry Scott died in January 2017 in Bangkok, where he had lived for many years. Many tributes were paid to Harry's creative genius. SDR benefited from his creative talent in countless campaigns, innovations and ideas. At SDR I developed the concept of Vertical News Display which led the way for, and has now been copied by, just about every other newspaper publisher in the land. Traditionally newspapers were displayed at ground floor level, usually on a plinth below the magazine rack. I researched this in some detail and discovered that if a title were displayed at eye level, it resulted in an increase in sales of up to 15%. Harry built some prototypes which we installed at several retailers, and which validated the concept. The fact that its fundamental design is much the same now as it was 30 years ago is testament to Harry's vision. Many of his best ideas were spontaneous. You would discuss something with him, he would take out his pen and a sheet of paper and sketch something which would, more often than not, closely resemble the eventual finished article. Gordon and Sandra Adams[12] talked to Harry when they were setting up their estate agency business. Pen and paper produced, Harry drew two houses, side by side, a G in one and an S in the other, and joined them up. 30 years later the business is using that same logo, which still looks fresh and up to date. When John Welsh was opening an antiques shop in Bearsden it was to be

---

[10] Raymond Stern b.1948, Co-founder Scott Stern 1972, subsequently acquired by WPP Group 1987
[11] Above the line promotes products on radio, television, billboard, print and film formats. Below the line advertising seeks to reach consumers directly instead of casting a wide net to reach mass audiences.
[12] Gordon Adams b.1946 m. Sandra (née Henderson) 2s. one of the West of Scotland's leading estate agents since 1979 (G&S Properties) and property/land development (Comstock)

called Bearsden Antiques. Harry disagreed, "Don't be so stupid, there's only one name for that business - Welsh Rare Bits". It's still there 30 years later.

For most of his life Harry lived in a world where, as the owner of a relatively small business, he could dictate everything that happened. He was a true Glaswegian in everything he did (including his language!) For his 50th birthday his employees produced 'The Little Orange Book – the sayings and philosophy of Harry Fletcher Scott.' In the chapter devoted to "friendly and helpful advice to suppliers" are the following gems:

"I don't want to pay for this – lose it."
"Sack them."
"Hide this on that effin' job you're doing for nothing."

Sometimes his advice was contradictory.

"He's a wa*ker – don't use him."
"He's a wa*ker but we've no choice but to use the c**t."

The book was produced with the following acknowledgement, "Printed (for nothing) by David J. Clark, Glasgow (who's hiding the cost on another job he's doing for nothing)."

Harry also had huge motivational skills:

"Look at that and tell me what's wrong with it."
"Who put all this sh*te on my desk?"
"What would you do if I wasn't here?"
"I don't need an effin' computer. I can do it quicker by hand."

Finally, Harry was always full of reassurance, "Don't worry, it'll effin' work." Rest in peace, Harry.

My first major shock on joining SDR was to witness the power and greed of the trade unions. Although I had worked in the newspaper industry since 1971, nothing had prepared me for the state of almost industrial scale anarchy at MGN. Although the misuse of power by the Fleet Street unions was well known, I had assumed that Glasgow would be different. Wrong! As part of MGN, SDR was a replica of Fleet Street, with the same union structure, attitudes and practices and with the print unions at the vanguard of the whole process. At SDR every group of the workforce was represented by a Chapel, headed by the Father of the Chapel. SDR's Managers even had their own Chapel – surely a contradiction in terms if there ever was one? The print unions were the most vicious of the lot with little subtlety in their negotiating style, just brute force and threats.

In my first year there I started to record the various sales losses resulting from interrupted production. As the person ultimately responsible for maximising sales, I found it incredibly frustrating to see the company's efforts frequently negated by the belligerence and sheer bloody-mindedness of the print unions. Between 11th April and 13th July 1984 when Maxwell bought the company, there were eight occasions when disputes led to major losses of production. In hindsight, this was mere skirmishing; the big battle with the print unions lay ahead. Right now, this was old-style trade unionism, a recipe for inefficiency, inertia, and a stranglehold on any management initiative or change. It was greed and self-interest at their very worst. The print unions were almost Luddite in their relations with the company. For example, no IBM manufactured product was permitted within SDR, despite IBM being a major employer in Greenock, less than 20 miles away. This was because IBM did not recognise trade unions. In another example, in 1985 the Chairman took delivery of the latest piece of technology, a facsimile transmission (Fax) machine. It was installed in his office and very nearly brought the company to a standstill, as until then all communications to the company had gone through what was called the 'Wire Room'.

The major challenge I faced on joining SDR was its sales policy. Virtually every other newspaper in the marketplace operated a policy of full sale or return - i.e. the retailer received full credit for any unsold copies. The Daily Record's policy meant that for every unsold copy the retailer received credit for only one third of the net cost. The effect of this was to curtail severely availability of the paper, as many retailers made sure that they sold all their supplies and incurred no returns (or losses as they saw it). On the other hand, SDR felt there was an acceptable level of availability and that financially this was the best outcome.

I spent an enormous amount of time looking at this, viewing evidence in the field and monitoring sales levels hour by hour throughout the day. The conventional arguments supporting the current policy were twofold. The first one was financial. By only giving the retailer partial credit on unsold copies the publisher benefited. In crude terms, retailers were "swallowing" the major part of the cost of unsold copies. Only a significant market leader could operate such a policy. The second argument was that an enormous number of factors influenced the sale of newspapers. Operating a policy of full sale or return was therefore high risk, as it was impossible to predict sales levels accurately - or so the argument ran. However, there were many predictable trends. Sales of newspapers were cyclical; Saturdays were the highest sales day, Tuesdays and Wednesdays the lowest. Sales were also affected by content - a good news or sports story could have a significant effect. Sales promotion was also a major contributor with the advent of newspaper bingo and similar promotions.

These then were the main reasons for maintaining the existing returns policy at SDR - the system was fit for purpose and fluctuating market conditions meant that sales levels could never be accurately predicted. It was against this background that I began assembling a case for change. I did so by re-analysing existing data. It was already established that the Daily Record's availability level was 100% up until around 11am, after which it started to decline significantly. The lack of availability was determined by newsagents deliberately ensuring that they had sold their entire supply, thus guaranteeing no loss to them. What hadn't been taken into account was that most of them kept one copy which they read in the evening and subsequently returned to the publisher. In previous analyses, a return of one copy indicated maximum availability. When the returns data was reanalysed and one copy returns counted as sell outs, availability levels plummeted.

I initiated new research which analysed the sales pattern throughout the day on an hourly basis. This reinforced some information that everyone was aware of i.e. that the bulk of morning newspapers were purchased before 9.15am, with home deliveries included in this figure. The new data however, was startling in that it showed that as much as 30% of sales were after 11am. Prior to this, SDR's thinking was that it was sufficient if 100% availability could be guaranteed up until 11 am. The new data showed a significant level of sale being lost by lack of availability, particularly if there was a major story or significant sales promotion on that day. SDR at the time was spending between £1-1.5 million per year on sales promotion and that investment was being diluted by the paper's lack of availability. Potential new readers simply weren't able to sample the paper.

I provided two further facts: for all the efforts of the biggest sales force in Scotland and despite the efforts of our wholesalers, the huge gaps in availability were not remotely being plugged. Secondly, SDR's large sales force was supposed to cultivate good relationships with its retailers. I analysed the scale of news trade promotions and found that we were spending about £250,000 a year building this supposedly great relationship. The reality, however, was that the average retailer did little to promote the Daily Record actively over any other title, because to do so incurred a financial loss. In numerous meetings with individual retailers, with groups of multiple retailers (such as RS McColl) and with the collective trade body the National Federation of Retail Newsagents, I was to hear that the main feature of their relationships with SDR was one of grievance. The company through its returns policy was "cheating" them and more than anything else they wanted a full sale and return policy from SDR, just as they had from everyone else. So much for the "cosy" relationship that everybody within Anderston Quay talked about.

By my second year I had persuaded the Board that the SDR should change its sales policy and move to full sale or return (SOR). Derick Henry the Finance Director was vehemently opposed to it as there was an immediate and easily calculated financial downside, offset against unknown (and to an accountant incalculable) future sales increases, which in turn would also lead to increased advertising revenues. Vic, a cautious man by nature, could also see this argument but, to his credit, supported my proposal.

To maximise the benefits, much faster and more accurate processing of unsolds was needed. That led to the company re-examining the fundamental relationship between the publisher (ourselves), the wholesalers (predominantly John Menzies), and 6,000 odd retailers. In my time with SDR I renegotiated our wholesaler contracts in Scotland twice, with a major change being that wholesalers were now required to pick up unsolds on a daily basis instead of weekly and to process them faster. To do this they also had to invest significantly in IT systems and we in turn helped by introducing barcodes to our titles, enabling electronic scanning of unsolds. The most controversial part of the new contracts was that I introduced individual targets for both unsold levels and availability, with financial penalties for non-achievement.

Sales levels continued to be impressive throughout the mid and late 80s. Indeed, sales rose virtually continually in my first eight years with the company. I certainly can't claim sole credit for this, but many of the measures that I introduced made a positive contribution. I also gradually assumed more responsibility for the overall marketing strategy, which was reflected in my being appointed Circulation and Marketing Director.

After several years, my secretary retired and Janis Judge [13] joined SDR in May 1993 and became a key part of my team. She shone during the recruitment process and was not put off when I told her one of the qualities I required was psychic powers. Janis was to work with me during my remaining time at SDR and then at News International. She later described me as a first-class communicator, always conveying at least 95% of the information required to complete any task. Sometimes however it was the crucial 5% that I omitted to tell her about, hence the need for her psychic powers.

Throughout the mid-80s both Maxwell and Murdoch [14] in their separate ways were preparing for the final battle with the trade unions. Maxwell's strategy is detailed in Chapter 15. Murdoch was also encountering the same industrial anarchy. In early 1995 in Warrington the then unknown Eddie Shah had commenced his battle and the first violent picket lines that later became common place at Wapping were first seen there. There are many excellent accounts of these battles, the best of which are by Linda Melvern [15], Charles Wintour [16], and Brian MacArthur [17].

From SDR's perspective, the company had always known that one front of Murdoch's battle would be in Glasgow. From the early 1980s News International (NI) was flying newspapers into Scotland at enormous cost, particularly if their paper failed to be published, as happened on 25 occasions in 1985 alone. In the late 1970s NI had purchased an old engineering foundry at Kinning Park in Glasgow and installed some fairly ancient presses. There was no doubt that eventually Scottish editions of News International's titles would be printed there.

In some ways, the early departure of Bernard Vickers was a prelude to this. Endell Laird was not an easy man to work for and was nowhere near as revered as Bernard, but he brought, in his own style, strong leadership to the Daily Record editorial team. The heavy drinking culture of Bernard's reign was gradually reduced. Endell was not a man to be crossed and he laid down his marker early on what was acceptable and what was not. In many ways, his troops were in constant fear of him as he was not the most forgiving person. As a thrawn Forfarer, once he became

[13] Janis Judge, b. 1951, my PA 1993-94, 1995-2007
[14] Rupert Murdoch AC, KCSG, b.1931, Australian born, American media mogul
[15] 'The End of the Street' Linda Melvern, 1986, Methuen London Ltd.
[16] 'The Rise and Fall of Fleet Street', Charles Wintour, 1989, Hutchinson
[17] 'Eddie Shah: Today and the Newspaper Revolution', Brian MacArthur, 1988, David and Charles Publishers Ltd.

convinced of something, no amount of evidence would persuade him to change his opinion.

I worked with Endell over a number of years and I had enormous respect for him. Although we developed a very close working relationship in those critical years it would be wrong to describe it as cosy. We were both very strong characters, often with opposing points of view, but nevertheless we greatly respected each other.

As an editor, Endell had a very clear view on the type of paper he wanted to produce, but his vision was very different to Bernard's. For Endell the Daily Record, as the dominant player in the market, had to dominate the news agenda. Endell's yardstick of success was that the average Daily Record reader, whether at home or in the pub after work, should be discussing either that day's Daily Record's stories or its viewpoint on a particular subject. If they weren't, we had failed. If they were discussing anything that was in the Scottish Sun, all hell would break loose and there would be a major inquest the following day as to how this had happened. Endell could instil infinitely more fear on the hapless hack who had missed the story than Bernard's "You're fooking fired" could ever do. He was also the first to recognise the importance of female readership and developed a number of brilliant female journalists, including Elsa McIlonan[18] and Melanie Reid[19], both of whom are still at the forefront of their trade almost 30 years later.

I wasn't the only Board member to have confrontations with Endell. In 1985, whilst still Editor of the Sunday Mail, he single-handedly caused a furore that resulted in SDR's single biggest advertiser withdrawing all their advertising overnight, a situation which continued for almost a year and ultimately accounted for almost £1million of lost revenue. Endell had commissioned a feature on the costs of car maintenance. The Sunday Mail obtained an elderly vehicle and had it thoroughly checked by the RAC to ensure that it met all legal requirements. Journalists then took the car around a number of branches of different Tyre and Accessory Depots to have it checked. The outcomes were fairly predictable, with various establishments claiming that the car was deficient in a number of areas which would require rectifying – in some cases at considerable cost. The results were then published in a major piece in the Sunday Mail. Amongst the 'offenders' were several branches of Kwik Fit, then owned by Sir Tom Farmer[20].

The following morning, Farmer phoned his advertising agency and instructed them to withdraw all advertising from our titles there and then. Gordon Terris and Vic were horrified and tried to contact Farmer, but he refused to take their calls. At about 3 o'clock that afternoon, I happened to look out of my office window and noticed some television cameras setting up on the quayside opposite SDR's main entrance. Shortly afterwards a number of coaches drew up and offloaded some 400 Kwik Fit employees, who started chanting, "You can't get better than a Kwik Fit fitter!" as Farmer himself was being interviewed by said T.V. crew. It was a fantastic

---

[18] Elsa McIlonan feature writer, beauty columnist, Associated Newspapers
[19] Melanie Reid MBE b.1957, journalist, author and writer of Spinal Column, The Times Magazine
[20] Sir Tom Farmer, CVO, CBE, KC*SG, FRSE, DL, b 1940, entrepreneur, founder/CEO, Kwik Fit 1971-2002

bit of PR. Farmer was able to pour scorn on the Sunday Mail article and, in doing so, enjoyed 60-seconds of prime-time advertising on the evenings news bulletins free of charge. The Sunday Mail story was completely accurate and had detailed all the recommendations made by Kwik Fit staff, but of course this evidence was ignored by Farmer in his moment of glory. He also publicly threatened legal action but, not surprisingly, it never materialised. He did however stick to his guns and despite an intensive SDR campaign to woo him back, no Kwik Fit advertising appeared in the titles for several months. Eventually Gordon Terris managed to negotiate a new (and I am sure highly favourable to Farmer) contract. Throughout, Endell maintained the position of editorial integrity and never acknowledged any role in the lost revenue - which of course was the Advertising Department's problem.

Meanwhile, the battle between the Daily Record and the Scottish Sun continued to rage. Endell's main contribution was to reassure Daily Record readers constantly that they were getting the best quality newspaper and the latest, most comprehensive news and sports coverage. He introduced a series of new sections for women and for business. We also launched new regional editions for Aberdeen and Inverness, beefing up editorial content for both areas. I obtained significant increases in marketing expenditure.

One area where Endell and I were to clash was on the start time of the Daily Record. Endell was by nature a 'tinkerer', forever making amendments or last-minute changes in an effort to produce the best possible paper. As a result, his 'off stone' (last copy released) performance was lamentable. The first Daily Record copies were supposed to roll off the presses at 9:50pm, but Endell rarely achieved that, with post 10pm much more the norm for him. I was increasingly concerned about the inevitable arrival of a Scottish Sun and (correctly as it turned out) anticipated that News International would also produce a 'Streets Edition' in an area where previously the Daily Record had had the market to itself. I did not want to be disadvantaged when it came to who would have the first copies on the streets.

The major battle with Endell to improve his off-stone times would go on for several months, but I felt that I was gradually gaining the upper hand and would bombard Endell when his performance lagged. To his credit, he managed to improve the situation significantly and was regularly hitting his off-stone target. All was well between us until one Thursday night when, by sheer chance, he happened to be in the production area and encountered a hapless Advertising Representative putting through some last minute (and totally unauthorised) copy changes to an Arnold Clark advertisement for the following day's paper. All hell broke out and from that day onwards, Endell would always blame advertising for a late off stone time, even though there was not a shred of evidence that this was the case.

NI started printing at Kinning Park on 26th January 1986, the same night as at Wapping. As I had predicted, once the Kinning Park production schedule started settling down, the Scottish Sun wanted to join the well-organised street sales network that the Daily Record had spent many years creating. Glasgow was one of the few cities in the country with such a network, a myriad of vendors who permeated the city's nightlife, giving people the opportunity to 'buy tomorrow's paper today'. Unsurprisingly, NI put enormous pressure on our Street Wholesaler George Proudfoot to join what we regarded as our exclusive network. Proudfoot was an extremely interesting character. He and SDR went back a long way and he had, over the years, built up an extensive network of Glasgow street vendors. Many were minors, and he was frequently in trouble with the authorities over this. Fortunately for him, in those days regulation was still fairly light-touch, but nevertheless SDR spent an enormous amount of time keeping track on what Proudfoot was up to. Furthermore, although he was licensed to distribute and sell the streets edition solely through a vendor network, he was also supplying a whole range of unofficial outlets who went on to sell this edition throughout the following day, to the combined fury of SDR, John Menzies, and the news trade. To top it all, Proudfoot regarded himself as a sort of self-styled 'gangster' and I have no doubt that he maintained extensive contacts with the Glasgow underworld. He was by now a very successful businessman and maintained an extremely high profile, driving around in his Rolls Royce. From the start I was extremely wary of him but I realised that many of my staff were enthralled by him, his reputation no doubt greatly assisted by his considerable largesse with them. As a consequence, I became convinced that, where possible, SDR turned a blind eye to many of his activities. Proudfoot's long-term objective was to become an official wholesaler in his own right. I was equally determined never to allow that to happen as the result would have been complete chaos in the marketplace. Also, entirely predictably, once NI arrived on the scene, Proudfoot was determined to get a slice of their business and SDR had to pull out every trick in the book to prevent this. Our lawyers had ensured that our contract with Proudfoot was watertight and I tightened things up even further each time I renegotiated it. Nevertheless, one couldn't relax with him, never knowing what he would be up to next. In some ways it could be highly entertaining watching him constantly trying to outwit us.

I suppose it was inevitable that, with the rationalisation and major changes in the wholesale market and the various marketing initiatives I was now involved in, I would make a few enemies along the way. But none of that could have prepared me for a chilling episode in 1988. In the middle of the night, I received an anonymous phone call telling me, "McClatchie, you're a dead man", followed by two similar calls the following nights. The company consulted with the police and some measures were put in place to 'protect' me. Our security staff escorted me to my car each evening and I was instructed to vary, as much as possible, my journey home (this is all very well but there was no way to vary the final part of my journey up Barclaven Road). The local police in Kilmacolm were also informed and were to keep an eye on the house. Finally, the police, through British Telecom, installed a special device on my home phone that would enable them to trace any subsequent threatening calls. All I had to do was dial 3 after such a call and the trace mechanism would kick in. Although reassured by the police that the vast majority of these calls were hoax ones, it did concentrate the mind and, for a while, I became very aware of people in my immediate vicinity. The threatening calls then ceased. Two weeks later, I had a call from the police to tell me that there had been another one and that they had traced the number and asked me if the number was known to me. I listened with keen anticipation, as I was pretty sure who the caller had been but I was flabbergasted when they gave me my own mobile number! It transpired that I had called Claire from the car on the way home that evening and five-year-old Amanda had picked up an extension and by sheer chance dialled three. I never officially learned the identity of the original caller but I remain convinced of his identity. Thirty years later my then two-year-old granddaughter Tarryn did something similar. I was in the middle of a very important conference call when I and everyone else gradually became aware of someone else joining the call. Various distinct sounds now permeated our conversation with everyone wondering where these were coming from. To my horror I realised that Tarryn had picked up the upstairs extension and was increasingly loudly contributing to our deliberations!

Meanwhile, the pace of the war between the Daily Record and the 'Scottish' Sun was now picking up. As the established and dominant player, the Daily Record had to take the high ground - and drive the agenda and be all things to all people – no easy task. Again, Endell and I worked very closely, particularly on the marketing side and he was always helpful in ensuring that our promotions were prominently displayed throughout the paper with maximum editorial support, but his enthusiasm could occasionally be a major problem. Even if he liked a concept which was being developed, he might lose interest as the final details were being shaped. As far as he was concerned, it should already have been in the paper. This was in the era when The Daily Record and Sun camps were closely monitoring each other's activities and our intelligence network was running on overdrive. One day we got wind of a massive national Sun promotion to be launched in the near future – free life insurance for every reader. Endell was determined that the Daily Record would not be disadvantaged and thus work started on a similar scheme (known in the trade as a 'spoiler'). Negotiations immediately commenced with General Accident to launch a similar or, better still, superior scheme for Daily Record readers. Despite the fact that the Sun had probably been working on their promotion for several weeks, Endell was determined not to be outdone and although the discussions with General Accident were well underway, they were far from complete. To everyone's horror, Endell took it upon himself to splash the promotion the very next day, even before the Sun had launched theirs. The massive coverage which dominated the front page completely spooked the General Accident team and to say they were less than amused is an understatement. Nevertheless, it was a fait accompli and they were now forced to stitch up the final details of the promotion quickly. Despite a major inquest afterwards as to how to avoid this happening again, I remained convinced that Endell would have done the same again given the opportunity.

The Glasgow Garden Festival took place from April to September 1986. It was the third of five such events and by far the most successful. It was the first event of its type to be held in the city since the Empire Exhibition of 1938 and, combined with Glasgow becoming European City of Culture in 1990, did much to enhance the city's national and international reputation. The Garden Festival site was almost on our doorstep and it was an event that SDR had to be involved in, but how? After extensive research, the company decided to maximise its presence by taking a unit at the very centre of the site in the retail village. It was an enormous project. The exhibition ran over 152 days and just staffing our unit required four full-time people. Initially I had reservations about it, but in the end, I recommended that we should go ahead. In hindsight, our involvement in the Garden Festival was probably more dictated by keeping NI out rather than on the merits of SDR's own involvement. Harry Scott was in his element, his creative talents in overdrive and Scott Stern came up with a large range of merchandise to sell in our 'shop' and thus make a profit on the entire venture. It did not take my accountant Jim Frew too long to realise that this was a pipedream. Realistically we looked at it as an investment rather than being a remotely break-even venture. Harry's range of coffee mugs, posters, promotional material and personalised front pages all looked great but the litmus test was whether the 28,000+ visitors each day would want to buy them. There was even a specially commissioned 2x1½ ft. colour poster by the renowned cartoonist Malky McCormick[21], celebrating the Garden Festival itself. McCormick was notorious for adding minute appendages to his cartoons (usually a penis) and many a sub-editor had been taken to task by Endell for failing to spot and remove these before publication. I therefore assigned a squad of people to scrutinise thoroughly Malky's original submission for the garden festival and managed to remove three penises and a pair of copulating dogs before it was finally sent for print.

One idea that I became involved in was in the production of a coffee table book 'Front Page Scotland', which reproduced a whole series of front pages from 1900 onwards. I spent many hours in our library going through the bound volumes of back issues to make the final selection. I had two criteria - each page should be dominated by details of an extremely well-known event, but somewhere on the page there should be at least two other small short stories that would also interest the reader. For example, the front page of the Daily Record on 27th February 1950 was dominated by the death of Harry Lauder [22], but had also three short stories, one entitled "A 175lbs very hungry killer leopard is loose somewhere in Oklahoma City but the place is like a circus, everyone wants to see it". As the book's introduction said, "They [the front pages] show that whilst some things have changed out of all recognition, others have not changed at all. The only element that does is time itself." Readers would have noted that front pages from the 1920s included a plug for 'Today's Wireless Programmes". By the 1930s this had become, "Today's Radio". By the 60s, it was "T.V. and Radio", and by the 80s, "Big Weekend T.V. guide".

As an aside, I was to discover that the only front page missing from almost 39,000 issues in the Daily Record library was the account of Rudolph Hess'[23] landing at Eaglesham on 10th May 1941. That front page had been cleverly removed with a scalpel, but I only discovered it because I was specifically looking for it. The following day I went to the Mitchell Library in Glasgow, the only other place where there are bound copies of the Daily Record, and discovered that someone had done

---

[21] Malky McCormick, 1943-2019, cartoonist and caricaturist
[22] Sir Harry Lauder, 1870-1950, Scottish singer and comedian, described by Churchill as 'Scotland's greatest ambassador'
[23] Rudolph Hess, 1894-1987, German politician, Deputy Führer

exactly the same to their copy. The inevitable conclusion is that in at least one household in Scotland there must be a copy of that front page, perhaps framed over the fireplace. Hold on to it - it's now worth a lot of money.

As it turned out, 'Front Page Scotland' was by far the most popular item within the Daily Record 'shop'. All 5,000 copies of the initial print were sold and another 5,000 were printed and eventually sold. I wish I could say the same for the rest of Harry's merchandise. There was so much of it left over that at the end of the festival we had to hire storage space for it. Eventually a massive campaign of promotional give-aways managed to shift most of it.

Although the company never publicly acknowledged the presence of the Scottish Sun, it maintained an intelligence network on full alert, always trying to second guess them and, where possible, spoil whatever they were up to. Sometimes it could be really simple. At an event in one of Glasgow's hotels, I noticed that a number of senior London News International personnel were present. Towards the end of the evening, I chanced upon a vendor carrying in some bundles of that evening's Scottish Sun first edition and quickly established that he had been asked to give everyone at the event a complimentary copy. I made a quick decision, purchased the entire supply from him and dumped said bundles out of sight in the corner of the cloakroom. I then phoned the office and had a supply of Daily Records sent round in double quick time. Within 15 minutes, every guest at the function had a copy of the Daily Record – much to the initial puzzlement, and subsequent fury, of the NI team.

I realise that I am moving slightly ahead of myself in this account of life at the Daily Record. Less than three months after I joined the company, MGN was bought by Robert Maxwell and life was never to be quite the same again. Much has been written about Maxwell but the following chapters deal exclusively with him and his dealings with SDR.

Chapter 14   INTRODUCTION TO MAXWELL

"I keep on repeating, I'll say it again for the last time- I am not on some ego trip."
Robert Maxwell

Robert Maxwell acquired Mirror Group Newspapers (MGN) from Reed
International for £90 million on the evening of 12th July 1984. To many, MGN was
an unsellable business. Reed had toyed with the idea of flotation but their advisors
thought it was unlikely to raise much more than £45 million. It was a company
dominated by the trade unions, Reed considered it almost unmanageable and over
60% of the workforce earned over £20,000 per year (The equivalent of £75,000 today).
Mike Malloy[1], when he became editor of the Daily Mirror in 1975, found that his
gardening correspondent owned only a window box, his motoring editor was
banned from driving, his travel editor was banned from flying with BA after cabin
rage and his features editor hadn't written a piece for five years. All this took place
during what was called the golden age of Fleet Street!

Others considered Maxwell's purchase of MGN one of the bargains of the century.
The Mirror building in Holborn Circus alone was worth more than £90 million. The
extremely profitable Scottish titles (SDR) would also have realised more than that.
Furthermore, Maxwell had discovered that the MGN pension fund had a significant
surplus and over the years of his ownership he (quite legally) took an employer's
pension "holiday".

Despite specifically being asked by Reed to stay away until the following day,
Maxwell, true to form, simply ignored this and entered the Mirror building at
11:45pm. He walked into the office of Douglas Long, Chief Executive, went straight
to his cocktail cabinet and said "I'm going to have a drink, anyone want one?" Joe
Haines[2], although not present, describes the scene as follows, "The offer was much
more than an act of courtesy, Maxwell may not even have wanted a drink. What
Long and others assembled there thought that he was demonstrating was that it was
his drink, in his cocktail cabinet, in his building, which housed his newspapers, and
their acceptance of his hospitality was also an acceptance of that fact."

Mike Malloy[3] describes it; "Maxwell turned up in the small hours to claim his new
toy. Douglas Long invited him into his office where Maxwell immediately
demonstrated his new powers and his lack of grace – by striding to the open drinks
cabinet and pouring himself a large whisky. He then pointedly sat down in Long's
chair, squatting like some gigantic cuckoo settling itself into a new nest."

Maxwell convened an MGN Board meeting at 3am, 13th July and another later that
day. At the second meeting our (SDR) chief executive Vic Horwood informed

---

[1] Mike Malloy b.1940, Editor Daily Mirror 1975-85, Editor in Chief MGN 1985-90
[2] Joe Haines, b. 1928, Chief Press Secretary to Harold Wilson 1969-76, Assistant Editor; Daily Mirror 1984-90, Director SDR 1986-92
[3] Mike Malloy, 'The Happy Hack', Paperback Edition 2016, John Blake Publishing Ltd.

Maxwell, "I must tell you that the entire staff of the Daily Record and Sunday Mail has taken a hall in Glasgow for a mass meeting to decide whether they are going to work for you". This was typical Horwood. He could have expressed this more diplomatically but he was a straight and honest man and wasn't going to soften the reality of what was happening. Maxwell's reaction was equally predictable "You'd better get on the first available plane, mister, and tell them that if they don't return to work, I will close down their papers and they won't open again."

The Daily Record was published the next morning despite the meeting, but from that moment the battle ground was being prepared for a showdown between Maxwell and the unions. We on the SDR senior management team were about to enter into the world of Maxwellia which was to last until, and in fact well beyond, his death on 6th November 1991. It felt sometimes like a world suspended from reality and, as in Star Trek, going where no man had gone before.

Maxwell's life has been extensively chronicled by biographers and in the autobiographies of some of those who worked for him. The only official biography was written by Joe Haines[4] and many believe that it was quickly assembled to counter another biography being written by Tom Bower[5]. Maxwell issued 12 writs to prevent publication of Bower's book, not only against Bower himself, but also against his publisher, the wholesale distributors and, finally, the book sellers. As Bower comments, "Maxwell's writs transferred the book into an author's dream, a number one best seller. The only handicap was that the book was gradually no longer on sale". The only consolation for Bower was that many book sellers retaliated by refusing to stock the Haines biography. A third book by Peter Thompson and Tony Delano[6] was never published, having been prevented by writs from Maxwell, who also thought that every copy of the book had been pulped. In fact, the book was stored and reissued after Maxwell's death. Later Roy Greenslade[7], a former Daily Mirror Editor, published his account of the Maxwell years – again after Maxwell's death. Both Greenslade and Bower are critical of Haines' biography – it was written when Maxwell was still alive and, as the official biography, it was never going to be over critical of the man himself. The autobiographies of Daily Mirror editors Richard Stott[8] and Mike Malloy also detail their experiences of working under Maxwell.

I do not propose to write my own version. Rather I have chosen to record my experiences and those of a number of my colleagues in dealing with Maxwell. First, a brief biography of the man himself. Born in poverty in Czechoslovakia in 1923, his father was a labourer and part-time smuggler. When the Nazis invaded in 1939, Maxwell joined the Czechoslovakian Army in exile, eventually fighting bravely with the British Army in Germany – where he was promoted to Captain and won the Military Cross in the process. He demonstrated a gift for wheeling and dealing, which stayed with him for the rest of his life. In post-war Germany he started selling

[4] Joe Haines, 'Maxwell' 1988, Macdonald & Co. Publishers Ltd.
[5] Tom Bower, 'Maxwell. The Outsider' 2nd Edition, 1991, Mandarin Paperbacks
[6] Peter Thompson and Tony Delano, 'Maxwell. A Portrait of Power' 1998, Bantam Press
[7] Roy Greenslade, 'Maxwell's Fall', 1992, Simon & Schuster Ltd.
[8] Richard Stott, 'Dogs and Lamposts' 2002, Metro Publishing Ltd.

the rights to German scientific journals and quickly went into scientific publishing, creating Pergamon Press, a major publishing house which became a public company in 1964. A dispute during a takeover bid by the US company Lesco led to Maxwell being accused of making false claims about Pergamon's profitability. This led to a Board of Trade enquiry in 1971, which famously concluded, "He is not, in our opinion, a person who can be relied on to exercise stewardship of a public company." His reputation in tatters, Maxwell was effectively cast aside by the business establishment, but all this was to change when he acquired the near-bankrupt British Printing Corporation in 1981. In this he was backed by the National Westminster Bank, which had been badly exposed by the company. Against all odds, and crushing the print unions in the process, Maxwell successfully turned round the company, made it extremely profitable and renamed it The British Printing and Communications Corporation. In the process, he re-earned the support of the city and, after a number of false starts in 1984, acquired a national newspaper group, Mirror Group Newspapers. In the process, he became possibly the biggest self-publicist the media has ever known. Nicknamed the Bouncing Czech, Private Eye thereafter called him Captain Bob, a title actually created by the columnist Keith Waterhouse[9], who later regretted it as he felt the title gave Maxwell "a patina of avuncular geniality".

When Maxwell bought Mirror Group Newspapers in 1984 my colleagues and I at SDR knew relatively little about him. The DTI report was the one piece of information on record but his meteoric rise from that period had been astonishing. Much of what has been written about Maxwell appeared after his death, with in some cases the benefit of much hindsight and, because the dead can't be libelled, I suspect with a great deal of embellishment. I do not seek to defend him – the man was a monster – but none of us had the benefit of that hindsight. We learned as we went along and there certainly was never a dull moment

From the onset we had many advantages over our colleagues in London. We were a profitable business, over 450 miles away and thus away from the day to day scrutiny and actions of the man himself. In London his hand was on everything – every detail and aspect of the company. He imposed authority levels on expenditure which meant that every decision, however minor, had to be approved by him personally, hence the permanent long queue of people outside his office.

The Stott autobiography deals extensively with his time under Maxwell. He was the longest serving editor during the Maxwell era and perhaps managed him better than any of those around him. Unlike any of the editors before or after him he miraculously managed to negotiate an arrangement to reduce Maxwell's level of involvement in the paper (and his desire to appear in it). Self-confident almost to the point of being arrogant and extremely sarcastic, I encountered Stott on several occasions and never took to him.

---

[9] Keith Waterhouse, CBE 1929-2009, British writer, newspaper columnist and author

Vic once took me to Maxwell's famous Tuesday lunch and, as we were walking into the dining room, whispered in my ear, "Colin, tuck in behind me, there are those here who will almost shove each other out of the way to get close to Maxwell. I sit halfway down one side which means I can ease back just out of his line of sight if the going gets tough." At that lunch Stott and Eve Pollard[10] vied for the honour of sitting next to Maxwell. At another Tuesday lunch, shortly after Peter Jay[11] had joined as Maxwell's Chief of Staff, Stott asked him why, as he was one of the 100 cleverest people in the world according to Time Magazine, he didn't wear a condom when he got his au pair pregnant. Jay laughed and, instead of punching him, confessed that he had often wondered the same thing himself. Another reason for Stott's survival was that as well as being an excellent editor, he stood up for staff and faced down Maxwell when necessary. He also detailed how he managed to perfect the technique of slamming down the phone after a fierce argument before Maxwell himself did the same thing.

The Malloy autobiography, the most humorous of all, contains the least detail on Maxwell. Malloy had been editor of the Mirror for nearly ten years prior to Maxwell buying the company. He was later made Editor in Chief, clearly not an onerous role since he managed to write three novels over this period and was well into his fourth before his departure. Malloy best sums up life within Maxwellia, "One of the most frustrating aspects of dealing with Maxwell was his attention span; he didn't have one at all. He also ignored the systems used for administration in all normal organisations. Refusing to read written information, he nevertheless insisted that even quite minor decisions be made by him. Therefore, all communications with subordinates had to be either face to face or by telephone. Queues of people would gather outside his office holding papers for him to sign, while several at a time reluctantly might be inside. Favourites would be given precedence over those out of favour but their supplications would be constantly interrupted by long telephone calls that Maxwell insisted on taking."

Our first meeting with Maxwell was a short Board Meeting in Glasgow a few days after the takeover. It turned out to be the only Board Meeting he ever attended in Glasgow. Both Gordon Terris and I were invited to it. Not much happened, introductions were made but, significantly, Maxwell sat in Derek Webster's seat. Although it was always going to happen, Webster symbolically sacrificed himself at that very meeting by removing his company tie and presenting it to Maxwell who promptly put it on (with some difficulty as I recall). As predicted, Webster was gone within a very short period of time – there were never going to be two Chairmen at SDR.

My next meeting with Maxwell was when Gordon Terris and I were appointed to the Board in early September, just weeks after Maxwell's acquisition of the company. We flew to London with Vic and all three of us sat in the queue outside Maxwell's office for what seemed a very long time before each of us was brought in separately

---

[10] Eve Pollard, Editor, Sunday Mirror 1988-91
[11] The Hon. Peter Jay, b. 1937, US Ambassador 1977-79, Maxwell's Chief of Staff 1986-89

by Vic. I cannot recall much of what happened. I certainly was extremely nervous but I do remember that Maxwell spoke for about 95% of the time, about himself and what he was going to do with the company. He asked me one question about my role. Gordon had a similar experience but afterwards the three of us were ushered into Maxwell's large sitting room and served champagne and caviar to celebrate our appointments. So far so good!

At SDR, I joined what was to be an extremely well-run Board. Vic Horwood the chief executive was a very effective leader and I learned a lot from him. He was an excellent communicator and moulded the Board into a cohesive unit. Coping with Maxwell was easier if we all pooled information, thus ensuring there were never any surprises. Vic held a short morning briefing daily (which also took place in his absence) so that everyone knew the bigger picture. Vic was also extremely effective in teasing out any potential flashpoints. It was an excellent management style and one that I adapted for the rest of my career. It meant that Maxwell could never surprise us with something going on within our own company, although that didn't stop him from constantly second guessing us on other matters. The other great strength of Vic's management style was that communication was a two-way process meaning we could all consider the major implications of MGN decisions for SDR.

One of the great challenges was that Maxwell automatically assumed that all policies and decisions about Mirror titles would also apply to SDR. Here we also had another major advantage over our colleagues in London. Our two titles dominated the Scottish market. At the time, the Daily Record sold around 750,000 copies per day compared to the Daily Mirror's 30,000. Although it was difficult, we tried to make Maxwell understand that Scotland was a very different market to the rest of the UK and therefore our approach should be different (or am I deluding myself that he ever actually grasped this?). Endell Laird became particularly adept at keeping Maxwell - related activities out of the paper. In that first year all the Mirror editors had a terrible time. Pictures of Maxwell with various world leaders appeared in the Daily Mirror on an almost daily basis and keeping them out of the Daily Record and Sunday Mail was a formidable challenge.

Many of the SDR battles with Maxwell were conducted by phone. On editorial matters the editors and HR professionals became increasingly aware that there always appeared to be someone who could be heard in the background. It was as if this person was supplying the ammunition for Maxwell's arguments. Step forward Joe Haines.

Haines was a strange character – the MGN equivalent of SDR's Hugh Currie (see chapter 21). Originally vehemently opposed to the Maxwell takeover of MGN, he quickly became his confidante and consigliore and of course was entrusted with the official biography. He was also someone who nursed a grudge to keep it warm! As press secretary to Harold Wilson he had frequently clashed with Marcia Falkender[12] and in his memoirs gave a trenchant account of this period. When Falkender died in

---

[12] Baroness Falkender, CBE 1932-2019, political secretary and head of the political office of Harold Wilson 1964-70 and 1974-76

early 2019 her corpse was scarcely cold before Haines delivered another withering assessment[13]. First damning praise, "After her election to the peerage, she became a devoted member, sitting in the House of Lords for 40 years, and regularly drawing her £300 a day allowance despite never making a speech" before wielding the stiletto, "although she accepted the Labour Whip, she secretly approached Margret Thatcher offering her help to defeat Jim Callaghan in the 1979 General Election – a monumental treachery." Like Maxwell, Haines clearly was not a man to be trifled with.

One incident stands out from Maxwell's early days at MGN. Bingo as a newspaper promotion was just developing and Maxwell decided to escalate the stakes by offering a £1 million first prize. Like everything else, he fronted the television commercial, standing in front of a pallet of £1 million worth of bank notes. We had to agree to carry this promotion but we topped and tailed the commercials exclusively for the Daily Record and Sunday Mail and ran them with a separate voiceover (by Maxwell of course). Who would get the £1 million winner? Some background to this promotion - most newspaper promotion games at this time, be they bingo, scratch cards or whatever, were strictly controlled in terms of winners. They were in no sense fixed in that there were winning tickets for all the cash prizes promoted, but the distribution of the winning tickets was tightly controlled, particularly geographically. A relatively small number of cards were winners and most weren't. In the case of the £1 million bingo game, there was a huge argument between MGN and SDR as to how the potential prize winners would be divided. We had to concede that the £1 Million winner would be a Daily Mirror reader but after much negotiation SDR secured two £100,000 runner-up prizes. These would be the biggest amounts ever won in any individual newspaper game in Scotland. Another huge row developed after the Mirror eventually declared a prize winner – a chain smoking widow, Maudie, who was eternally accompanied by her spaniel Trumper. She was whisked to Blackpool to receive her £1 million during a party-political conference. Maxwell wanted this event published in all of his papers. As far as SDR was concerned, the last thing the paper wanted was to publicise that a Daily Mirror reader had won the £1 million prize. We were only interested in promoting our two £100,000 winners. Managing Maxwell at these times was hell. However, some hilarious stories emerged from Blackpool. Meeting Maudie for the first time in her hotel suite, Maxwell sat down on the edge of her bed and with his great bulk instantly propelled her three feet into the air. Marje Proops[14] the veteran agony aunt also accidentally managed to sit on top of the wretched Trumper. There was an open top bus ride along Blackpool promenade - it was a circus with Maxwell as ringmaster at the centre of everything. As Richard Stott puts it, "There can't be a ringmaster if you don't want acrobats, clowns, high-wire acts and dangerous animals in the show."

During the seven plus years of the Maxwell era there were most definitely many dangerous animals at large. Vic and Endell as the two Board members most in

---

[13] "Life at Number 10 was Ruled by Marcia's Tantrums.", The Mail on Sunday 17th February 2019
[14] Marjorie (Marje) Proops OBE, b.1911-1996, agony aunt; Daily Mirror 1962-1996

London would describe current events at the circus, which brought some light relief to having to deal with him on a regular and highly unpredictable basis. I should not misrepresent the situation as us being in a permanent state of fear. He left us alone for long periods in relative calm and stability, but the Maxwell threat was always there. In their individual ways, Vic and Endell became extremely adept at managing Maxwell. One of the great frustrations was that Maxwell insisted on signing off personally any staff recruitment. A form had to be filled in and, without Maxwell's signature, no replacement staff could be hired. Over the years this could virtually paralyse parts of the organisation at critical periods. It was rumoured that Endell always carried around several blank forms and, if he judged Maxwell to be in a good mood, he'd get him to sign these, promising to fill in the details later.

People have over the years constantly asked me "But you must have always known that he was a bully and a crook?" I can honestly say that until the last few months of his life, when we did note a significant behavioural change, there was little or no evidence of wrongdoing as far as SDR was concerned. We were a well-run and profitable company before Maxwell and continued to be so. The issue is that many of those who ask me these questions do so with the benefit of massive hindsight. When Tom Bower wrote his book in 1998, he was the first journalist to hint at Maxwell's increasingly fraudulent activities, but it took the second edition of the book, published after Maxwell's death, to expose many of the actual details. With the exception of the DTI report some 30 years earlier, not one major institution, regulator, any part of government, or the UK's best investigative financial journalists managed to expose the true picture of what was going on. Mostly it has to be said that was because of the intricate web of companies he had created. Even the hundreds of advisors, accountants and lawyers working on the MGN flotation in 1998 only scratched at the surface. It took the DTI ten years to publish their investigation of Maxwell's downfall. As Richard Stott comments, "As so often happens with DTI reports, it has been rendered irrelevant by time and the watering down of its findings by the consistent picking over of it by expensive lawyers representing powerful financial institutions. In spite of its marathon examination of the flotation...it remains true to this day that the biggest corporate fraud in British financial history did not procure one criminal conviction." Fast forward a decade and is much the same not true of the recent British banking crisis? At the time both before and during the Maxwell meltdown, I felt that Bronwen Maddox[15], who led the Financial Times' year-long award-winning investigation, was consistently closest to the scent of what was going on. I met her several years later when she was Foreign Editor of the Times and suggested that she should have written a book on the situation. Sadly, she chose not to do so.

Modern corporate governance largely did not exist in that period. The Cadbury Report[16] and The Higgs Review[17] were some years away. Nevertheless, Vic insisted that monthly Board meetings were properly minuted. Maxwell of course never

---

[15] Bronwen Maddox, b. 1963, Foreign Editor, The Times
[16] The Cadbury Report, 'The Financial Agenda of Corporate Governance' 1992
[17] The Higgs Review, 'Review on the Roles and Effectiveness of Non-Executive Directors' 2003

bothered to attend. I believe he only ever attended four formal SDR Board meetings and three of these were in London. In the Maxwell era SDR also had a non-executive Board member. Sir Alwyn Williams[18] was the first, followed by Sir Kenneth Alexander[19]. (Joe Haines was also a Board member from 1986-92) Being academics, Maxwell would have come across the first two via Pergamon Press. Williams was by far the more effective of the two, Alexander's main contribution being his ability to hoover up significant quantities of food and drink at board lunches. Alwyn also had a delightfully indiscreet wife, Joan, who became the life and soul of several Board functions, with endless tales of scandal. She was not overly keen on Maxwell and was not afraid to say so.

In these early Maxwell days, tales of his eating habits started to emerge. David MacKay tells of being invited for dinner at Holborn Circus and sitting next to him. The main course was guinea fowl and Maxwell had consumed his portion in two bites, spitting out the bones onto his side plate. I suppose it was no surprise that when we attended our first Board meeting in London something similar should happen. Maxwell didn't join the meeting until after lunch – we were to learn that this was common. At any given time, he might host two or three lunches simultaneously, joining each at some stage. Once our lunch had finished, Maxwell appeared and sat down at the head of the table. Josef, his tiny Portuguese butler, brought in an enormous platter of fruit which he held in front of Maxwell, who selected a large peach and proceeded to shove the entire fruit into his mouth and start chewing, with juice running out from either side of his mouth. Everyone watched spellbound, knowing what would happen. Suddenly Maxwell spat out the stone (which pinged loudly off his plate), looked down the table at Bob Lindsay[20] and said, "And how are things in Scotland Bob?" What an opening question! I found myself barely able to suppress laughter but with a huge sense of relief that I hadn't been asked that first question. Josef served coffee to everyone in normal cups but Maxwell, served first of course, had his in the most enormous three handled cup. Inscribed around it was, "I am a very important person".

Other stories emerged over the years. Richard Stott described being served with a rather good piece of lamb while he was talking to the person on his left and, when he was ready to eat, discovered that Maxwell, on his right, had already eaten most of it. Maxwell also smoked Cuban cigars and was fond of first sucking the tip of the cigar and then dipping it into a glass of brandy. It was not unheard of for him to dip said cigar into the glass of the lady sitting beside him. The most frustrating part of any meal was that Maxwell always had to be served first. He then of course couldn't be bothered to wait for anyone else, with the result that by the time the last person at the table had been served, Maxwell had finished his food and was ready to open the discussion.

The lunches themselves could be interesting, or combative or - at the extreme - precipitate the end of someone's career. Inevitably the standing joke before lunch

---

[18] Sir Alwyn Williams, 1921 - 2004, Principal and Vice-Chancellor, University of Glasgow 1976-88
[19] Sir Kenneth Alexander, 1922-2001, Chancellor, Aberdeen University 1986-96
[20] Bob Lindsay, Managing Director BNPC (Scotland) Ltd.

became not 'What's on the menu?' but 'Who's on the menu?' People would sometimes appear at the lunch and never be seen again. Others were humiliated by Maxwell and even threatened with dismissal.

All this was faithfully chronicled by Vic and Endell to ensure that the rest of us were in touch with anything of significance. Endell told a hilarious story of one such lunch when Maxwell was ranting about the excesses of his executives with their chauffeurs and limousines saying that all this would now stop – with immediate effect. Unusually, Maxwell then walked with Endell and Vic to the ground floor of Maxwell House. Just as a chauffeur called out, "Car for Mr Horwood!" Maxwell momentarily stopped to talk to someone. Endell and Vic went outside, where an enormous stretch limousine was waiting for them. Endell describes Vic as almost throwing himself onto the floor of the back seat (quite a task as he was 6'3") and ordering the chauffeur to drive off immediately.

I spent a very short time working under the Reed International regime. It was typical of a parent/subsidiary company relationship at the time. What didn't help was, that by almost any indicator, SDR outperformed MGN – in profit, market dominance, circulation, penetration etc. Whereas the Daily Record outperformed every other title in the marketplace and so was a clear market leader in Scotland, the Daily Mirror's dominance had been eroded over the years by News International and The Sun had a healthy sales lead over the Daily Mirror. Several authors of the Maxwell era have tried to justify the Reed years by pointing out that the company actually made a profit for several years before the Maxwell takeover. The truth is that the vast majority of these profits were generated by SDR and that MGN was a poorly run company in the Reed era. SDR's success was resented by the senior team in London – Webster, Vic and his team were regarded as a bunch of "smart-arsed Jocks" who had somehow inherited their dominance but were still very much the country cousins. The relationship was toxic prior to Maxwell taking over and was certainly not helped by Maxwell himself after the takeover. Maxwell's style of management of being involved in every decision, big or small, ensured constant chaos in London. SDR had to manage its way round that and Vic Horwood deserves huge credit for managing to run a stable company in the midst of it. In Harry Reid's book, I am quoted some 25 years ago, saying, "the already toxic relationship between the two companies only got worse, not helped by Maxwell's infuriating solution to occasional crises 'We're in trouble – send for the Jocks'".

A measure of how MGN regarded SDR is in Malloy's, Stott's and Greenslade's books. SDR is mentioned only around five or six times in each. Even in Haines' book, bearing in mind that he was a Director of SDR, the company is mentioned no more than a handful of times. Crucially none of them would ever acknowledge the success of SDR. Stott even went so far as to argue in the aftermath of the Maxwell years that MGN should not provide the finance to re-equip the SDR with new presses. "I was appalled at the bare headed stupidity of raising the price of the Daily Mirror at such a time, particularly as it wasn't just to generate more cash flow but to re-equip the Daily Record plant in Scotland, an absurd priority given the beleaguered state of the company." So much for a collegiate approach and one of the reasons I never had a particularly high regard for Stott.

Maxwell was credited with transforming Mirror Group Newspapers and turning it into a profitable company. He had the vision to re-equip both MGN plants with full colour presses, well ahead of Murdoch. Unfortunately, as we were to discover later, he had run out of money and his empire was collapsing by the time he finally committed to re-equipping SDR itself. Therein lies another tale.

Bernard Vickers' Farewell Dinner 1986

Back row l-r: Kevin McMahon, Gordon Terris, Bob Lindsay, Derick Henry,
June Laird, Sir Alwyn Williams, Alistair Liddell, Vic Horwood, Claire,
Helen Liddell, CMcC.

Front row l-r : Joan, Lady Williams; Julie Horwood, Bernard Vickers,
Mary Vickers, Margaret Lindsay, Frances Henry, Shelagh Terris and
Bronwyn McMahon

Chapter 15   MAXWELL vs. SDR UNIONS

"Whatever his weight in pounds, shillings and ounces
he always seems bigger because of his bounces" AA Milne[1]

When Robert Maxwell purchased SDR in July 1984 the entire staff held a meeting to decide whether they wanted to work for him. Maxwell's view was, "If you don't work, I'll close the place down and never reopen it." Two utterly conflicting viewpoints and from that moment onwards, war was effectively declared. Over the coming months there was a series of skirmishes and some minor battles, but everyone was aware that there would be, at some stage, a final battle and only one winner. At SDR, in the case of the print unions, the battle was about gross over-manning, the numerous "Spanish" practices[2] and the inevitable introduction of new technology. For the journalists it was the maintenance of a lifestyle that suited them - a four-day week, sabbaticals and unchallenged expenses.

Unlike MGN, SDR was then a relatively modern company. A substantial amount of new technology was introduced in the 1970s and, at the time, SDR's titles were some of the few newspapers produced in colour and making reasonable profits. Early 1986 saw the first move towards the final battle. In classic Maxwell style, he wrong-footed the unions (in this case SOGAT82[3] and the NUJ[4]) almost from the start. In return for agreeing to changes in working practices and the elimination of unnecessary overtime and casual staff working, he offered a 10% increase in salaries and guaranteed all existing employment. Astonishingly the unions rejected this. Most commentators believe they should have accepted the overall package and negotiated out the most unpalatable parts later. Experienced Maxwell watchers could have told them "his first offer will always be the best one – grab it."

Thus on 22nd February 1986 all staff received a letter. In typical Maxwell it started, "I wrote to you on the 17th of February that I did not intend to go the Murdoch way and that I prefer to safeguard jobs rather than end them, to give security rather than create insecurity." (The context of this was Murdoch's move to Wapping on 26th January 1986). The last line was classic Maxwell, "P.S. London printers and journalists have accepted the fact of life that the Fleet Street gravy train has finally hit the buffers. The workforce at Anderston Quay must also accept that the Flying Scot cannot steam on in the old way."

The letter of course detailed the consequences of the rejection of the earlier offer, "...are that in order to safeguard the survival of this company, we have no

---

[1] AA Milne, 1882-1956, 'The House at Pooh Corner'
[2] The term 'Spanish practice' is a British expression that refers to irregular or restrictive practices in workers' interests. Typically, these are arrangements that have been negotiated in the past between employers and unions.
[3] The Society of Graphical and Allied Trades.
[4] The National Union of Journalists.

alternative but to notify the Department of Employment that we will need to declare redundant between 300 and 400 of our 1050 strong workforce."

The journalists were sidetracked into fighting on a separate issue – the production of an Irish edition of the Daily Mirror. In reality of course Maxwell only wanted greater productivity which would mean the end of the four-day week. The journalists were sucked into an expression of Scottish nationalism, which resents outsiders (i.e. Englishmen, whether native-born or naturalised) having control over a Scottish institution. Joe Haines (an Englishman) describes the issue, "But in refusing the Irish edition of the Daily Mirror the journalists, without a shred of evidence, were claiming that what Maxwell really had in mind was to anglicise the Record and the Mail to a point that most pages of the paper would be prepared in London and their Scottish identity lost. It was the kind of fantasy to which the Scots are prone. The fact that there was never a word of truth in it did not lessen the repeated assertion that it was so. There is nothing so powerful as a rumour whose time has come" (Shades of the modern SNP and independence here?).

In the long established tradition of kicking your competitor when he's down, the rest of the press waded in and stirred the nationalist pot - conveniently ignoring the fact that News International was owned by an Australian (soon to be an American) citizen and that three of the other four major Scottish newspapers were owned by a German (Outram's), and a Canadian (The Scotsman and The Press and Journal). Never let the facts get in the way of a good story! As Joe Haines put it, "I tried to convince them (the journalists) that this was ludicrous. Why should a newspaper which sold 760,000 copies per day in Scotland be remodelled along the lines of an English paper which sold 15,000 there? But they were not willing to listen. The rest of the Scottish press continued to report the dispute as if the fantasy was the fact."

"The 1,000 production staff dug in last night in a determined attempt to prove that they are ready to work and save the separate identity of the newspapers" (The Scotsman 25th February).

The dispute rumbled on through February and into March. After a walkout by both the journalists and the print workers they returned, still facing the threat of 330 redundancies and an Irish edition. Events took another turn for the worse when the print workers refused to set an article which criticised them unless they were granted the right of reply. This would have led to blatant censorship of the worst kind but it was another trial of strength. Maxwell held firm and again the print workers and journalists walked out, this time over Maxwell's alleged failure to negotiate. As this was happening, we (SDR management) were now having to prepare to dig in for a long dispute. Maxwell, true to form, sent up an alleged industrial relations expert to advise the Board on how to manage a strike. You can imagine how this went down. We all sat around the Boardroom table listening to this buffoon with his manual in front of him, lecturing us on what we should be doing. He had already incensed Vic by sitting in his seat at the top of the table. This went on for a couple of hours with frequent references to his manual. This, he left us in no doubt, contained the answer to every possible situation. Around 4pm the phone went at the end of the room. Jack Anderson[5] answered it and said, "How interesting, thank you for letting me know." On putting down the phone Jack stared at the 'expert' and said, "the printers have just barricaded themselves inside the press hall." We then had the wonderful sight of our hapless visitor frantically leafing through his manual, only to discover that this situation didn't seem to be covered.

Things moved on to a different footing thereafter. Maxwell decreed that senior management should occupy the plant 24 hours a day and a rota was drawn up for it. He continued to bombard the strikers with all sorts of communication. On 14th March he issued a further statement, "The Board of the Daily Record and Sunday Mail deplores the useless action of our 230 journalists going on strike on the instructions of union bosses in London. Our journalists who are paid on average £23,000 per year for a 36-hour four-day week have turned down three realistic proposals..." (A deliberate attempt to lose journalists their public sympathy, which turned out to be exactly the correct card to play) By 29th March Maxwell had racked up the stakes even higher. "It is now clear beyond doubt that the Daily Record and Sunday Mail are being prevented from publishing by a conspiracy between officials of SOGAT82 and National Union of Journalists. They are ready to fight to the death of the papers to maintain the ruinously expensive four-day week. The company has no option but to resist the threat posed to its future by the perversion of trade union power, a combination of muscle and madness which will bring about unemployment where none was ever contemplated or necessary." What Maxwell was now doing was closing the company down. SDR would cease to exist at midnight 31st March 1986. All staff were deemed to have dismissed themselves by refusing to work and would have to reapply for their jobs in one of two new companies – Scottish Daily Record and Sunday Mail (1986) Ltd. and the British Newspaper Printing Corporation (Scotland) Ltd. by 3rd April. "...for employment in the new companies on the conditions contained in the new house agreements. There will be no further negotiations with the Chapels of the old companies. They too will cease to exist on 31st March. The new companies will be open for a single new union agreement at Anderston Quay." The reason for the battle and the rules of engagement were restated, "Over several weeks the SDR and SM have been enmeshed in a pointless struggle by dinosaurs who believed that the company owed them a living. Unlike Rupert Murdoch's News International, the company had offered them excellent conditions, excellent salaries, excellent holidays and a secure future with no compulsory redundancies. All this they took as weakness and they spurned it. Instead they chose the path of personal abuse, lies, defiance of the law and intimidation. This was their gravest mistake. The unions of Anderston Quay are solely responsible for destroying the jobs of hundreds of their members. Events will prove that that was their only success."

There was to be a final sting to the tail. Still in my sleeping bag on the settee in Vic's office, I was awakened by a phone call at 7am on Easter Sunday. No 'Happy Easter' Colin or no 'good morning, how's it going up there?' Instead good old Maxwell speak, "What the f**k are you people doing up there?" The essence of the

---

[5] Jack Anderson, b.1939, SDR Production Director 1985-2002

conversation was that he had been told that the printers occupying the Press Hall were doing so with minimum numbers and were being relieved by their mates. Access was gained via a ladder over a wall at the back of the Press Hall into a nearby street. Maxwell left me in no doubt that he wanted the access and the ladder removed and barbed wire in place along the top of the wall, and he wanted it done by early afternoon. With that he hung up.

Calls like that certainly focus the mind. How was I going to find someone to carry out this task on Easter Sunday? After many inquiries I was able to track down a friend of a friend - Neil Howie[6], who was able to arrange for someone to carry out the work. By early afternoon the work was complete - needless to say at a premium price, given the short notice of the project. All this was being done in advance of the letters to strikers arriving at their homes the following day. I reported back to Maxwell that the work was now completed and he told me that a new security team would be arriving on site at 6am the following morning. Our own security staff, believed to be sympathetic to the strikers, would then be relieved of their duties. True to form, a squad arrived the next morning, including a huge Alsatian dog, subsequently christened Snapper. Snapper was deployed to roam free in the yard outside the Press Hall. It was a salutary message to those inside, they could no longer be relieved by their comrades and were now stuck inside a building that was never designed for comfortable living. Meantime Snapper happily roamed just outside in full view of all.

Maxwell was slowly but surely racking up the pressure. Negotiations were continuing in London with the two full time officials of the unions, Mike Smith[7] NUJ and Allan Watson[8] SOGAT82. In the case of the print workers, matters were not helped by the fact that Watson and the Daily Record's SOGAT82 Father of the Chapel Harry Templeton[9] couldn't stand the sight of each other.

The reaction of the Scottish press to the appearance of the barbed wire was predictable and outrageous. A page 2 picture in The Herald under the caption 'Fortress Anderston Quay' was typical. A short length of barbed wire, in the hysteria that gripped the Scottish press, was transformed into something similar to the hundreds of yards of razor wire that surrounded Murdoch's Wapping printing centre. Even Tom Bower comments, "As the dispute stretched into the third week, barbed wire appeared round the premises and emotions became inflamed."

Cue for another rant from Maxwell, this time at 6am on Wednesday morning

RM: Who the f**k put up the razor wire?

CMcC: No one, it's barbed wire

RM: Who the f**k authorised that?

---

[6] Neil Howie b.1953, Director and Co-owner, Howie of Dunlop
[7] Mike Smith National Officer NUJ
[8] Allan Watson b.1948 full time official, latterly Scottish Secretary, SOGAT82 1975-1994
[9] Harry Templeton FOC, SOGAT Chapel, SDR, now Scottish Director, Public Concern at Work

CMcC: You did

RM: Get it down – now!

(End of call)

What followed on Wednesday morning was identical to Sunday morning: same phone call to same contractor, another enormous sum of money changed hands and the same barbed wire was removed before midday. By a strange coincidence, Snapper was also removed from the premises at exactly the same time. Perhaps I should have asked Maxwell, "Who the f**k authorised the dog?"

My guess is that negotiations in London had reached a critical stage and Maxwell was not going to let a small thing like a piece of barbed wire interfere with the bigger picture. Ultimately the strike was to no avail. At last the strikers realised that Maxwell had outwitted them and that they were out of work unless they agreed to return. That return was swift. For the journalists it was the end of the four-day week and for the print workers it was the end of the Spanish practices that had plagued the newspaper industry for years. Negotiations now began on redundancies and sensible manning levels in every department.

There is a certain irony that Rupert Murdoch had been an even earlier mover in this area. He had taken on the journalists and their excesses at The Times and The Sunday Times in 1981. In his book[10], Bill Bryson[11] describes his time as a sub-editor at The Times – the long lunches and the lavish expense accounts. "Nothing that good can last forever." Within days of buying the paper, the building was full of mysterious tanned Australians in white, short sleeved shirts who began roaming with clipboards "looking as if they were measuring people for coffins." Although Murdoch is generally credited with leading the Fleet Street revolution through the move to Wapping in January 1986, he was not the sole contributor. Eddie Shah[12] and Maxwell also played significant parts.

Eddie Shah in a much smaller way had taken on the unions in Warrington in 1983. Shah won what is now known as the Battle of Warrington, not just by outfacing the pickets but by using the new Thatcher government trade union laws to maximum effect, winning more than £1 million in fines against the National Graphical Association (NGA), mainly for illegal picketing and contempt of court. Mr Justice Eastham[13] in his summing up said, "Any law-abiding citizen would have been shocked that such a thing could have happened in England and should take place at the instigation of union leaders responsible to their members. They succeeded in drumming up a demonstration which got 4,000 people when inside there were only ten workers, six security guards, and two dogs." (Clearly Maxwell must have got the

---

[10] Notes from a Small Island, Bill Bryson 1995 Doubleday.
[11] Bill Bryson OBE, Hon. FRS, b. 1951, Anglo-American author of books on travel, English language, science and other non-fiction topics.
[12] Selim Jehan 'Eddie' Shah, b.1944, owner, Messenger Group Newspapers, Manchester, founded 'Today' in March 1986
[13] Sir Michael Eastham, 1920-1993, High Court Judge

idea of Snapper from here!) Shah went on to launch Today, a national newspaper, in March 1986. His story is well documented in Brian McArthur's[14] account.[15]

Maxwell also played his part in the Fleet Street Revolution and, in doing so, turned MGN into a properly managed and profitable company, something Reed International had abysmally failed to do in the years prior to the takeover. At SDR Maxwell won the battle, not only by brute strength, but also by outmanoeuvring and out-thinking the unions.

We now turn to the pleasures of working with working with Maxwell on a day-to-day basis....

---

[14] Brian McArthur, 1940-2019, Editor, Times Higher Education Supplement, Editor, Western Morning News Plymouth, Founder Editor, Today
[15] 'Eddie Shah. Today and the Newspaper Revolution' Brian McArthur, 1988, David and Charles Publishers Plc. Newton Abbott.

Daily Record, Anderston Quay, Glasgow 1984

Derek Webster, SDR Chairman and Douglas Long's, Chief Executive MGN
Farewell Dinner 1984

l-r: Sheleagh Terris, Mary Wilson, Gordon Terris, Mrs Long, Vic Horwood,
Douglas Long, Ann-Marie Kane, Derick Henry, Julie Horwood, Liam
Kane, Endell Laird, Ann MacLennan, Bernard Vickers,
Murdoch MacLennan, Sir Alwyn Williams, Frances Henry,
Joan, Lady Williams, CMcC, June Laird and Derek Webster.

Front of menu for Maxwell's 40th Wedding
Anniversary, 1985

Chapter 16   DEALING WITH MAXWELL

"You are as safe with me as you would be in the Bank of England." Robert Maxwell

Many people have asked me, "What was it like working for Maxwell?", "What was he really like?", "How could you work for such a despot and sup with the Devil?" and so on. Even now, almost 30 years after his death, people continue to be fascinated by him.

My first head-to-head encounter with him came after a long negotiation to rationalise SDR's distribution system, when we awarded a single contract to Scottish Road Services (SRS). As part of the settlement, a second company was due a substantial compensation payment which would ultimately have to be authorised by Maxwell. As the payment became due, Vic was on holiday and Finance Director Derick Henry did not fancy asking Maxwell's approval for it. He confessed that he was terrified of the man and had had a very bruising encounter with him the previous week. Maxwell had phoned him at home at 7am and harangued him for two or three minutes before Derick, not having a clue what he was talking about, eventually blurted out, "Mr. Maxwell, this is Derick Henry the Finance Director," whereupon Maxwell hung up. It later transpired that Maxwell meant to ring Vic Horwood and had simply pressed the wrong button on his speed dial, hence the call to Derick. Derick therefore asked if I would go instead of him. I readily agreed. I didn't see a problem as distribution was top of the industry's agenda at the time and the entire industry had recently moved from rail to road with enormous savings. At the last negotiations British Rail proposed charging £102 per tonne for newspaper distribution and when the publishers moved to road the cost was £27 per tonne. I often wonder where the current enthusiasm for renationalising the railways comes from – many of us still remember the quite appalling level of service provided in those days.

I duly phoned Maxwell's PA and explained the urgency for getting the documentation signed. She agreed to try to find a slot for me the following day and accordingly I arrived at Holborn, expecting a long wait. As it turned out, I was ushered in almost immediately. I had prepared a short, one-page summary of the issue, pointing out that it was an excellent deal for SDR with some significant cost savings and therefore I walked into Maxwell's office feeling quietly confident. Ten minutes later I was on my way back out after a huge bollocking. I was subjected to a barrage of abuse, mainly about the incompetence of 'you f*ckers in Scotland". My 'crime' was that I hadn't realised that MGN were about to rationalise their own distribution system under a new company called Newsflow, part of the National Freight Consortium. Par for the course, none of our colleagues in London had bothered to share this vital piece of information. Maxwell, as the originator of this great plan, expected me to be psychic and have deduced what he was up to. Being rather hacked off at the situation, I was perhaps a little bit sharp in my first response, telling him that there wasn't really any problem as SRS was a separate division of the National Freight Consortium. This was a big mistake and led to him almost foaming at the mouth and I left to another torrent of abuse. The result was inevitable. Maxwell contacted the head of NFC to insist that both arrangements must be part of the Mirror Group deal with Newsflow. As a consequence, senior executives of both divisions had to structure a complicated and totally unnecessary intercompany arrangement, not helped by the fact that there was no love lost between the two companies in the first place. The only upside for me was that I ended up forming an excellent relationship with the Managing Directors of both companies – Doug Cartin of Newsflow and Bill Glenroy of SRS. Both realised from the onset that the situation had not been caused by me.

In those days, corporate entertainment was a device that glued relationships together. This seems to be no longer the case and seems to be both frowned upon and totally discouraged. After the fracas of Maxwell's intervention, Doug Cartin invited Claire and me to Henley Regatta. As this was on a Friday, we decided to treat ourselves to a weekend in London. On Friday morning, a Newsflow driver picked us up at Heathrow and delivered us to a lock on the Thames where we linked up with a large party on a boat on which we were to remain for the entire day. I had booked tickets for a play in central London that evening and the driver had calculated that there would be adequate time to get us there. We had a great day at Henley. None of us was particularly interested in the rowing, but drinks and an excellent lunch facilitated lots of networking and I made several new contacts. By the end of the day, I had also built an excellent relationship with Doug Cartin and his wife, which was to endure for several years. On the way back, we realised that the timescale was starting to slip. A change of plan was now necessary and we were picked up at a remote lock where disembarkation was not easy. Claire and I had to be lowered off the boat, causing great amusement, and we drove off through a cornfield to rapturous applause from all on the boat. Happily, we were on time to see a memorable performance by Dustin Hoffman as Shylock in the Merchant of Venice. He was the first Oscar winner I'd ever seen perform live. Geraldine James and Ian Lavender were also part of the cast and the following evening we saw Kenneth Branagh and Emma Thompson in John Osborne's Look Back in Anger. All in all, a memorable weekend.

Two other Maxwell incidents further illustrate the man. He never bothered to question or validate any information he was given before launching a full-scale attack, usually via the early morning weekend phone calls for which he was famous. The first had the usual niceties of a Maxwell greeting, "What the f*ck are you people doing up there?" I had no idea what he was going on about as he continued with a torrent of abuse. Eventually I deduced that he suspected that SDR was somehow trying to dilute one of his major promotions for which television commercials were running all weekend. Maxwell was to some extent correct in that we didn't slavishly follow everything the Mirror Group did, but all SDR commercials were topped and tailed with a separate voiceover and our strapline 'Your papers, made in Scotland.' In this case, someone had clearly leaked some poison suggesting that we had substantially changed both the promotion and the commercials and so after his initial 'pleasantries', I told him in no uncertain terms that this was not the case and that our version was essentially identical to the Mirror's. Not convinced, he ended the call by saying, "Send me the commercial - now!" and hung up. The solution was simple; indeed I wish they had all been as easy as this one, I booked a return flight to Heathrow for Claire, picked up the cassette of the commercial and drove Claire to the airport. A limousine picked her up at Heathrow and drove her to Maxwell House where she delivered an envelope marked for Maxwell's urgent attention. She then spent a very pleasant afternoon shopping and the limousine took her back to Heathrow. I never heard anything more about the matter. I doubt Maxwell even opened the envelope or viewed the commercial.

The second example was yet another early morning call with the usual pleasantries and then, "The Editor of the Sunday Mirror tells me that you people are deliberately disadvantaging her paper by ensuring that it suffers from a lack of availability." Again, this was easy to deal with. Eve Pollard was complaining about the Sunday Mirror selling only 30,000 copies in Scotland, compared to the Sunday Mail's 700,000. Spread over 6,000 retail outlets it would be extremely difficult to generate the same level of availability for the Sunday Mirror without a huge level of unsolds, perhaps as high as 50%. Crucially the Sunday Mirror's print figure was the responsibility of the MGN Circulation Department and thus it was their problem. The result was that I confidently said to Maxwell, "Well, you tell the Editor of the Sunday Mirror that she's totally wrong on this and that if she wants to get more availability then it's her prerogative to increase her print figure – she sets it, I don't." He hung up without another word and I never heard anything more about it. I subsequently found out that the Sunday Mirror, presumably at Eve Pollard's direction, had commissioned a team of merchandisers to carry out retail calls the previous weekend and clearly didn't like what they had found. The whole exercise must have cost a fortune and the same information would have been available from their wholesalers two days later. But hey ho, this was the world of Maxwellia.

Maxwell never relaxed. He slept little and therefore worked around the clock, seven days a week. Every executive had the same experiences - weekends, Bank Holidays, Christmas, New Year were all the same to him. Roy Greenslade was even interviewed by Maxwell for the editorship of the Daily Mirror on Boxing Day. It was said that Maxwell was at his most dangerous during these periods and on one occasion, six senior executives were fired. Just before Christmas, six forms were put on his desk urgently requesting authorisation to purchase six new company cars. Reflecting on this on Christmas Day, he decided to fire the six people instead.

Kevin McMahon[1] tells a great story from his BPCC days in London. His phone rang early one morning on a Bank Holiday weekend. Knowing it could only be Maxwell, Kevin told his wife Bronwyn to answer and tell Maxwell that he had gone on a rugby tour for the weekend. Maxwell reluctantly accepted this but demanded she give him the phone number of another executive. Needless to say, that executive had

---

[1] Kevin McMahon b.1948, m. Bronwyn (née Price), SDR Director of Manpower 1986-98 Director of Manpower and Industrial Relations 1988-93

to spend the entire weekend sorting out some mess for Maxwell only to discover that Maxwell himself had gone away and no longer needed the information. For weeks afterwards, the executive quizzed Kevin as to why Maxwell hadn't phoned him first, but remained none the wiser.

The Maxwell stories are legion. Here was a man who had had five different names by the time he was in his twenties. He eventually stuck with the name Ian Robert Maxwell before dropping the 'Ian', finally preferring to be called Captain Robert Maxwell. As Mick Malloy pointed out, "No author of espionage thrillers would dare to invent such a baffling background for one of their thrillers."

Roy Greenslade sums him up, "Robert Maxwell was an inventor. He invented himself not once, but many times over. He invented his name, his history, his voice, his persona. He invented the past and the present. If his invention led to a dead-end, in other words if the invention didn't fit the current charade or take him to where he wanted to go, then he would simply reinvent it. He stood reality on its head over and over again. But Robert Maxwell was more than an inventor, his artful fabrication provided him with the tools with which he could deceive everyone including himself. He was arguably the greatest confidence trickster the world has ever known, an illusionist so clever that he fooled the world's biggest banks, the world's leading politicians and hundreds of thousands of people the world over. He posed as a powerful man but it was a figment of his imagination. He posed as kindly saviour but was totally unjust to those closest to him."

On one occasion, Maxwell was invited to Poland to take part in a World War II remembrance service and had a British Army uniform made especially for the occasion. In typical Maxwell fashion, he showed this to his editors, although it had to be pointed out to him that the Sam Browne belt was the wrong way around. Joe Haines asked Field Marshal Lord Bramall[2] if Maxwell was entitled to wear this uniform. Bramell confirmed that the only people allowed to wear military uniforms in perpetuity were members of the Royal Family or Field Marshalls. Maxwell clearly regarded himself as one of these two - which one I wonder?

There was a degree of chaos at the ceremony. All those in uniform laid wreaths on the memorial but, because Maxwell had not been expected to be in uniform, there was no wreath for him. Maxwell commandeered the wreath of the man standing next to him, who just happened to be the American Ambassador, who now realising that he had no wreath, pinched that of the man next to him and so on down the line until the last, and presumably the most junior, representative could do nothing but bow in front of the memorial.

Another favourite Maxwell story, possibly apocryphal, concerns him getting into a lift on the top floor of Holborn Circus and being joined by a boiler suited man who was contentedly smoking a cigarette. Maxwell demanded to know how much the man earned. When he was told £100 a week, he put his hand in his pocket and

---

[2] Field Marshall Lord Bramall KG, GCB, OBE, MC, JP, DL. b.1923 Chief of the General Staff 1979-82, Chief of the Defence Staff 1982-85

peeled off ten £50 notes, telling the man he was fired as he couldn't stand the smell of cigarette smoke. Exit one very happy man from the building. He was a contractor who had been called in for some emergency painting duty.

Opinions of Maxwell at that time vary;

"He's a bastard but he's fair." - Sir Tom McCaffrey[3]

"With Bob, what you see is what you get. Of course, you might get something different the next day, or the next minute, but it's all out there. By the way don't believe a word he says." - Anon

"A dose of Maxwell will do you good." - Margaret Thatcher[4] to an MGN journalist

"Maxwell could charm the birds out of the trees and then shoot them." – Bill Keys[5]

"He only likes taking over companies. He and his sons gallop across the plains like Genghis Khan and his horde and they conquer a new city but they don't actually know what to do with it so they sit in a circle in their houses and they say 'let's leave someone incompetent in charge' and off they gallop to the next conquest" – Peter Jay

Maxwell spoke nine languages, fathered nine children and, some would say, lived nine lives. Surprisingly, for all his linguistic ability, his grasp of English was, at times, fairly limited. His sayings became legendary:

"They are all running around like chickens with no necks."

"Jerusalem wasn't built in a day."

"They have made their apple pie now they must live in it."

"You can't change heads in midstream"

" You would have needed to be a blind Turk with one leg not to have known."

"Even Winston Churchill couldn't have understood that with the aid of a shepherd guide dog and a Chinese dictionary."

"They locked the stable horse after the door was bolted."

"There's more than one skin in catching a cat."

I hope this provides some sense of what life under Maxwell was like for me and my colleagues at SDR. There certainly never was a dull moment and in Chapter 19 I provide my own personal assessment of him, but before that two remarkable stories of life at SDR.

---

[3] Sir Tom McCaffrey 1922-2016 former press secretary to James Callaghan
[4] Margaret, Baroness Thatcher LG, OM, DStJ, PC, FRS, HonFRSC, 1925-2013, Prime Minister 1979-90
[5] Bill Keys, General Secretary, SOGAT (1975-85)

Early Daily Record days 1984

Colder Scottish Winters - 1988

Chapter 17   MAXWELL FREE NEWSPAPERS 1989 - 94

"Impossible is a word to be found only in the dictionary of fools."
Napoleon Bonaparte[1]

Sometimes in life, two events happen in close succession, appearing completely unrelated, but one subsequently emerges as a direct consequence of the other. Two such events happened to me in late 1988. Tudor Hopkins, now NI's HR Director, phoned me and we met at a hotel in Glasgow to talk about an unspecified role within NI. We agreed to discuss the matter further at a later date. I returned to SDR shortly before lunch and, to my horror, by mid-afternoon rumours started circulating around the building that I was moving to NI. There had to have been a leak from NI in London. Vic asked me to come and see him at the end of the day and broached the subject. We had a long discussion about my role in the company and he assured me that I had a very bright future there. Without promising anything, he thought it would be in my best interests to be patient and something might happen in the near future. I trusted Vic as he had always been very straight and honest with me. On that basis I phoned Tudor that evening, told him I had been badly compromised and that I was not interested in pursuing matters any further.

In early 1989 we attended an SDR Board meeting in London. Maxwell asked us our views on free newspapers, a subject on which we had already done a considerable amount of research. Glasgow was then one of the few major cities in the United Kingdom without a citywide free newspaper. We had concluded that, whilst there was an opportunity, it would be extremely difficult to make any proposition stack up, mainly because SDR's existing cost base was too high. In typical Maxwell style, he told us we were "a bunch of complete dickheads", that he wanted a free newspaper launched within three months and to get on with it. Back in Glasgow, Vic told me that he wanted me to be Managing Director of the company's new Free Newspaper Division. This sounded fantastic, until I discovered that this new role was to be in addition to my existing role as Circulation and Marketing Director. Vic had discussed this with Maxwell and, if I agreed, Maxwell wanted to see me as soon as possible to formalise the arrangement. Vic and I therefore went to London the following Tuesday, when I attended the famous Tuesday Lunch and was to see Maxwell immediately afterwards. After the relatively uneventful lunch, we went to Maxwell's office where it was confirmed that we would see him shortly - and so we waited and waited and waited. Along with an ever-lengthening queue of others, we were there all afternoon. I met Peter Jay, Kevin Maxwell, Ian Maxwell, Ernie Burrington[2] and a host of others but not the publisher. This of course was a perfectly normal day and an example of inefficiency on the grandest scale.

At around 6.30pm, after waiting almost five hours, we were finally shown in to see the great man, who apologised profusely for keeping us waiting. We had a brief

---

[1] Napoleon Bonaparte, 1769-1821, French statesman and military leader
[2] Ernie Burrington, 1926-2018, Editor, The People 1985-86, Joint Managing Director MGN 1991-92

discussion (brief on my part since Maxwell did most of the talking) and I was awarded a reasonable salary increase. At the end of the meeting, in a typical Maxwell gesture, he picked up the phone and asked if the pilot was still around. Having established that he was (I suspect that this was a bit of showboating as the pilot was probably around all the time), he arranged for us to be flown out to Heathrow in his helicopter and shortly afterwards we took off from the helipad on the top of Maxwell House. We landed at Heathrow just next to Concorde, where a limousine was waiting to take us over to Terminal One for our flight to Glasgow. All in all, a day of pure theatre in the world of Maxwellia.

Reality very quickly set in on my return, since an enormous task lay ahead and one that we were starting from scratch. Some decisions were quickly made: Maxwell Free Newspapers would be a stand-alone company as we knew that a free newspaper company was unsustainable if it inherited SDR's cost base. The next decision was that the company would be located on the fourth floor of the SDR's building, a floor which was now vacant, having been formerly leased to Clyde Cablevision. This meant we could start to recruit staff immediately without looking for premises first. The final decision was that although we couldn't use SDR staff we could tap into the experience of group staff not based in Scotland on a short-term basis. I met soon after with John Welsh from BPCC who agreed to lend us Peter Wilkinson on a temporary basis. Peter had experience in the free newspaper market. Others arrived as we neared the launch date, including Norman Walker, a Production Manager from MGN.

Distribution was always going to be key and we temporarily transferred George Easton, Deputy Circulation Manager, Sunday Mail to work on the project. The precise distribution area was to be critical and, although the working title of the paper at this stage was The Glaswegian, we had yet to decide if this would limit its distribution to the City of Glasgow boundaries, or whether we should include some suburbs of the Greater Glasgow area. We subsequently decided to include a large section of East Renfrewshire (Giffnock and Newton Mearns) and finally arrived at a distribution figure of 320,000 copies, making the publication then the largest free newspaper in the UK.

As the project started to take shape, I decided that we needed to put in place a management team, as we could not depend on the services of the secondees forever. I appointed Ann Wood, then SDR's Tele-Ad Manager, as General Manager, Alastair Wilson became Distribution Manager and David Mill the Launch Editor. The next key task was working out how we would produce the paper. Here we were able to reach agreement that it would be printed on SDR presses with The Glaswegian being treated as a contract print customer. However, page makeup, typesetting and distribution were subcontracted to minimise cost. The final part of the jigsaw was editorial and here David Mill produced a number of 'dummies'. We decided to settle for a 30:70% editorial to advertising ratio. This was a slightly higher editorial ratio than in most free newspapers but we wanted to achieve a high level of readership as quickly as possible. The final decision was on the recruitment of journalists and here we demonstrated lateral thinking of the highest order, combined with a large slice of good luck. We effectively rounded up the entire final year of the journalism course at Napier University and signed up the most promising graduates. David Mill was succeeded by Jack Wright. The management team was relatively young with great enthusiasm, drive and energy but with very limited experience, but the old hands in the team Peter, Norman and Daily Record reporter Tom Grant were able to provide experience.

Things fell into place reasonably well. I decided to stick rigidly to our original timeline and The Glaswegian was launched on 5th April 1989. Maxwell himself attended the launch in great form. True to form, he claimed that the paper was very much his baby and that The Glaswegian would be the first of many new titles (short gulp of breath by all involved in the launch, having only now got to the starting line – just). Equally true to form, we had set up the company, Metropolitan Free Newspapers Ltd. as a wholly owned subsidiary of SDR. Somewhere along the line this was changed to Maxwell Free Newspapers – I wonder how?

Regardless of Maxwell's views, I was quite clear on The Glaswegian's objectives. First and foremost, there was a market gap in Glasgow for a free newspaper, which made the Evening Times our principal target. Surprisingly, Outram's had previously made the strange decision not to have a defensive free sheet to protect it and therefore left the field clear for a predator (us) to move in. The prime objective for The Glaswegian was to secure local advertising revenues from the Evening Times, or from other free or local paid-for newspapers. SDR's titles occupied a space further up the food chain and Gordon Terris and I had a clear agreement that we both understood the bigger picture and would try to avoid conflicts with individual advertisers. The Glaswegian appointed a National Sales Agency in London and there was a potential source of conflict here with MGN's own National Sales Force, but Gordon and I managed our way through that.

The first year of the paper was an unqualified success. We had sufficient confidence to release some of those seconded for the initial launch. Ann Wood was now in place and Alastair Wilson was constantly refining the distribution area, adding and dropping G postcodes. The strike rate for copies delivered increased all the time, with fewer and fewer 'dumpings' and rogue distributors being replaced. We quickly got our first official stamp of approval - a VFD (Verified Free Distribution) certificate for 320,000 copies. At the Association of Free Newspapers awards in 1990, The Glaswegian won the title of Free Newspaper of the Year with Ian Maxwell[3] picking up the award at a ceremony in Birmingham.

Less than a year later Maxwell Senior was at it again. Out of the blue, he phoned Vic to say he had been offered another free newspaper - this time the Edinburgh and Lothians Post, then owned by Reed Publishing - and we should have a look at it. Off we went to Edinburgh. This proposition was a totally different one to that of The Glaswegian. Edinburgh was the heartland of Scotsman Publications and, unlike Glasgow, they had already ring fenced their evening newspaper The Evening News

---

[3] Ian Maxwell b.1956 Chairman MGN November 1991

with a number of free newspaper titles. The Herald and Post series circulated in Edinburgh, Lothians and Fife. On closer analysis, the words 'ring fencing' or 'protecting' were rather wide of the mark. The Herald and Post competed ferociously with the Evening News, its sister title. Quite why Reed thought there was a gap in this market escaped me, but they had nonetheless launched the Edinburgh and Lothians Post in March 1988, distributing it to 200,000 households in Edinburgh and the Lothians, but not Fife. Now, less than two years later, they were proposing to offload (sorry, sell) it to us. We didn't particularly like what we saw. The papers were run by husband and wife team, Earl[4] and Sue Black[5]. We weren't overly impressed by them, even less so with their advertising revenues and profit (or lack of it). I reported all this to Vic and told him that it would not be a good acquisition for us, but too late. Maxwell had already bought it "over a very good lunch" with Sir Peter Davis[6]. Maxwell reported that he had secured the titles for a bargain price. Believe me, the bargain was entirely on the part of Sir Peter Davis, who offloaded a major heap of crap for some £650,000, a fantastic deal for Reed. We were left to pick up the pieces and, when the transaction was completed in March 1990, we tried to consolidate it into our existing structures, removing as much cost as possible, but the scope for this was negligible.

What we were unable to do was to grow its advertising revenues. Our competitor The Herald and Post had a formidable General Manager, Bernadette Nicol who took no prisoners, particularly from within her own camp. The general strategy of having a protective circle of free newspapers is to protect the parent publication. This policy clearly didn't operate here in the case of the parent, The Evening News. Long before Reed had launched the Edinburgh and Lothians Post, Bernadette had virtually stripped all the key categories of classified out of the paper and into The Herald and Post series. Reed, and subsequently Maxwell Free Newspapers, entering the fray had made matters worse by opening up another front on which to fight. Advertising rates came tumbling down even further, leaving the Evening News a husk of its former self. Starved of advertising revenue, pagination of the Evening News fell rapidly and the paper continued its slow, agonising decline in both sales and influence.

For us, worse was to follow. Just after MGN's flotation in 1991, when Maxwell was sinking under a huge wave of debt, he instructed us to launch yet another free newspaper, this time in Aberdeen, where he claimed to have been in touch with senior councillors in both local authorities. They allegedly had told him of their frustration with the almost monopolistic position of the Aberdeen Press and Journal Group, particularly its evening newspaper The Evening Express. Maxwell claimed that the local authorities had promised him a significant amount of advertising support for any new publication in the marketplace that would challenge this monopoly.

[4] Earl Black, General Manager, Edinburgh and Lothians Post 1988-90
[5] Sue Black, Advertising Manager, Edinburgh and Lothians Post 1988-90
[6] Sir Peter Davis, b. 1941, Chief Executive, Reed International 1986-92

Astute readers can guess what happened. We spent three months preparing for the launch of The Aberdonian. I spent a lot of time with the senior officials and councillors in both local authorities, but could secure no commitment whatsoever for advertising or the other 'significant financial help' that Maxwell had promised. In fact, I was unable to find anyone who would admit to having been in contact with Maxwell at all and Vic's attempts to probe Maxwell on who these mysterious people might have been were all to no avail. By that summer, Maxwell's financial problems were closing in on him and, much to our relief, we were able to abandon the entire project quietly.

After Maxwell's death, it was no surprise that our holding company was renamed Metropolitan Free Newspapers Ltd in 1992.

AFN Conference Birmingham October 1990
Celebrating The Glaswegian's award of
Free Newspaper of the Year

l-r: Alastair Wilson, Jack Wright, David Mill,
Ian Maxwell, Ann Wood and CMcC.

Chapter 18   THE SUNDAY SCOT 1991

"Those who fail to learn from history are condemned to repeat it." Winston Churchill[1]

In the autumn of 1990 SDR started picking up intelligence that a competitor to the Sunday Mail was being planned, with a launch date sometime in early 1991. The new title, to be called The Sunday Scot, appeared a credible threat but, more importantly, if it was successful in a Sunday format there was a strong possibility that it would become a daily newspaper. From that moment on, we treated the threat of The Sunday Scot as a military exercise. There was about to be a war and SDR's objective was to kill off the enemy as quickly as possible.

A key taskforce headed by Gordon Terris and me was set up to coordinate our response. The first thing we did was to ensure that every scrap of intelligence, however big or small, was collected, analysed and added to our overall knowledge of what was happening. It was later acknowledged that the SDR team spent more time analysing the business model of The Sunday Scot than the title's actual management team.

The Sunday Scot was the brainchild of two ex-Daily Record and News International journalists Jack Irvine[2] and Steve Sampson[3]. They had persuaded the Scottish businessman and then steel tycoon, David (later Sir David) Murray[4] to back them. Murray was also the owner of Rangers Football Club and it was perhaps there that he became involved with Irvine and Sampson. Murray was an interesting character. During his time at Rangers he had frequently fallen out with sections of the Scottish media and had a reputation for banning journalists when he didn't like something that they had written.

David Murray was not the first business tycoon to have become seduced by the idea of owning a newspaper. As I have detailed earlier, Robert Maxwell, similarly obsessed, had endured many failures in his attempts, prior to acquiring Mirror Group Newspapers. A few years later, Sir Tom Hunter[5] invited me to lunch, mainly to ask me about starting a newspaper. His motivation was more philosophical and he had become concerned that many newspapers focussed on covering 'bad' news, with very little emphasis on providing 'good' news. We had a most agreeable lunch, during which I think I persuaded him that 'good news' doesn't necessarily sell newspapers and that newspapers themselves are enormously complex businesses. Launch costs can be extremely high with no guarantee of success, as many have

[1] Sir Winston Churchill 1874-1965. Prime Minister 1940-45, 1951-55. House of Commons Speech 1948. Churchill adapted the quote from one by George Santayana, 1863-1952, a Spanish philosopher. The original quote was, "Those who cannot remember the past are condemned to repeat it."
[2] Jack Irvine, b. 1949, Managing Director, NI Scotland; latterly Founder and Executive Chairman of Media House International
[3] Steve Sampson, former Assistant / Northern / Scottish Editor, The Sun. Founder First Press Publishing, Director Trinity Mirror
[4] Sir David Murray, b.1951, Chairman, Murray Capital Ltd.
[5] Sir Tom Hunter, b. 1961, entrepreneur and founder of West Coast Capital

found out to their cost. In the intervening years, Tom appears to have taken my advice.

The reason for the high rate of failure was that starting such a venture was prohibitively expensive and required very deep pockets. In the late 80s, both Maxwell and Murdoch had smashed the power of the trade unions and, combined with advances in new technology, the entry cost came tumbling down.

By the end of 1990 we had started to build up a more exact picture of what was about to happen. The newspaper, now definitely to be called The Sunday Scot, was to be launched "soon" and would be based in premises in St Vincent Street in Glasgow, where all pre-production would be based on Mac technology. It would then be printed on the new Herald presses in Albion Street. This would have been an extremely lucrative piece of business for Outram's, particularly as their own Sunday Herald (eventually launched in February 1999) was probably not even on the drawing board at this stage. Of most concern to us was that the target audience of The Sunday Scot was virtually identical to that of the Sunday Mail. The Sunday Scot team had identified the increasingly ageing readership of the Sunday Post and new, younger readers were effectively being offered only one choice - the Sunday Mail. From this they had identified a supposed 'gap' in the marketplace, specifically a younger audience who might want something different to the Sunday Mail. The logic was based on the fact that the Sunday Mail, now straddling the entire popular Sunday newspaper market in Scotland, had to be all things to all people. I'm not sure there ever was such a gap, but one thing that The Sunday Scot team might have identified was that the Sunday Mail was looking rather tired and had perhaps slightly lost its way editorially. Sales of the Sunday Mail had been increasing every year from 1982 but sales had declined in 1989 and had not yet recovered in 1990.

There were those who would suggest that the best years of the paper, under Endell Laird, had not been replicated by Noel Young's[6] recent editorship. The result was that a new Editor for the Sunday Mail, Jim Cassidy[7], was appointed in early 1991 and Noel Young moved to become Managing Editor of SDR. Although that decision would ultimately have been taken by Maxwell and Endell, it was supported by the SDR Board. We were nervous about the ability of the Sunday Mail in its present format to withstand the coming challenge of The Sunday Scot. Noel Young would have considered himself unfortunate to be replaced, particularly since he had taken the paper to an all-time high sale of 907,000 copies per day in 1988. He thus defied the old newspaper maxim, "When sales are up, lavish praise on the Editor. When sales are down, fire the Sales Manager."

Jim Cassidy hit the ground running in January 1991, two months before the launch of The Sunday Scot. I had already secured a significant promotions budget for the first six months of that year, although at this stage we did not know the exact launch date of The Sunday Scot. By now, new staff were being signed up by The Sunday Scot on almost a weekly basis. SDR lost some very capable people during this time

---

[6] Noel Young, Editor, Sunday Mail 1988-91
[7] Jim Cassidy, b. 1950, Editor, Sunday Mail 1991-99

across almost all departments and we were becoming increasingly concerned as to what damage the new paper could cause the Sunday Mail.

In the meantime we continued to pick up and analyse every scrap of intelligence. By this stage The Sunday Scot was starting to promulgate the message that the paper would be something completely new and different to any other newspaper. Although it was building a great public relations campaign, it was always a little short on detail. We were using every trick in the book to determine their launch date, which was of crucial importance. It would mean we could direct our firepower in one massive initial blitz and blow them out of the water right at the very start. Try as hard as we might we were unable to determine the date. The reality was that The Sunday Scot didn't decide the date themselves until the last possible moment, mainly because they were unprepared in a whole series of areas and kept postponing it.

At this stage SDR changed its strategy. We decided, rather than waiting to determine the actual specific launch date, we would base our assumptions on a time window. We eventually worked out (totally accurately as it turned out), that the launch would have to occur within a four-week period if The Sunday Scot were to take advantage of the traditional spring period of rising sales

At this time our above the line advertising agency Shaw Advertising then brilliantly executed one of the smartest moves in the battle. The agency was run by the mercurial David Shaw[8] and he booked every single commercial break on Scottish Television, Border and Grampian Television for a six-week period. This of course was at our very favourable rates as the biggest player in the market. When The Sunday Scot settled on their 8th March launch date and tried to book their campaign, every commercial break already contained one newspaper within it. The only way they could have access was by a process called 'pre-empting' i.e. offering a much higher price to secure the break. It was a major triumph for us and a massive psychological (and expensive) blow for them.

The truth of the matter was that The Sunday Scot was launched too late. For a spring launch, conventional marketing wisdom is to be ready to go as soon as the effects of the Christmas and New Year holiday period are over. The market starts to rebuild then, hence the Sunday Herald was launched on the 7th February 1999, so in effect, The Sunday Scot lost four weeks of a rising market.

Our first major media campaign began two weeks prior to the launch of The Sunday Scot. We therefore had a free two-week period to extol the virtues of the Sunday Mail and emphasise the core values of the paper. We launched a whole series of new promotions, along with an extremely innovative (and, coming from Scott Stern, very expensive) retailer incentive scheme. For retailers, the scheme had a large number of valuable quick-win incentives already in the bag before The Sunday Scot launch.

---

[8] David Shaw, 1944-96, Managing Director, Shaw Advertising and amateur drama Impresario

This meant the retailers' feel-good factor for the Sunday Mail was well-established before The Sunday Scot's launch.

Once we had finally established their launch date, we not only had a major series of promotions but Jim Cassidy also had a record number of 'exclusives' for the paper. Just over a week before the launch, we managed to 'acquire' some waste samples of The Sunday Scot's first dummy print run. It was a veritable treasure trove of intelligence, providing us with the likely format of the paper, the ad shapes, editorial features etc. Our overall reaction to the dummy was that it looked like an extremely ordinary, very conventional Sunday tabloid newspaper. At that stage we all had a slight sense of relief, as we had been fearful of something absolutely groundbreaking, but we remained on high alert.

On the evening before the launch day, The Sunday Scot started printing at around 9pm and we had our first copies back in Anderson Quay by 9.30pm. I was with Jim Cassidy as we looked at those first copies. Jim's first reaction was that this must be a 'spoof' edition as the lead front page story was so weak. Increasingly worried that they must have a major exclusive, we anxiously awaited the second edition, which we acquired just before midnight. Lo and behold, it contained exactly the same lead story, which indeed was used for the entire print run. As they had had months to prepare for this event, Jim was expecting some earth-shattering stories - and there simply weren't any. All in all, the verdict on the first issue of The Sunday Scot was that it was hugely disappointing.

On the morning of the launch, the full force of the SDR's field team swung into action, backed up by as many other people as we could lay our hands on. There was a further range of updated point of sale material, again reinforcing the weekend's television and radio promotions. Our people on the ground did a magnificent job and I concede that in the heat of battle there may have been cases where some copies of the Sunday Mail were accidently placed on top of the entire supplies of The Sunday Scot.

In summary it was a very promising start to the battle and we now awaited sales figures. Each of our team – editorial, advertising, circulation, marketing and finance – had in the meantime meticulously analysed the new arrival. We did some extensive financial modelling on what their bottom line might have looked like and noted that their ad content was significantly lower than we had projected.

The second phase of the operation now swung into place. We had analysed every newspaper launch in recent history and had concluded that, in most cases, there was a high level of launch 'hype' that would continue for up to six months afterwards. In particular, there was a tendency to overstate sales figures and revenues excessively and praise the launch of the new project. Again, in almost all cases, this euphoria lasted only until the publication of audited sales figures.

Our strategy was not to allow this period of euphoria to gain any traction. And so we issued our own weekly bulletins to retailers, wholesalers, advertising agencies, other media - or indeed anyone who was prepared to listen. Our bulletins contained our own estimates of what was happening both to the sale of the Sunday Mail and of course The Sunday Scot. Needless to say, our predictions were a lot more pessimistic than those being bandied around by The Sunday Scot. The main target audience for all this, though we carefully never alluded to it, was the staff of The Sunday Scot itself. We wanted to create as much self-doubt as possible within the camp. However, the top target was David Murray himself and we had assumed that, without any previous experience of launching a newspaper, he would be relying heavily on what he was being told by Messrs Irvine and Sampson. We were determined to provide him with an alternative view of events.

The war of attrition continued throughout spring and into early summer. The Sunday Mail emerged virtually unscathed from the whole exercise - not surprising as we had spent almost £1.5 million promoting it. Our view had always been that we were in for a long battle. Sales of The Sunday Scot, against their own target of 250,000, never reached anywhere near that and, after the initial launch blitz, started declining each week. From the middle of June onwards, the normal summer seasonal overall sales decline would accelerate the trend even further. We had calculated that, in early September, they would need a re-launch campaign and to counter this we had already earmarked a further £1.5 million for an autumn campaign for the Sunday Mail.

Astonishingly, after only 17 issues and in the second week of July when traditionally sales of all newspapers in Scotland are at their lowest for the entire year, David Murray threw in the towel and announced that he was closing the paper with immediate effect. Staring at losses which we estimated to be around £5 million, there would be no autumn re-launch and no future Daily Scot. Over the following years I met David Murray a number of times and from our conversations I am convinced that he had been badly advised on the predictable trends when launching a newspaper. Basically, it requires a significant level of resources and a willingness to launch and re-launch on a number of occasions before finally gaining a meaningful foothold in the market. I think Murray was simply unprepared for all this; no one had told him that this was the likely outcome and with his first £5 million gone already, he simply had no appetite to go any further. I have no doubt that The Sunday Scot might have eventually established a foothold but it was never going to achieve the 250,000 sales target that had been set. Readers purchased more Sunday newspapers than dailies and I admit the Sunday Mail, embracing such a wide parish, could have been vulnerable. My later experience in NI demonstrated that we were less successful in the battle between the Scottish News of the World and the Sunday Mail than we were in the one between The Scottish Sun and the Daily Record. I am absolutely convinced that, although there might have been a small gap in the Sunday market that The Sunday Scot might have productively occupied, there would have been no such gap in the daily market should they have gone on to launch a daily. The all out war between the Scottish Sun and the Daily Record would have prevented any other player successfully competing in that market.

The final postscript of The Sunday Scot episode was that both Jack Irvine and Steve Sampson went on to other successful careers but the fallout between the two of them was enormous. For many years afterwards each would badmouth and blame the other for the failure of the ill-fated Sunday Scot.

To all potential marketeers, I commend that they look at what happened to The Sunday Scot. It is a classic case study of how to see off a competitor by good intelligence, detailed analysis, inspired marketing - and a large dose of good luck.

Headington Hill Hall, Oxford

Chapter 19   MAXWELL- A FINAL ASSESSMENT

"The thing I would most like to see invented is a way of teaching children and grown ups the difference between right and wrong."   Robert Maxwell

Despite his murky past and having been written off by many after the Board of Trade Report some 15 years earlier, by the time Maxwell had acquired Mirror Group Newspapers his stock was at an all time high. One example of this was at an event in his home Headington Hill Hall in Oxford on 7th June 1985. Claire and I, along with the SDR Board and more than 500 others, were invited to his 40th Wedding Anniversary dinner.

We stayed at the Randolph Hotel and were bussed to the event. Gaining access proved tricky and the security was incredibly tight – maybe because Prince Charles was rumoured to be attending. As we later learned, it was to protect Maxwell, now a multi-millionaire, who hadn't exactly helped himself when, on television recently, he had proclaimed that IRA bombers should be tried by court martial and, if guilty, immediately shot. In the house we joined a line to be presented to Robert and Elizabeth Maxwell[1] and were then served from magnums of fine champagne by a host of waiters. The famous harpist Jeannette Cordrey played in the background. Headington Hill Hall was a magnificent mansion on the outskirts of Oxford but, in true Maxwell style, he leased it from the local Council at a peppercorn rent. In the huge salon, cynics in the party immediately moved to the bookshelves and confirmed what had been long rumoured – most of the impressive volumes were simply spines pasted on backings.

We were then guided via a covered walkway to an enormous marquee which had been erected around the swimming pool in the grounds. The Salon Orchestra of the Royal Airforce played throughout dinner. A seating plan directed us to Table A1, where we met four other couples, all from Maxwell companies. I still have the guest list and table plan provided at each place setting. Among the guests were a former Prime Minister, 23 Peers of the Realm, 21 Knights, several Ambassadors (mainly Eastern Bloc) and an impressive gathering of tycoons, bankers, media celebrities, academics and trade unionists. For people watchers like us it was a fascinating evening. After dinner, Elizabeth Maxwell was the first to speak and took us through the menu (see page 160) which had been created to reflect the occasion. Terrine de Homard Normandie was to commemorate her husband's part in the Invasion; Selle d'Agneau Cancellier and Panaché de Legumes Versaillais were named after the places of their early meetings; Le Plateau de Fromages Parlo celebrated the town where he had won his Military Cross and Bombe Glacée Queen's Royal recognised his regiment.

For me, the evening also turned out to be significant event, but for an unusual reason. After the first course of terrine I asked Claire what was in it and to my horror

---

[1] Elizabeth Maxwell, (née. Meynard), 1921-2013 m. Robert Maxwell 1945

realised that I had eaten lobster. For 20 years I had avoided shellfish, having had two violent reactions to them in my early twenties. After that evening I tentatively sampled seafood again and now enjoy it enormously with no repercussions. After Betty Maxwell's speech about the early years of her relationship and marriage, their eldest son Phillip[2] spoke. An academic, he appeared rather nervous and tellingly informed the audience that what he was going to say had "not been submitted for official clearance" – a clear reference to his father's controlling nature. He described his childhood, with his father portrayed as a demanding, but indulgent tyrant. The "demanding tyrant" certainly chimed with most of the audience, "indulgent" rather less so. He movingly referred to his brother and sister who had died – Michael[3] the firstborn and Karine[4].

Finally, Maxwell rose to respond and, as well as charting a lengthy catalogue of his achievements, insisted on introducing the other six sons and daughters and demanded that they each stood up. In turn, Anne, twins Isobel and Christine, Ian, Kevin and Ghislaine all did so.[5]

Finally, Maxwell asked the former Prime Minister Harold (later Lord) Wilson of Rievaulx to speak. This clearly came as something of a surprise to Wilson, since he then commenced a rambling speech. With hindsight many concluded that he was showing the early signs of the dementia which was to devastate his last years. Others felt that he simply could not recall the name of his host. He ploughed on and concluded that, if Maxwell had stayed in politics, then he too would have been a Prime Minister. Maxwell positively beamed at this suggestion. Speeches over, dancing commenced to the music of Joe Loss's Ambassadors. After the event we all repaired to the Randolph to reflect on the evening. Everyone had a story to tell. At the next table was a collection of what I would describe as seasoned Mirror hacks, led in their revelry by the most seasoned of all – the legendary Keith Waterhouse. Amongst them was also Sir Robin Day[6] entering into what was now early morning with great enthusiasm. There was only one slight problem – Day had brought along a young, female companion, who was, as the night porter had to remind him on several occasions, awaiting him in their room – presumably for an entirely different type of activity. Sadly, for the young lady, as the evening wore on, her prospects of such activity were rapidly diminishing and as we left at around 1.30am, the party was still in full flow.

We were to return to Headington Hill Hall on two further occasions: the first an anniversary lunch to celebrate 40 years of Pergamon Press. I was particularly taken by the then elderly Margaret, Duchess of Argyll, still elegantly turned out and accompanied by her pet chihuahua, which sat on her lap for the entire lunch. Our final visit was for a Christmas dinner and dance on 15th December 1990 when, although Maxwell was ill and didn't attend, we were served from Salmanazars of

---

[2] Phillip Maxwell, b. 1951
[3] Michael Maxwell, 1947-68
[4] Karine Maxwell, 1954-57
[5] Anne Maxwell, b. 1949, Isobel and Christine Maxwell, b. 1950, Kevin Maxwell, b. 1958, Ghislaine Maxwell, b. 1961
[6] Sir Robin Day, 1923-2000, British political broadcaster and commentator

vintage champagne and magnums of Gevrey Chambertin 1978. Less than a year later Maxwell was dead and his empire had crashed.

There is no doubt that, at the time of his acquisition of MGN, Maxwell was an extremely successful businessman, with his large group of companies making significant profits. The 40th wedding anniversary dinner in 1985 demonstrated how powerful he had become, but there were still doubts concerning his methods and the complex relationships between his 400+ companies. His "need to know" management style meant there was a total lack of transparency and a lack of knowledge of the overall health of the Group. What eventually brought him down was over-ambition and his obsession with being seen to be more successful than Rupert Murdoch. Murdoch himself had nearly gone under in the Great Crash of 1987, losing an estimated $1 billion (almost half his fortune), but he had survived. Maxwell, cash rich at the time, had emerged nowhere near as damaged but had realised that, in order to build a bigger company than Murdoch's, it could not be in Europe alone. He would have to switch his attention to the USA. He wasn't helped by making a series of bad decisions from 1987 onwards. He launched a 24 hour newspaper, The London Daily News, which swallowed £50 million in its short lifetime. The European, launched three years later, was to lose £150 million.

Maxwell's first foray in US in 1987 also ended in failure. He had bid $2 billion for the mammoth US publishing conglomerate Harcourt Brace Janovich (HBJ), but it fought him off at great cost in a bitter battle which ended up in the US courts. Part of HBJ's defence was Maxwell's ownership of his Liechtenstein Trusts. These mysterious trusts, which Maxwell had earlier used as a strength, were to prove a significant problem to him in the last years of his life. I watched Brian Walden[7] interview Maxwell on television in early 1988. He mercilessly goaded Maxwell about his ambitions, his lack of success in expanding his empire (Murdoch had also thwarted him at the eleventh hour in his bid for the Today newspaper) and particularly his failure to acquire HBJ. Maxwell glowered at him and his final, angry response to Walden was "Just watch this space, Mister." I believe that this was a most significant statement and that Maxwell's attempt to recover the perceived loss of face and damage to his ego would play a part in the future downfall of the entire Maxwell Empire.

In July 1988 Maxwell made his second American bid. When he entered the race to acquire MacMillan, the giant US publishing company, its shares were trading at $50. An initial hostile take-over offer from Bass Group had been at $64 a share, eventually rising to $73. Maxwell entered the battle in July, offering $80 a share. In a fierce battle which also ended up in the US courts, Maxwell finally acquired MacMillan for $90.25 a share. He had paid $2.6 billion for a company which many regarded as worth $1 billion less. Equally astonishingly, one week before completing the MacMillan deal, he had acquired the Official Airline Guides for $750 million. For good measure, around the same time he had also bought AGB Market Research for

---

[7] Brian Walden, 1932-2019, journalist and broadcaster, Labour MP 1964-77

£134 million and the Pannini Stickers Company for £60 million. All in all, he had taken on £3 billion of debt.

The reasons for Maxwell's downfall are very simple. In 1988 he took on massive debt for those deals and he was unable to service it. The series of poor acquisitions and launches drained cash from the organisation at the very time when it was required to service the new debt. He wasn't the first businessman to make this mistake, nor was he the last, but for Maxwell the consequences were devastating. All that happened subsequently can be traced back to the MacMillan acquisition – simply a deal too far.

For us in SDR, one consequence was the flotation of MGN in April 1991. Although we did not know it at the time, the flotation was just one of a series of moves by Maxwell to raise cash to stave off the inevitable demands of the banks. For many of us, it was our first and only experience of being involved in the flotation of a public company. As well as running the day to day business, for months we were to have hoards of advisors asking us endless questions about the business. Every small detail of our business was challenged by a legion of so-called experts. From this, the long form prospectus eventually emerged. The list of advisors was impressive and they were allegedly from the top tier in the City. They included Samuel Montague and Co., Smith Newcourt, Salomon Brothers, Coopers and Lybrand, Clifford Chance, Linklaters and Paine, with the National Westminster Bank as principal banker.

The purpose of this mammoth exercise was to ensure that the information presented to potential investors was accurate and represented a true picture of the company and its dealings. The subplot was that the team of advisors had to pick their way through the myriad inter-company relationships between MGN and the numerous other Maxwell companies. They also had to ensure that, after flotation, all transactions were transparent and that MGN was ring-fenced from all the other entities. The attempt at ring-fencing continued right up to the launch of the prospectus. The SDR Board was in London on launch day to hear the presentation by the advisors. Maxwell was attending another event, but was still creating mayhem. I recall Sir Michael Richardson[8] of Smith Newcourt, the brokers, being in mid flow of his presentation, when an aide whispered in his ear. Richardson, his microphone unfortunately still switched on, was heard to say incredulously "He said what?" Maxwell, at his other meeting, allegedly stated that the Mirror building was not included in the share offer, despite the prospectus definitively stating that it was. Cue chaos. History would seem to point out that the team of advisors spectacularly failed to achieve the desired ring-fencing. In his subsequent need for cash, Maxwell was also to plunder the MGN Treasury and Pension Fund and the supposed ring-fence turned out to be virtually non-existent.

For SDR the creation of the prospectus had some benefits. It was designed to define precisely what was being offered for public subscription. To do this, the advisors had to examine minutely the company structure and we were horrified to discover

---

[8] Sir Michael Richardson, 1925-2003, Chairman, Smith New Court 1989-95

that our free newspaper company had been placed within Maxwell Communications Corporation (MCC), an entirely separate company, and had to be redirected back into SDR. The most disturbing fact to emerge was that the titles themselves (the Daily Record and the Sunday Mail), upon which was based the good will value of the company, had somehow also found their way into MCC and had to be retrieved.

The whole exercise was not without its amusing moments. The case of Helen Liddell[9] is an example. Helen joined the SDR Board in 1988 and her actual appointment was pure Maxwell theatre. Although it had been rumoured for some weeks that she would be joining, it was only confirmed at a board meeting in London. Shortly before the meeting Maxwell had taken aside Kevin McMahon, the Human Resources Director, and told him he now had a new title – Director of Manpower and Industrial Relations. At the end of the Board meeting, Maxwell announced "Gentlemen, I am appointing a new member to your Board." Cue the double doors at the end of the Board Room to open as he continued "Mrs Helen Liddell will be your new Director of Personnel." Everyone in the room looked aghast, thinking "Surely Kevin McMahon is our Director of Personnel?" Quick as a flash, Vic Horwood nudged Maxwell, who, without a pause continued, "and Public Affairs." This seeming duplication of titles continued for the next three years until, not surprisingly, one of the advisors at a pre-flotation meeting, innocently asked "I see that you have a Director of Manpower and Industrial Relations and a Director of Human Resources and Public Affairs. Can you explain the difference in these two roles?" All eyes swivelled to Vic, who eventually announced a short adjournment and took the advisor into his office. 15 minutes later the meeting resumed with a new title for Helen – Director of Corporate and Public Affairs.

If the flotation was an example of Maxwell desperately trying to raise cash, the knock-on effect for SDR was a lack of capital investment which was increasingly becoming a major problem. Since the mid-80s, demand for colour advertising had been fast outstripping supply and as a result of this our presses no longer had the capacity to produce the amount of colour required. The presses were effectively becoming obsolete and would need to be replaced. Maxwell had re-equipped both MGN's printing sites with new colour presses but had increasingly been prevaricating on the issue with us; with hindsight it's easy to understand why.

Nevertheless, we thought that we were finally moving him towards a final decision. The flotation prospectus in April 1991 stated "SDR is making a major capital investment in four new Koenig & Barr Commander Web-offset colour printing presses to replace the existing plant, which is now 20 years old. The new equipment is expected to be fully operational in 1994. It will allow SDR to produce newspapers with more pages and double the existing colour capacity. Together with the infrastructure, it is expected to cost approximately £83 million (of which £37

---

[9] The Rt. Hon. Helen, Baroness Liddell of Coatdyke, b. 1950, Labour MP 1994-2005, Secretary of State for Scotland 2001-03, British High Commissioner Australia 2005-08

million has already been spent). SDR is committed to acquire a fifth press at a further cost of £10 million, which it intends to sell."

The astute reader would surely have asked two obvious questions at this point. Firstly, why buy K&B presses, when the rest of the Group is operating with MAN Roland equipment? Secondly, why buy five presses when you only need four? The answer, of course, is that in the world of Maxwell nothing was ever straightforward. In the late 80s Maxwell had decided to launch a French national newspaper and had acquired the five presses for that purpose. He had subsequently fallen out with the French trade unions, the project was abandoned and the presses were now stored in Germany. Since cash was already in short supply, Maxwell had not purchased the presses outright, but had leased them through the Royal Bank of Scotland (a fact strangely missing in the prospectus). Vic Horwood, having tried and failed to re-equip SDR at the same time as MGN, had subsequently heard about these presses and persuaded Maxwell to install four of them in Glasgow. The only snag was that it would take another £45 million to rebuild a large part of the Anderston Quay plant to accommodate them. Although the prospectus referred to the capital investment as reality, Maxwell had not yet formally signed it off. Vic, now based in London most of the time as Joint MD of MGN, was still very much on the case and so was feeling very pleased with himself when he asked us to attend a meeting in Anderston Quay one Sunday morning in early October 1991.

Maxwell was coming up to sign off the project. Ahead of the meeting the SDR Board spent a great deal of time in preparation, trying to anticipate every conceivable question the great man might ask. Maxwell arrived at 10.30, looking for all the world like a tramp, in a baseball cap, a loose-fitting, very crumpled polo shirt and a baggy suit. I am perhaps being unkind to him. At this stage he must have been under relentless pressure from the world's banks and financial institutions, all chasing him to honour his commitments and he was, as we now know, fast running out of options. What we were not prepared for was the pantomime which took place over the next 90 minutes. Vic gave an impressive presentation, unveiling a scale model of the building and revealing considerable innovative thinking on manufacturing process. He finished by flourishing a single piece of paper and saying "All we need, Bob, is for you to sign this and we can start the project immediately." There was a lengthy silence as Maxwell stared at the model and his first question should have given us a clue as to what was to follow. "Where is the helipad?" "What helipad?" was definitely the wrong response and resulted in a lecture from Maxwell about modern travel. We were now on the back foot. Maxwell rejected the first suggestion of a helipad in the car park. The second suggestion of the flat roof on the new press hall then prompted a series of questions on the load-bearing capabilities of the roof, to which of course we did not have the answer. He then looked at the model again and prodded the new newsprint storage facility (currently our garage). Question: "What's this beside it?" Answer: "That's Cheapside Street, which runs along our building (again, the wrong answer). Question: "Don't you realise you can't close a public highway, but strikers and a picket line could blockade it and prevent raw materials getting on to your site. You must build a tunnel." By now the engineers were reeling. Next question: "How much newsprint can you store in that building?" Answer: "About two weeks' supply." Question: "Where is it replenished from?" "It comes to Grangemouth by boat and is transported to the site by lorry." Question: "How far away is Grangemouth?" Answer: "About 30 miles." Maxwell's final response was "You're all complete dickheads. Don't you realise you've got a canal right beside you? (We assumed he meant the River Clyde). You will need to think about taking delivery of your newsprint supplies by boat. Why haven't you thought about that?" By this stage, the project team were almost jibbering wrecks. The rest of us wondered if there was any point in telling him that the reason our newsprint came into Grangemouth was that most of it came from Scandinavia. Why would we then ship it round the north coast of Scotland and down the west coast into Glasgow to save a 35 mile road journey? The final question was: "Where's the nearest railway station? Have you considered how you could get our supplies to that nearest railhead?" (Glasgow Central). The fact was that the station was more than half a mile away, in a built-up part of Glasgow. Of course, the wrong answer was to say that the entire newspaper industry had just moved from rail to road; why would we want to move back to rail? By this stage the atmosphere was tetchy and Maxwell was in his element. "Don't you crowd of dummies realise that you're asking me to spend £45 million on a project which will accommodate our needs for the next 25 years and you crackpots think you know what's going to happen during that time?" At this he threw his briefing papers on to the table and walked out, his parting shot ringing in our ears. "It seems you people still need to answer a lot of questions about this project. I suggest you'd better get on with it." We were shell shocked – almost three years' work and still no nearer getting the decision to go ahead. Of course, it was all Maxwell bluff – he didn't have the money to fund the project and, if he had, although we didn't know it at the time, there were many, many others well ahead of us in the queue for that money. Vic had laid on an impressive buffet lunch, hoping (wrongly as it turned out) that the project would have obtained its final approval. Maxwell eschewed the buffet, instead ordering that a plain omelette be prepared. Curiously he then started to reminisce about the Park Royal days and his battles with the trade unions there. He was unable to remember some of the individuals concerned and Kevin McMahon had to prompt him on more than one occasion. Unusually, when he departed, he went into the kitchen to thank the lady who had prepared the omelette.

Less than a month later Maxwell was dead. Kevin and I have talked recently about that day's events. Why did he fly to Glasgow in the first place? After all he was notorious for cancelling meetings at the last moment. Why all the recollections of times past? This was unheard of for Maxwell. Our conclusion was that for him the net was tightening and there was no way out. Alone, what else was there to do on a bleak Sunday in October?

The pressure on Maxwell continued to mount and now reached a crescendo by the end of the month. The share price of both his public companies continued to fall and it now emerged that he had been illegally supporting it through a number of financial institutions. These same institutions were now threatening to dump the shares on to the market. Maxwell had also removed large amounts of cash from the MGN Treasury and its pension fund. There seemed no way out. In Gibraltar on the evening of 31st October the captain of his yacht Lady Ghislaine was told Maxwell would arrive the next day. Unusually, he was alone. His movements over the next few days are well charted, as he cruised, seemingly at random, in the Canaries. He was last seen alive at 4.25am on 5th November 1991. His body was found shortly after 6pm that day. In Glasgow we had been alerted to his disappearance just after 3pm. Shares in MGN and MCC were suspended on the Stock Exchange. We had previously been aware that all was not well in London and that Vic and Laurie Guest[10] were extremely concerned about the situation.

Maxwell was buried on the Mount of Olives in Jerusalem, overlooking the Garden of Gethsemane.   It is the most coveted burial site for followers of Judaism, as those buried there will be the first to hear the call of the Messiah on the Day of Judgement. Cynics said "Trust Maxwell – making sure he would be at the front of the queue." Television viewers seeing Endell Laird representing SDR at the funeral asked, "Who is that bloke with the tartan bonnet and Canon Sureshot?"

Less than a month later it emerged that the organisation had debts of over £1 billion and the administrators were called in on 5th December. I recall two things from that time. The first was the initial praise and positive assessment of his career, even by some of his opponents. The great British characteristic of never speaking ill of the dead emerged in spades. In his own paper, he was the man who saved The Mirror and "a giant with vision." "His death removes a Colossus from the scene." (Joe Haines) "The nation's headlines will be much poorer with his passing and the length of his journey from the place and circumstances of his death demand respect from all of us who have had to travel much less high." (Max Hastings[11]). "A great character and a charismatic figure." (Ted Heath[12]). Only The Independent on Sunday broke ranks. Maxwell was "a liar, a cheat, and a bully... His untruthfulness was not a matter of occasional slips. It was an instinct, a habit and, above all, a weapon."

The second thing I recall are the conspiracy theories. As details of the scale of his fraud gathered pace, The Sun's headline expressed what many were thinking: "Did he fall, or did he jump?" All in all, there were around 10 different versions of what might have happened, some more fanciful than others. A genuine accident, a heart attack and suicide were the most common. More disingenuous were those who suggested that he was assassinated by The Mafia (because of his involvement in The New York Daily News), or the KGB (misappropriation of funds). The most elaborate theory of all was that he faked his own death and lived contentedly in the Paraguayan jungle for several more years on the proceeds of an undetected Liechtenstein trust. Aside from the admittedly not impossible necessity of substituting a 22 stone corpse, this theory surely falls on the unlikely premise that Maxwell could have lived anywhere quietly and contentedly.

---

[10] Laurie Guest, b. 1936, Finance Director, MGN 1977-92
[11] Sir Max Hastings, b. 1945, author, journalist, broadcaster, Editor, Daily Telegraph 1986-95
[12] The Rt. Hon. Sir Edward Heath, 1916-2005, Prime Minister 1970-74

Suicide remains the most likely possibility. As well as seeing the crash into bankruptcy of the business he had spent a lifetime creating, the inevitable personal vilification would have been huge. His raiding of the pension fund created outrage. On top of that, the likelihood was that he would have faced a long prison sentence for fraud. I suspect the warm waters of the Canaries were much more appealing that early morning. Roy Greenslade summed it up "The 20th Century's most monstrous confidence trickster, braggart, bully, liar, cheat, thief drowned himself because he was about to be found out at last."

Tom Bower surprisingly produced a more measured opinion: "Maxwell could not have intended to bequeath a debt-ridden conglomerate, at the mercy of those whom he despised, as his memorial. But, by the nature of the man, it could never have been different. Certainly, by normal criteria, he was dishonest, but it is questionable whether he consciously intended to be dishonest. In his own terms, Maxwell could probably not distinguish right from wrong, for everything which he did was, by definition, right. When the smoke has passed and the dishonesty is forgotten, he will be remembered in equal measures for his failures and success, but most of all for his success in overcoming failures which would have crushed other mortals forever. There are many mortals of Maxwell's kind who have sought in their lifetime to ensure a secure place in posterity. Maxwell was unusual in many ways, but not least because he sought to write his own epitaph in his lifetime and then enjoy his self-assessment for many years to come. His great dream of a permanent worldwide communications group bearing his name is dead."

In a second book on Maxwell[13] published five years later, Bower was much more critical of him, "even though in Maxwell's case, his propensity to commit a fraud had been obvious since 1954 it was almost impossible for any journalist to produce the evidence contemporaneously." "Maxwell prospered because hundreds of otherwise intelligent people wilfully suspended any moral judgement and succumbed to their avarice and greed."

 The last word was from one of his employees: "We feel like digging him up and hanging him."

At SDR we had many issues to contend with – the plundering of the MGN pension fund, the appointment of an administrator and the prospect of a very uncertain future. My colleagues and I were delighted to see the end of the Maxwell era, with all the bullying, interference and, latterly, fraudulent behaviour which accompanied it. Little did we know that less than a year later we would have to contend with a different type of monster – David Montgomery[14].

---

[13] Maxwell: The Final Verdict, Tom Bower 1995, Harper Collins
[14] David Montgomery, b.1948, CEO Mirror Group Newspapers 1992-99

Gala Dinner and Dance
to celebrate

**Bob and Betty Maxwell's
40th Wedding Anniversary**

*Headington Hill Hall, Oxford
Friday 7 June 1985*

*Dancing to the Music of
Joe Loss's Ambassadors*

MENU

Terrine de Homard Normandie
Meursault-Charmes 1979

•••

Selle d'Agneau Cancellier
Panaché de Légumes Versaillais
Nuits Saint Georges 1978

•••

Le Plateau de Fromages Parlo

•••

Bombe Glacée Queen's Royal
Möet et Chandon Brut

•••

Gâteau du 40e Anniversaire

•••

Café et Liqueurs

Menu, Headington Hill Hall, Oxford 1985

Chapter 20   ADMINISTRATION AND MONTGOMERY

"Age wrinkles the body. Quitting wrinkles the soul."   Douglas MacArthur[1]

After Maxwell's death and the collapse of the Maxwell Empire just over a month later, MGN entered into administration. As the full extent of Maxwell's machinations was revealed, all sorts of questions were asked about how he had been able to plunder the MGN treasury and its pension fund without being challenged. What was the role of the two Senior Non-Executive Directors Alan Clements[2] and Sir Robert Clark[3]? What of the Executive Directors – Vic Horwood, Laurie Guest, Ernie Burrington, Roger Eastoe[4], Endell Laird, and Charlie Wilson[5] – and why hadn't they challenged him? The subsequent DTI inquiry extensively examined all this. At the last MGN board meeting, six days before Maxwell's death, no one raised the matter. Clark and Clements had a meeting with Maxwell afterwards and allegedly demanded that an audit committee be set up to examine financial controls within the Group. Maxwell's response was to tell them that Michael Stoney[6], his lackey as Finance Director, would draft the terms of reference. The net result of the DTI inquiry, though it criticised many of the individuals concerned, did not result in a single criminal conviction in what surely must rank as one of the greatest financial frauds at that time. Astonishing! Indeed, one wonders if Maxwell might have been better taking his chances with the inquiry rather than jumping off his boat, but he was not to know that. Within MGN no one emerged with any credit. The banks had lent recklessly, the Board had not tackled him sufficiently robustly at critical times, and the auditors had been duped. Most of all, the city advisors in the flotation had created a ring fence, which in the words of Richard Stott, "was effectively paper bars to cage a tiger," whilst picking up huge fees for the exercise.

The banks, true to form, wanted their money back. MGN was the best asset within the old Maxwell Empire, but its share price was languishing at around half of its £1.25 flotation price. What was required was someone to come in and up the profit level from the organisation and the banks themselves knew of only one way to do this – cut costs.

At SDR the existing Board made an excellent job of continuing to run a still very profitable business under very trying circumstances. Despite all sorts of recriminations taking place over Maxwell's activities, it seemed obvious that MGN would end up under some form of new management and SDR along with it. As Directors of SDR, the best run and most profitable part of the organisation, it occurred to us that we were perfectly capable of continuing this situation and could probably do so far better than anyone else. We talked to Vic about the possibility of a

---

[1] General Douglas MacArthur, 1880-1964, American five-star General
[2] Alan Clements CBE, b. 1928, Non-executive Director MGN 1991-93, Finance Director ICI 1979-90
[3] Sir Robert Clark, b. 1921, Non-executive Director MGN 1991-92, Chairman 1991
[4] Roger Eastoe, b. 1951, Deputy Managing Director MGN 1990-93
[5] Charlie Wilson, b. 1935, Editor, The Times 1985-90, Editorial Director MGN 1991
[6] Michael Stoney, b. 1949, Director MGN 1991

management buyout of SDR. We had to be extremely careful; very often failed management buyouts result in the losing team being summarily dismissed by the eventual winners. All of us, Kevin McMahon, Derick Henry, Gordon Terris, Jack Anderson and I, were very happy in our current roles and our overriding objective was not to put that in jeopardy. Vic agreed to set up a meeting with Ernie Burrington, now MGN Chairman, for us to make our case and I suppose, not surprisingly, shortly afterwards Ernie wrote to each of us saying that MGN did not consider the disposal of SDR to be in its best interests. That was the end of the matter, or so we thought.

Vic Horwood was now permanently in London. Helen Liddell, used by Maxwell in his last months for all sorts of projects including establishing a Maxwell empire in Bulgaria, remained with Vic in London, straining our resources even further. In some ways, Vic should have appointed a successor in Glasgow but he seemed reluctant to do so. I am convinced that he knew that his days at MGN were numbered, particularly if new management arrived, and coming back to Scotland might have been an option. To the rest of us, it seemed extremely unlikely that would happen and, in the end, we were proved right.

Vic's position was not helped by a separate Ernst and Young report into the MGN flotation. Burrington and Guest resigned just before its publication. The report was particularly critical of the failure of the MGN Board to prevent the ring fencing being breached i.e. to keep Maxwell's private companies at arm's length. It criticised the Independent Directors for failure to have a system to monitor transactions with the Maxwell private companies. The consequence was that funds were moved on the authority only of Directors who also worked for the private companies themselves.

Burrington was succeeded by Sir Robert Clark, one of the same Independent Directors who would eventually be criticised by both E&Y and, subsequently, the DTI. Relations between MGN and SDR, toxic at the best of times, were now at an all-time low. Maxwell's predilection for saying "send for the Jocks" at times merely increased the mutual loathing between the Boards. Vic and Helen being in London at both the end of the Maxwell era and during the period of administration most definitely didn't improve matters. I am not criticising them for this. It was just a fact of life but amongst my SDR colleagues and me there was a considerable degree of apprehension about the future.

It's worth reflecting on the following. The SDR Board survived the Maxwell era largely intact. Derek Webster the Chairman was axed almost immediately and Bernard Vickers replaced as Daily Record Editor soon afterwards. Liam Kane had departed of his own free will shortly after the Maxwell takeover. The rest of us remained in post but after the period of administration, all of us, with the exception of Jack Anderson were gone, victims of what has been described as the vicious post-Maxwell ethnic cleansing of SDR by David Montgomery.

The banks saw MGN as the one of the best assets in the smouldering remains of the Maxwell Empire. Reviving its share price gave them the opportunity to get at least some of their money back. Out of the ashes emerged Hambro's Bank and Lord (Clive) Hollick[7]. Hollick had fancied running MGN himself, but in the end he came in as a Non-executive Director and installed David Montgomery as Chief Executive with Murdoch MacLennon appointed as SDR Managing Director. Vic had voted against Montgomery's appointment and was the first to go. The move was approved by the rump of the old MGN Board, which included Clark and Clements (aptly named the "watchdogs who didn't bark" by Richard Stott), Charlie Wilson and Roger Eastoe, none of whom was exactly friends of SDR, and so the scene was set for - even by Maxwell standards - one of the greatest bloodbaths in the history of Fleet Street, which in turn also engulfed us at SDR.

I have to say that I took an instant dislike to Montgomery the second I met him and I can think of very few other people that I have ever felt this way about. He was, without a doubt, the most humourless man I have ever encountered and from day one he revealed a ruthlessness that matched Maxwell's. Smallish, always immaculately dressed, and with a large pair of spectacles, there was always a hint of menace about him as he set about SDR, effectively blaming us for everything that Maxwell had done. He turned out to be an obsessive control freak with a self-belief in himself that even exceeded that of Maxwell. He knew it all, he had all the answers and was in no mood to tolerate anyone who disagreed. Unfortunately, a number of us at SDR did precisely that.

Montgomery, a right-wing Ulsterman, had started out at the Mirror Training scheme in Plymouth and had worked his way up the MGN editorial ladder before leaving to become Editor of the News of the World. Many of his critics grudgingly admit that he did a good job there, but his ultimate ambition was to run his own newspaper and Murdoch gave him that opportunity when he purchased Today from under Maxwell's nose.

Things didn't work out and Murdoch eventually fired him. Thereafter came an obsession (another Maxwell-like trait?) to prove Murdoch wrong. By the time he became Chief Executive of MGN, his reputation had preceded him and the editorial floor rebelled. It tried to have him removed. Having failed, they demanded assurances about jobs. Montgomery, again in true Maxwell style, promised them everything they wanted, "I have no difficulty or reservations in giving you the assurances for which you ask. The editorial independence of our newspapers will be preserved and vested in the Editors." (Very similar to Maxwell's 'Editorial on Top, Management on Tap'?) "…. with continuing support for the Left of centre and tradition of our titles, I have definitely no plans for job cuts in editorial departments, nor has the Board considered any…. Union recognition will continue… the Editors of all titles will remain in their positions."

Richard Stott, himself sacked less than three weeks later, presents a totally different picture, "He walked like a crab, often with his hands clasped in front of him, and when he spoke he turned his face and spoke to you sideways in his broad, clipped

---

[7] The Rt. Hon. Clive, Baron Hollick of Nottinghill in the Royal Borough of Kensington and Chelsea, b. 1945, Chief Executive, United News and Media 1986-2005

Ulster accent... his spiritual home was with the Red Hand of Ulster, a hard-line Protestant and a natural descendant of Carson." Of his assurances Stott wrote "Nevertheless what he did showed a breathtaking disregard for keeping his word and a merciless savagery unheard of, even by Fleet Street's blood-soaked and hypocritical standards. Within weeks, every one of his assurances had been torn up. Two editors gone, staff - both regular and casual - summarily sacked, Union officials victimised and forced out, and the papers in chaos with circulations plunging."

My first meeting with Montgomery was not a good one. I had put together a detailed briefing on where SDR stood from a sales and marketing viewpoint and the challenges ahead. My almost instant impression was that he would not be a good listener and I was right. Almost immediately he launched into an almost Maxwellian torrent of criticism of SDR – we were underperforming, producing poor quality newspapers, and had demonstrated appalling judgement in not re-equipping years earlier. We apparently were totally out of step with our competitors and were turning away advertising on a daily basis. I found Montgomery singularly unimpressive and he was clearly irritated by my parting shot that his greatest priority should be in securing the investment necessary for us to complete our re-equipping. Little did I realise that we had twin forces operating against us. Montgomery had it firmly in his mind that he would be able to renege on the RBS leases on the five K&B presses and thus get out of this commitment entirely. The second force against us was Richard Stott who, prior to his dismissal, was also urging MGN Chairman, Sir Robert Clark, against <u>any</u> new investment in Scotland. Arguing against a price rise for the Daily Mirror, his note to Clark left no doubt where his priorities were, "The price rise will be seen as an attempt to pay for the refinancing of the company by the banks at interest rates that have already raised many eyebrows in the press. It will also be seen to be using the Daily Mirror to finance the reequipping of the Daily Record at a time when the Daily Mirror needs all its resources to protect itself."

From the onset, it was clear that Montgomery had a completely different view on SDR redevelopment. His plan was to negotiate his way out of the RBS leases and sell off the Anderston Quay site, which would finance the construction of a smaller building on a greenfield site. There was nothing wrong with this concept, indeed I supported it, but he effectively blamed the SDR Board for its appalling lack of vision for not having had the same idea themselves. The RBS leases proved impossible to get out of, as Derick Henry had told Montgomery at their first meeting. As a result, after the dismissal of Helen Liddell, Derick was next and Kevin McMahon departed shortly afterwards.

Montgomery had a solution to solving the colour capacity problem in the short term, whilst installing the new presses, but it was one that we had considered before and rejected. By changing the configuration of the printing presses, it was possible to run 'collect'. In effect, this halved the output of the press but doubled the pagination of each copy. Instead of producing a maximum of 48 pages, with 16 in full colour, it was possible to produce 96 pages, crucially with 32 in full colour. However, the number of copies produced was halved. Even if we started printing earlier and finished later, we could not produce enough copies this way. Furthermore, the print window itself was predetermined by the need to have copies in retailers at specific times in order to meet demand. In many ways this was non-negotiable, as all newspapers had a collective agreement with their wholesalers on delivery times. Montgomery was also ignoring one other major factor, which was that the colour capacity problem only existed on Thursdays and Fridays on about 40 weeks of the year. Gordon Terris had managed the problem extremely effectively and could continue to do so, providing there was an ultimate solution. Again, in his first meeting he told Montgomery this, but he was not for listening. Montgomery announced that SDR would commence printing 'collect' immediately with a modified print schedule and any shortfall in capacity would be made up by also printing the SDR titles at the Mirror plant in Oldham. We were utterly opposed to this, as it meant that around 250,000 copies would be printed up to five hours earlier and would therefore be a vastly inferior product to the present one. Furthermore, to accommodate distribution needs, both plants would need to begin printing some 30 minutes earlier. To claim, as Montgomery did, that readers somehow wouldn't notice the difference, was quite absurd.

We all vehemently opposed this 'solution'. Gordon Terris again maintained that he could hold the line on the colour shortfall in the short term, whilst Endell and I argued that the diminution in the quality of the product by printing earlier would have disastrous consequences, particularly in those areas being serviced by copies from Oldham. In a heated discussion with Montgomery, Endell didn't exactly boost our argument by suddenly stating that we would be unable to print the results from 'The Flapping Tracks'. These were unlicensed greyhound tracks mainly in Fife and Lanarkshire. Montgomery looked aghast at this irrelevance. Unfortunately, Endell had missed the far more important point - we would miss evening football results, parliamentary divisions and any late breaking stories. It was all to no avail. Montgomery accused us of being one dimensional. From that moment, Gordon's, Endell's, and my own days were numbered. Montgomery, like Maxwell before him, did not like any counterargument to his ideas. There was only ever one solution to any problem – his.

Montgomery's plan was implemented and, as predicted, it was a disaster. In January 1994 the SDR Board had a strategy away day and I was able to demonstrate that in those areas provided by the Glasgow presses, sales had declined by 1.2% compared to the previous year, whereas in the areas supplied by Oldham, sales had declined by 5.5%. Who said that the readers wouldn't notice the difference? Montgomery's obstinacy was very much in evidence. If only he could have accepted that the leases for the K&B presses were non-negotiable and had listened to his people on the ground about the folly of 'collect' running, SDR might have been in a better place. But, like Maxwell before him, he simply wouldn't listen. What was even more disappointing was that Vic's successor Murdoch MacLennan and his assistant Kevin Beatty[8] were unwilling to stand up to him.

---

[8] Kevin Beatty, Managing Director, SDR 1994-96; latterly Chief Executive, DMG Media and Director, DMGT

Those last 18 months at Anderson Quay were the unhappiest of my working life. My proudest achievement was that I had increased sales of the Daily Record in each of my first seven years there, getting it to its highest ever sale of 770,000 copies per day in 1990. This had also happened when the overall sales of newspapers in the United Kingdom had started to decline. In the case of the Sunday Mail, I had increased sales in six out of the seven years, achieving an all-time high sale of 907,830 copies in 1990. The deregulation of television listings in 1991 resulted in some bad decision-making in the newspaper industry as a whole and thus lost sales. Montgomery's management at SDR started a much longer-term decline. In hindsight, Montgomery simply couldn't accept that SDR was a well-run company, both during and after the Maxwell era, and he did more to destroy the business than Maxwell had ever done. He also continued to purge the SDR Board.

Gordon Terris and Endell Laird were dismissed in 1994. Endell to his credit, having fought Maxwell over the years, continued to do so with Montgomery, but in that particular battle there was only ever going to be one winner. Montgomery was not for listening and Endell was replaced by Terry Quinn[9]. Gordon Terris departed in September, dismissed by Kevin Beatty.

To his credit, Murdoch MacLennan, having being instrumental in bringing me to SDR in the first place, was to provide me with a parting gift, for which I am eternally grateful. In the summer of 1994, he informed me that he had decided that both Kevin Beatty and I would attend the month-long Advanced Management programme at INSEAD, the leading European business school at Fontainebleau in France. He decided that I should go first and I duly went there from 3rd to 28th October 1994. The month at INSEAD turned out to be one of the best things ever to happen to me and was to make a significant impact on my future career.

---

[9] Terry Quinn, b. 1952, Editor, Daily Record 1994-98

Chapter 21   'NORMAL' LIFE AT SDR

"Always forgive your enemies; nothing annoys them so much."   *Oscar Wilde*

It is important to put into context the pervasive interference of Maxwell, and latterly Montgomery, on SDR's business. It was potentially there all the time. One phone call could lead to weeks of work on some harebrained scheme, yet for those of us managing the business on a day to day basis, life had to go on as normal. During most of my time as Sales and Marketing Director, sales of both titles had increased, often in spite of both Maxwell and Montgomery and other 'colleagues' in London, who could also throw a spanner in the works at any time.

In the case of the Sunday Mail, we had been spectacularly successful in building its sales south of the border, particularly in London with its large ex-pat community. This was an extremely costly exercise, as all supplies to the south of England were flown to Luton, initially on one aeroplane, but as we became more successful we had to rent a second plane in October 1985. Onward distribution to London wholesalers was also extremely expensive, as we were at the mercy of the London Central branch of the trade unions. After Maxwell had successfully taken on the unions, we were able to get out of these arrangements and employ our own distributors, Peter and Mark Treadwell from Thames Distribution. Around this time, new technology meant that the concept of facsimile transmission would eventually enable us to print the Sunday Mail at the Mirror's new plants in Watford and Oldham. Negotiating such an obvious way to reduce our costs significantly should have been an easy exercise, except that I was to encounter Patrick Morrissey[1] for the first time. Morrissey had been recently recruited by Maxwell from Glaxo SmithKlein Beecham and came with a marketing background. He soon brought in a colleague, Ricky Elliot[2]. Morrissey got off to a bad start with the London editors, always referring to the newspapers as 'products'. Very quickly he and Elliot were nicknamed 'The Beecham Pillocks'. Morrissey also got off to a bad start with Vic and a mutual loathing soon developed. This did not make matters any easier for me, as I was trying to sort out printing arrangements for the Sunday Mail (and eventually the Daily Record) at both plants. This finally happened in early 1987 but sadly there was never much of a collegiate approach to it.

After Liam's departure at the end of 1984, Vic had not replaced him as Deputy MD but had grown increasingly reliant on Hugh Currie[3], the Daily Record's Managing Editor. To his credit, Hugh was an excellent wordsmith and of great help to Vic in his various dealings with Maxwell, but to the rest of us he was a viper who could strike at any moment. Currie's well-honed animal cunning was developed during his time as Chief Reporter of the Daily Record. Malcolm Speed[4] recalls an example of

---

[1] Patrick Morrissey, Managing Director, Mirror Group Newspapers
[2] Ricky Elliot, Circulation Director, Mirror Group Newspapers
[3] Hugh Currie, 1923- 2018, former Chief Reporter, Daily Record, SDR, Managing Editor
[4] Malcolm Speed b.1941, SDR 1966-2006, News Editor Daily Record 1983-1994, latterly Managing Editor SDR 1994-2006

this, "The press pack was at a hotel in Mull on a story and the Scottish Daily Express team of that era was cockahoop at having nailed the story at the expense of the others. The pack was all having a drink together afterwards and the cunning Hugh Currie had the hotel clock put forward, convinced one of the Express team that the edition deadline was passed and persuaded the hapless Express man to tell the tale. Currie immediately phoned the Record and caught the edition."

Bernard and Endell were very uncomfortable with Hugh's appointment as 'Consigliere', but there was very little they could do about it. For the rest of us, it became a considerable source of annoyance that, when seeing Vic about something, Hugh would inevitably be in the office. It is fair to say that everyone was very much looking forward to Hugh's retirement in early 1988, with the exception of Vic, whose crutch was about to be removed. Vic organized a lavish farewell for Hugh at Gleddoch House near Langbank on 4th March and his speech reflected on Hugh's great qualities, his long service, his loyalty to the company, and so on. Imagine then Vic's humiliation and embarrassment when, the following Monday morning, Hugh turned up at Kinning Park to take up his new position as Managing Editor of The Scottish Sun. Many wondered how Hugh could have possibly sat through Friday evening's proceedings knowing what he was about to do and the effect that it would have on Vic personally.

In 1987-88, I presided over an extremely successful collaboration between SDR and another Maxwell company, which, most unusually, happened without any involvement from Maxwell himself. In late 1987, I met Martin Heller and George McVicar from the British Magazine Publishing Company (BMPC) which was part of Maxwell Communications Corporation. BMPC produced partwork publications and had developed a series on the history of Scotland. They proposed that it be should be marketed as 'The Sunday Mail Story of Scotland'. As Sunday Mail Editor, Endell was extremely enthusiastic about the concept and I eventually negotiated a deal enabling the Sunday Mail to share the kudos of publishing, over 52 issues, one of the most successful partworks ever produced in Scotland. The first issue was given away free with the Sunday Mail, giving the paper a major sales boost. It was a win/win situation for both parties and, of course, when Maxwell eventually heard about it, he claimed all the credit.

The biggest operational challenge was yet to come. In 1992 plans were announced for the deregulation of TV listings. Until then, the listings were tightly controlled, with two monopolistic publications, Radio Times (BBC) and TV Times (ITV), published weekly as paid-for magazines with full seven-day listings. Newspapers were licensed to publish daily listings for the next 24 hours only, but the marketplace was starting to experience major changes. Rupert Murdoch's Sky Television, founded in 1988 and launched on the Astra Satellite Network in January 1989, required a circular receiving dish for reception. The British Satellite Broadcasting (BSB), founded in 1986, launched in March 1990 with the slogan, 'It's smart to be square' referring to its 'Squarial' receiving dish. In October 1990 an enterprising manufacturer came up with a dual satellite dish which could be used to receive both

Sky and BSB services and, with both companies struggling with huge losses, they completed a 50/50 merger in November 1990, operating as British Sky Broadcasting but marketed as Sky.

This increased capacity inevitably led to the end of the monopoly of the BBC and ITV on the listings market. Deregulation led to the appearance of several new paid-for listings publications but, more significantly, newspapers, in return for a significant increase in the licence fee, were also now allowed to publish full seven-day listings.

This was greeted enthusiastically by the sector. Every publisher now rushed into planning how best to deal with seven-day listings. Rival daily and Sunday publications argued fiercely as to how each could provide the best service, determined to compete as ferociously against their own stablemates as against their competitors. Most publications planned stand-alone listings magazines, all at enormous cost.

All in all, it led to some of the worst decision making ever made in the sector and some would say it precipitated a significant sales downturn which, although already in existence for several years, now rapidly accelerated.

There were several individual changes across the sector, some with disastrous consequences:

Most Sunday publications, already offering more than one section, now added a separate TV Guide.

A multi-section Saturday publication now became the norm, again with a separate TV Guide.

One of the bedrocks of daily newspapers was regular six-day-a-week readership. Until then, for a fraction of the combined cost of both Radio Times and TV Times, a reader could find out what was on television and radio that day for the price of their daily newspaper. Now a weekly TV guide meant that all they had to do was buy the paper once a week for this same information.

The final consequence was that, in an effort to defer the costs of all this, some titles started differential pricing, with a different cover price on Saturdays than for the Monday-Friday issues

At SDR the same scenarios played out. Both editors were extremely enthusiastic about the potential, but each wanted a separate listing magazine for his publication. Hence the company would have to pay twice to achieve this, in addition to the significant hike in the licensing fee. The consequences for SDR were also the same as for everyone else. It was a disastrous decision. The Daily Record, having increased in sales in each of my first seven years there, peaked and started to decline. The very solid platform of regular six-day-a-week readership disintegrated and we never managed to pick up the pieces again. I do not seek to distance myself from the collective decision making, although I was opposed to the Sunday Mail having a separate listings magazine. From a business point of view, it made no sense and my preference would have been to enhance the existing offering in a different way. However, I regard myself as equally guilty in not having thought through the consequences of our plans, although in some ways the actions of our competitors forced our hand anyway, as we had no option but to follow everyone else.

The other issue I had to deal with was the pending retirement of my deputy Tommy Mansbridge. Tommy had been an extremely loyal employee, adequate in what he did but, as Liam had identified long before I arrived, he was never going to be the head of the department, mainly because he never wanted to take responsibility for making decisions. An example was when he once phoned me in my hotel room in Dallas at 5am during an international conference to impart an important piece of market information. From previous experience, I knew the purpose of the call. Once he had informed me, the responsibility for the consequences of it was mine and not his. He had passed the buck up the line and could now rest easy.

There was no obvious internal successor to Tommy, so for several months I did an extensive search to seek out potential candidates and eventually settled on Kevin Beatty, who had originally started his career at the Belfast Telegraph after I left and was now Field Sales Supervisor at the Evening Gazette, Teesside. Kevin joined SDR in September 1990. He was an excellent choice and quickly got to grips with running the department far more effectively than Tommy had ever done. In some ways I had recruited someone with too much ability, because no sooner had Murdoch MacLennan joined in 1993, than he made Kevin his Executive Assistant and I was back to square one.

In 1993 I reviewed all aspects of SDR's advertising. There was a feeling that "Your Papers Made in Scotland" was becoming increasingly dated. To provide some fresh thinking I briefed four of Scotland's leading advertising agencies to present some ideas. By far the best came from The Leith Agency run by John Denholm.[5] For the Daily Record they proposed to make brand television commercials which would also be used for breaking news stories and promotions. "A brand sandwich with hard news or content as the filling," as Gerry Farrell[6] described it. The concept was blindingly simple, using visual metaphors of everything that tabloid newspapers do - letting the cat out of the bag, opening a can of worms, keeping your eyes peeled,

---

[5] John Denholm, b. 1950, Managing Director, The Leith Agency 1984-90; Chairman 1990-2006
[6] Gerry Farrell b. 1957, Creative Director, The Leith Agency 1987-2014, Founder and Creative Director, Gerry Farrell INK 2014

spilling the beans, skeletons in the cupboard and so on. They then filmed these in close up. For example, the 'eyes peeled' idea involved two oranges unpeeling to reveal a pair of eyeballs. The campaign was launched with a massive television blitz backed by 48 sheet posters. The 'eyes peeled' was also used as a car sticker "Daily Record: Keep your eyes peeled" and within a short time it seemed every second vehicle in Scotland had this sticker on its back window.

The Sunday Mail campaign was equally dramatic. The concept involved wrapping objects that the paper was known for. The standout idea was an AK-47 Kalasashnikov rifle representing Scottish crime stories. Pages of the Sunday Mail were wrapped around the rifle, the 'parcel' was suspended in mid-air and the gun would fire, ripping apart the parcel to reveal the commercial's strapline.

The presentation was made to the full SDR Board in September 1983. Montgomery was in town that day and attended the presentation. Unknown to us the agency had purchased a replica AK-47 which fired blanks. As Gerry Farrell was introducing the campaign, he took the 'parcel', unwrapped the rifle and fired it. Montgomery was particularly tickled by this and asked for the gun. He pointed it around the Boardroom, taking careful aim at a number of us including Endell, Gordon and myself. He gave us all a sinister stare and said to Farrell, "I could be firing some of these people shortly. Did you bring any bullets?" Since Montgomery was not known for his sense of humor these was a ripple of nervous laughter around the Boardroom.

Murdoch MacLennan and Kevin Beatty got on so well together that when Murdoch left SDR, Kevin followed him to Associated Newspapers in early 1995 and he ultimately became Managing Director there after Murdoch moved to the Telegraph Group in 2004. I was proud to have unearthed and developed Kevin, but he did not impress me during my last 18 months at SDR when, under the Montgomery administration he and Murdoch did not demonstrate much independent leadership or thinking and became the henchmen for some of Montgomery's stranger decisions. It is important to record that these were anxious times for everyone at SDR. Maxwell's plundering of the pension fund had a devasting effect on staff morale. All the employees' entire futures were at risk and the SDR Board, not unreasonably, was asked how it had allowed this to happen. Kevin McMahon's last months revolved around a never-ending series of Chapel meetings with extremely disgruntled employees.

I became part of a regime that I gradually began to despise. Typical was the end of a meeting where a business associate said, "Of course Colin I'll see you this evening at the launch of SDR's sponsorship of…" The look on my face clearly indicated I was unaware of the event and hadn't been invited, leading to acute embarrassment for both of us. This type of behavior was indicative of a lack of common courtesy and decency on the part of those above me. It was a depressing period. Claire remembers me arriving home on more than one occasion looking ashen and down-hearted. On meeting me during this period Bronwyn McMahon reported to Kevin that I seemed far removed from my normal buoyant self.

Thankfully life has moved on from those depressing days. It was somewhat ironic that it was Kevin Beatty who sacked me and as I shall describe later, it was with some pleasure that I got my own back during my time at NI, when I know that Kevin was frequently extremely irritated by our antics and, most importantly, by our success.

Chapter 22   SDR - THE FINAL CHAPTER 1994

"Whatever you can do, or dream that you can do, begin it. Boldness had genius power and magic to it." James Anster[1]

I returned to the Daily Record from my four-week spell at INSEAD on Monday 31st October 1994 and was promptly sacked. For the company it was an extremely poor rate of return of an investment of £20k but a fantastic outcome for me.

That morning at a 9.30am meeting Kevin Beatty trotted out a well-rehearsed speech about the need for change and exciting new plans for the future, but unfortunately, I was not going to be part of that change. The company felt that my capabilities did not match those needed for the future and that someone younger would be appointed. At 45, I was clearly too old for this job and discrimination on the grounds of age was being healthily embraced at Anderston Quay. Naturally the real reasons for terminating my employment were never mentioned. Montgomery was continuing to purge the MGN ranks of all those associated with Maxwell. I was the eighth Board member to depart. The entire meeting took less than 15 minutes and I returned to the building the next day to collect my personal effects to discover that the locks in my office had been changed shortly after I left and my PA Janis had also been dismissed. A Stalinist culture was alive and well.

To their credit, the company honoured my contract to the letter of the law. After negotiation on some minor points the severance package was sorted out relatively quickly. I signed the normal confidentiality agreement and a sizeable sum of money was deposited in my bank account within three weeks. That chapter of my life was now closed.

My 10 years at SDR were mostly positive and rewarding. I was part of team which built an incredibly successful business. We had navigated our way through the Maxwell era, a successful flotation, Maxwell's death, the appointment of an administrator and, finally, Montgomery. On a personal basis, I had helped see off the first assault from the Scottish Sun and the News of the World, destroyed the Sunday Scot in 18 weeks and built the circulations of both our titles to record levels. I had also overseen the creation of a free newspaper division in which I had successfully established a low cost financial and production model different to that of the parent company. My personal development had also continued, culminating in my outstanding experience at INSEAD, thus I was well equipped to deal with the challenges that lay ahead. As David Brinkley[2] said, "a successful man is one who can lay a firm foundation with the bricks others have thrown at him."

---

[1] James Anster 1793-1867, Irish poet. This quote was originally attributed to the German writer Johann Wolfgang von Goethe 1749-1832 but is actually from a translation of part of his work by Anster in 1835
[2] David Brinkley 1920-2003, American newscaster for NBC and ABC 1943-97

Some people told me that I had stayed with the company two years longer than I should have. Hindsight is a wonderful thing. I had seen the way things were going, with the inevitable purge of those associated with the Maxwell era and old scores being settled from London. Those last two years were difficult, constantly fighting battles that I knew I was going to lose, but that didn't stop me sticking to my principles. Furthermore, my dismissal gave me the financial security to pick and choose what I wanted to do without having the pressure of having to take the first job offer that came along.

After calling home, I returned to Kilmacolm to give Claire a full account of events. At 45 I was unemployed for the first time in my life, with a hefty mortgage and two children at an independent school. The reality was that I would have short-term financial security and I had, thanks to INSEAD, total confidence in my own ability. Quite what the future was going to hold, I was not so sure of.

Three major things happened over the following months, each of which was to change me and shape the rest of my life. The first was the fantastic support of most of my friends. I classified my experience of people in those first six months after I left into three categories. The first was those who went out of their way to extend friendship and offer help, some tangible, some intangible. I particularly single out Geoffrey Holliman[3] and Steve Sampson, who in totally different ways helped me shape what I was going to do in the short and medium term. The second group were the "neutrals" – people I had known who after my departure continued our relationship, unaffected by recent events. The third category needless to say I had not bargained for were those who simply walked away never to be seen again. It was as if I was no longer of any use to them, no longer "one of us". Happily, there were very few in this category but I had thought some to be close friends upon whom I could depend in a time of crisis. They know who they are!

The second thing that happened was that, thanks to the many people who helped me, I was able to put together an action plan of how to move forward, with guidelines based on others' experience of the same situation. In later years I would use these principles to help and advise other people who found themselves in a similar situation. The six main principles were:

1. Never look back. Every minute spent looking back is one minute less spent planning the rest of your life. There is no point spending time analysing what happened, what could have been avoided, or what you might have done differently. On the day I walked out of the Anderston Quay building for the final time I regarded it as the end of one period of my life and I now had to plan the next stage. As Tom Stoppard[4] wrote, "look on every exit as being an entrance somewhere else."

---

[3] Geoffrey Holliman, b.1945, Sales and Marketing Director, Radio Clyde 1984-98
[4] Sir Tom Stoppard OM, CBE, FRSL, b. 1937, British playwright and screenwriter. Quote from 'Rosencrantz and Guildenstern are Dead'

2. Don't hang about. One ex-colleague said to me after being fired, "I'm going to take six months out, take stock and then look for another job". Wrong move! You're at your most marketable right now. The longer you stay out of the public gaze, the sooner you are forgotten and become yesterday's person. Out of sight is out of mind. My advice therefore is not to waste a moment before moving into the next phase.

3. Maintain as high a public profile as possible. I made sure that in those first few months I attended as many events as possible. Barry Norman[5] brilliantly dealt with the same subject in his autobiography. After an initial period of depression on being made redundant by the Daily Mail in 1971, he came up with a plan. He purchased a couple of good suits, shirts and ties, polished his shoes and hung out with Fleet Street's movers and shakers at El Vino's. He went there twice a week, arrived early, selected a prominent table, ordered a bottle of champagne and started The Times crossword. When people asked him how he was doing he would say he was busy and over a period of time he gradually picked up quite a lot of freelance work, which put him back on his feet. He never looked back from there.

4. Be positive. Losing your job is not a pleasant experience and it can have a devastating effect on self-confidence. I was lucky. I had just returned from probably the most intellectually stimulating experience of my life and I was brimming with confidence. My wife and family were wonderfully supportive and I received a huge amount of sound advice from many friends. That is not to say there were not some dark moments in the ensuing weeks, when that confidence was severely tested, but in general I was more than motivated to hit the ground running.

5. Plan for the future. Redundancy is one of the few occasions in your life when you can start with a blank sheet of paper and write down what you'd like to do. I call this constructing your own personal balance sheet and I have recommended this approach to many people over the years. On one side of paper list all the positive things you would like in a job. The list is endless - or should be if you're thinking properly about it. On the other side, list all the things that would prevent you from taking a job. This list probably won't be as long but will include things that you are not prepared to do. The whole purpose of the exercise is to think outside the box, think the unthinkable and consider every aspect of a career. It's also a very useful tool for those considering a career change. It helps to underline skills shortages and development needs and is also a positive influence at a time of great stress and possible low self-esteem. It should produce a series of propositions,

---

[5] Barry Norman 1933-2017, 'And Why Not?' 2002, Simon & Schuster UK Ltd.

indicators about who you are or would like to be and the environment in which you would like to operate. The litmus test is "Does it work?" and the general feedback I have is that it does. No particular job will have all the positives and none of the negatives, but the balance sheet approach will give an overall positive/negative scoring ratio. In my own particular case, for example, it helped me turn down a job offer with too few positives and too many negatives.

6. Network. Don't wait for the world to beat a path to your door. In other words, don't wait for employers to come rushing to you to secure your services – it rarely happens. You must chase jobs or, equally importantly, ensure that as many potential employers as possible are aware of your availability in whatever sector you want to be in.

In the last 25 years I have seen many other people go through the same experience as I did. I have tried to help them with advice and contacts for them to talk to and many emerged successfully from the experience. Irving Berlin[6] once said, "life is 10% what you make it and 90% how you take it." I have equally seen the effects losing one's job can have on family life and the feelings of depression, despair and worthlessness that it can cause.

The third thing that happened to me was that I became a consummate networker. When most people are made redundant, they look for a new job as quickly as possible. In my own case, one option would have been to scan the recruitment sections of the various newspapers, dust down my CV, and start making as many job applications as possible. At the time, I felt this was a rather scattergun approach and I decided to get out and about and have a cup of coffee with as many of my existing network as quickly as possible. Thankfully I have met very few people who refuse to have a coffee on request and I have never refused anyone who asked me.

How that 10-15 minutes opportunity over coffee is used is equally important. In my own case, I would discuss my circumstances, what I was hoping to do, what my skill set was, and what type of role I was interested in. I hoped to emerge from the meeting with two or three further people to contact and ideally a personal introduction to them. I should emphasise that this exercise will very rarely produce instant results and it can sometimes take three to six months to find the right position. Many people simply don't have the patience and grab the first opportunity that comes along. The chances of that position being the perfect one are low.

In summary, this process is called 'putting yourself about in the marketplace'. As the saying goes, there are many different ways of skinning a cat. Barry Norman did it by lunching twice a week at a prominent table at El Vino's. I did it with a huge intake of caffeine over a six-week period, learning a lot as I went along, and with a high level

---

[6] Irving Berlin 1888-1989, American composer and lyricist

of self-confidence that was to be seriously tested a few times along the way. With some irony, I ended up going down a totally different path to the one on which I had set out. So much for taking my own advice!

The first McClatchie pyramid California, 1990.
Top row: Sharon.
Second row: Adeline, Claire,
Third row: Ted, Iain, CMcC,
Bottom row: Amanda, Milena

Amanda 1990   Milena 1990

CHAPTER 23   INSEAD OCTOBER 1994

"Successful workers will be those who embrace a lifetime of learning. Those who don't will be left behind." **Rupert Murdoch**

I devote this short chapter to my time at INSEAD because, coming as it did immediately prior to my departure from SDR, it was one of the most significant experiences of my life. I had arrived there after two very unhappy years of the Montgomery era, during which I felt many of my values, beliefs and even my management style were being constantly questioned and often criticised. However, I arrived at INSEAD determined to make the most of the opportunity. As Gandhi[1] said, "live as if you were to die tomorrow. Learn as if you were to live forever."

INSEAD, the European Institute of Business Administration, is a graduate European business school based in Fontainebleau, south of Paris. Its name is originally derived from an acronym for the French 'Institut Européen d'Administration des Affaires'. In 2017 the Financial Times ranked it first in global MBA schools.

I participated in the Advanced Management Programme in October 1994. The four-week programme - based over 23 days - included modules in Marketing, Organisational Behaviour, Strategic Cost Management, Operations Management, Strategic Management, Global Assessment (Politics), Finance, and Global Assessment (Economics). In my programme there were 100 participants, divided into two groups. They came from 36 different countries, 64 from Europe (including 20 from the UK), 13 from the Americas, 13 from Asia and Africa, seven from the Middle East and three from Australia and New Zealand. Unsurprisingly, for an event taking place some 25 years ago, the male/female ratio was 95/5. The programme's eight modules were delivered by academics from the UK (2), USA (3), France (1), South Korea (1) and Belgium (1). All the sessions were in English.

Intellectually it was an incredibly stimulating experience. In my application form I listed the reasons I wished to attend; 'To further develop business skills', 'To enable me to make a smooth transition to Senior General Management' and 'for further career development'. I had also written, 'To consider my present and future roles', clearly reflecting the state of mind that I was currently in.

I quickly discovered that I was one of the most junior participants. In the group were five Presidents, five Senior Vice-Presidents, three Vice-Presidents, six Managing Directors, 12 General Managers, and two Senior Civil Servants from the Hong Kong and Malaysian Governments.

We started each morning at 8am with a very short break for lunch and finished around 6.30pm. There was further evening study with follow up reading and case-studies. The only leisure time available was for an evening meal. During the plenary

---

[1] Mahatma Gandhi 1869-1948, activist and leader of the Indian Independence Movement against British Colonial Rule

sessions I was in a group of 50, but in the various break-out sessions and discussions we were split into groups of between six and eight. In this way I got to know particularly well a group of around 15 people and it was from this group that our 'dining club' emerged. Fontainebleau, in typical French style, had a huge number of restaurants so we never ate in the same restaurant twice. We sampled some fabulous French cuisine, but two particular evenings stand out. Rodegang Erlenbruch[2] took us to an Alsace restaurant where he guided us through a first-class dining experience. Alan Lai-Nin[3] organised an evening at a Chinese restaurant, where, in advance, he had specifically ordered three different types of duck. We had five separate courses as we worked our way through the birds, all closely supervised by Alan. One Sunday six of us organised a round of golf at a nearby club and, almost as an afterthought, decided to lunch there as well. We experienced a superb Michelin star quality lunch. I can't think of many UK golf clubs which could emulate that.

Also in the course was a Health Management module, run by an American doctor Michael McGann and his French wife Juliette. In the first week I had a full medical examination, the results of which were discussed with Doctor McGann at a private session. He was a specialist in preventative medicine. From my results, McCann's hypothesis was that at 45, I had a 'health-age' of 49, "Your lifestyle has a major influence on your health status. In whatever way you are living your life, you are doing so in a style that is more physiologically aged than your actual age." My potential health age was 36.8 years. This is how young one's body could be if you were to gradually improve your lifestyle habits, thereby protecting your most important core assets, your health and fitness. It was an extremely useful exercise and I returned to Scotland determined to improve my lifestyle. The McGanns also conducted group sessions on relaxation and exercise techniques. One relaxation technique was how to catnap and where possible, throughout my subsequent NI years, I would have a 10-15 minute catnap in the middle of the day. It proved invaluable for general concentration levels.

The entire INSEAD experience was extremely challenging. The programme included self-analysis and analysis by a peer group. By the end of the four weeks my self-confidence was completely restored. What I learned from the whole experience was that my self-belief, moral code and values were shared by a great number of fellow delegates. More importantly, despite being dismissed by SDR upon my return, I was able to take so much of what I had learned and apply it during my period as a Marketing Consultant. Equally importantly, the whole experience prepared me perfectly for my first experience in general management with News International.

---

[2] Rodegang Erlenbruch, Senior Vice-President, Deutsche Bank
[3] Alan Lai-Nin, Senior Civil Servant, Government of Hong Kong

Chapter 24   MARKETING CONSULTANT 1994 - 95

"Failure is simply the opportunity to begin again, this time more intelligently."
Henry Ford

Two days after leaving the Daily Record I was offered a new job. Although I had yet to draw up my personal balance sheet, there were enough pointers to tell me this was not the right position for me and I turned it down. When I arrived home and told Claire, I could see a look of apprehension on her face. She made the perfectly reasonable point that surely it would be better to be in a job when looking around, rather than being "unemployed", a reasonable response as there was still a stigma to this status.

As time progressed, I realised that it could take some time to find the "right" job. This opinion was reinforced by a number of people whose judgement I trusted. I did worry how Claire might react if I kept turning down offers, although my severance package gave us the financial security to ride out the storm.

Other events that November included buying a car and in this area Glen Gall[1] of Arnold Clark was very helpful. Interestingly there is a lesson to be learnt here – the first purchase of a vehicle, if handled properly, can lead to a lot of future business. We went on to buy several more cars from Arnold Clark solely on the basis of our relationship with Glen. When Glen retired, the relationship with Arnold Clark faded and Joe O'Donnell[2] of Shields took over. That relationship also continued for several years.

The other major event that occurred within the McClatchie household was that we decided to get a dog. Amanda and Milena were now ten and eight and the time seemed right, so we set off (minus the children) to see a litter of black Labrador pups in Ralston. We purchased a delightful little puppy, Newmilns Jade (her official kennel club name), whom we renamed Purdey and who was to be picked up on Christmas Day. Claire's mum Olive and I set off for Ralston that Christmas morning at 7am and returned just after 9am. When we arrived back with the dog, I hid in the kitchen until the girls came down and amidst joyous scenes met Purdey for the first time. Purdey turned out to be a most lovable and good-natured dog and gave us all fantastic pleasure and fun for over 13 years.

In December I started on the networking circuit. Three meetings were to change the direction of my life in the short term. The first was with Steve Sampson, Managing Director of First Press Publishing, who had been a friend ever since we worked together at the Daily Record. A larger than life character, Steve had gone on to become Editor of the Scottish Sun, then Editor of the short-lived Sunday Scot and

---

[1] Glen Gall, b. 1935, Former Managing Director, Arnold Clark, retired 1999
[2] Joe O'Donnell, b. 1955, Founder, Shields Automotive 1994

had now set up his own publishing company. One of Steve's major clients was The Herald, for whom he produced and formatted the Property section. Steve and I met on 19th December and, in addition to providing me with some very good advice and making some useful introductions for me, he asked if I would be available to handle a short-term assignment for one of his clients. This turned out to be the Glasgow Association of Estate Agents who had been reviewing the property market. The Herald was then the dominant advertising platform for property and, although the estate agents were reasonably satisfied with their relationship with The Herald, not everyone was happy with it. Their main competitor was the Glasgow Solicitors' Property Guide which was steadily increasing its market share. The estate agents decided to have a thorough review of the market and wanted an external perspective. The terms of reference included a detailed analysis of the marketplace and the current marketing structure and a report that would make recommendations for future action. In short, they were after a marketing plan and Steve asked me if I would undertake this exercise.

The very next day I attended the Edinburgh Publicity Club's Christmas lunch and met for the first time Tom Hunter[3], who was the first Managing Director of Scot FM, an Edinburgh-based commercial radio station, which had launched a few months previously. Tom was concerned that advertising revenues were below plan and was beginning to question the sales and marketing strategy. He wanted to test the perception of the company amongst a cross section of the advertising community, in particular the main advertising agencies. Tom asked me to come and see him in early January to talk about it.

At the same function I also met Charlie Birrell[4], General Manager of Scottish and Universal Newspapers, based in Irvine. He was responsible for a range of titles, most of them in Ayrshire. He was looking for some strategic marketing advice and knew that I was between jobs. He also asked if I would come and talk to him in early January.

By mid-January I had secured all three projects, started work for the estate agents and the Scottish and Universal (a total of 15 days work) and Tom Hunter wanted the Scot FM project (10 days work) completed by early February.

I had to make some very quick decisions. I met Colville Johnston[5], the Chairman of the Glasgow Association of Estate Agents. Colville scoped out the details of the project. I was to write the marketing plan but work closely on the financial details with Alan Malcolm[6]. We agreed that my part of the work would take 10 days, whereupon Colville asked me my daily rate. I have to confess that this was an area in which I had nil experience so I thought of a figure, doubled it and announced my rate (excluding VAT). When Colville didn't blink an eyelid, I realised I had probably pitched the rate too low, but at least I was up and running.

[3] Tom Hunter, Managing Director, Scot FM, launched 1994; Chairman, National Broadcasting School
[4] Charlie Birrell b. 1960, Commercial Director, Scottish and Universal Newspapers 1994-2000
[5] Colville Johnston, Managing Director Slater Hogg and Howison
[6] Alan Malcolm, Partner, KPMG 1994-97

On the subject of pricing, it also reminded me of our window cleaner in Kilmacolm. He announced one day that he was increasing his prices and I quickly worked out that this represented a 25% increase. When I asked him about the rationale behind such a whopping increase, he simply answered, "It's £1 for the small hooses, and £5 for the big ones." Not a bad reply! On the same subject is the story of an Englishman in Utah who was called to fix a broken pump. He simply gave said pump an enormous whack with his sledgehammer and it jolted into action. He subsequently sent an invoice for $100 for his services, a large amount at the time (the 1930s) and unsurprisingly was asked for an itemised bill. The mechanic wrote, "For hitting the pump with hammer – 50 cents. For knowing where to hit it - $99.50."

For me the decision to set up on my own as a consultant therefore evolved rather than being a conscious decision. I had secured three contracts but quickly learnt that the number of days agreed is never an exact science. These three projects took until early March to complete, but the upside was that I had earned substantially more than I would have done had I been still working for the Daily Record.

As a result, the career of Colin J S McClatchie, Marketing Consultant was born. I didn't rule out going back to full time employment but for now there seemed potential in working for myself. As well as working flat out on the three projects, I had to create the infrastructure for setting myself up as a "sole trader". I acquired a financial advisor, Alan Brown[7] (like myself, just setting up with Karen Muir as Muir Brown). I also found an accountant, Sandra Mackie[8]. Sandra still keeps me on the straight and narrow. She was also extremely helpful in briefing Claire on getting the new business up and running. Claire in quick succession became a secretary, bookkeeper, office manager, receptionist and everything else required in running a small enterprise and she performed it all admirably. It was not easy, particularly working for me, but she was a rock throughout this period.

One particular challenge was registering for VAT quickly – a slight contradiction in terms. I already had the clients but couldn't invoice them until I had a VAT number. To short-circuit matters, Claire and I visited the local VAT establishment, then based in the magnificent Custom House in Greenock. No amount of cajoling could get us through the wall of bureaucracy that was HMRC and we emerged with nothing more than a vague promise to try and shorten the six-week registration period.

In early March, having been working flat out for seven weeks and having completed and presented the initial reports for both GAEA and Scot FM, the inevitable happened: there were no more assignments in the pipeline. In devoting all my time to these projects, I had not been prospecting for any further business. I learnt the hard way that in a start-up consultancy business time has to be divided between working on the existing project and on future development. There and then I decided that, for the rest of my time as a consultant, I would allocate a minimum of one and a half days a week to investigate further work.

---

[7] Alan Brown and Karen Muir, Partners, Muir Brown Plc. est. 1997
[8] Sandra Mackie, b. 1954, Partner, Parkhill Mackie est. 1989

Following my work with Scot FM, Tom Hunter proposed that I should have a short, weekly radio programme commenting on current media events. The format could include guests and over the following six months I interviewed many senior figures from the Scottish media sector. I also contributed occasional articles to The Drum, the media magazine run by Nina Young[9] and her family, and periodically did a newspaper review on Sunday mornings on Real Radio.

By now I was beginning to enjoy the relative freedom of working for myself, with all the associated advantages – to work at whatever pace was required, answerable only to myself and only working on assignments where I liked the people involved. Financially so far it was also rewarding and in the coming months would be even more so. There were of course downsides – financial uncertainty; no regular long-term income or benefits, such as pension contributions, holidays and a company car, but by in large I was very happy with my lot. I was also starting to look ahead to year two. I had decided I would continue to be a one-man operation with no aspirations to develop a company.

After the initial hiatus of too much work preventing sales development, matters settled down with a fixed pattern of work regularly interspersed with prospecting for new work and making new contacts. I subsequently built up a range of clients in a variety of sectors. Claire often asked how I could make a contribution to businesses I knew nothing about or had no experience in. The answer to this was that product knowledge is relatively easy to acquire. The skills that I had were transformational ones – how to take an existing business and make it better or how to create a new one by the application of sound business principles, coupled with the marketing skills to make them work. The time I spent as a marketing consultant in 1995 helped cement some principles that have stayed with me ever since. My time at INSEAD was also a huge help. Lack of marketing skills and knowledge is a significant impediment to the success of many, many companies. Marketing is about assessing opportunity and grasping it.

Six months after starting, I acquired my first customer outside Scotland and did a project in Birmingham with a motoring publication, Micromart, run by Sarah Wilde-McKeown[10]. I also had initial discussions in London with three potential clients and was actively developing proposals for them. As I approached the final quarter, I did so with optimism, particularly because I had not yet had to touch any of my severance settlement from the Daily Record.

And then News International came calling and life changed yet again. My nine months as a marketing consultant following on from my sacking from the Daily Record were some of the happiest of my life. At the onset, someone had said to me that everyone should experience being made redundant at least once in their life, that it was good for the soul and a great learning experience. Someone else pointed

---

[9] Nina Young, journalist and publisher
[10] Sarah Wilde-McKeown, Trinity Mirror Group 1993-2013, latterly as Commercial Director

out that being sacked was a fantastic opportunity to make some serious money, especially since the first £30,000 of any settlement is tax free.

What did I learn from the experience? Firstly, a lot about myself. In some ways my redundancy couldn't have come at a better time. I had returned from INSEAD with my confidence sky high and had spent a lot of time there thinking about the future. Redundancy gave me the opportunity to adjust the compass and set myself on a different course. By and large I think I coped with the trauma of redundancy pretty well. There were some low periods but I emerged from the experience stronger. Secondly, working for myself from home was a new experience for both Claire and me. As well as acquiring a whole new range of skills, we had to adjust to being together much more than previously. Claire would say that for her it was a horrendous experience, with my impatience and intolerance regularly demonstrated. She often wondered how on earth Janis had put up with me. My response was to explain that Janis possessed the great quality of patience and was also psychic! Thirdly, working for yourself imposes a level of self-discipline seldom experienced in corporate life and the fact that you are required to do everything for yourself is certainly a new experience. However, the downside is that self-employment can be very lonely and is in stark contrast to being part of a large organisation. Another reality of self-employment is having to provide everything yourself - a fact that escapes many of those in full-time employment who often take for granted the many things their employer provides for them.

The final benefit was being removed from what I call the silo effect of fulltime employment. In many ways employees are cogs in the wheel of the company. Cogs are dependent on each other, but in most cases have only one function. Being self-employed removed all these restrictions and provided a freedom that I had never experienced before. I emerged much stronger, with new experience that was to serve me well in the next phase of my career. I also learned that I had not networked sufficiently up until then and I was determined never to let that happen again.

Finally, I was extremely lucky that my period as a marketing consultant was financially rewarding. Several months after joining News International, we moved home within Kilmacolm and I was able to erect a small plaque in one part of the house that said, "You're now entering the Daily Record wing" in recognition that the company's severance package solely financed that part of the house.

Hugh Currie Farewell Dinner 1988 - just before he joined The Sun !

l-r: CMcC, Vic Horwood, Bernard Vickers, Hugh Currie, Endell Laird, Derick Henry, Kevin McMahaon, and Gordon Terris.

Note how happy Bernard and Endell look !

Daily Record International Show Jumping Masters, 1984

Back row l-r: Protection officer, June Laird, Endell Laird
Front row l-r : Raymond Blin PKF, HRH The Princess Royal,
CMcC and Claire

Rex Stewart Golf Day 1987, l-r Norman Lawson (MD Rex Stewart),
Glen Gall (MD Arnold Clark), CMcC and John Greig (Rangers FC)

Golf swing c. 1990 - not improved much since then!

The SDR Board, 1990.
Back row l-r: Kevin McMahon, Gordon Terris, Helen Liddell,
Jack Anderson, CMcC, Derick Henry, Endell Laird
Seated: Sir Alywn Williams, Vic Horwood

Reception, Palace of Holyroodhouse, Edinburgh 1998
l-r: Elsa McIlonan, CMcC, Claire, HRH The Prince of Wales and Murdoch McLennan

Childline Reception, Downing Street 1990, l-r Norma Major, Esther Rantzen,
John Major and CMcC

Claire's family at Neil and Anne's Wedding 1992.
Back row l-r: CMcC, Claire, niece Sarah, sister Joan, brother Neil and Anne.
Front row l-r: Milena, parents Olive and Stewart, and Amanda.

Guest Speakers, Press Fund Lunch 1999

Richard Littlejohn and Elaine C. Smith

Buckingham Palace Garden Party 1998

Chapter 25   HEADHUNTED 1995

"Coming together is a beginning, staying together is progression and working together is success." Henry Ford

I spent ten years focussed on limiting the development of The Sun and the News of the World in Scotland. It had been at times a battle of savage intensity and I had no doubt that I had emerged on the winning side.

On a personal level NI and I had circled each other on three separate occasions to discuss the possibility of my joining them. The first abortive move by Tudor Hopkins is described in Chapter 17. The second was initiated by me in 1995 as a result of meeting Liam Kane while I was a Marketing Consultant. Liam had given me some excellent advice and also offered to set up a meeting with Gus Fischer[1], then NI's Chief Executive. This took place in London in mid-February 1995. I had provided my CV in advance, but turned up not knowing what to expect. I found Fischer cold and totally lacking in empathy. The meeting had no obvious structure or conclusion and I emerged somewhat baffled and wondering why it had taken place. However, I was invited to go immediately afterwards to meet with Chris Maybury[2], then Commercial Director with responsibility for Circulation and Marketing. Months later I was to work with Maybury when he was General Manager of Times Newspapers, but even from that first meeting, I simply didn't warm to him. As I left Wapping that afternoon, I felt slightly depressed that what should have been a golden opportunity for me to impress and possibly land a job had come to absolutely nothing. I put the thought of News International out of my mind and went back to building my consultancy business.

As it turned out, Fischer departed in the middle of March. At the same time John Dux[3], Managing Director, was also fired. Fischer was eventually replaced by Les Hinton and John Dux was replaced by his deputy Doug Flynn[4].

In late summer, I took a phone call from Ian McDonald[5]. Ian and I vaguely knew each other and had met several times at functions. He was interested to know what I was up to and we had a fairly lengthy conversation about life in general and that was that, or so I thought. Within days Ian rang, suggesting that I meet Doug Flynn in Glasgow. The result was that I turned up at 1 Devonshire Gardens on the evening of 15th September 1994 for a meeting that was to shape my life for the next 13 years. I warmed to Doug immediately. He had a twinkle in his eye, was most engaging and we had a lengthy discussion.

Initially it centred around what I had been doing and moved on to what I thought about the current NI operation in Scotland. Doug stressed that he wanted to hear an

---

[1] Gus Fischer, b. 1939, Chief Executive, News International 1992-95
[2] Chris Maybury, b. 1960, Commercial Director, Sales and Marketing, News International
[3] John Dux, b. 1952, Managing Director, News International 1990-95
[4] Doug Flynn, b. 1949, Managing Director, News International 1995-1999; latterly CEO, Aegis and Rentokil plcs.
[5] Ian McDonald, b. 1940, Operations Director, News International 1993-2010

honest, no holds barred appraisal on my part so I opened by saying, "NI in Scotland feels like a company that has its finger up its backside." I explained that, when I had been at SDR, I had devised a very clear strategy for dealing with The Scottish Sun. The Daily Record was the clear market leader, and, as such, the rules of engagement meant that it should never acknowledge The Scottish Sun or even mention it in any of its newspapers. I remember one particular incident during Endell's editorship when this policy was severely put to the test. During the Glasgow Fair, The Scottish Sun had run a story about the donkeys on the beach in Blackpool and as part of the story they had named one donkey Endell. Endell was incensed by this and threatened all sorts of revenge and we had to prevail upon him not to publish anything in retaliation.

The strategy for a Number Two in the market is completely the opposite to that of market leader, which is what I tried to impress on Doug. The Number Two has no position to protect so should constantly be challenging the market leader in all sorts of ways, in the case of The Scottish Sun putting major doubts in Daily Record readers' minds as to whether they had made the right choice. I told Doug that my perception in the year that I had been away from the business was that The Scottish Sun had been giving the Daily Record a pretty easy ride. Challenging the Number One is not just about editorial content; it is also about marketing, PR and point of sale, among other things. I also made the point that behaving like a Number Two was clearly not part of The Sun's culture and that part of the problem might be that, because they dominated the tabloid market by such a wide margin in the rest of the UK, they perhaps did not understand the principles of being Number Two in Scotland. He seemed to grasp this immediately. He then explained the purpose of the meeting. News International in Scotland was currently headed by Jim Neil[6], brother of Andrew, a former Editor of the Sunday Times. I did not know Jim, but his reputation was that of a very honourable man – I believe his nickname was 'Gentleman Jim'. Doug felt it was time for change and, assuming that they could find a suitable replacement, Jim would be retiring in the near future. I am not sure if Jim Neil was yet aware of this. There and then Doug offered me the job of General Manager of News International in Scotland. I said that I genuinely was enjoying what I was doing and was already well on my way to building a successful consultancy business. I was also abundantly honest and said that running News International in Scotland was something that I was very interested in. Having spent a decade as part of a team which had established total market dominance for the Daily Record, it would be a huge challenge to try to reverse that trend.

There were clearly a few more hurdles to overcome before anything could happen but by the end of the evening Doug was clear that he wanted me. I would have to see some of other senior people within the organisation before he could make an offer. Two weeks later I was in Wapping (again!) and met Les Hinton, Stuart Higgins[7], Ian McDonald, Clive Milner[8], and Chris Maybury (again!). This time I felt

---

[6] Jim Neil, 1939 - 2009, Managing Director, NI Scotland 1988-95
[7] Stuart Higgins, b.1956, Editor, The Sun 1994-98
[8] Clive Milner, General Manager, NGN; Managing Director, NGN 1999-2001, Managing Director, TNL 2001-04; NI Managing Director 2004-08

that I had given a pretty good account of myself and shortly afterwards there arrived a most attractive offer which I had no hesitation in accepting.

On 6th November 1995, almost exactly a year after I left the Daily Record, I joined News International. My initial meeting with Doug coincided with a time when I was extremely busy and, as the talks with NI progressed, it became clear that it would be a problem to complete all my current projects and wind up my consultancy business. As NI started to press me on a start date I had one brief conversation with Doug about perhaps being allowed to continue the business in my spare time. Let's just say it was a very brief conversation and my suggestion was a non-starter. October 1995 was thus an extremely busy time and, before NI announced that I was joining them, I had to tell my existing clients that I could no longer work with them beyond their present projects. I also had to contact several prospective clients. The result was that I had to turn down what would have been two immensely profitable assignments.

The reason that NI were pressing for a start date was that looming on the horizon was the prospect of a Labour government. Within the Labour manifesto was a clear commitment to reform trade union legislation and, prior to this happening, NI had already started to consider the implications (see Chapter 31) and a conference had been organised in Cumbria for the 7th/8th November. It was essential that I be part of it.

My new contract with NI provided me with a very clear job description. I was to be General Manager of News International (Scotland) Ltd and would be responsible for the development of all five titles in Scotland - The Scottish Sun, the News of the World, Today (which ceased publication on 17th November 1995), The Times and The Sunday Times. I had responsibility for 370 people and my key tasks included maximising the company's sales and advertising revenue and promoting its image within Scotland. This last item was of great interest, bearing in mind how under-networked I had felt as a consultant, so I was determined to rectify that shortcoming from day one. All was therefore set fair for the next stage of my career and I eagerly awaited joining NI. As it turned out, it was one of the most stimulating periods of my life.

Chapter 26   EARLY DAYS AT NI 1995-96

"Anyone can hold the helm when the sea is calm."   **Publilius Syrus**[1]

I joined NI with a very clear job description, but what was not so clear was the reporting structure. In London NI operated within a fairly rigid structure, with all editorial staff reporting through the Editors who, in turn, reported directly to Les Hinton. The four editors at that time were: Stuart Higgins (The Sun), Phil Hall (News of the World)[2], Peter Stothard (The Times)[3], and John Witherow[4] (The Sunday Times). One other person, Rebekah Brooks (then Wade)[5], was Deputy Editor of the News of the World (and features prominently later.)

All commercial and support function staff reported directly to Doug Flynn. Among the senior executive team were Ian McDonald, Clive Milner, Chris Maybury, Andy Kemp[6], Dick Linford[7], Toby Constantine[8], Ellis Watson[9], Ian Jackson[10] and Alasdair MacLeod[11]. Doug had decided that I should report directly to Ian McDonald, partly because Ian had identified me in the first place and secondly because he was responsible for the Knowsley Plant. Both Glasgow and Knowsley were printing plants but Glasgow also had a complete commercial and editorial operation. Ian seemed happy with this arrangement and, as we got to know each other, we got on well. The arrangement worked well for me. Ian gave me a reasonable amount of freedom and we were easily able to establish basic ground rules. Ian was very political and, in many ways, similar to me in that he didn't like surprises. He was quite happy to let me run my own show, but if anything was about to veer off track, he wanted to know about it first.

One of the first issues I had to contend with was a suggested four-week handover with Jim Neil. In the end we compromised on two weeks, during which I was either in London or Cumbria, while Jim had a number of farewell functions to attend. Jim behaved impeccably, personally coming to the company's reception area the first morning to welcome me. He took me into 'my' office (theoretically still his) and insisted that I sat in 'my' chair (ditto). The handover was both smooth and amicable.

I recognised that if I were to create change quickly, I would require someone who could understand what I wanted and also organise my day-to-day workload. As Jack Welch[12] put it, "You've got to eat while you dream. You've got to deliver on short-range commitments while you develop a long-range strategy and implement

---

[1] Publilius Syrus 85-43BC, Syrian slave and Latin writer, quote from Sententiae
[2] Phil Hall, b.1955, Editor, News of the World 1995-2000
[3] Sir Peter Stothard, b 1951, Editor, The Times 1992-2002
[4] John Witherow, b. 1952, Editor, The Sunday Times 1994-2013, The Times 2013-Present
[5] Rebekah Brooks (née. Wade), b. 1968, Editor, News of the World 2000-03, Editor, The Sun 2003-09
[6] Andy Kemp b. 1950, Director of Human Resources NI 1998-2002
[7] Dick Linford, Chief Financial Officer, NI 1999-2006
[8] Toby Constantine, Marketing Director TNL 1995-99
[9] Ellis Watson, b. 1947, Marketing Director NGN
[10] Ian Jackson, Circulation Director, Newsgroup Newspapers
[11] Alasdair MacLeod, Circulation Director, latterly General Manager, TNL
[12] Jack Welch, b. 1935, business executive, author, Chairman and CEO, General Electric 1981-2001

it." Janis Judge joined me at NI in late December 1996. Claire's response was to say that she must have been quite mad - when she started working for me at SDR, she had no idea what to expect; now she knew exactly what she was letting herself in for! Janis was to stay with me throughout my entire time at NI and was extremely well regarded by everyone she came into contact with, both within Kinning Park and at Wapping.

One of my first impressions was that NI was grossly over-managed. It was split in two divisions, News Group Newspapers (NGN), the tabloids and Times Newspapers Ltd, (TNL) the broadsheets. It was a huge organisation with around 4,000 employees, yet more than 400 people held the title 'Director' or 'Manager'. I became increasingly convinced that removing half these people would result in far faster, more effective decision making, less politics and much greater efficiency.

The second impression was that the parent/subsidiary company issue I had already encountered at MGN was much worse at NI. The company was M25-centric. Scotland was regarded as being in 'The Provinces' - worse still, over the border. Unlike MGN, NI had market dominance within its tabloid titles everywhere except in Scotland, also contributing to a perception of inferiority.

The main consequences of having 400 'Executives' was that the organisation was structured vertically, inevitably creating a silo mentality. This had led to the creation of many individual fiefdoms, each extremely well protected, and turf wars were inevitable. All in all, NI was an extremely political organisation. Sadly, what I regarded as my company, News International Newspapers (Scotland) Ltd (NINS), was seen in London as merely a subsidiary company and therefore the potential for conflict was enormous. I later discovered that there were 12 other Directors of NINS, all based in London.

I inherited a relatively small executive team of eight people. Within the overall NI structure, each one of the eight people had a direct line report to someone in Wapping and, as Doug explained, (with the exception of the Editors) a dotted line responsibility to me. In theory I was responsible for managing them on a day to day basis. They were employed to work for the Scottish company to maximise its impact, but ultimately they reported to someone in London. It was a crazy situation and inevitably created friction and conflict. In fairness, most of the London management team recognised the structure and accepted that they would need to work closely with me, and I in turn with them, to avoid conflict. In turn, each of the Kinning Park employees recognised that in theory they were serving two masters, but the potential for playing two ends against the middle was enormous. To avoid this I made it abundantly clear to them from the onset that there would only ever be one winner in that situation – me.

As time went on I was delighted to know that I had Ian McDonald's complete backing, that it was ultimately my show and I had the freedom to operate as I saw fit. After all, I was there to drive the company forward from what Doug himself had acknowledged had previously been a stagnant operation. Doug on one occasion told

Ian McDonald that he thought I was doing a great job in Scotland and his barometer for judging how well I was doing was based on the number of complaints he heard from London staff about what I was up to. The more complaints there were, the more effective I was - a very backhanded compliment. Colin Powell[13] put it another way, "Pissing people off doesn't mean that you're doing the right things, but doing the right things will almost inevitably piss people off."

From the first day I sought to create a team in Scotland, a team that would unite and drive the company forward. I sat down with each person and explained my management philosophy. After we agreed a common set of goals, I gave them complete freedom to implement them and manage their people. I would always back someone who tried to do this to the best of their ability. George Bernard Shaw[14] once said, "a life making mistakes is not only more honourable but more useful than a life spent doing nothing at all." However, what I would not tolerate was, in the event of something going wrong, the person involved trying to bluff their way out of the situation. I demanded honesty and transparency and, if I got it, I would always support them. I also demanded no surprises. If something was awry, I did not want to find out second hand. As Theodore Roosevelt[15] once said, "the best leader is the one who has the sense to pick good men to do what he wants done and the self-restraint to keep from meddling with them while they do it."

In the decade I was there, I built a team which achieved great things. There were some personnel changes, but it was a team of which I felt extremely proud and I was confident that 'my people' inevitably acquitted themselves well in group situations.

However, the road to this was not without problems. Three of the original eight were simply not up to the standards required and departed, usually unwillingly, and inevitably after a major battle between myself and their 'boss' in London, who thought they had been hard done by. In the fourth case, the person was sacked by his superior in London but much to my delight.

This may seem harsh and brutal. It was not. They were well rewarded and perhaps it had not been made clear to them in the past what standards were expected, in return for a remuneration package second to none in both the sector and the world at large. NI was an excellent employer and for my part I was simply insisting on perfectly reasonable levels of attainment and behaviour to justify the remuneration. I also made it clear that I would not carry passengers. It was not a regime of fear and overall the team worked tremendously hard together. Jack Welch, whose management theories I greatly admire, had two things to say on this subject, "You've got to be rigorous in your appraisal system. The biggest cowards are managers who don't let people know where they really stand." "Protecting underperformers always backfires."

---

[13] Colin Powell, b. 1937, 4-Star General, Chairman, Joint Chiefs of Staff 1989-93, 65th US Secretary of State 2001-05
[14] George Bernard Shaw 1856-1950, Irish playwright, critic, polemicist and political activist
[15] Theodore Roosevelt Jr. 1858-1919, American statesman, conservationist and writer. 26th President of the United States 1901-09

Chapter 27   EARLY BATTLES

"I can't give you a sure-fire formula for success but I can give you a formula for failure: try to please everybody all the time."   Herbert Swape[1]

I settled in at Kinning Park very quickly, coping with the constant frustration of the reporting structure. Early on, the Editor of The Sunday Times in Scotland, Will Peakin shared with me his battle to make local decisions on content. The main team in London had a sizeable number of editorial managers with authority for various parts of the Scottish edition. Many had little knowledge of the market there - indeed some had never visited Kinning Park - but all had opinions on what was suitable for the Scottish edition. For example, it was said that The Sunday Times' Managing Editor only ever came to Scotland to sack people. Tony Baimbridge's arrival was always preceded by huge speculation that a hanging was about to take place. He would arrive immaculately attired in a Saville Row pinstriped suit with the only thing missing being the black cap to pronounce sentence.

I was to have many battles over the years, but only ever seriously fell out with two people, ironically the Marketing Directors of TNL and NGN, Toby Constantine and Ellis Watson respectively. They prided themselves on being part of the notorious 'Wapping terrible twins act'. As Campaign magazine[2] said at the time, "the pair could afford to make jokes about mortality back then because they were by most people's reckoning immortal."

Constantine and I got off to a bad start and never really recovered. The same Campaign article described him, "They say the manic aggressive (and somewhat juvenile) posturing demanded by News International tended to obscure the more natural urbane and sophisticated facets of Constantine's character." I recognised all of the former traits but very few of the latter ones. I suspect that no one in the entire Sunday Times operation had ever been seriously challenged and consequently the new whippersnapper in Scotland needed to be put in his place. There was no shortage of volunteers to do this, so the ensuing contretemps with Constantine was highly predictable.

I cannot even remember what triggered it, since it was a relatively minor issue, but what enraged me was that Constantine had gone behind my back and complained to Ian McDonald. Ian and I agreed that it would be best for me to go to London and the three of us try to resolve the issue. I suspect that Ian recognised that this needed to be hit on the head immediately or he would find himself constantly as mediator. He, after listening to both sides, totally backed my decision, the issue was resolved and, although not happy, Constantine and I shook hands at the end of the discussion.

---

[1] Herbert Swape 1892-1958, US journalist and editor. First and three-time winner of the Pulitzer Prize for Reporting
[2] Campaign, 27th November 2003

Worse was to follow, this time with Chris Maybury. There was always an edge to our relationship. I was starting to build other relationships within the company and I always felt that some senior commercial people in Wapping resented it. I met John Witherow, Editor of The Sunday Times, and we seemed to strike up a positive rapport. I think Witherow enjoyed our meetings. He would have already been briefed by a number of his team on matters Scottish – by the very people who were driving Will Peakin to distraction. I was now giving him some alternative views on what was happening in the Scottish marketplace and at the same time floating a number of other ideas. All was going well until I had a call from Maybury, apoplectic with rage, accusing me of interfering with matters which had absolutely nothing to do with me. What he was effectively saying was that I should not contact any senior individual in Wapping without informing him first. We had an extremely 'robust' conversation on this and I, in turn, had an even more robust one with Ian McDonald. There was no way that I was going to accept that, as the senior person responsible for Scotland, I would have to clear with Maybury anytime I wanted to talk to someone in Wapping. Ian absolutely backed me to the hilt on my right to pursue any initiatives that I felt appropriate.

The real problem was that I didn't fit into the traditional Wapping model and, clearly, in recent years Scotland's voice had been neither strong nor vociferous. I was challenging that and constantly putting forward new ideas and 'they' didn't like it. Ian and Doug between them ensured that I was given my head to develop Scotland but I always felt a sense of edginess in my dealings with those underneath them. I built a reasonable relationship with Clive Milner the then General Manager of NGN, but never with Maybury.

Ellis Watson and I also got off to a bad start. The NGN marketing function in Scotland was represented by a junior News Group Executive Douglas Rodger. In my initial meeting with him, he said, "You do realise that I work for Ellis and everything I do has to be cleared by him?" As far as I was concerned, his fate was sealed from that moment onwards.

From the onset I was determined to send a very strong signal to the Daily Record that, regardless of any cosy relationship in the past, things were going to change and we were going after them with a vengeance. Marketing would play a key role. In my first week I contacted Julia Crossthwaite[3]. Scotland were playing San Marino at Hampden Park on 15th November and I did a deal to purchase the entire track-side advertising sites for The Scottish Sun. I phoned Ellis to tell him what I'd agreed and asked if he could arrange to make this happen. I suspect that Ellis did not like this one bit but as I had just been appointed, he was sufficiently unsure of his ground to be seen to oppose it. The impact from the live television coverage of the game was enormous.

Ellis and I soldiered on for a while but the relationship did not flourish. Early in 1986 I was in his Wapping office when he suddenly said, "You don't really like Douglas,

---

[3] Julia Crossthwaite, Sales Manager, Morton Sports Media

do you?" I replied, "No, I don't rate him at all." Ellis then threw his can of Diet Coke straight at me. As I ducked, the can splattered all over the wall behind me. Almost foaming at the mouth, he shouted at me, "Don't ever speak to me like that about a member of my staff!" I stood up, reached over the table, resisting the temptation to grab him by the throat, and responded, "If you ever try to do something like that again, you will regret it", and walked out. It was a bit of handbags at dawn and the relationship deteriorated. We tolerated each other and worked together as best we could. Ellis was an incredibly bright young man full of ideas, but he loved playing to the gallery, like a court jester. To his credit, he came up with some great ideas in our battle with the Daily Record and I recognised his considerable talent. The postscript was that he and Rodger eventually parted company and I can't say I shed any tears at his departure.

Kinning Park press hall 1995

Chapter 28   KINNING PARK REFURBISHMENT

"Do not wait to strike until the iron is hot but make it hot by striking."
W.B. Yeats

After just a few days with NI, I began to have serious misgivings about our premises. Portman Street in Kinning Park was an old Foundry and Engineering Works. In 1995 Kinning Park, just over a mile from Glasgow city centre, was a rundown area and even now, more than 20 years later, urban regeneration had yet to reach it.

The manufacturing part of the business was adjacent to the M8 motorway whilst the commercial and editorial half of the factory adjourned Milnpark Street. The premises were spartan and extremely shabby. In my first week there, I asked to see the visitors' book and discovered that very few people ever visited us - not surprising as there didn't appear to be any meeting rooms. Catering facilities were also basic – just a works canteen providing extremely mediocre fare.

I realised that I would need to address these shortcomings fairly quickly. In my early visits to Wapping, I couldn't help but notice its excellent facilities. In moving to Wapping, NI had managed to build extensive and impressive office facilities. Greatly encouraged by this I enthusiastically set about planning an extensive upgrade to the Kinning Park facilities. In exploring the building, I discovered an old crane at the Milnpark Street end of the plant, now completely encased. Helped by our facilities team, I envisaged restoring the crane to make it a focal reminder of the former glory of the building, whilst showcasing an extensive entrance hall with a mezzanine floor created around it. Combined with refurbishing the entire ground floor, this would cost just over £1 million.

When Doug Flynn next came to Glasgow, I enthusiastically outlined my proposals to him. Much to my surprise he was almost apoplectic and curtly told me not to have such grandiose plans. I subsequently found out that his reaction was probably based on recent events at Wapping. There a new entrance had been created with a double set of escalators running through an extensive waterfall feature over two floors leading up to the main entrance hall and foyer for the building. The project had ended up massively over budget, costing over £1 million. Although I am not sure how closely Doug had been involved, the sacking of his boss John Dux had led to the entrance hall becoming known as 'Dux's Folly'. I suspect being even remotely associated with this had made Doug very nervous about creating a 'Flynn's Folly' in Kinning Park.

Forced to downscale my ambition, I came up with a revised plan to refurbish the ground floor, creating additional office space, a boardroom, much needed meeting rooms and a new visitor entrance in Portman Street. All in all it presented a much softer image of the company. More importantly, our staff would feel comfortable inviting people to visit. In addition we created a small kitchen area. Until then all NI visitors to Kinning Park were served lunch or light refreshments supplied from the canteen. Everything seemed to be deep-fried and it had become something of a standing joke in the senior executive Wapping team. I already knew Suzanne Ritchie[1] who had her own professional catering business and she agreed to be our chef when required. Suzanne significantly upgraded the catering for visiting Wapping "firemen", providing another subtle reminder that a new regime was in place.

Doug on his next visit pronounced himself well satisfied with my modified proposals, now costing just over £300,000. The only remaining hurdle was having it all signed off by Rupert, since major capital projects had to be authorised by him. Rupert considered all News Corps' Capital Expenditure requests in New York at 5pm on a Wednesday. My continued pressure on Doug clearly worked and, one Monday morning shortly afterwards, I had a phone call from Dick Linford confirming that the CapEx would be presented that Wednesday and, since they didn't anticipate any problems, I should go ahead and start organising the refurbishment. Not one to hang about, I had a squad of contractors on site by mid-morning.

At 8am on the Thursday, I had a call from an extremely worried Dick Linford. Rupert had apparently been in a foul mood and had thrown out the Kinning Park proposals with the words, "And how many extra copies is that going to sell for us?" Dick said that we needed to call a halt to any work immediately whilst they reconsidered the position. Too late - the entire ground floor has already been gutted, since the easiest part of any project is ripping out what already exists. The contractor, knowing my pressing desire to get the project completed, had moved extremely quickly. Not a trace remained of what had been. Ian McDonald was dispatched from Wapping that very same day and reported back that everything I had said was completely true.

I relentlessly kept up the pressure on Doug who accepted that we couldn't have a shell of a building in the long term. On the other hand, no one seemed willing to get another 'doing' from Rupert. Eventually, after much deliberation, it was decided to proceed with the project, now divided into five phases.

In the end, the project was completed within six weeks and everyone agreed that it transformed the building. It also enhanced my reputation as someone who got things done quickly. Almost immediately lots of visitors appeared and Kinning Park's reputation for producing fried Mars Bars became a distant memory.

---

[1] Suzanne Ritchie, b. 1960. Owner, Mise En Place 1990-2012

New Kinning Park reception area at last !

Chapter 29   INDUSTRIAL RELATIONS AT NI

"The simple fact of paying positive attention to people has a great deal to do with productivity." Tom Peters[1]

Observant readers will have noted that I joined News International on a Sunday. The date, 6th Nov 1995, is a significant one because it was then that NI first devised its strategy for dealing with the new employment legislation looming on the horizon. By now it was clear that Tony Blair and New Labour proposed to reform many parts of the current trade union legislation put on the statute book by the Thatcher Government. Although the election was still 18 months away, to me it was an early indication of the forward thinking of my new company. All the key human resources and manufacturing management teams were meeting at a hotel in Cumbria for a two-day seminar to consider the implications of the proposed legislation and to plan the future strategy in order to be compliant with it.

That Sunday I travelled with Allan Boyd[2], my new Human Resources Manager, and he briefed me on who would be present. To illustrate just how seriously the matter was considered, Bill O'Neill[3], Rupert's senior HR man in News Corp, had flown from the US to be there. A tough no nonsense Australian with little evidence of a sense of humour, I met O'Neill that evening for the first time and his opening gambit was, "Well Colin, how does it feel to be in charge of the first plant throughout the whole of the organisation that's going to let in the trade unions?" It was a crass cheap shot based upon his totally outdated perception that our workforce was likely to exhibit the old 'Red Clydeside' mentality. There was not a shred of evidence to support this view and, as I was to remind him frequently in later years, it was totally inaccurate. Of NI's three manufacturing plants, Glasgow would eventually vote by the highest margin to create an internal trade union rather than recognise an external one.

This was at the heart of the proposed new legislation. Labour, if elected, would create employment legislation giving individual workers the right to belong to a trade union. The legislation would mean that with any organised group of workers, of whom a majority (50% +1) chose to be represented by a trade union, the employer would by law have to recognise that union and negotiate with it. Although it was a radical step, it was a shrewd move by Blair not to hand back complete power to the trade unions. New Labour had realised that, in the Thatcher era, the pendulum had swung too far the other way and their proposed legislation was an attempt to reset the compass on a more reasonable course.

The task for our group was to examine our entire industrial relations strategy to ensure that it was sufficiently fit for purpose and that our staff would not feel the

[1] Tom Peters b.1942, American writer on business management practices
[2] Allan Boyd b.1957, HR Manager Kinning Park 1992-2000, latterly HR Director, Morris and Spottiswood
[3] Bill O'Neill, b. 1936, Australian-American, Vice-President (Global Human Resources), News Corp.

need for external trade union representation. At the heart of the new strategy was that we should be more proactive and create our own internal trade union and formally conduct all our collective bargaining arrangements through this body.

The bones of a new structure emerged from our discussion – a new body called the News International Staff Association (NISA). There would be a number of constituencies covering all members of staff and members would be elected from those constituencies annually. The elected body would meet monthly with senior NI management in London, Knowsley and Glasgow. All meetings would have pre-agreed agendas and be fully minuted, with minutes freely available. In later years, the level of transparency increased even further with any member of staff able to attend a meeting as an observer.

Over the years the NISA structure was refined but many of its processes were formalised at that original meeting. For example, NISA would become an integral part of NI's disciplinary process and, in the event of a member of staff being dismissed, a final appeal would be heard by a panel comprising of two members of management and three members of NISA. The panel itself, chaired by a member of management, would have the final say on whether the dismissal was fair or not and thus could uphold or reject the appeal. The members of the panel would be drawn from the other two sites and would never sit in judgement on anyone from their own site, thus ensuring total impartiality. In my time I chaired two such appeals, one at Knowsley and one at Wapping. In both cases the panel unanimously rejected the appeal. The Wapping case then went to an Industrial Tribunal which also found in favour of the company.

This was extremely heartening, but in those early days it was recognised that if NISA were to have any chance of success, NI's management culture would need to change drastically. In our management teams, we had to realise that we had some managers whose style was simply not fit for purpose. In some cases there existed a culture of bullying, in others an overly autocratic style that had to be changed. Our task in the relatively short window of opportunity was to change the culture, which meant ultimately changing some of the people if they didn't buy into it. At heart was a desire to make the company a model employer, with whom all members of staff would feel confident that their rights and conditions of employment were being looked after as part of an internal process, without the need to be represented by a third-party.

As the details of the proposed new arrangements emerged there was a massive communications exercise throughout the company to ensure that every member of staff understood them. The new body NISA was thus well-established before the new legislation came into effect. It was interesting to note that the eventual members of the NISA team took their responsibilities very seriously but recognised the central principle that consensus rather than conflict was more likely to produce results.

The other major advantage from the company's point of view was that, by having the new structures up and running long before the new legislation, all members of staff, when they voted on whether to recognise external trade unions or not, did so on an informed basis and with sufficient experience of the company's proposed system. When the vote finally took place, it was with some personal pride that Kinning Park voted almost 80% in favour of an internal staff union. The Knowsley vote was 70% in favour and Wapping, somewhat surprisingly, voted with just under 60% in favour.

The structure, now known as the News Union is still in place and flourishing. That it does so is testament to the individuals who met in Cumbria some 20 years ago to consider how best to organise and treat employees fairly, and to a desire to manage the business through consensus rather than conflict.

For me, my small part in the organisation at Kinning Park was the first time I had ever run a company, albeit a relatively small division of a much larger company. I took great pride in my workforce and constantly strove to be as inclusive as possible in my dealings with them. NI was structured along vertical lines and I wanted to explore ways of breaking the silo mentality.

In 1997/98, I instituted a series of employee get-togethers, inviting every member of staff to breakfast in groups of around 15. People were not chosen along departmental lines, guaranteeing a reasonable cross-section of staff each time. They were informal occasions with bacon rolls and coffee. Allan Boyd and I hosted each one. As an ice breaker, after everyone had introduced themselves, Allan had organised a simple exercise of naming a colour and asking each individual to think of an associated word or phrase. For example, 'Blue' could lead to 'Blue Moon', 'Blue Peter', 'The Blues', 'Blueprint' and so on. People started to get the hang of this quickly, the level of participation increased and, more importantly, any initial nervousness disappeared. I then invited each person to talk about the company and any ideas he or she had on how to make it a better organisation or how it might be more effective. I should add that there was an incentive. At the 1998 Football World Cup in Paris, Scotland were to play Brazil at the Stade de France on 10th June. I obtained tickets and offered to take the two staff members who made the best contribution during the sessions. As an exercise it was a great success and produced several major benefits. For my part, I met every member of staff. All those participating met people in other departments whom they had not previously known. Most importantly, in the various responses, people began to realise the interdependency they all shared. Everyone was part of a structure which produced a new newspaper every day and each contributed to how successful that process could be. The endeavour was judged by most people to be thoroughly worthwhile. We had some great suggestions on how the company could operate more effectively and two people went on a three-day trip to Paris - and of course on their return told everyone about their experience. I thought it so worthwhile that I repeated it the following year and took another two people to the Rugby World Cup Final in Cardiff.

Chapter 30   LET BATTLE COMMENCE

"If things seem under control, you're not going fast enough."   Mario Andretti [1]

I was a man in a hurry and sometimes you have to take risks to make things happen quickly. Much as taking the entire track-side advertising at Hampden was about telling the general public that there was a new 'noisy neighbour' in town, it was also sending a warning to SDR that things were about to change and Kinning Park was no longer the sleepy hollow they thought it to be.

On my first Saturday, Bob Bird[2] invited me to address The Scottish Sun's senior editorial team at an away day at Cameron House, Loch Lomond. I found Bob's senior team of Bruce Waddell[3], Derek Stewart Brown, Alan Muir and others to be extremely enthusiastic. In a rallying call, I told them that they had already made significant inroads into the Daily Record's supposed superiority, and that the sales trend was positive, but most importantly, that they were capable of taking market leadership. It would take some time, it would be a long journey, but it was achievable. I used the words that I was to use many times, "You are competing for the hearts and minds of Joe Public in Scotland. You must aim always to be one step ahead of the Daily Record, but you have the great advantage that, as Number 2 in the market, there is no level playing field, and as such you can do pretty well what you want. As Number 1, they cannot retaliate." My reasoning that the Record couldn't retaliate on a like-for-like basis was that it would have given the oxygen of publicity to the very thing that they could never admit – that the Daily Record and The Sun were equals playing on the same pitch. I explained that the strategy was based on a number of things. Firstly demonstrating that The Scottish Sun was superior to the Daily Record editorially and showing that the gap in sales between the two had significantly diminished and would continue to do so. Another factor was that the Daily Record's sales were being boosted by their giving away an ever-increasing number of free and sponsored copies and claiming them as sold copies. I wanted to establish a Daily Record figure for its Scottish sale, excluding these 'bulk' sales, and thereafter to compare this figure with The Scottish Sun.

Bob and his team were quick to grasp this and instantly unleashed a ferocious campaign against the Daily Record, its track record, its sales losses and its missed stories, but all done in the humorous style for which The Scottish Sun was famous.

In my second week, with the Daily Record celebrating its 100th Birthday, Bob ran a full page headlined, "100 TEARS OF THE DAILY RECORD – HUNDREDS AND HUNDREDS DUMP PAPER". Included were such gems;

"Canny Scots are deciding in their droves that The Sun's the one for Scotland"

---

[1] Mario Andretti, b. 1940, Italian-born American racing driver, F1 World Champion 1978
[2] Bob Bird b. 1956, Editor The Scottish Sun 1990-98, Deputy Editor the News of the World 1998-2000, Scottish Editor 2000-11
[3] Bruce Waddell, b 1959, Deputy Editor, The Scottish Sun 1994-98; Editor 1998-2003; Editor, The Daily Record 2003-11

"While the OAPs at Anderston Quay were collecting a telegram from the Queen, The Sun was collecting more readers"

"They never did have a sense of humour at the Record and, after these dismal sales figures, you'll never get a laugh out of them or their paper again"

That week Bob and his team launched a campaign, "Spot a free Record and win a tenner" "The dishonest Daily Record is conning readers and advertisers by giving away copies for nothing at exhibitions, conferences and even through doors. Why should readers pay 27p for the Record if other folk get it for nothing? We want you, our loyal readers, to tell us every time you see a free copy of the Record, so that we can expose them for the cheats that they are."

The campaign began to take off. Within days there were further headlines like, "BAN THE DAILY RECORD JUNK MAIL" and, 'SUN READERS BRAND OUR RIVAL A DEAD GIVEAWAY'. Naturally each article always had quotes from Sun readers, "The Record is rubbish, that's why I buy The Sun. Not even being offered it for free would tempt me to pick it up." Bob's campaign soon unearthed another unexpected bonus. In the first week of December, another headline read, "IT ASDA BE ANOTHER FREE DAILY RECORD, 30,000 COPIES TO BE HANDED OUT IN PAISLEY AREA TODAY. We ASDA warn you – the Dreary Record's planning another giveaway rip-off by handing out 30,000 free copies today, sponsored by a supermarket. So, if you live in the Paisley area and you know a sad soul who buys the Record, do them a favour. Warn them that they don't have to fork out 27p for the usual dose of day-late news – just sit tight and they'll get one free. Those naughty snoozepaper people don't plan on handing out their free copies until this afternoon. That's so some of their unsuspecting readers will still go out and buy it in the morning as usual – what a swizz! Mind you, you'd be off your trolley to read it."

The feedback was incredibly positive. People loved the campaign, absolutely adored the humour of it and the readers themselves maintained its momentum. In some ways, it was similar to the ethos of Terry Wogan's[4] radio shows where his listeners provided much of the content of the show.

Bob's team maintained the humour of the campaign. More headlines soon appeared, "10 WAYS TO GET RID OF A FREE DREARY RECORD". Amongst these were, "Cut out the title and see which words you can make from the letters Daily Record'. Examples are; Dreary, Dire, Idle, Dear, Dead, Old." "Save them, and within days, you'll have enough to start your own lucrative paper recycling business." "Tear them into tiny pieces and organise a daily paper chase. The finishing line will be somewhere on the outskirts of Sydney."

The team were even able to mimic the Daily Record's recent advertising campaign created by the Leith Agency (Chapter 21). Using almost identical images, they

---

[4] Sir Terry Wogan KBE DL, 1938-2016, Irish television and radio broadcaster, voted the BBC's greatest radio presenter

exhorted readers to; "Keep your eyes peeled or your ear to the ground for Daily Record giveaways."

There seemed no end to the brilliance of The Sun's journalists. At the time, the Daily Record's most used strapline was, "Real Scots read The Record". Around this time, Alan Muir discovered that Glasgow's first gay restaurant was about to open quite close to the Daily Record building. Headlined, "REAL BOTS FEED THE RECORD", it continued, "The diner is the perfect spot for Record top brass to plan a rear-guard action and to stiffen up their limp circulation. Their daily sale has drooped to 670,000 despite massaging the figures by dishing out free copies." I'm not sure how this might have gone down in the politically correct world of some 25 years later.

The pressure continued unabated. One of the most read parts of The Sun was its Agony Aunt's cartoon, 'Deidre's Photo Casebook'. Bob commissioned a storyline about two young women; the boyfriend of one of them had just switched to buying The Sun and was now a different man, while the other continued to buy the Record. "What a plonker", says one. In her final advice Deidre wrote, "This is a familiar problem played out in many homes across Scotland. If you know someone who is listless and down-in-the-mouth all the time, it could be down to the fact that they've had a bellyful of the Daily Record. Get them to try The Scottish Sun. Remember 'No Sun, no fun'."

NI's 10th anniversary of printing in Scotland was in January 1996. For some time, The Sun's cover price was 2p less than the Daily Record's but, astonishingly, the latter chose to increase its price to 28p just as the 10th anniversary celebrations were in full swing. Swiftly The Sun dropped its price to 10p on the actual anniversary date and sold a then all-time high figure of 446,000 copies.

The 10th anniversary provided my first opportunity to showcase both our position and, more importantly, our aspirations to become an even bigger player in Scotland. To mark the occasion, we organised a significant 'party' and invited more than 300 guests to Hopetoun House in South Queensferry. No expense was spared and word quickly spread round that this would be a prestigious occasion. In addition to the national editors, I also invited three of the titles' best known columnists, Deidre Sanders[5] (The Sun), Alan Clark[6] (News of the World) and Mary Anne Sieghart[7] (The Times). Alan Clark's appearance certainly caused a stir. He was no longer in the Cabinet but had attracted massive coverage over his extracurricular activities. When word spread that he was there, it was fascinating to see numerous female guests literally elbowing each other out of the way to meet him – having a reputation as a serial philanderer was clearly not a disadvantage!

For me, the evening was memorable for a number of things. Les made an excellent speech, pitching the message just right. We were here and we were only going to go one way – upwards. Sir Timothy Clifford[8] made an impromptu thank you speech,

---

[5] Deidre Sanders b.1945 'Dear Deidre' Agony Aunt, The Sun 1980-
[6] Alan Clark 1928-99 MP, Plymouth Sutton 1974-92, Kensington and Chelsea 1977-99 Junior Minister and Diarist
[7] Mary Anne Sieghart b.1961 English journalist and radio presenter, former assistant Editor, The Times
[8] Sir Timothy Clifford b.1946 British art historian, Director National Galleries of Scotland 1984-2006

manfully delivered, despite being heckled by an incredibly drunk Sun journalist. Janis also delivered a great put-down line to estate agent Ian Robb[9]. As he was registering, she said that he looked familiar. Ian drew himself up and said that perhaps this was because he was very often mistaken for Gavin Hastings. "No," said Janis, "That's impossible, he's not here this evening." Eddie MacKechnie[10] embellished the story some years later, suggesting that Robb couldn't possibly be mistaken for Hastings as the latter was not known to apply hair gel so liberally.

In the meantime, the editorial war against the Daily Record continued with a vengeance. As part of the 10th anniversary celebrations I arranged to have a giant billboard erected on the main facade of our building next to the M8 motorway, showing The Sun's upward sales graph literally bursting through the roof.

This was the last straw for the Daily Record. We had been deliberately provoking them to retaliate and when they finally did, their response gave us priceless publicity. In a Scotland on Sunday (SOS) major article headlined, "SOARAWAY SUN REACHES ITS ZENITH. RUPERT MURDOCH'S UPSTART HAS HIT A SALES PLATEAU" Terry Quinn, Editor of the Daily Record, and Jack Irvine (yes, the former MD of the Sun but now heading the Daily Record's PR agency) argued that we had shot our bolt. When asked for comment on the piece, I was quoted thus, "An 8% year-on-year increase doesn't sound like plateauing. OK, the gap between the Daily Record and The Sun is still large, but not half as big as it used to be. If we make the same progress in the next ten years, we'll have them." Irvine's hypothesis was, "McClatchie is a master at manipulating non-verifiable figures but his latest porky cannot disguise the fact that The Sun has plateaued." Quinn, in true tabloid prose, opened, "If in the late 80s and early 90s there was a real Sun-rise, it has turned into a real Sun-set." Irvine added a particularly tasteless remark about editing The Sun, "I'm not sure that anyone can do that for more than a couple of years without wrecking their health or their marriage." Bob Bird had been Editor of the Sun for five years and his marriage at that time was indeed under strain but he refused to rise to the bait and was quoted, "Compare the Record with The Sun day-by-day and you'll see, we'll wipe the arse off them." Despite Irvine's poorly disguised jibe at the state of Bob's marriage, Quinn claimed that The Sun's increasing viciousness stemmed from commercial desperation. "In their continuing frustration at our continuing strength, they have turned to standard Sun tactics of smears, distortions, and downright lies."

It was fantastic publicity and Plan B now swung into action. I demanded the right to reply to some of the inaccuracies in the article and, astonishingly, the following week, SOS agreed to publish my lengthy reply word-for-word in a prominent article running to almost a third of a page.

---

[9] Ian Robb b.1958, estate agent since 1979, Director Robb Residential 2013-
[10] Eddie MacKechnie b.1951, former partner McGrigor Donald

I was able to get across three main points:

1. The Scottish Sun sales were going up and the Daily Record's were going down, hence no zenith, plateau or sunset.

2. Most importantly we had now successfully got into the public realm a Daily Record sales figure that excluded 'bulk' sales. This was a major breakthrough and, from then on, we always quoted that figure. The Scottish Sun's spotlight on the Daily Record's and other publishers' activities in this area became a hotly debated topic and, eventually, the Audit Bureau of Circulations (ABC) passed new rules requiring publishers to provide details of these bulk sales and ABC figures now listed those copies sold at less than full-rate. Happy days!

3. I was able to focus on the ongoing battle. "At no stage have we set out to suggest that the Daily Record is not the largest selling newspaper in Scotland. What we do suggest, is that its sales are haemorrhaging rapidly and that, far from plateauing, The Sun will continue to erode the Daily Record's existing dominance.

Most pleasing of all was that SOS headlined the article, "THE SUN HAS ITS SCOTTISH READERSHIP FIGURED OUT: CIRCULATION STATISTICS SHOW WHICH TABLOID IS REALLY WINNING THE READERSHIP BATTLE". Game, set and match, and even better, there was a sting in the tail of the article. I said, "Finally, I note that these comments on non-verification come from Jack Irvine. Could this be the same Jack Irvine, former Managing Director of the ill-fated Sunday Scot, whose sales forecasts for that newspaper are so fondly remembered by many in the advertising industry as being wildly optimistic – so much so that the paper closed after 18 issues?"

Astonishingly the story rolled on for a third week much to our delight. Rob Brown, author of the two SOS pieces, wrote a full-page article for the UK Press Gazette giving us priceless national publicity within our sector. Many of the key quotes in the original pieces made it into the article.

The main theme was that the battle was between Terry Quinn and, most surprisingly, myself and not Bob Bird as it should have been. "A cold war between these two titles has raged across the Clyde for a decade, but it has caught fire in the past few months since Colin McClatchie was appointed MD of News International's Scottish Operation. The 46-year old Ulsterman was sacked as Circulation and Marketing Director of the Record and Sunday Mail around the same time as Quinn's appointment. Now, McClatchie's declared mission is to get even, rather than mad, with his former employer." "No one can deny that The Sun's satellite plant on the south bank of the Clyde is now a serious and successful force in Scottish newspaper publishing." Particularly pleasing for us was, once again, that the Daily Record's sales figure (excluding bulks) was extensively quoted. Finally, the article, which opened with Quinn saying he had only ever wanted to edit the Daily Record and the Manchester Evening News, concluded, "Being the constant target must at times make Terry Quinn fantasise about editing the MEN."

The overall point was that in a relatively short period of time we had the Daily Record completely on the back foot. We had exposed their falling sales, established a sales figure less 'bulks' and planted the thought in everyone's mind about the ever-shrinking gap between the Scottish Sun and the Daily Record, while constantly extolling the superior qualities of the former.

The battle had well and truly commenced.

I can't be bothered to see any crazy salesman – we've got a battle to fight!"

The Scottish Sun purchased the gun, whilst the Daily Record continued to fight the battle in their own way.....as per usual !

Chapter 31   THE INFLUENCE OF RUPERT

"There are two parts to influence, first influence is power and second influence is subtle." Jim Rahn[1]

When Caxton[2] brought the first printing press to England in 1486, he quickly became the largest and most influential retailer of printed books. Rupert Murdoch reached that position in the media sector by the early 1970s and his operations have dominated the marketplace since then. He is regarded as either the Devil Incarnate or a media mogul who expresses and leads opinions on any number of issues, including politics. As Rupert himself says, "I did not come all this way not to interfere." An article by Julian Crowley[3] summed it up thus, "Since the dawn of mass media, newspapers, radio and television have all been used to inform and educate the public. They have also been used to whip mobs into a frenzy, control the world of politics and consolidate their owners' power. These media moguls all straddled the line between entertainment and politics, preaching to the public and wielding an immense influence over lawmakers and politicians." Crowley goes on to rank the ten most influential media moguls in history. Needless to say, Murdoch tops the list, followed by Michael Bloomberg[4], Henry Luce[5], Frank Ernest Gannett[6], James Gordon Bennett Sr.[7], Joseph Pulitzer[8], Lord Beaverbrook[9], William Randolph Hearst[10], Ted Turner[11], and Silvio Berlusconi[12]. I have provided extensive footnotes of all ten and I am sure that Crowley's ranking has caused endless debate on the relative positions of the individuals and, more importantly, who was not on the list.

---

[1] Jim Rahn 1930-2009, American author and motivational speaker
[2] William Caxton,1422-1491, diplomat, writer, printer
[3] 'Ten Most Influential Media Moguls in History', Julian Crowley, 20th July 2011, BusinessPundit.com
[4] Michael Bloomberg, b.1942, Mayor of New York City; Founder owner of Bloomberg; a global financial services, mass media and software company, 10th richest person in the world
[5] Henry Luce, 1898-1967, Publisher, Editor in Chief of Time, Fortune, Life, and Sports Illustrated magazines
[6] Frank Ernest Gannett, 1876-1957, Founder, Publisher of US media corporation Gannett, now publishes 92 newspapers, including USA Today, and 23 television stations
[7] James Gordon Bennett Sr, 1795-1872, Founder, Editor and Publisher, The New York Herald
[8] Joseph Pulitzer, 1847-1911, Publisher of St Louis Post Dispatch and The New York World, best known for the Pulitzer Prizes, endowed in 1917 given annually to recognise and reward excellence in American journalism, history, poetry, music, and drama, Founder, The Colombian School of Journalism 1912
[9] Max Aiken, The Rt. Hon. First Baron Beaverbrook, 1897-1964, Canadian-British Newspaper Publisher, an influential figure in British media and politics in the first half of the 20th century through Express Newspapers.
[10] William Randolph Hearst,1863-1951, Founder, The Hearst Corporation. Along with Joseph Pulitzer, he is credited with the creation of 'Yellow Journalism', in popular media by emphasising sensationalism and human-interest stories
[11] Ted Turner, b. 1938, Founder, Cable News Network (CNN), the first 24hr cable news channel, gifted $1bn to create the United Nations Forum to broaden domestic support for the UN
[12] Silvio Berlusconi, b. 1936, Italian media tycoon (Finivest), Politician, Prime Minister of Italy in 4 Governments. Owner of AC Milan FC 2006-2012

Les Hinton, for example, compiled an even more international list but confined it to press barons, including Rothermere[13] , Northcliffe[14], Ochs[15], Sulzberger[16], Packer[17], and Fairfax[18].

When I joined NI I was extremely impressed by its substantial influence in the marketplace. This manifested itself in a number of people whom I would encounter on my regular visits to Wapping. In its corridors I would regularly see cabinet ministers, politicians and major figures from the world of business, show business and culture, no doubt all there to try to influence the UK's leading media company. Influence is of course a two-way commodity. I attended both Les Hinton's and John Witherow's Christmas parties, and very impressive and high profile gatherings they were. Like everyone else, I worked the rooms diligently, making some very useful contacts for my Scottish division. Les hosted one particularly glamorous affair at the Royal Opera House in Covent Garden, whilst John Witherow's parties were equally impressive, with the Princess of Wales[19] being a guest at one. On another occasion I witnessed a memorable spat between Michael Winner[20] and the doorman of the club where the party was being held. Winner had the reputation of being extremely obnoxious and he was certainly in his element on this occasion. He had driven up in his Rolls Royce and thrown the keys at the doorman, who had promptly thrown them straight back at him and told him to move on (that was the polite version of the conversation!).

The most significant event I attended was the News International Conference in Cancun, Mexico in February 2004. I had heard about previous conferences such as the 1986 one on Hayling Island, Australia, where Tony Blair had made his pitch for New Labour, so was therefore very much looking forward to the occasion. I was not disappointed. It was a most impressive three days with several high profile speakers. One of the first was Roger Ailes[21] of Fox. Ailes had built up Fox News since 1996 after a career as a political consultant and was one of Murdoch's highest paid executives, allegedly earning $21 million a year. He later became one of the first high profile figures in the US to be accused of sexual harassment. He resigned in July 2016. Ailes was followed by a live video presentation/ Q&A with Condoleezza Rice[22], US Secretary of State. Rice, if I remember correctly, got a grilling from Alastair Campbell. I had met Campbell earlier that year, liked him and found him hugely entertaining. His various diaries are the definitive account of New Labour and the Blair years in government[23].

[13] Harold Sidney Harmsworth, 1st Viscount Rothermere, 1868-1940
[14] Alfred Charles William Harmsworth, 1st Viscount Northcliffe, 1865-1922
[15] Adolf Simon Ochs, 1858-1935, Newspaper Publisher and former owner, The New York Times
[16] Arthur Ochs Sulzberger Jr., b 1951, Publisher, New York Time since 1993
[17] Sir Frank Packer, 1906-1974, Australian Media Tycoon, father of Kerry 1937-2005
[18] John Fairfax, 1804-1872, English-born journalist and founder of John Fairfax and Sons, Sydney
[19] Diana, Princess of Wales, 1961-97, m. HRH Prince Charles 1981-96
[20] Michael Winner, 1955-2013, film director, producer, Sunday Times restaurant critic
[21] Roger Ailes, 1940-2017, Chairman, CEO, Fox News and Television.
[22] Condoleezza (Condy) Rice, b. 1954, 66th US Secretary of State, First (of two) female members of Augusta National Golf Club 2012
[23] 'The Blair Years', Alastair Campbell (2007), Hutcheson, London

The after-lunch speaker that day was General Tommy Franks[24]. Franks had a distinguished war record and had led the attack on the Taliban in Afghanistan after 9/11. He also led the 2003 invasion of Iraq and the overthrow of Suddam Hussein. He had recently written a memoir, 'American Soldier', published by Harper Collins (no surprise there!). Although the book displaced Bill Clinton's at the top of the New York Times' bestseller list, one reviewer concluded that it, like the plan for and execution of the Iraqi War, "begins better than it ends." That equally summed up Franks' post-lunch speech. It promised much but failed to deliver.

One of the most fascinating presentations was by Jack Welch of General Electric. During Welch's 20-year tenure at General Electric the company's market value rose by 4000%, no mean achievement. When he retired in 2001, he received a severance package of $417 million – then the largest ever. What I learned from his presentation was that, in any company, 80% of the employees are drones, essential but never going to set the heather on fire. It is the key 15% of employees who should be nurtured and given the opportunity to develop – both themselves and the organisation. The remaining 5% are non-achievers and should be fired annually to create turn-over and the opportunity to refresh the organisation – an interesting theory! Many of these theories appeared in his autobiography[25] which I read later. A number of them certainly struck a chord, particularly on leadership. He placed people at the very heart of his organisation. "Getting the right people in the right jobs is more important than developing a strategy." "The team with the best players usually does win - this is why you need to invest the majority of your time and energy developing your people."

The most interesting guest was Michael Howard[26], recently elected leader of the Conservative Party, who was clearly there to sing for his supper. He came with his wife Sandra and was the first speaker in Day 2. Despite there being an audience of over 300, in reality he was addressing one member of the audience only – Rupert who was sitting directly in front of him. The Murdoch Press was still supporting Blair but here was the leader of the opposition being given a golden opportunity to lay out his credentials. Howard gave a flawless speech, delivered extremely eloquently, and was then closely questioned by a number of the political journalists present, including Trevor Kavanagh[27]. It was interesting that Howard and his wife were seated beside Rupert at the Conference Gala Dinner that evening, clearly the principal guests of honour.

Everyone repaired to the bar at the end of the evening and, at around 1am, I accidentally bumped into someone behind me, and turned around to find out that it was Rupert. When I introduced myself, he claimed to know exactly who I was and I asked him what he had thought of Howard's speech. He said that it was fine but that the trouble of being in opposition was that you were inevitably a bit of a one-man-

---

[24] General Tommy Franks, b. 1945, US 4-Star General, last command was Commander of US Central Command overseeing US Military Operation in 25 countries, including the Middle East
[25] 'Straight from the Gut' Jack Welch (with John A. Byrne), 2001, Warner Books
[26] The Rt. Hon. Michael Howard, Baron Howard of Lympne, CH PC QC, b. 1941, Leader, Conservative Party, November 2003 – December 2005
[27] Trevor Kavanagh b. 1943, Political Editor of The Sun 1983-2005

band. Howard's problem therefore was that no one knew much about the Tories, their policies, or even who else was in the Shadow Cabinet. He said, "Can you name me four members of the Shadow Cabinet?" As I reeled off Michael Ancram, Oliver Letwin, Liam Fox, and David Davis, he was momentarily startled. He smiled and told me that I was very much an exception. (I took this to be a great compliment!).

London Press Fund Ball 2000

Chapter 32   THE NEWSPAPER PRESS FUND

"My mother died when I was very young. I didn't want to be in the position I was in but I eventually pulled my head out of the sand, started listening to people, and decided to use my role for good. I am now fired up, engaged and love charity stuff."
Prince Harry[1]

In November 1996, just one year after joining NI, I received a phone call from the legendary "Jolly" Jim Rodger[2], elder statesman of the West of Scotland sports journalists. Jim, then 74, worked for the Daily Mirror and claimed to have the largest contacts book in the business, including Prime Ministers, politicians, celebrities, football managers, players, and royalty. Most of these claims came from Jim himself, one of the world's best self-publicists. Known as 'The Wee Man from Shotts', Jim's other abiding passion was the Newspaper Press Fund (NPF), a charity for retired journalists in need of help – and there were plenty of them.

Jim was the Secretary of the West of Scotland branch of the Fund. On reflection, that is a gross understatement – he ran the committee lock, stock and barrel and nothing happened without his approval. The West of Scotland branch of the Fund in the 1980s ran four main fundraisers each year – two lunches, a ball and a pantomime – and raised £40,000 per year.

I was a regular attendee at the lunches, which attracted big audiences mainly due to the quality of the speakers. They were then held in the Marriott Hotel in Argyle Street, which was also Jim's "office." Over the years I heard some outstanding speakers, including Jeffrey Archer[3], Margaret Thatcher, John Major[4], Lord McCluskey[5] and John Birt[6] and it is no exaggeration to say that the lunches were the hottest tickets in town.

Jim's greatest coup was to get Margaret Thatcher as guest speaker at the lunch in February 1989. Just prior to it, I was present when Jim was asked how he had persuaded the Prime Minister to speak at the event. His answer was highly predictable: "I've always had her private number and when I phoned her she instantly agreed to come, as a special favour to me." Thatcher in her speech perpetuated the myth by glowingly referring to Jim – quite a love-in!

Mrs Thatcher was very impressive. She was in the West of Scotland and, although at the peak of her powers, she was addressing what can only be described as an extremely hostile, cynical audience. On the way in, Jim had to rescue her from overzealous snappers saying, "Follow me, hen, and you'll be fine." By the end of her

---

[1] HRH Prince Harry, Duke of Sussex, KCVO ADC b.1984, younger son of HRH The Prince of Wales
[2] Jim 'Jolly' Rodger OBE, 1923-2007, Daily Mirror sports journalist
[3] The Rt. Hon. Jeffery, Baron Archer of Western-super-Mare, b. 1940, novelist, politician
[4] The Rt. Hon. Sir John Major KG CH, b. 1943, Prime Minister 1990-97
[5] John, Baron McCluskey, 1929-2017, Senator of the College of Justice 1984-2004
[6] John, Baron Birt, b. 1944, Director General, BBC 1992-2000

speech she had the audience eating out of the palm of her hand and received a tremendous reception. Her speech over, she stood up, stepped off the platform and spoke to Jim. She then immediately jumped back on to the platform, grabbed the microphone from the startled Toastmaster and offered her best wishes to the Scottish football team, several of whom were present. Again, she brought the house down.

I now turn to the phone call in which Jim asked me to be the 'Chairman'. When I asked what he meant, he said "You're going to be the Chairman of the West of Scotland branch of the Newspaper Press Fund for the next two years." I pointed out to him that traditionally the Chairman had always been an editor of a Scottish newspaper. He said, "Never mind that, all you have to do is speak at a couple of lunches and chair the Committee." I told him that I didn't even know there was a Committee. Jim was having none of this. "Son, you can do it. It's all decided and I will give you all the help you need." Who can say no to an offer like that? In truth, I was enormously flattered to be asked and very proud to be the first Chairman who was not an editor.

After my meeting with Jim, I told my long-suffering PA Janis about what I had agreed to. I knew Janis would inevitably have to do a lot of the spade work. In selling the proposition to her, I said, "Don't worry, it's a well-oiled organisation and there will be lots of existing files and infrastructure." Janis was later to say, "When Colin tells me not to worry, that's when I start to worry."

Tragically, two months later on 2nd January 1997 Jim Rodger died of a heart attack. Swiftly I tried to establish the infrastructure of the organisation. My first point of contact was Lorraine Woods[7] who is still involved with the Fund some 25 years later. She was enormously helpful, but sadly there were no files. We did get a list of who had taken tables at some previous lunches and balls, but that was it. Janis's prediction about being worried had come true.

And so to the Committee. Again, Lorraine was able to help us on who the current Committee members were. I had anticipated that most of the current crop of editors would be members and perhaps the odd past Chairman, which would have given an element of continuity. Naively I also thought that my successor would already have been identified and I also expected that we would have a long list of potential future speakers for consideration and that the speakers for the next few lunches would be in the bag.

In fact, this all turned out to be not quite as I hoped. My first problem was that I had never met most of Committee – Jim had promised to introduce me to them. It comprised mainly former senior journalists and editors who had, in most cases, been retired for some time – Ian McColl[8], then in his 80s, Jack Campbell[9], Stuart "Bullit"

---

[7] Lorraine Woods then PA to the Editor, Sunday Mail
[8] Ian McColl, 1915-2005, Editor, Scottish Daily Express 1961-71, Editor, Daily Express 1971-74
[9] Jack Campbell, 1914-2004, Editor, Evening Citizen & Scottish Daily Express

McCartney[10], Martin Frizell[11], Alan Herron[12] and Alex 'Chiefy' Cameron[13]. At my first committee meeting I had barely introduced myself when I heard a plaintive voice from the other end of the room whispering loudly "I can't hear what he's saying." Lesson number one learned immediately – put Ian McColl near the top of the table. Lesson number two was the need to draft in some new blood - and urgently.

Another task was to recognise the enormous contribution made by Jim. Murdoch MacLennan had suggested an annual award to the best young sports journalist and was prepared to donate a trophy. Ross Wilson[14], ex Daily Record journalist and now fledgling PR executive, agreed to organise it. Funded by the Scottish Newspaper Publishers, each year a committee would consider nominations and select a winner of The Jim Rodger Memorial Trophy. It would be awarded to a sports journalist under 35 years of age currently writing for a Scottish newspaper. Thus Jonathan Norcroft of The Sunday Times was presented with the trophy by Alex Ferguson[15] (Chairman of the judging panel) in November 1998. Jonathan was the first two-time winner of the Trophy (1997, 1998) whilst Moira Gordon of Scotland on Sunday was the only female winner (2003).

One of Jim Rodger's greatest ideas in organising the lunch was to have perhaps the longest top table ever seen – sometimes well over 20 people. This was to accommodate several categories of people – the current Chairman, guest speaker(s), previous Chairmen (if still in favour), sponsors, representatives from The Newspaper Press Fund in London (if in favour), politicians (same rule applied), and 'important' people. This last category was a very flexible arrangement to give the occasion some star quality, but I suspect it also gave Jim the opportunity to repay favours. At one end was the Minister of Glasgow Cathedral for over 40 years the Very Reverend William Morris[16], who was superb at delivering a specially commissioned Grace, and at the other end, to balance the ticket, the Bishop of Motherwell, the Rt Reverend Joe Devine[17].

Bill Morris was a great character and delivered graces at functions throughout Scotland. He eventually published them in an excellent book, 'Amazing Graces'[18]. His Press Fund utterances were particularly memorable;

---

[10] Stuart McCartney, senior reporter, Scottish Daily Express
[11] Martin Frizell, sports journalist, News of the World
[12] Alan Herron, sports journalist, Sunday Mirror
[13] Alex Cameron, 1934-2007, Sports Editor, Daily Record
[14] Ross Wilson b. 1965, Founder (1996) and Managing Director, Ross Wilson Public Relations
[15] Sir Alex Ferguson, b. 1941, Manager, Manchester United 1986-2013
[16] The Very Reverend William Morris, 1925-2013, Minister of Glasgow Cathedral 1967-2005
[17] The Rt Reverend Joseph Devine, 1937-2019, Bishop of Motherwell 1983-2013
[18] 'Amazing Graces, Pre-Prandial Words of Spiritual Uplift to Grace any Gathering'. The Very Reverend William J. Morris 2001, Neil Wilson Publishing Ltd.

"Lord, Our thanks for those with skills,
Who entertain us, give us thrills,
We thank thee, too, for those who write,
Help us relive each game, each fight.

Our thanks for those who write no more,
No longer play, nor ever score.
Remembering those from whom we've learned,
May we be blessed by grace unearned."

Keeping the old Scottish tradition of clapping this lot in to lunch required a strong pair of hands. After completing my term as Chairman, I found myself still seated beside some really interesting people, but gradually moving outwards from centre stage. The day of reckoning came a few years later, when I found myself sitting beside the Bishop of Motherwell and knew that the end was nigh – back to the ranks!

At a Press Fund Ball in the spirit of Bill Morris I used a grace that seemed appropriate for a room full of thirsty journalists:

"Lord Almighty, Lord Divine,
Who turned the water into wine,
Look down upon thy mortal men,
As we try to turn it back again."

Jim Rodger had left a tremendous legacy and was awarded an OBE in recognition of his contribution to the Fund. Although attendances had started to decline, the functions were still reasonably attended and continued to raise significant funds for the charity. I reviewed everything and created an action plan based on achieving a number of key objectives:

- The NPF was first and foremost a charity, so the main objective was to raise more money for it. By the time I completed my term of office, we had raised the bar from £40,000 to £55,000 a year for the Fund.
- Membership of the committee hadn't changed a great deal over the years, but I concluded that the way forward was not to retire existing committee members, but to introduce a few new, keen helpers and let natural wastage take its course. Matt Bendoris[19] and Janette Harkess[20] joined the committee and began to revamp the Ball.

[19] Matt Bendoris, b. 1970 Chief Features Writer, The Scottish Sun
[20] Janette Harkess, b. 1964, journalist, Sunday Mail, Daily Mail, Deputy Editor, The Herald 2006-09

- The lunches offered the greatest potential for increasing revenue. I felt that attendance was directly dependent on the quality of the speakers and a key objective was therefore to continue to attract high-profile quality speakers.
- Audiences were attracted not just by the quality of the speaker, but also by the profile of the event and we needed to ensure that they continued to be attended by more well-known "names." It's a simple fact of life that most people love to rub shoulders with the great and the good. We had them, not just at the top table, but throughout the audience and so a further key objective was to continue to sprinkle 'Pixie Dust'.

On becoming Chairman and realising that there was no pipeline of future speakers, I needed to rectify the situation very quickly, particularly with the first lunch less than six months away. I targeted two extremely high-profile people, Tony Blair and Sir Richard Branson[21], and set about securing their services. Branson had huge charisma, particularly as he was going through the daredevil stage of his career, having recently completed the Blue Riband, the fastest trans-Atlantic boat crossing, and was about to embark on his balloon phase. The key (or so I thought) to attracting high profile speakers was to have someone on the inside – a senior person within the individual's organisation, who could cut through the red tape and secure a date in their diary. The previous Autumn I had attended the Entrepreneurial Exchange Annual Dinner and sat beside Will Whitehorn[22], a senior Virgin executive. We had exchanged cards so I was able to contact Will several months later with an invitation for Richard to speak. All went swimmingly well at first. Richard was delighted and instantly agreed to speak. What we had not foreseen was that in the coming months Richard was attempting to go around the world by balloon which presented major problems in securing a date. This took almost a year and he spoke at my second lunch as Chairman in November 1998.

On the day, Richard was due to arrive on the 11.40am by Virgin Train from Newcastle which was cutting it fine as the Chairman's pre-lunch reception started at noon. His train was late and he eventually arrived at the hotel at 12.10pm. I added a line recording his tardiness into my speech. I always felt an enormous sense of relief when our main speaker arrived, especially in this case, after so many false starts, but finally there was Richard Branson. He immediately moved round the room, mingling with the guests and everyone was happy.

The top table was eventually clapped in to lunch and in my introductory speech I welcomed everyone and introduced the top table guests. During lunch Richard and I chatted amicably, but it was then that he confessed to me that he was a very nervous speaker and had great difficulty in speaking to audiences of this size. He had therefore decided to make a short speech and take questions for the rest of the time, despite the fact that he had been exhaustively briefed on making a speech of 25-30

---

[21] Sir Richard Branson, b. 1950, Founder, Virgin Group
[22] Will Whitehorn, b. 1960, joined Virgin Group 1987, Head of Public Affairs, President of Virgin Galactic (until 2010)

minutes. I then discovered that he had read my introductory speech, sitting on the table between us, and was not happy that I was going to refer to his train being late. I didn't change my speech and his lasted nine minutes – slightly longer than my introduction. It was rather disappointing as it was almost entirely devoted to the challenges of running a rail network. He then invited questions. The first was from Tom Shields, who asked: "Mr Branson, given your great experience with balloons, would you be prepared to give some advice to those running Celtic Football Club?" Richard was like a rabbit caught in the headlights – he clearly didn't understand the nuance of the question – and so started a whole series of off the cuff responses, which ultimately culminated in him giving tacit support to the concept of an independent Scotland. It was this answer which provided the headlines and a major story in the papers and Richard's press team had to dance around the issue for several days before it died down.

The one major lesson for me from this lunch was never to invite a keynote speaker unless someone has heard them speak elsewhere. The general conclusion was that Richard's speech was underwhelming and the audience felt short changed.

The first lunch during my Chairmanship of the Press Fund featured Tony Blair, supported by Donald Dewar[23]. Blair, since becoming Prime Minister in 1997, had seldom spoken in Scotland and the Press Fund Lunch, with its high profile media audience, would have been an attractive proposition. In terms of securing the speaker this was a far simpler exercise than the Branson saga – we made a reasonable assumption that Blair would not turn down the opportunity to talk to the Scottish press in the lead-up to the first elections to the Scottish Parliament and, after minor negotiations, the date was set for 30th April 1998, a mere six days before polling day. When the Prime Minister is the speaker, you pray that no earth-shattering event will occur just before or on the day. There were many conversations between Janis and Number 10 about logistics, security, timings and so on, so when Blair's office asked for a list of the top table guests about a week before the event, we were happy to oblige.

What then occurred was not so happy. On receipt of the list, Blair's office immediately contacted Janis and demanded that one of the guests, Alex Salmond[24], be removed from the list. Janis explained that this was impossible, as he had already accepted his invitation. There then was what I can only describe as a forceful exchange between myself and Anji Hunter[25], Blair's Chief of Staff. The thrust of her argument – actually, her demand – was that, since this was a period leading up to an election, there were well established protocols in place on what was acceptable and that an opposition figure could not be present when the Prime Minister was speaking. For my part, I argued that this was not a political occasion; it was a charity lunch and the Prime Minister had been invited on that basis; we were not expecting a political speech from him (she snorted at that!). I also pointed out that Alex

[23] The Rt. Hon. Donald Dewar, 1937-2000, Inaugural First Minister of Scotland 1999-2000
[24] The Rt. Hon. Alex Salmond, b. 1954, MP, Banff and Buchan 1987-2010, First Minister of Scotland 2007-14, MP, Gordon 2015-17
[25] Anji Hunter, b. 1955, Tony Blair's Director of Government Relations 1997-2001

Salmond was a regular guest and supporter of the Press Fund. Finally, I told her in no uncertain terms that it was not up to the Prime Minister who the Press Fund invited as guests to its lunch. She didn't quite hang up at this point, but I suspected that this was not going to be the end of the matter and indeed it was not. Behind my back, Downing Street contacted the local branch of the Press Fund, and also the London office, with the same demand – that Alex Salmond should be removed from the list of guests, or the Prime Minister might not attend. Fortunately, I had already been in touch with London and they wholeheartedly supported my stance. In the end, I'd like to be able to say common sense prevailed. In a way it did, but Downing Street accepted the situation with very bad grace.

I'm perhaps being uncharitable when I suggest that Blair extracted revenge by his behaviour on the day. He was due to arrive at around 12.15pm, enabling him to make his scheduled appearance at the Chairman's Reception. The guest list for this exceeded 50 people due to the prominence of the speaker and all expected to rub shoulders with the great man himself. In some ways I was not surprised when Janis whispered to me that the Prime Minister was running late. No cause for panic, as politicians are rarely on time. I also became aware that Alex Salmond was behaving strangely and seemed to be following me round the room. Everywhere I went, he was directly behind me. On a couple of occasions, I deliberately made a point of introducing him to a guest and extracted myself to get back to the door to await the Prime Minister. Two seconds later he would appear beside me again and I'd have to divert him to meet someone else.

By 12.40 there was still no sign of the Prime Minister. The hotel management were getting very agitated, as they needed to start to move the 700+ guests into the room. We held off for a few more minutes and were relieved to hear that the Prime Minister's party had now arrived at the hotel, but were demanding a separate room, in which to attend to some last-minute matters. By 12.45 everyone should have been seated and the top table guests introduced by me. By now Alex Salmond was almost perched on my right shoulder. A further complication was that the time was rapidly approaching when the seafood first course would have to be removed and scrapped, because of the time it had already been on the tables. We quickly made some alternative plans: The Banqueting Manager would immediately bring in the guests, followed by the top table guests, minus the Prime Minister and Donald Dewar, and I would start proceedings without them. I was absolutely furious. It was well after 1pm before everyone was seated and I could introduce the top table, which, because of the speaker, was the longest in the history of the NPF. The Bishop of Motherwell was so far away that I could hardly see him! The Toastmaster would alert me when Blair arrived. I had just started my speech by apologising for Blair's absence when I received the signal and saw him standing in the doorway at the back of the room. I ignored the signal and continued to introduce the entire top table, leaving the Prime Minister to cool his heels at the back of the room. Revenge for such discourtesy was sweet.

Blair was due to fly to Wales in a private plane immediately after lunch, but was now so seriously behind schedule that we had to accept yet another change to the plan: Blair would speak after the main course and leave immediately afterwards and Donald Dewar would also speak.

I had very little time for a one-to-one conversation with Blair, who seemed preoccupied, but we did manage to discuss Northern Ireland affairs for a short time. I had admired him for his tenacity in keeping the Peace Process going, when at times it seemed as if it was an impossible task (See Chapter 3).

The first part of Blair's speech was devoted to an appraisal of events in Kosovo. The second part of his speech was a blistering attack on the SNP, whose manifesto had been launched that morning. We now understood the real reason for the Prime Minister arriving late – he was rewriting his speech. The final insult was that the Press Fund subsequently received a bill for the room hire, sandwiches and coffee for the Blair entourage – so much for charity! During the fiercest part of his attack on the SNP the entire audience suddenly burst out laughing. Most of the top table, including Blair, had no idea what caused the laughter, until we realised that Salmond, who had appeared on the television programme 'Call My Bluff', was holding up a large card bearing the word "BLUFF." More importantly, he must have pre-warned photographers of what he intended to do, as the following day's newspapers all carried at least one photograph of the bemused and totally upstaged Prime Minister and a grinning Alex Salmond holding up his card. It was an extraordinary move by Salmond in its planning, timing and execution. With 734 attendees, the Blair lunch was the highest number of guests ever at a Press Fund lunch and is still a record.

Ten years later, Salmond was himself the chief guest at the NPF lunch. I couldn't attend, but my daughter Amanda was there. I was flattered to hear that he mentioned me in his speech, not to recall the "Bluff" incident, but to acknowledge my part in ensuring that his invitation to the Blair lunch was honoured. I wrote to him and received a letter thanking me for my courtesy on the day. Ramsay Smith[26] succeeded me as Chairman and as I gradually moved down the top table, I sat beside many people including Robin Cook[27], Wendy Alexander[28], Rosie Kane[29] and finally, as I've already mentioned, the Bishop of Motherwell.

The Christmas pantomime was also a huge success. Each year the organisers of the main Glasgow pantomime donated the dress rehearsal evening to the Press Fund and hosted a drinks party for the committee and friends afterwards. For Amanda and Milena this was the highlight of their year and they met Elaine C Smith[30], Gerard Kelly[31] and a host of other stars over the years. One year I asked Gerard to read out a message for one of my friends Sandro Formisano[32]. Sandro at the time was

[26] Ramsay Smith, b. 1955, Director, Media House International
[27] Robin Cook, 1946-2015, MP Livingstone 1983-2005, Foreign Secretary 1997-2001
[28] Wendy Alexander FRSE, b. 1963, MSP, Leader, Scottish Labour Party 2007-08 Vice Principal (International) University of Dundee
[29] Rosie Kane, b. 1961, MSP 2003-07, Scottish Socialist Party
[30] Elaine C Smith b.1958, Scottish actress and comedienne
[31] Gerard Kelly 1959-2010, Scottish actor
[32] Sandro Formisano b. 1955, Cavalieri de Lavoro, founder and CEO New Concept m. Beverley (née Hopkinson)

in his late forties and Gerard in front of the whole audience wished him a happy sixtieth birthday. Sandro was to extract revenge many years later.

The Press Fund is now known as The Journalists' Charity. The change was described at the time as a move to make it more inclusive, encompassing all media. I suspect it was an acknowledgement of the declining influence and importance of print media.

In the West of Scotland the charity went through a period of steady decline, not helped by the severe recession of 2008 and the continuing decline of the industry itself. The lunches stopped in 2010 and only recently resumed. In December 2018 I attended my first lunch since leaving NI and witnessed Michael Gove[33] deliver an underwhelming speech – he'll never be a stand-up comedian. Stuart MacQuarrie[34] continued Bill Morris' great tradition with another fine grace, perhaps reflecting the changing world of the media.

"Oh Lord, we're here for the Journalists' Charity Fund,
The nation's favourite hacks, some slim, some sleek, but mostly rotund,
The institution dates back to Dickens' day,
Pickwick Papers, poorhouses, all work no play,
Much the same for us today."

---

[33] The Rt. Hon. Michael Gove MP, b. 1967, Secretary of State for Environment, Food and Rural Affairs
[34] The Rev. Stuart MacQuarrie, b. 1952, Chaplain, University of Glasgow 2001-

With Elaine C. Smith, Press Fund Pantomime 2000.

Chapter 33   RUPERT MURDOCH - AN ASSESSMENT

"We have no intention of failing. The only question is how great a success we will have." Rupert Murdoch

There continues to be a fascination with Keith Rupert Murdoch. His grandparents had emigrated to Australia from Cruden Bay in the north of Scotland and he was born south of Melbourne in 1931. He is now in his late eighties.

His father Keith had built up a smallish group of newspapers in Australia which Rupert, named after his maternal grandfather, inherited on the sudden death of his father when Rupert was 22. By the age of 37 he had expanded the company rapidly, mainly through acquisition, and now owned a sizeable newspaper empire in Australia valued at A$ 50 million.

In 1968 he moved to England where he purchased the News of the World, followed by the ailing Sun, both transformed with a by now well-tested and successful formula of sex, sport, and crime. A series of US acquisitions followed from 1973 onwards and in 1979 News Corporation (News Corp) became the holding company for his empire. In the UK he had acquired The Sunday Times and The Times. He diversified rapidly in the 1980s, purchasing 20th Century Fox Film Corporation in 1985 and several independent radio stations, the group eventually emerging as Fox Inc., a major American television network. From 1974 Murdoch was based in the US, initially in New York, and became a naturalised US citizen in 1985. Book publishing followed and numerous acquisitions, including Harper & Row in the US and William Collins in Glasgow, eventually becoming Harper Collins, based in the UK. In 1989 he created Sky Television, merging it with British Satellite Broadcasting to become B Sky B. Star TV in Hong Kong was purchased to create a pan-Asian television network. Other significant acquisitions along the way included: Fox News in 1994, MySpace.com in 2005, and The Wall Street Journal in 2007. In 2013, News Corp split into two separate companies, News Corp and 21st Century Fox. In 2017, Murdoch sold most of the holdings in 21st Century Fox to Disney for $66bn.

Murdoch, like many others, was always highly leveraged. In 1990 News Corp's debt stood at $8.1bn and most of it was now due. Murdoch restructured the debt, diluted his shareholding and convinced the consortium of banks to give him extensions until 1993. The negotiations went to the wire and it was said that the whole organisation could have collapsed had a Pittsburgh bank, owed a mere $10 million, refused to join in the restructuring. In the end he succeeded and, less than two years later, had bought back control of the company.

The few mainstream biographies about Murdoch are by William Shawcross (1997)[1], Neil Chenoweth (2001)[2], and Michael Wolff (2008)[3]. Andrew Neil's autobiography[4] in 1996 provides a close insight into his relationship with Murdoch during his years at The Sunday Times. Perhaps Les Hinton's 2018 autobiography[5] reveals the most intimate portrait of him. At the other end of the spectrum, there are some publications whose very titles give a clue to the authors' opinion of Murdoch. Amongst these are 'Murdoch's Politics; How One Man's Thirst for Power and Wealth Shapes Our World.' 'Breaking News; Sex, Lies and the Murdoch Succession.' 'The Rise and Fall of the Murdoch Empire. and 'The Fall of the House of Murdoch.'

He is essentially an extremely private person but much has been written about his personal life. He has been married four times - to Patricia Brooks (1956-65, 1 daughter; Prudence), Anna Torv (1967-99, 2 sons: Lachlan and James, 1 daughter: Elizabeth), Wendy Deng (1999-2014, 2 daughters: Grace and Chloe), and Jerry Hall (Jan 2016 – present).

Many observers have made comparisons between Murdoch and Maxwell. Julian Crowley (Chapter 31) ranked Murdoch as the most influential media mogul in history. I'm not sure Maxwell would have made the top 50. There are significant differences between the two men. In my years at MGN Maxwell was referred to by everyone in the company simply as 'Maxwell' and regarded with fear, loathing, and suspicion. He was brash and full of his own importance. Murdoch on the other hand within the company was almost universally referred to as 'Rupert', even though most of the staff had never met him. He was not necessarily regarded with affection - more a deep-seated admiration for what he had achieved - and a sense of pride in belonging to a successful organisation. News International tended to be well-ahead of MGN in its remuneration levels. Its Sharesave[6] scheme introduced in 1997 meant a significant number of staff had a personal stake in the company. In the first five years of the scheme, News Corp's share price rose significantly, to the enormous benefit of those in the scheme.

The second major difference was that Maxwell's management style meant he was involved in everything within the company. Part 4 of this book illustrates Maxwell's micro-management style and I frequently found myself involved both with him and with the consequences of his decisions. During my time with NI, I only met Rupert on a handful of occasions, because NI was a far more structured and infinitely better managed company. Despite this, he could still instil a different type of fear and apprehension in his senior management team. He visited Wapping perhaps five or six times a year, usually for a week or two at a time, and both before and during those periods there was a totally different atmosphere throughout the building. 'Rupert's coming in next week' or 'Rupert's in town' was usually part of any

[1] 'Murdoch', William Shawcross 1997, Simon and Schuster, New York
[2] 'Rupert Murdoch; The Untold Story of the World's Greatest Media Wizard', Neil Chenoweth 2001, Random House, New York
[3] 'The Man who owns the News; Inside the Secret World of Rupert Murdoch', Michael Wolff 2008, The Bodley Head, London
[4] 'Full Disclosure', Andrew Neil 1996, Macmillan, London
[5] 'The Bootle Boy: An Untidy Life in News', Les Hinton 2018, Scribe UK
[6] Sharesave: the News International Sharesave Scheme, a share option scheme enabling employees through regular savings to take up a shareholding in News Corp

conversation. The entire organisation focussed solely on his visits and it sometimes felt that the actual running of the business was on hold during them.

I first met him during the budgetary round in early 1996. For the coming financial year I was trying to persuade Les and Doug to drop the price of The Scottish Sun for three months. It had been tried before and the results had been encouraging, but it had never been used as part of a long-term strategy. Even in my short time with the company, I felt Bob and Bruce had aligned the paper editorially to fight the Daily Record effectively. A significant price differential would exert even more pressure and achieve results much faster.

I was invited to join the final budget process in which Rupert would approve the 1996/7 business plan. I was wheeled into the boardroom towards the end of an all-day meeting on NGN's plans and the final session was to be on Scotland. I was extremely nervous but had prepared extensively. At the top of a long table sat Rupert with an empty seat directly to his left, where he indicated I should sit, and around the table were Les, Doug, Clive, Ian and two or three accountants. After a brief introduction, Rupert fired at me a series of pertinent questions about the Scottish market place. I was comfortable as I could provide all the answers, but even within that short period, I could see an intellectual rigour about the man that was streets ahead of the hot air and bluster of Maxwell. All the time Rupert sat slightly back from the table with a yellow legal pad on his knees and every time I answered a question he would write something down. Finally we got to the crux of the matter – pricing. Until then, everyone's focus had been on considering up to three months of reduced cover price. Out of the blue Rupert asked, "What would this cost if we were to do it for a year?" Cue accountants lunging forward, calculators whirring and everyone working to establish the answer to the question. It was not an easy calculation as it involved a complex equation of both retailer and wholesaler discounts and the probability of maintaining the retailer's margin throughout the period. Rupert continued doodling on his pad and quite quickly said, "I guess it's around £5.1 million." It was almost a minute before one of the accountants answered, "It is actually £5.06 million, Mr Murdoch." Afterwards there was a brief discussion about what level of sales uplift we could expect to gain. I said that with a fair wind we might get to 450,000. Rupert's passing shot as he indicated the discussion was over and the decision made was, "Don't come back until it's 475,000." As I was leaving he smiled. Passing him, I glanced at his yellow pad and saw what I can only describe as hieroglyphics – doodles with the odd number here or there.

That early meeting with Rupert aptly demonstrated for me the huge difference between him and Maxwell. He was an intellectual Colossus by comparison. He has built a business on an extremely sophisticated weekly financial reporting system. Combine this with his incredible grasp of numbers and it in part explains how he has been able to keep track of almost everything within his empire. As Andrew Neil puts it, "He is one of the smartest men in the business with a restless, ruthless brain that is more than a match for any British competitor in newspapers or broadcasting.

His mind is always buzzing, always up on the issues and always original which means his editors have to be on their toes if they are to keep up with him."

How to assess the man himself? Andrew Neil said, "When you work for Rupert Murdoch, you do not work for a company, a chairman, or a CEO, you work for a Sun King. You are not a director or manager, or an editor; you are a courtier at the court of the Sun King, rewarded by money and status by a grateful king, as long as you serve his purpose; dismissed outright or demoted to a remote corner of the empire when you have ceased to please him or outlived your usefulness." Neil himself became Icarus to Rupert's Sun King with predictable consequences. Others have made similar comments,

"Don't fall in love with Rupert, he turns against lovers and chops them off," wrote Bruce Matthews[7]. In Matthews' obituary, Michael Leapman[8] wrote, "The court of Rupert Murdoch is much like the court of Henry VIII. Men and women are promoted to positions of great power, only to be felled on the royal whim, either because they cease to be useful or because they threaten to gain more fame than the monarch himself. Bruce Matthews was Murdoch's Thomas Cromwell. As Henry had Cromwell executed after doing his dirty work on the monasteries, so Matthews fell from grace only months after engineering the supreme coup of Murdoch's career, the move of his papers to Wapping to escape the stranglehold of the print unions. The irony was that, having masterminded the most ruthless stratagem in modern industrial history, he was not tough enough to survive in the harsh environment he helped to create."

"He has built his empire by using people then discarding them when they have passed their expiration date. It's not the sort of management style which lends itself to lasting friendships. In fact Rupert is a lousy manager, he terrifies those under him when he makes one of his flying visits. It takes weeks to restore their morale." Gus Fischer

"The management style of News Corporation is one of extreme devolution punctuated by periods of episodic autocracy. Most company Boards meet to make decisions, ours meets to ratify Rupert's." Richard Searby[9]

In Rupert's defence there is an element of predictability in all this. Many of the above quotes are from senior ex-employees, perhaps sad and bitter, who were not running the business the way Rupert wanted. After all, he was the major shareholder, he certainly regarded it as 'his business' and it was therefore his prerogative to do things as he wanted. To use the Colin Powell phrase again, "Doing the right things will almost inevitably piss people off."

One area of the business where Rupert's decision was non-negotiable was in the political support given by his newspapers at any given time. For example, in Scotland in the late 1990s Bob Bird had persuaded him to let the paper support the

[7] Bruce Matthews, 1925-96, Managing Director, NI 1983-87
[8] Michael Leapman, The Independent, 26th October 1996
[9] Richard Searby, 1931-2018, Legal Advisor, Chairman, News Corp 1977-92

SNP. Bob's argument was that it offered The Scottish Sun a significant point of difference to the Daily Record. During that time, the Sun was nationally pro-Thatcher and the cynics said that Murdoch allowed Bob to take the SNP line because, during any election if the SNP won any seats, the likelihood was that they would be from Labour, thus helping the Conservatives nationally. From 1995 onwards, Blair courted Murdoch, who by now did not think very highly of John Major. The Hayling Island Conference sealed the betrothal and, during the 1997 election, The Sun switched its support to Labour and Rupert told Les to ensure that The Scottish Sun followed suit. I remember Les visiting Kinning Park and telling Bob and his team what had to happen. Naturally it did not go down well; The Scottish Sun editorial team were very unhappy but they accepted the proprietor's prerogative. To his credit, Bob skilfully changed the paper's stance without in turn 'pissing off' too many readers.

In his 2018 autobiography Les Hinton provides a much more measured view of Murdoch. Referring to him as 'Rupert' throughout, his are the recollections of a man who worked for him for 52 years and was eventually, in his own words, made the scapegoat for the phone hacking scandal and so resigned. "His success has not met with universal admiration. Rupert could be hell to work for and 60 years of success and tough tactics yielded for him a bitter harvest of enemies." "As a boss, he could be hands-off or autocratic, charming or irascible, forgiving or fierce, and sometimes just a comprehensive pain but he also imbued his companies with a fantastic sense of possibility and got big results. Working for him could be very tough, and the attrition rate was high."

Rupert visited Kinning Park once during my tenure. In 2001 at relatively short notice I was told that he was coming for a 'visit', we should expect him around 4pm, and he would stay on for dinner with the senior management team. The last part turned out to be the biggest headache of the entire visit. Logistics dictated that we had to be in a restaurant by 6.30pm. Unbelievably in the middle of a recession, finding a top-quality restaurant in Glasgow that would serve dinner at that time for a private party of 20+ people with no expense spared proved almost impossible. Thankfully The Corinthian came up trumps and looked after us extremely well, but the whole exercise left severe doubts in my mind about the overall efficiency of the restaurant sector in the West of Scotland. Further details about the visit emerged over the final two days. Rupert was coming with his son Lachlan[10], Les Hinton, and Ian McDonald. We were to make a short presentation about what we were doing in Scotland - the strategy for the business etc. - and he would then go on a tour of the plant. I felt reasonably relaxed about the whole occasion, as I had an extremely capable management team whom I more than trusted to give a good account of themselves. For the formal meeting in the boardroom I arranged copies of every daily and Sunday newspaper to be on the table. Once again, Rupert was extremely impressive. To put things in perspective, my subsidiary company in Scotland was considerably less than 1% of his entire business but he was more than familiar with the marketplace and fired a whole series of questions and a really good discussion

---

[10] Lachlan Keith Murdoch, b. 1971, Executive Director, News Corp 1996-2000, Deputy Chief Operating Officer 2000-05

ensued around the table. Again, Rupert's intellectual rigour shone through the entire visit. On the walkabout there was lots of Glaswegian banter, which he seemed to like. I may be biased but Rupert could not have failed to have been impressed with my team. In the Press Hall we witnessed a classic set piece test when Rupert whispered something to Lachlan, who then peeled off from the party. We knew exactly what he was doing - inspecting the 'cores' (the ends of the massive newsprint reels). The best printers leave an absolute minimum amount of paper on the core. Lachlan re-joined the party shortly afterwards and whispered to his dad that, "They're very good." Richard Bennett[11] and I smiled at each other. We knew they would do it; they knew they were going to do it, but it was immensely satisfying that they witnessed our efficiency. During dinner Rupert was an excellent host and the conversation covered a wide range of subjects. We waved goodbye to him just after 7.45pm – the end of a momentous day. I interpreted Rupert's visit as a thank you to the Scottish team who had performed extremely well over the years in one of the last great tabloid battles in the UK.

And Rupert himself? My final assessment was that Julian Crowley's ranking of him as the world's greatest ever media mogul was totally accurate. The term 'press baron' could be substituted for media mogul but what is increasingly emerging is that he will be the last of that ilk. As I shall describe in Chapter 40 the press barons of the 20th Century were operating in a business already showing signs of decline that will eventually become terminal.

---

[11] Richard Bennett b.1952 Production Manager, Kinning Park 2000-12. m. Janis Judge 2013

Chapter 34   LEGAL ANECDOTES

"Ethics is knowing the difference between what you have the right to do and what is right to do."   Potter Stewart[1]

In the Noughties, at a Press Fund Lunch in Glasgow, Kelvin MacKenzie[2] made a highly amusing speech in which he talked about a number of the libel cases The Sun had been involved in during his editorship. He referred to the Elton John case which cost the Sun £1 million in damages. At the end of the case Rupert had arrived in London and, less than amused at the outcome, instructed MacKenzie and Phil Hall to meet him first thing Monday morning to review all outstanding legal cases. MacKenzie described spending a sleepless weekend assembling all the material and was nervously walking towards Rupert's office at 7.55 am Monday morning, his files under his arm, when his mood was considerably lightened by the sight of Phil Hall in front of him with someone wheeling a large trolley containing the News of the World's files.

In Scotland, the issue of defamation was never far from editors' minds, particularly those of the tabloids (Note: defamation in Scotland covers both the written wrong and the verbal/ spoken wrong, whereas in England the former is libel, the latter slander). Our various night lawyers would arrive in the early evening, their job being to peruse every controversial piece of copy and guide the editor(s) as to its legality, particularly in the area of defamation. Many lawyers and QCs built extremely successful careers by specialising in this area. Despite all these checks and safeguards, a regular stream of people continued to sue NI.

Scotland was no different. Resorting to legal action was the ultimate sanction, but a lot could happen before it reached that stage. I was constantly reminded of Rupert's remark to Les Hinton. "Complaints will pour your way from important people annoyed at the way they have been treated in our pages." To this I would add another category: attempts by people to prevent publication of stories about them. I am sure that our editors had to deal with this on a daily basis but occasionally I also found myself involved. It would usually be from someone I knew personally or professionally. Could I possibly use my influence, a friendly word in the editor's ear etc. to prevent a story from appearing? Most cases were fairly predictable - an affair about to become public knowledge, or some questionable behaviour. Sometimes the explanations for such behaviour were hilarious, "A wet bottle, that slipped from my hand and accidently struck someone on the head." To all these pleas I had a standard approach. First, I would tell the person totally truthfully that I had absolutely no influence in what appeared or didn't appear in the paper. The company had clear lines of demarcation between commercial and editorial functions and I had no influence over an editor. Furthermore, I stressed that any interference

---

[1] Potter Stewart 1915-87, US Supreme Court Judge 1959-81
[2] Kelvin MacKenzie, b. 1946, media executive, Editor, The Sun 1981-94

from me could be counterproductive. A story might have no chance of being published, but suddenly be reassessed in the light of my interest. Regardless, the outcome was the same – I could not and would not interfere. My advice would be for the person to hope that another major story develop. If that happened, and their story still appeared, it might be relegated from the front of the paper to some obscure position in the back. If they were really lucky it might not appear at all, dropped for some much bigger and more important event. My best advice was that if it did appear, then they should lie low for a few days and be unavailable for comment. In 1999 I was asked to write a piece for the Institute of Directors Magazine. Headed 'PR Should Be Top of the List For Business People' I offered similar advice. "Finally, what do you do when you're caught with your pants down? There can only be one piece of advice here - shut up shop, disconnect the telephone and treat yourself to that long-deserved break in a far flung place. A week might be a long time in politics (as Harold Wilson famously once said), but when there is a good sex scandal on the go, the media has an avaricious appetite."

Most people accepted my course of action with good grace. Some did not, sometimes making threats – the end of a friendship, or, in the case of some advertisers, the withdrawal of all their advertising. All rather sad. Some went to extraordinary lengths to prevent people from seeing what was in the paper. In my village, one person whose family appeared in a particularly salacious story in the News of the World allegedly set off early in the morning and purchased every copy of the paper. Needless to say, news spread rapidly and the story was discussed in minute detail throughout the village.

The threat of legal action certainly concentrated the minds of editors. Often the cases could take several months or even years before coming to court, with much serious negotiation between the parties in the interim. I was involved in a case between Fred Goodwin and The Sunday Times. I was aware of the details and when I met Fred at a function in Edinburgh, I asked him why on earth he was pursuing such an action. He rather sheepishly admitted that in fact the case was being pursued by his legal team and not him personally. I suggested that a better course of action might be to contact Les Hinton. After the function I relayed the contents of the conversation to Les and happily the action was dropped a short time afterwards, I believe to the satisfaction of both parties.

I often met people who had been, or were currently, involved in legal actions against us. In 2003, I was a member of the Royal Society of Edinburgh (RSE) committee organising a media symposium. At the first meeting one attendee arrived late and sat in the empty seat beside me. After the meeting we introduced ourselves and I met for the first time Alistair Moffat[3], then involved in an action over a story that had appeared in the News of the World. Alistair and I maintained cordial relations during the lengthy organisational period of the RSE event. In the event the matter never ended up in court.

---

[3] Alistair Moffat, b. 1950, award-winning Scottish writer and journalist

One defamation case which did dominate the headlines was the case of Father Noel Barry[4], a Roman Catholic priest and press secretary to Cardinal Thomas Winning[5], head of the Catholic Church in Scotland. The case involved Father Barry and Anne Clinton[6]. In September 1996 The Scottish Sun implied that they were involved in a long-term, secret sexual relationship. Each sued the paper for £200,000 damages and, after a ten-day trial, the judge awarded Ms. Clinton £125,000 and Father Barry £45,000. Both admitted spending nights under the same roof but denied that there had ever been a sexual relationship. It was an extremely high-profile case and many observers were astonished at its outcome. This was because of the testimony of a former nun Caroline Brown, who told the court that she lost her virginity to Father Barry in a Preston hotel room in 1985. She said that Father Barry had lied under oath and she claimed that they had been in love and planned to marry, but their relationship eventually floundered after he refused to leave the priesthood.

Mrs. Brown was particularly critical of Cardinal Winning, who she said had been unsympathetic when she approached him. She said that he asked her if she had any tape recordings. She told the court that she had become quite upset and said to Winning, "I don't think you realise how difficult this is for me to come here." Winning replied, "What do you want, tears?"

This was all particularly interesting because many observers could not understand how Barry and Clinton were taking this action on their own. Winning said that the Church had not paid anything towards the costs incurred by his press secretary in fighting the case and refused to be drawn into any debate. Barry was sacked as the Cardinal's spokesman shortly after the case. Winning did not emerge well from it. Many thought that Mrs. Brown had emerged as a woman of great integrity and that the case should not have gone to court. 'Barry won a battle but lost a war.' Winning maintained his stance that the arch-diocese of Glasgow had no involvement in the case, which was a personal matter between Barry and the newspaper.

[4] Father Noel Barry, 1956-2015, Catholic priest and Press Secretary to Cardinal Winning
[5] Cardinal Thomas Winning, 1925-2001, appointed Cardinal in 1991 by Pope John Paul II, the second ever Scottish Cardinal
[6] Anne Clinton, Glasgow Head Teacher, former Education Advisor, Glasgow City Council

Burns Supper Blairquhan Castle Ayrshire, January 1999
l-r: Jack McConnell, Amanda, Donald Dewar and Milena....

.... Bruce Waddell, Les Hinton, Ian and Myra McDonald.

Chapter 35   CONTINUING THE BATTLE

"If you are first, you are first. If you are second, you are nothing." **Bill Shankly**

Kelvin MacKenzie was one of The Sun's most successful editors but had retired before I joined NI. He continued to contribute to the paper periodically but his public utterances certainly did not help our cause in the ensuing years. He developed a clear aversion to Scotland and Scots, referring to them in one column as 'tartan tosspots' (The Sun, July 2006). By 2012 he was expressing opinions on Scottish independence. "My sense about England right now is that they wish Scotland to be independent. They want them to go out there and make their way in the world and see if they are as clever as they think they are (BBC Question Time). In 2015, he suggested that Scots living in England should be shipped back home, "load up all the jocks and drop them off in Edinburgh."

The 'Kelvin Factor' was but one example of the dangers constantly lurking in our quest to produce a relevant regional edition of a national newspaper i.e. how to ensure our papers were regionally relevant without losing the essence of being a national title. In marketing terms, it was about creating a 'regional brand' to sit alongside the 'national brand'. The Daily Record's 'Your Papers Made in Scotland' was a clear brand statement - it spelt out in large letters exactly what the paper stood for.

The tried, tested and very successful formula that successive editors of The Scottish Sun created was as follows. They took the very best content from the national edition and added the very best stories and features from Scotland. Then there was one more check: re-examine all the national material and omit anything gratuitously English. This was what other nationals didn't do – often to their cost. After Scottish devolution, this became even more important. There is no point in extensively reporting matters in the rest of the UK if the subject is a devolved matter. Readers would inevitably become confused. Another example was seasonal differences between the rest of the UK and Scotland. For example, every year national advertising would be promoting 'back to school' offers, sales etc. when Scottish schools had already been back for three to four weeks. Although the Advertising Department didn't like it, they would be asked to contact the advertisers and 'offer' a copy change for the Scottish edition. Our potential Achilles' heel in all of this was what I subsequently called the 'Kelvin Factor'. This is where there would be a radical difference between the stance that The Sun was taking nationally and that of its Scottish counterpart. We had to find a way of addressing this.

Bob Bird was well aware of the problem and gradually got on top of it. A classic example was the England versus Scotland football games – of huge interest to most male tabloid readers. The game in 1996 was no exception and, as the day approached, the Daily Record joyfully quoted the 'English' Sun's comments about the Scottish team.

On Saturday 15th June Bob devoted a full-page leading article to the subject and delivered a knock-out punch. Headlined, "For the Record, We Back Scotland and We're Proud of It!" It went on to say,

"We recently celebrated our 10th anniversary of writing and printing our paper in Glasgow. Our office is stuffed with Scots and we're the only paper fighting for Scotland's independence. It would be odd then – would it not? – if we did everything other than put all of our weight behind the Scottish team today. Well, we think so, no doubt you think so. But the tired old Daily Record doesn't seem to think so. Yesterday, as part of a cheap attempt to halt its diving circulation, it devoted almost an entire page to attacking us. Its complaint? That The Sun in England supports the English football team whilst The Scottish Sun backs Scotland. The Record, for some reason known only to itself, seems to think this makes us 'two-faced traitors'. Funny that. Most normal people would think it's perfectly sensible and logical for the workers of a newspaper to back their home side. Our London paper has every right to support the England team – just as we're absolutely determined to stand foursquare behind the Scots boys. This isn't two-faced, it's not hypocritical. It's about being proud of your country and being on the same wavelength as your readers.

The BBC do exactly the same thing in England and Scotland, they will have different commentators tomorrow for different audiences. Incredibly, the Record seems think that we should be SHAMED because we support Scotland while our London Sun colleagues back England.

Shamed? We are PROUD we take this stand because we are serving up a great paper in Scotland for a great country. The Record are taking cheap pot-shots at us because there are one or two Englishman working in our Glasgow office. We don't care what nationality people are. Of course, we could sink to their level, we COULD point out that The Daily Record's news editor is English, that their executive editor is English, that their editor has Irish roots, and their London based overall boss is from Ulster – but we won't. We COULD point out that their own sister paper, the London based Daily Mirror, has run a string of anti-Scotland based jokes this week, such as the old one of our goalie putting his head in his hands and missing – but we won't. We COULD point out that their circulation has tumbled to its lowest ever level and that they are resorting to giving papers away to try and keep it up – but we won't. The Daily Record claims to fight for Scotland, but it turns its patriotism off and on like a tap. At least we're consistent at The Scottish Sun, all day, every day The Scottish Sun supports Scotland. The Record engages in false patriotism when it suits them. But at least The Record has finally got one thing right, The Scottish Sun is different to the English one."

I congratulated Bob on dealing with the issue brilliantly. What he had also done was to illustrate perfectly how, in a relatively short period of time, we had got the Daily Record onto a level playing field and they were now frantically defending themselves against us. As market leader, they should have ignored us and been above it all. The outcome was that the average tabloid reader perceived it to be a battle between two equals and, happily, we were able to remind them constantly who was winning. The old adage that nobody wants to be on the losing side ensured that The Sun's sales continued to rise as the Daily Record's declined.

Bob Bird moved to London as deputy editor of the News of the World and was succeeded by Bruce Waddell, with Rob Dalton[1] appointed as his deputy. As with Bob, I got on extremely well with Bruce and we forged an excellent relationship, united against a common enemy and constantly refining our successful battle plan. Throughout my time in the company there were further editorial changes. In 2003 Bruce was succeeded by Rob Dalton, who in turn was succeeded by David Dinsmore[2] in 2006.

At Wapping, Clive became Managing Director and was replaced at News Group by Mike 'Lavish McTavish' Anderson[3], known as Lav to his close friends. I formed a satisfactory relationship with Mike and he was to be a strong ally in providing the last tranche of cover price investment, enabling us to overtake the Daily Record finally – but more of this later.

In the battle, constant sniping was also a tactic and the continuing enhancement of imaging technology presented us with many new opportunities. Reporting on Walter Smith's[4] testimonial game, surprisingly part-sponsored by the Daily Record, we swapped the Daily Record logo on the player's shirts with the Daily Ranger, much to the amusement of both the blue and green sides of Glasgow, whilst at the same time neatly raising a large question mark about the Daily Record's impartiality. Never mind reality, perception is all important! Whilst publishing a picture of a crucial incident at a Hearts versus Celtic match, there was unfortunately a large track side advertising board for the Daily Record in the background but, using new technology, we were able to substitute it with a Scottish Sun image. Needless to say, both incidents resulted in a string of lawyers' letters from the aggrieved parties, but the public loved it.

Sport frequently provided an opportunity for The Scottish Sun to prove its superiority over its rival and its Sports sub-editors surpassed themselves with their 9th February 2000 headline on Celtic's 1-3 defeat by Inverness Caledonian in a Scottish League Cup game, 'Super Caley Go Ballistic; Celtic Are Atrocious'. The headline was later named by The Guardian as the World's Best Sporting Headline ever.

Legal skirmishes between the two sides were also frequent - usually the result of something that NI had done. As the sales gap between the rivals continued to narrow, it became increasingly obvious that The Scottish Sun would eventually overtake the Daily Record and we were sufficiently confident to press our M8 gable end into service once more, with a massive graph of both sales figures showing a

---

[1] Rob Dalton, Editor Scottish Sun 1993-96
[2] David Dinsmore, b.1968, Editor of The Scottish Sun 2006-10, Editor, The Sun 2013-15, Chief Operating Officer, News UK 2015
[3] Mike Anderson, Managing Director News Group 2005-09, Founder, Chelsea Apps Factory
[4] Walter Smith, b. 1948, Manager, Rangers Football Club 1991-98, 2007-11

crossover in 2-3 years time. Cue yet another lawyer's letter, this time from the Planning Department of the Glasgow City Council.

As I have mentioned, the price differential increasingly became the main promotional weapon and The Scottish Sun used this tactic frequently as part of the long-term strategic plan to achieve market leadership. My old friend Ellis Watson surpassed himself when he hired a truck with a massive spotlight and projected the image of 'The Scottish Sun 10p tomorrow' onto the Daily Record building for an entire evening. Not unexpectedly, the police, no doubt after a tip-off, eventually appeared but could not find any transgression of the local by-laws. For good measure, the same image was projected onto the ramparts of Edinburgh Castle. Both pictures appeared prominently in The Scottish Sun the following morning.

Sometimes matters became very serious. One Friday, just as we had launched a massive promotional game, supported on television and radio all weekend, we discovered the SDR had applied for an interim interdict preventing us from running the game, claiming that we had lifted the idea from them and were thus illegally passing off their intellectual property. I was particularly impressed with the speed of The Scottish Judiciary when three senior judges convened at the Court of Session on Saturday morning to hear the case. I attended and, after some quite obscure legal jousting, our QC presented a crucial fact – that the concept for the game itself was not originated by the Daily Record but had been used by Walker's Crisps some three years earlier and was therefore not the intellectual property of the Daily Record. Soon afterwards 'm'lords' took a swift adjournment and quickly returned to announce that the interdict would not be granted. Our QC immediately applied for costs, which were awarded to us. It was calculated that the whole affair cost SDR around £250,000, which included the costs of us having to cancel the advertising campaign in the light of the original interdict.

In 2003 Bruce Waddell was offered the job of Editor of the Daily Record. SDR would have regarded this as a considerable coup but I believe that Bruce had severe doubts as to whether he was doing the right thing, although I suspect a significant salary increase might have been the clinching factor. Bruce was and remains a friend. I didn't try to talk him out of the move but put as many doubts in his mind as possible. Just to be difficult, NI insisted on holding him to his 12 months' notice period and took an interim interdict preventing him from joining SDR. Lord Drummond Young[5] ruled that Bruce had broken his contract and that the interim interdict for NGN should be awarded but with the 12 months reduced to four.

Bruce remained SDR editor for eight years. I suspect he always knew that the job had a limited shelf-life but that he couldn't turn it down. Throughout the battle, we kept in touch and he once remarked to me, "I wonder who will get to 500,000 first – you on the way up, or us on the way down." True to form, the Daily Record was the first to reach this milestone in July 2002.

---

[5] Lord Drummond Young QC, b. 1950, Judge of the Supreme Courts of Scotland, formerly Chairman of the Scottish Law Commission

Caricature: International Newspaper Conference c 2002

Chapter 36 ESTABLISHING MARKET LEADERSHIP

"The world is changing very fast. Big will not beat small anymore. It will be the fast beating the slow." Rupert Murdoch

My first job description was abundantly clear about my priorities. I was there to increase the market penetration of our four titles and, if possible, achieve the market leadership enjoyed in the rest of the UK. One suggestion on how I might achieve this was by increasing the company's profile within Scotland.

The primary reason the NI titles did not have market leadership then was the incredibly strong, indigenous Scottish Press. When I joined NI in 1995, the five Scottish morning titles (The Scotsman, The Herald, The Courier, The Press and Journal, and the Daily Record) between them sold over 70% of all daily newspapers. The figure now stands at 45%.

Let's take The Times first. Shortly after I joined, I attended a media conference in London where Andrew Neil was a speaker. Then at Scotsman Publications, his main theme was that Scottish devolution would 'completely marginalise' the 'English' quality press. The Herald, and particularly The Scotsman, would emerge triumphant in this new era. I told the conference that I thought the reality would be exactly the opposite. I can say now that I was proved totally right. My view was that the onset of devolution would mean the indigenous Scottish Press would become ever more parochial and that there would be an increasing market opportunity caused by people wanting a national UK perspective in their daily newspaper. Following devolution, The Times, under the editorship of John Mair, maintained its sales position, while both The Scotsman and The Herald declined. During that entire period, there was almost no sales promotion of The Times in Scotland. It was not until the editorship of Magnus Linklater[1] (appointed just as I was leaving NI) that the paper actively promoted itself and, by 2017, The Times outsold both The Herald and The Scotsman. After I retired, having sifted through every Sunday and daily newspaper every day for 12 years, I purchased only The Times, The Herald, and The Scotsman. However, I dropped The Scotsman several years ago.

In 2004 The Times was an example of the fast, decisive decision making that the NI was famous for. The issue of converting from broadsheet to compact (tabloid) format had been carefully researched. At the end of 1983 The Independent suddenly made the first move in this area. Astonishingly they decided to produce both formats for an unspecified period of time. For The Times there was no confused thinking in trying to please everyone. The decision was made and executed to change to compact format overnight. The result was an extremely well received and ultimately very sucessful new format. Interestingly The Daily Telegraph chose not to follow suit and has continued to haemorrhage readers at an alarming rate ever since. In the

---

[1] Magnus Linklater, CBE b.1942, Scottish journalist, writer and former newspaper editor. Scottish Editor of The Times 2007-12

Republic of Ireland, The Irish Independent was guilty of even more confused thinking and produced broadsheet and compact versions for over eight years.

Marketing The Sunday Times was most frustrating, with so many individual protective fiefdoms in London. My early battles with Toby Constantine (Chapter 28) were merely a foretaste of things to come. After a battle royal, we settled on a separate Scottish section, Ecosse, and a tiny front-page lozenge under the masthead containing the word 'Scotland'. In later years, we made a major effort to capture the property advertising market from The Herald with a quite revolutionary proposal for a standalone section. In the end the project never came to fruition because of the battles we had with the west coast estate agents. They could never agree anything between themselves, even as the market was collapsing around them. The reality was that these battles were mere skirmishes compared to the real ones we had with our 'colleagues' in London in getting approval to plan for another section of the paper.

The major achievement for The Sunday Times was keeping its market position after the launch of the Sunday Herald in February 1999. Outrams had already failed with their first attempt to launch a Sunday. The ill-fated Sunday Standard, launched in 1983 under Charlie Wilson's editorship, lasted a mere two years. I had considered a Sunday version of The Herald a major threat to The Sunday Times so you can imagine my amazement when I lunched with Des Hudson[2] (my counterpart at Outrams) and he explained their rationale just after the launch. To me, the obvious course of action would have been to tap into The Herald's loyal, long-established readership but, amazingly, Outrams decided to have as much product differentiation as possible between The Herald and The Sunday Herald. Equally astonishingly, they recruited an entirely separate editorial team - when there would have been a considerable benefit in having some shared seven-day editorial resource. The Sunday Herald never managed to pull through regular six-day Herald readers into Sunday. Prior to its closure it was still selling 30% less than its daily counterpart.

Postscript: I wrote the draft of this chapter in 2017, reflecting on a lunch that took place in 1999. On 24th April 2018, The Herald announced, "Newsquest Scotland is to produce a Sunday edition of The Herald. The move is in response to reader demand for a seven-day offering of both titles and closer alignment of the Herald brand. The launch of The Herald on Sunday will mean the closure of The Sunday Herald." Graham Morrison[3] said, "It has been clear for some time, that Herald readers want a seven-day offering with clearer alignment of the brand and the titles editorial values on a Sunday." Donald Martin[4] said, "The Herald on Sunday will take the best of our journalism and columnists and offer a weekend package unrivalled for the Scottish market." Plus ça change, plus c'est la même chose!

---

[2] Des Hudson, CEO, Scottish Media Group, publishing division 1999-2004
[3] Graham Morrison, Managing Director, Newsquest Scotland
[4] Donald Martin, Editor in Chief, Newsquest Scotland

As far as the Scottish Sun is concerned, the News International Years (Part IV) extensively detail the massive battles between the Scottish Sun and the Daily Record, which eventually resulted in my proudest achievement - gaining market leadership in 2007.

Marketing the News of the World in Scotland was a totally different matter. Right from the start I sensed its proposition did not fit well with the hard and inflexible underbelly of Scottish Presbyterianism and, to my frustration over the years, this turned out to be the case. Having looked on enviously at what was happening with The Scottish Sun, it did not take Phil Hall (News of the World Editor) long to decide that the title should have a Scottish Editor. A very young Rebekah Wade was dispatched to Kinning Park where she and I interviewed a number of candidates, eventually appointing David Dinsmore as the first Scottish Editor of the News of the World. But even he and his successors, including Bob Bird, could never get sufficient traction to take on the Sunday Mail seriously. The Scottish Sun made significant inroads into the Daily Record's market dominance. Despite considerable promotional support, the Scottish News of the World, although achieving steady increases in sales, never seriously threatened the Sunday Mail's dominant market position.

In his autobiography, Les Hinton remarks that when he was appointed as Executive Chairman in 1995, "He (Rupert) said I should prepare for an onslaught of flattery from politicians, Royal Family acolytes, company bosses, and every civic leader with a cause to promote. As well as flattery, complaints would pour my way from important people annoyed at the way they had been treated in our pages. Don't get too close to these people." In Scotland at that time, the situation couldn't have been more different. Here this same group paid homage at the headquarters of SDR, Outrams and SPL. As the visitors' book showed, few ever came to Kinning Park; we were total unknowns. Over the years I sought to change this. As our market position gradually improved, I kept telling our editors and senior staff that we had to prepare for market leadership. We had to have a seat, not just at the table, but eventually at the head of it. In those days, we weren't even at the table. Establishing that position took a long time, a huge number of man hours and occasionally some reluctant passengers on the journey.

Over the years I hosted a regular series of lunches. Some were for senior politicians and amongst our visitors were Donald Dewar, Jack McConnell[5], Henry McLeish[6] (First Ministers), Gordon Brown[7] and Alistair Darling[8] (while each was Chancellor of the Exchequer). Dean Nelson[9], then Editor of The Sunday Times in Scotland, refused to attend the McConnell lunch. He told me, "My job is to bring him down, not to sit and have lunch with him." He also added that he didn't think I should be inviting politicians and 'forcing' editors to attend. I found this fascinating and momentarily thought about asking to see his job description to see if removing the First Minister

---

[5] The Rt. Hon. Jack, Baron McConnell of Glenscorrodale b.1960, First Minister of Scotland 2001-07
[6] The Rt. Hon. Henry McLeish b.1948, First Minister of Scotland 2000-01
[7] The Rt. Hon. Gordon Brown FRSE b.1951, Chancellor of the Exchequer 1997-2007, Prime Minister 2007-10
[8] The Rt. Hon. Alastair, Baron Darling of Roulanish PC b.1953, Chancellor of the Exchequer 2007-10, MP 1987-2015
[9] Dean Nelson, Editor Sunday Times Insight team, Editor Sunday Times Scotland

was a key task. Nelson made a great fuss about it. I certainly didn't force him to attend - indeed I couldn't have cared less whether he attended or not and, in my view, he was the loser in not being there. I subsequently found out that Les Hinton also got to hear of the altercation but interestingly at no point did Les tell me to cease having the lunches - or indeed any of the things I was doing to increase the company's profile.

Such activities are loosely called 'Networking' and in the early Noughties there emerged in some quarters a mood of disapproval. Around this time, Claire and I were guests of the First Minister Jack McConnell at a dinner in Bute House in Edinburgh. The Scotsman, using the new Freedom of Information Act, or as I called it 'The Charter for Lazy Journalists', obtained the guest list and ran it as a major news feature, with biographical details of everyone present. I was never sure quite what the purpose was, but running throughout the piece was inherent disapproval of the occasion. What wasn't mentioned was that such events were used by McConnell to showcase talent from catering students, designers, artists, singers and musicians, over and above the main objective of keeping in touch with what influential people thought about his administration.

I also organised a Burns' Supper at Blairquhan Castle in Ayrshire. Dewar and McConnell were the principal guests and both Les and Doug and their wives attended. Doug enthusiastically embraced the occasion. Janis had organised a kilt for him and he talked about this at Wapping for a long time afterwards.

If some of my Scottish based colleagues on the journey to market leadership were reluctant passengers, at national level there were even fewer supporters. I have already described how extremely M25-centric the company was. To their credit, Les and Doug recognised the need to put Scotland on the map, hence my appointment, and they were always supportive of my efforts to achieve increased market penetration. Sadly, very few others were as enthusiastic, particularly the editors. They were happy to come to Scotland for a 'jolly', put in an appearance and rally the troops. Few really understood the market or the many subtle differences between it and the rest of the UK. Some, like Kelvin McKenzie in his public utterances, were a severe impediment to the cause. The only national editor who ever took the trouble to come, talk to people and, more importantly, listen, was Robert Thomson[10] shortly after he was appointed Editor of The Times in 2002. I greatly admired him for it and perhaps it is no coincidence that he is now Chief Executive of News Corp.

Over the years, I organised many events which enabled us to move gradually from being the 'new kids on the block' to being one of the senior players in the market. I also found myself on the evening circuit, sometimes attending three or four events a week. It was hard work, but very rewarding. I always enjoyed meeting new people and the missionary work of spreading the NI gospel was never a hardship.

---

[10] Robert Thomson, b. 1961, Editor, the Times (2002-08), Managing Editor, Wall Street Journal 2008-13, Chief Executive, News Corp 2013 -

Many people visited us over the years. I particularly remember when Frank McAveety[11] and Alex Mossan[12] came to lunch and confessed that they had already been to Kinning Park on a few occasions – on the picket line in early 1986. How times change! Brian Souter[13], in his early Stagecoach career, arrived in jeans with his 'briefcase' – a Tesco carrier bag. Always ahead of the game, he simply wanted to meet the new kids on the block. I was to build a close friendship with Sir John Orr[14], then Chief Constable. John was an extremely effective leader and was also a great pragmatist, always willing to listen and, if persuaded, to take action. I cite two examples of this. I told him about a short slip road off the M8 leading to Seaward Street, close to our plant. It was always clogged with traffic in the mornings with long queues, as it was only one lane with a never used hard shoulder. Frequently frustrated motorists would drive down the hard shoulder and occasionally the traffic police waited at the bottom to catch them. It was a classic lose/lose situation. I suggested to John that it would improve the situation immeasurable if the section of hard shoulder was simply converted into an additional lane. He agreed and within a very short time 'made it happen'. Result – greatly reduced traffic jams. A few years later, for no apparent reason, someone on the City Council decided that Milnpark Street should have some 'traffic calming'. Quite why a quiet street in an industrial backwater of the city needed this was something of a mystery, but an extensive programme of work was carried out to create extended pavements and bollards. What no one had bothered to consider was the effect this would have on the huge HGVs delivering NI's newsprint supplies each morning. They could scarcely manoeuvre around the corner because of the new bollards. Another call to John and, within days, said bollards and extended pavements were removed.

One of NI's most high-profile events was its annual Christmas party. Claire and I decided early on to host these at our home, as it was the most cost-effective way of entertaining a large number of people. Eventually as the company's profile grew and NI became firmly on the radar of most of the important influencers in Scotland, we hosted two separate events and towards the end of my time there, had around 150 people at each – a pretty tight squeeze! 11 years later I still meet people who talk about those parties, how great they were and who was there. They even featured in the gossip columns of our competitors.

In February 2007 Gordon Brown invited David Dinsmore and me to breakfast in Edinburgh to discuss the forthcoming Scottish elections. It was a fascinating exchange of views. For me it also yet another example of how NI now had one of the very top seats at the table of Scottish influence.

---

[11] Frank McAveety b.1962, MSP 1999-2011, Leader, Glasgow City Council 1997-99 and 2015-17
[12] Alex Mossan, Lord Provost of Glasgow 1999-2003
[13] Sir Brian Souter, b. 1954, Chairman, Stagecoach 2013-
[14] Sir John Orr, OBE QPM 1945-2018, Chief Constable Strathclyde Police 1996-2001

Chapter 37

PLAN B- FIRST STEPS IN THE NON-EXECUTIVE WORLD

"Don't boast or get too cocky. The ideal non-executive director is apparently someone who is quiet, knowledgeable and competent. Modesty is a virtue, candidates should have a 'non-ego' and should not be dogmatic."
SpencerStuart

As I approached my fifties, I began to think actively about a non-executive career. I knew that I did not want to stay in full-time employment until my 65th birthday, then retire and do nothing. This was the norm for previous generations, as a two-stage career of work followed by retirement was usually the only option. I was considering a three-stage career - full-time employment, an active non-executive/consultancy career and, ultimately, full retirement. In an ideal world, the first stage would end sometime between the ages of 55 and 60 and the transition from the second to the third stage would mainly be determined by physical and mental capacity.

Happily, my life has gone according to plan in that I was able to move to the second stage at the age of 58 and, as I now enter my early 70s, I have no plans to move to the third stage just yet. I realise that I am not directly in control of events, but I am encouraged that my family and friends seem to agree that I haven't gone gaga just yet.

The first opportunity to start my non-executive journey came in 2000. I was asked to become Chairman of the West of Scotland branch of the Institute of Directors (IoD). There had been a Scottish division since the early 1970s with Sir Charles Fraser its first chairman. I had been an IoD member for several years and the Chairman's role was not particularly onerous. I had to organise a series of events and chair the committee. Speakers at early events included Wendy Alexander, Elish Angiolini[1], and the then-leader of the Conservative Party Iain Duncan Smith[2]. Within two years I was elected Scottish Chairman, succeeding Calum MacLeod[3], and I chaired the Scotland Committee and organised it's annual conference between 2002 and 2004.

The annual conference had traditionally been held at Gleneagles, but I decided to move it to the recently opened St Andrew's Bay Hotel. The deal included having the hotel's owner Don Panoz[4] as the principal after dinner speaker. I should have followed my instinct of always researching the quality of speakers before engaging them. Panoz broke the cardinal rule of after dinner speaking – alcohol and public

---

[1] Dame Elish Angiolini DBE, PC, QC, FRSA, FRSE b.1960, Solicitor General 2001-06; Lord Advocate Scotland 2006-11; Principal St Hugh's College, Oxford 2012-
[2] Iain Duncan Smith, b.1954, Leader of the Conservative Party and Leader of the Opposition 2001-03
[3] Calum MacLeod CBE, 1935-2013. IoD Scotland Chairman 1999-2002. Chairman Grampian Television 1993-97.
[4] Don Panoz, 1935-2018. American entrepreneur and founder of the Elan Pharmaceutical Corporation. Inventor of the nicotine patch.

speaking do not sit easily together. Having consumed a significant quantity of wine, he delivered a rambling diatribe against the Fife planning authorities. The content was quite interesting, but the delivery appalling. The only exception to the non alcohol / speaking rule was Derry Irvine,[5] whom I witnessed consume six glasses of claret at lunch, before delivering a flawless and most eloquent speech to the Newspaper Press Fund in London.

Being IoD Chair was interesting and presented a number of challenges. The Scottish Committee consisted of the chairs of all the IoD's branches in Scotland, each of whom had their own views on how the organisation should be run. Indeed, some of them thought that they should have been appointed Chairman! I also had to recruit a new Executive Director for Scotland, eventually appointing David Watt[6], who remained there until 2019, becoming a major and respected voice of the business community in Scotland. The role also brought me into close contact with the IoD national headquarters in London. I got on well with George Cox[7], the Director General, and Andrew Main-Wilson[8], Chief Operating Officer, but beneath them at the headquarters in 116 Pall Mall there was a vast bureaucracy. It had an almost identical silo structure to the one with which I was currently wrestling at NI. Creating meaningful change within such an organisation was not easy, but David Watt and I managed to up the profile of the Scottish division significantly. More importantly, we established its credibility with all parties in the newly devolved Scotland.

My first formal non-executive role was with Scottish Networks International (SNI) in 2001, chaired by Nick Kuenssberg[9]. SNI was co-funded by Scottish Development International and the British Council and it offered promising foreign Scottish university post-graduate students placements in Scottish companies, a small bursary and, most importantly, a two year visa. In any one year between 20 and 25 students out of around 70 applicants entered the scheme. Since candidates were usually at the very top level of achievement, many of them went on to operate at a very senior level when they returned to their own countries. The scheme had been in operation for a number of years and already some of the early scholars were CEOs of large organisations and, in at least one case, a government minister. For Scotland, the main benefit was in maintaining close links with past scholars, who inevitably became 'promoters' of Scotland throughout the world. SNI gave me an early entry into the non-executive world and, although extremely light-touch, it provided me with some very useful experience.

The next step was much more meaningful – Scottish Enterprise (SE). SE was Scotland's main economic development agency and a non departmental public body (NDPB) of the Scottish Government. It worked with partners in both the public and private sectors to identify and exploit the best opportunities to deliver significant

---

[5] Derry, Baron Irvine of Lairg, PC, QC, b.1940. Lord Chancellor 1997-2003.
[6] David Watt, b.1951, Executive Director IoD Scotland 2003-19
[7] George Cox, b.1941, IoD Director General 1999-2004
[8] Andrew Main-Wilson, b.1959, IoD Chief Operating Officer 1997-2013
[9] Nick Kuenssberg OBE, b.1942, Chairman, Scottish Networks International

lasting benefits to the Scottish economy. It then had an annual budget of £450 million and consisted of a parent body and 12 subsidiary local enterprise companies.

I had met Ron Culley[10], chief executive of Scottish Enterprise Glasgow (SEG), one of those subsidiaries, but it still was something of a surprise when he asked me to become a Non-Executive Director in SEG. The process involved an interview with the Chairman Tom O'Neill[11]. In those days there didn't seem to be any evidence of a Nominations Committee or similar form of governance. The position was unremunerated and, as I was to find out subsequently, there was a fairly eclectic Board, most of whom had been hand-picked by Ron and Tom. Naturally I had to clear the appointment with Ian McDonald but, as always, he was extremely supportive and considered it entirely consistent with my objective of raising the company's profile in Scotland. Indeed, NI continued to be sympathetic to my early forays into the non-executive world, provided they were within the public sector.

As a public body, SEG was a NDPB and therein lies a clue to one of the early difficulties I encountered. Everything in the organisation had an acronym and it took me months to understand the lengthy Board reports, as I had to work out what these acronyms stood for. Some 20 years later I became a Public Interest Member (PIM) of the Institute of Chartered Accountants in Scotland (ICAS). Its council reports had almost the same number of acronyms but, unlike SEG, ICAS helpfully provided an appendix in its board papers with details of all the acronyms.

Although SEG itself did a lot of good work, much of it was diluted because of an ongoing and increasingly bitter feud with SE. Ron and Tom were almost permanently at war with their counterparts at SE, Sir Ian Robinson[12] and Robert Crawford[13]. There was little sense of common purpose and Tom and Ron could whip up their troops into a frenzy every time SE tried to do something that they didn't like. To use a political analogy, in some ways SEG were like 'Old Labour' when Tony Blair and his 'New Labour' colleagues (SE) were trying to reform the party. SE was trying to create a uniform structure with cohesive and consistent policies throughout its network. It was like trying to steer a ship through very choppy waters, with 12 local crews operating at a level of almost permanent mutiny - particularly SEG. The 12 local enterprise companies (LECs) were very powerful fiefdoms, each with its own Board and each thinking that it knew most about its local marketplace. Robinson and Crawford became increasingly frustrated. Although there were undoubtedly faults on both sides and some of SE's communications were rather clumsy, SEG often behaved outrageously. At one of my last Board meetings, Ian Robinson tried to smooth relations, but was harangued throughout the meeting by O'Neill on the subject of SE's latest business plan. The plan detailed a whole range of efficiencies that could be achieved by centralising some activities. The estimated savings were heavily disputed by O'Neill and indeed after the meeting there followed a vicious exchange of letters, with each side maintaining its position. Later

---

[10] Ron Culley, b.1950, Chief Executive, Scottish Enterprise Glasgow 2002-06
[11] Tom O'Neill, b.1943, Chairman Scottish Enterprise Glasgow 1999-2005 and Chairman Thales Optronics
[12] Sir Ian Robinson, b.1942, Chief Executive, Scottish Power 1995-2001, Chairman, Scottish Enterprise 1999-2004
[13] Robert Crawford, b.1952, Chief Executive, Scottish Enterprise 1999-2003

that afternoon a friend was in the Departure Lounge at Glasgow Airport and found himself by sheer chance sitting very close to Robinson. He overheard him on his mobile venting his fury as to how he had been treated at the SEG board meeting.

One of the issues dominating Board time was the recently opened Glasgow Science Centre (GSC). It was already on its second management team by the time I joined the Board. From the onset I felt that the very name GSC was dull and boring, whereas Dynamic Earth in Edinburgh had a far more vibrant, positive image. GSC seemed doomed from the start, with its focal point of a rotating tower plagued with technical issues. The business plan was predicated on highly optimistic attendance figures provided by a firm of extremely expensive outside consultants. As a consequence, the plan was never on budget. As any shortfall was guaranteed by SEG itself, there seemed little incentive to get GSC to break even or, perish the thought, actually run at a profit. When the hapless third GSC Chief Executive appeared at the SEG Board, he opened his presentation with a series of slides demonstrating that GSC was the most successful of all similar operations throughout the UK, in that it lost less money than the others. I could hardly believe what I was hearing and suggested that he needed to change his mindset before he came back to us. In my view GSC was an appalling waste of public money - a public realm project worthy in its own right which would be a permanent drain on the taxpayer, mainly because of utterly unrealistic assumptions in its original business plan. I became an extremely vociferous critic of the management of GSC and, later on, of Loch Lomond Shores.

The structure of SE was deeply flawed. In a country of five million people, having a national and 12 local enterprise companies, each with their own Board, governance arrangements and management teams, was nonsensical. I served only one term on the SEG Board. I was disillusioned with the infighting. At the earliest opportunity I applied to join the main SE Board. I was interviewed by Sir John Ward[14] and Eddie Frizzell[15]. Also present, as part of the Government's new model of political correctness, was a representative of the Public Appointments Commission who contributed little to the interview. Indeed, much to my irritation, she asked me inane questions about my suitability to the post, including; "Was my chairmanship of the IoD not a conflict of interest?" When I asked why it might be, she couldn't provide a reason and I said that a more relevant observation might have been to note that my IoD term of office was due to end in less than three months' time. I could never fathom quite what value people like this added to the process, other than adding cost and ticking boxes.

However this was to be the start of the Government's obsession with the appointments process for public bodies. Having started during the Labour - Lib Dem Coalition, it continued to grow in the SNP era. Effectively the latter developed the proposition that NDPBs could not recruit people of their choice. That involved too much risk - it might encourage cronyism and lack of scrutiny. Worse still, left to their own devices the NDPBs might actually recruit people with skills which could

---

[14] Sir John Ward, b.1940, Chairman Scottish Enterprise 2004-09. Chairman European Asset Trust 1995-2015
[15] Professor Eddie Frizzell CB, civil servant, Head of Department of Enterprise, Transport and Lifelong Learning 1999-2006

add value to the organisation – and that certainly couldn't be allowed. The new process demanded complete anonymity; candidates weren't permitted to showcase their achievements and the whole process became nothing more than a box-ticking exercise, thus almost guaranteeing mediocrity.

Sometime later we were to witness a quite appalling consequence of this process. Jim McDonald[16], then Deputy Principal of the University of Strathclyde, had applied for a Board position. McDonald was one of the country's leading engineering academics with a significant skill set, so we were appalled to learn that he failed even to make the shortlist given to us by the civil servants. John Ward was enraged and queried the selection process. Although all the candidates' personal details were redacted he was able to work out which application was Jim's and demanded to see the marks awarded to him. It emerged that there had been a 'miscorrelation' in the marking process. Jim's name was then added to the shortlist for interview and, not surprisingly, he was appointed along with one other. It was an example of the folly of the Government's public appointment process.

The SE Board I joined was inspirational in experience terms. In my time there, Jim and Tim O'Shea[17] provided intellectual rigour, Fred Hallsworth[18], Charlie Morrison[19] and Iain McLaren[20] forensic accounting skills and Barbara Duffner[21] and Iain MacDonald[22] and others had a wealth of experience in the private sector. The consequence was that SE was like a private sector Board operating in the public sector and its non-execs were never slow in expressing opinions frequently at odds with the Government.

Robert Crawford had departed in 2003, just before I joined SE. I liked Robert enormously. He was exceptionally bright but I was unconvinced by some parts of his strategy. His Achille's heel was the media. He confessed to me his fury that someone had stopped his wife in the street to complain about something he was doing at SE, having read about it in their local newspaper. Sadly, Robert was very naive in his handling of and his reaction to what was written about him. He simply couldn't grasp that in an extremely high profile position like his, he would be constantly scrutinised and frequently criticised. In the end, he became particularly fixated by The Scotsman. I am told that he even banned copies of the paper from the SE building and almost developed a persecution complex about one particular Scotsman journalist. This led to even greater scrutiny from the journalist and the paper. Matters reached a head with further major criticism of SE in the paper. Robert felt that Ian Gray[23] did not sufficiently back him publicly on the matter and he resigned. It was a sad end for such a talented person.

---

[16] Professor Sir James McDonald, b.1957, Principal and Vice-Chancellor, University of Strathclyde 2009-

[17] Professor Sir Timothy O'Shea, b.1948, Principal, Vice-Chancellor, University of Edinburgh 2002-18

[18] Fred Hallsworth CA, b.1953 Arthur Andersen Ltd 1977-2007, latterly Managing Partner Scotland. NED specialising in tech/healthcare sectors

[19] Charlie Morrison CA, CCMI, OBE, b.1953. IBM 1971-2004, Vice President Operations Global Services Europe, business angel and software engineer.

[20] Iain McLaren b.1951, Senior Partner KPMG 1999-2004

[21] Barbra Duffner OBE, b.1946. Head of Personnel Royal Mail

[22] Iain MacDonald, b. 1944, computer industry entrepreneur

[23] Ian Gray, b.1957, Minister of Enterprise, Transport and Lifelong Learning 2002-03

Robert was succeeded by Jack Perry[24]. I had known Jack from his Ernst & Young days and also as Scottish Chairman of the CBI and was impressed by him. He set about restructuring his senior executive team, in particular reducing its overall size. He soon discovered, as I had done at the Daily Record, that it is extremely difficult to change personnel. At the Daily Record, the trade unions were the main impediment; at SE it was cost. The reality at SE was that, because of extremely generous redundancy and pension terms in the public sector, the departure costs for someone with, for example, 20 years' service could be up to seven times annual salary, compared to 1½ times in the private sector at that time. Because of the 2008 recession, the private sector cost has now probably shrunk by half but the public sector one is unchanged.

Little wonder then that successive governments have failed to tackle public sector efficiency and head count. I once challenged Gordon Brown on the subject. When I went into specific details about SE, he got extremely flustered and promptly finished the meeting by asking me to write to him. John and I crafted an extremely detailed letter but - no surprise – received only a standard acknowledgement.

What is palpable is that successive governments have known for the last 25 years that there would be a long-term problem with public sector pensions and that ultimately the situation would be unsustainable. The short-termism of the British political system means that no party has ever seriously addressed the issue. David Cameron's[25] lamentable performance in the 2012 General Election (when he threw away a healthy lead and ended up in a coalition with the Lib Dems) meant the last serious opportunity to address the issue had gone. With a reasonable majority Cameron might have been able to address it. The 2008 recession and subsequent freezing of council tax have certainly resulted in a massive shakeout in the public sector. However, there is little evidence of addressing the long term pension problem. I also doubt whether the recession has driven any high-level efficiencies in the public sector. Regrettably, reform of public sector pay and pensions is now firmly on the backburner, with Brexit likely to dominate the political agenda for years to come.

Jack Perry was successful in recruiting several new people onto his team, including Hugh Hall[26]. There is no doubt that the new regime was much more focussed strategically and began to develop a number of new initiatives. First and foremost was a determination to create, where possible, 'high-end jobs,' i.e. those that would create economic value. No disrespect to companies like Amazon, but the jobs created at their warehouses at Dunfermline and Greenock are certainly not the high-end jobs SE wanted. The high-value strategy was not without its problems. SE had to be seen to be all things to all people politically and one of its interventions, the Business Gateway scheme, had the target of creating 10,000 new jobs per year through start-ups. The reality was that the majority of these start-ups comprised one or two people and 95% never reached the VAT threshold, so these too were not high-value jobs.

---

[24] Jack Perry CBE, b.1954, Chief Executive, Scottish Enterprise 2004-09
[25] The Rt. Hon. David Cameron, b. 1966, Prime Minister 2010-16
[26] Hugh Hall b. 1958, Chief Financial Officer Scottish Enterprise 2006-10

Although this programme was necessary, it was incredibly labour intensive and costly. It was interesting that, when the SNP won the 2007 election, they immediately transferred the entire programme to the local authorities, leaving SE to focus on the high-end strategy.

During this time I was Chairman of SE's Remuneration and Nomination Committee, which was a fascinating journey through the world of salary and bonus awards. We helped to facilitate changes in personnel, whilst arguing all the way with politicians and civil servants who seemed to have a very different view of the world. In 2008 we had to make a difficult call on the annual bonus awards for the senior management team. SE had overspent its annual budget and was publicly heavily criticised for it. It was not a case of negligence, rather that some projects had to be re-phased which, coupled with changes in the government's resource accounting process, meant a significant overspend. The Finance Department had certainly not been on top of the situation and, as a result, and to make a very public statement, we awarded no bonus to Jack, Lena Wilson[27] and the other senior members of the team. Whilst they understood entirely the reasoning behind the decision, to say they were not particularly happy is putting it mildly. Indeed Hugh Hall, when he later joined SE, famously went on to say that bringing SE in on budget on 5th April each year was like trying to land a jumbo jet on a postage stamp. There was an unintended consequence to our actions. The following year, after the publication of SE's accounts, there was considerable press comment about the significant pay rises of SE's senior staff. I recall headlines of "Public Sector Fat Cats". Most financial journalists had missed the fact that there had been a zero bonus award the previous year.

One of the items which caused the budget overrun mentioned above was the Clyde Arc, affectionately known in Glasgow as the Squinty Bridge. A second public consultation had to be held after a single objector supposedly claimed that the water level of the Clyde would rise to dangerous levels following its construction. This single objection caused a nine month delay in construction, during which time steel prices rose sharply, resulting in its final cost rising by £650,000 - democracy gone mad.

The Enterprise Minister was then Nicol Stephen[28], described to me by one of his senior civil servants as, "one the laziest politicians of all time." It took Stephen 18 months to meet the SE board and he was just as unimpressive in the flesh as the civil servant's opinion suggested. At the Board meeting I asked him a relatively simple question and his response was so long and rambling that I eventually had to interrupt and say, "So I take it the answer is 'no' then?" The length of his title – Lord Stephen of Lower Deeside in the City of Aberdeen - might have indicated that brevity was not his strong point.

The whole issue of the LECs continued to ferment. SE wanted to operate as a single entity, with three or four 'Metropolitan' bodies providing regional strategic input

---

[27] Dr. Lena Wilson CBE FRSE, b.1964 Chief Executive Scottish Enterprise 2009-17
[28] Nicol, Lord Stephen of Lower Deeside in the City of Aberdeen, b. 1960, Minister for Enterprise and Lifelong Learning 2005-07

and governance. There had been a series of meetings between SE and the 12 LEC Chairs to try to facilitate progress, but what emerged was a vigorous rearguard action by the west coast group, led by Willie Haughey[29] (SEG) and including Kevin O'Sullivan[30], (SE Dunbartonshire), and Archie Bethel[31] (SE Lanarkshire). Others' responses were much more measured and many actually supported the proposal. After extensive local lobbying Nicol Stephen simply bowed to public pressure, took the easy option and refused to sanction the proposals. After the final decision had been made, a senior civil servant briefed the SE Board on the need to toe the party line and, although not quite threatening us, left us in no doubt that no one should attempt to brief the press or show any dissent. Nothing would be said on the matter, but some board members were astonished the following morning to see that virtually every newspaper carried the official government line. Such is the world of government briefing and spin doctors!

The 2007 Scottish elections saw a change in government and an SNP administration. John Swinney[32] was appointed Cabinet Secretary for the Enterprise brief and almost immediately abolished the entire LEC setup. The metropolitan entities were created and I became SE's representative on one of them - ACSEF (Aberdeen City and Shires Economic Future). This was an extremely impressive group which included the Leaders and Chief Executives of both local authorities, some extremely high-profile private sector individuals including Stewart Milne[33], Melfort Campbell[34], Colin Crosby[35], Stewart Spence[36] and a cluster of CEOs from the oil and gas sector. In my year there, there was a high level of debate focussed on how the region's future might look in 20-30 years time, when North Sea oil finished. It also showed how all interested parties could work together for a common purpose in a relationship far more effective than the former one.

The only downside for ACSEF was its failure to broker an agreement to facilitate Sir Ian Wood's[37] philanthropic offer of £50 million to transform Union Street Gardens in Aberdeen from an eyesore into a fantastic focal point to revitalise Aberdeen's main shopping street. This saga was to run for years. There were some in Aberdeen who saw it as an attempt by a rich man to impose his will on the city. Wood, anxious that his motives should not be misconstrued, financed a referendum to ensure that everyone could have a say on whether his gift should be accepted. Aberdonians voted with 52.4% in favour. Incredibly the majority Labour group in the City Council later set aside the referendum result. This was not directly the fault of ACSEF, but it does illustrate the difficulty of making things happen nowadays, even when an offer comes gift wrapped. A collection of crackpot local pressure groups prevented Sir Ian's vision becoming reality.

---

[29] The Rt. Hon. William, Baron Haughey of Hutchesontown in the City of Glasgow, b.1956, Chairman SE Glasgow
[30] Kevin O'Sullivan b.1949, Chairman SE Dumbarton
[31] Archie Bethel CBE, b.1953, CEO, Babcock International, Chairman, SE Lanarkshire
[32] John Swinney, b.1964, Cabinet Secretary for Finance, Constitution and the Economy 2007-16
[33] Stewart Milne CBE, b.1950, Founder, The Stewart Milne Housebuilding Group
[34] Melfort Campbell OBE, b.1959, Chairman IMES Group
[35] Colin Crosby, OBE b. 1955, investment manager Aberdeen Asset Management 1988-2006, Chairman ACSEF 2014-15, Director ONE 2015-
[36] Stewart Spence, b.1947, owner of Marcliffe Hotel, Aberdeen
[37] Sir Ian Wood, b.1942, Chairman and CEO, John Wood Group 1967-2006

Another issue was Aberdeen's Western Peripheral Route, completed in 2019 after 15 years. This is another example of Scotland's current planning regime, which still continues to thwart even the most necessary and vital public work programmes whilst ensuring democracy on a quite disproportionate scale. A recent National Infrastructure Commission[38] report is withering in its criticism on lack of progress for a number of national projects – new runways in the south east, the construction of the first rail link between Manchester and Leeds, a second cross rail link in London, and the laying down of a 5G superfast internet across the country. I find all this utterly depressing.

SE had created possibly one of the world's best business networks through its Global Scot initiative, which comprised Scots operating at very senior levels in over 100 countries throughout the world. At the top was the International Advisory Board (IAB), which was made up of CEOs of global companies in Silicon Valley, other parts of the US, and the Far East. At their own expense, these people came to Scotland once a year and met SE and its Board to discuss strategy and how they could help. Shortly after Alex Salmond became First Minister he created his own Council of Economic Advisors under Sir George Mathewson[39] and the inevitable happened. That year SE's IAB met in Edinburgh and Salmond was invited to address them. His speech was best paraphrased, "We know what we're doing, I've got some of the best people in the world on my side and, by the way, thanks for your minor efforts in helping us." At his table he continued to talk down to some of the group. The next morning several members of the IAB came to see John Ward. They were extremely unhappy about what had happened the previous evening and told him that they felt that they were no longer needed and, as they were doing this on a voluntary basis, they did not wish to continue. Scotland was the bigger loser. There is a certain irony, as I detail in Chapter 45, that the Republic of Ireland Government, when the Celtic Tiger collapsed in 2007, looked around the world to see how they could best leverage knowledge and experience and quickly established that the best current exemplar was Scotland's Global Scot Network and its International Advisory Board. Overnight they created the Global Irish Network and in 2009, 300 'ambassadors' were invited to Dublin for the first Global Economic Forum. The group was the catalyst for Ireland's recovery from the 2007-08 recession. This occurred at around the same time as the Scottish Government was ultimately responsible for the opposite taking place here.

A further example of SE wasting public money was what I call GSC Mark II. It was the Loch Lomond Shores project and again I found myself one of the sternest critics. Some of the principles were identical - a noble public realm work, developing a site that would give substantial access to one of Scotland's most famous iconic assets. Naming the project Lomond Shores was an early indicator of confused thinking and at the heart of the project was SE Dunbartonshire. There were many parallels with GSC - hopelessly optimistic visitor figures, another cinema complex, and an extremely large and expensive management team to guide the project. The cinema

---

[38] Report by Sir John Armitt. National Infrastructure Commission 2018.
[39] Sir George Mathewson CBE, b.1940. Chairman Royal Bank of Scotland 2001-06

complex in some ways illustrated the poor management thinking. It was the centrepiece of the sizeable tower complex designed to be the focal point. Instead of choosing the traditional IMAX wide screen format, the team chose an i-WERKS format (shades of VHS vs. Betamax). In addition, they commissioned content that did not showcase the outstanding beauty and quality of what they were trying to promote. Instead, they produced a drama film, 'The Legend of Loch Lomond'. It was dull and insipid, guaranteeing that no one would view it a second time. Ten years on, this time with an even worse performance. SE had to write off the entire project (around £30 million) and hand it over to a professional operator. I do not say that the project had no merits, particularly as the retail park created a facility which has been enjoyed by many, but it represented appalling value to the taxpayer. It was conceived and run by people with no concept of delivering value and who appeared not to care about financial success. In the public sector, when something goes wrong, there is always someone to bail it out – the taxpayer.

Sir John Ward completed his term of office in 2009. He had most effectively chaired an organisation that, because of its significant budget, attracted more than its fair share of public criticism. John was afraid of no one and could speak without fear of reprisal, hence his many clashes with government ministers and civil servants. Astonishingly the government took almost a year to choose his successor Crawford Gillies[40]. The inevitable conclusion had to be that either Gillies was not the first choice for the job or, perhaps more likely, that the Government's obsession with political correctness in public appointments had caused the delay. Either way, such incompetence would never have been tolerated in the private sector. I also know that I was not the only member to find it difficult when, as frequently happened, the organisation received a dressing down from ministers or civil servants who themselves couldn't run a whelk stall.

I served a relatively short time under Crawford Gillies and didn't particularly warm to him. He had a totally different modus operandi to John Ward. I attended one meeting with him in Edinburgh with other NDPBs. The whole bonus structure at the NDPBs had become a hot topic politically and there emerged a quite farcical situation in which, for political reasons, the Government, after many months of prevarication, had decided not to pay out the previous year's bonuses to Senior Executives of the NDPBs. In the case of the SE team, the bonus structure had been agreed almost two years previously and the Government was contractually obliged to honour its commitment. It refused to do so, virtually blackmailing the staff involved into 'voluntarily' waiving their entitlement to the payments. John Ward would have berated the hapless people trying to justify the Government's position. Crawford said nothing. I thought not to stand up for his team was a poor show. Prior to my departure from the SE board, I had a final review meeting with Crawford and, as Chairman of the Nominations Committee, I criticised the fact that the organisation no longer had any female non-executive directors. He blamed the public appointment system and looked aghast when I said that he needed to be more proactive and identify suitable candidates and ensure that they applied. In fairness

---

[40] Crawford Gillies, b.1956, Chairman, Scottish Enterprise 2009-15

to him, the shambolic nature of such a system would inevitably put many people off applying in the first place. However, it is interesting to note that four of the 11 members of the SE Board in 2019 are women.

After my time at SE I only applied for one other public appointment in Scotland and was again dumbfounded by the interminable application process. I didn't even make it to the interview stage and determined never again to go through such a farce. I know many highly capable people who felt and acted the same way. This is a waste of talent and a huge loss to the future well-being of Scotland.

Chapter 38   NI IN DUBLIN

"If it was raining soup, the Irish would go out with forks."   *Brendan Behan*[1]

"When you're lying drunk at the airport, you're Irish. When you win an Oscar, you're British."   *Brenda Fricker*[2]

In late 2004 Ian McDonald first mentioned a possible new role for me managing the Irish company in Dublin. Initially I was slightly suspicious of Ian's motivation. I had become increasingly vociferous in my criticism of some aspects of Project Hal which was the codeword for the re-equipping of NI's manufacturing side. Planning for it had started several years previously and it was a massive exercise requiring an investment of some £650 million. Its origins were threefold: a long-term requirement to upgrade NI's press capacity, as the existing presses were coming towards the end of their shelf-life with an inevitable decline in efficiency rapidly approaching; second, market demand for colour capacity continued to increase, particularly within the advertising sector and, alongside that, there was a trend for increasingly multi-section newspapers. The third factor was the relentless demand for operational efficiency. The move to Wapping had massively reduced the over manning of the old Fleet Street regime and the Teamwork 2000 project had made further inroads by ending the demarcation lines between manufacturing and engineering. Project Hal was to result in a massive technological breakthrough – the concept of high-speed triple-width presses not yet tested within the industry.

There were many compromises to ensure that the investment stacked up financially but I found myself utterly opposed to some of them. For example, in its early stages Project Hal could not accommodate any daytime printing. I already had a long-term contract with Dunfermline Press Group to print their titles during the day. It had taken me a long time to get this profitable business and I certainly didn't want to lose it in some transitional arrangements for the project. Furthermore, in an already declining overall market and with the best and most efficient presses, I could foresee huge opportunities for NI in the inevitable consolidation of the printing industry. This was the reason for my scepticism about the proposed promotion. Ian was intensely political, thus ridding himself of a perceived troublemaker in what was becoming an increasingly fraught project might appear attractive. In the end I decided my judgement was overly harsh. We had worked well together and in my new role he would have realised that I would be fighting, not just for the Scottish cause, but also that of the Republic of Ireland. To his credit, Ian was also to play a crucial role in finalising my new deal. He had told me that my new role would be as Managing Director (Scotland and Ireland) and that I would now report directly to Clive. I knew Clive reasonably well and did not think I would have a problem with working for him, but things did not get off to a great start. We immediately clashed on what my title would be. He wanted me to continue to be General Manager with a modest increase in my salary, which was not what Ian had described. Ian confronted Clive and quickly resolved the situation.

---

[1] Brendan Behan 1923-62, Irish poet, novelist and playwright
[2] Brenda Fricker b.1945, first Irish actress to win an Academy Award (Best Supporting Actress 'My Left Foot' 1989)

How the new arrangements were going to work had not been specifically mapped out in advance but, in some ways, this was a good thing. I sorted the logistics out quickly. I decided to spend Monday and Tuesday in Dublin, Wednesday in London, and Thursday and Friday in Glasgow. I tried to stick rigidly to this. The day in London was not a particularly attractive proposition. However, because of NI's major problem of far too many people involved in decision making. I would now have to deal with more people and, in my experience, face-to-face contact was the best way of resolving potential conflicts.

The second part of the logistics exercise was finding somewhere to stay. I had decided that renting a flat was the best option. In my first two weeks, I stayed in the Merrion Hotel, one of Dublin's best establishments which was very close to our offices. I then viewed three properties, the first of which was a new development just 150 yards from the office. Entry was by a concierge suite, there was an underground car park and gymnasium, and several penthouse flats were available. The only problem would be the rent. In 2004 the Celtic Tiger was roaring - I counted 29 major construction cranes from the front window and that was just one part of the city. Suitably impressed, I cancelled the other two appointments and started negotiating the rent downwards. The following day I was able to present to Clive a proposition giving him a considerable saving over my staying in the Merrion for two nights a week. It was a great apartment. I stayed there for over three years and it made the commuting so much easier. My occasional next-door neighbour was Jonathan Rhys Meyers[3] and it was about 200 yards from St Stephen's Green, right in the very heart of the city. I could walk everywhere but acquired Sean Bourne[4] to drive me to and from to the airport and for any out of town engagements. Sean was a great character, a source of information about everything happening in Dublin, up to date with all the latest scandal, through his vast network of other drivers, and all spun with typical Dublin humour. I tried to pack as much as possible into my two days in Dublin. I worked late on both evenings and normally tried to arrange a dinner on the Tuesday evening with major contacts – customers, politicians etc. Sean would pick me up at 6:30am on Wednesday and take me back to the airport. About a year after I arrived, I was asked how I was enjoying Dublin. I was able to reply, "It's wonderful. I'm gradually eating my way around St Stephen's Green."

Clive had warned me that I would not be welcomed in Dublin with open arms. The relatively small team in Dublin were Irish through and through. They worked for an 'English' company only because it was a well-paid job, but frequently put up with the rest of the experience through gritted teeth. As I had often found out in Glasgow, the team in London didn't help matters. Although they didn't quite regard the Dublin office as a 'bunch of Paddies', they totally lacked sensitivity in their understanding of Ireland. I once had to quell a major revolt when a Junior Marketing executive in London told her Dublin counterpart that they had a special promotion for 'the territories'. Another example occurred at a dinner in Dublin hosted by Tom Mooney[5]. One of Tom and Brenda's daughters was about to go to London having completed her secondary education. An English guest asked in all seriousness, "are you sending her there to be Anglicised?"

---

[3] Jonathan Rhys Meyers, b. 1977, Irish film actor
[4] Sean Bourne, b.1960, driver
[5] Tom Mooney b. 1951 m. Brenda (née Byrne) b. 1953 1s. 2d. Divisional CEO Print, Smurfit Kappa Group

The Dublin team initially resented my appointment. The most senior member of the team was Ken Hutton[6], who made no secret of the fact that he thought he should have got the job. The team's resentment was based on the fact that I was an outsider, an external appointment, from Northern Ireland and, probably worst of all, a Protestant. The Irish equivalent of Private Eye, The Phoenix, immediately called me Colin 'Jaffa' McClatchie. During my time there, The Phoenix regularly had a go at me, fed no doubt on scraps of gossip emanating from our Dublin office. I am very thick skinned and loved every moment of it! There is no such a thing as bad publicity and, as one part of my role was to increase the company's profile, this was as good a way as any of doing so. It reminded me of the story of John Witherow, who once asked his sports editor, "What do they think of me out there?" "They think you're a complete c**t," he replied. "That's fantastic," said Witherow.

One way in which my reputation preceded me favourably was the fact that I had successfully built NI's Scottish operation so, prior to my arrival, I had been thoroughly checked out in several conversations between the Dublin staff and their Scottish counterparts. Relatively quickly they came to understand that I was on their side and that what I was trying to do in Dublin would ultimately be to their benefit.

In some ways, NI had been too slow in entering the Irish market. Part of the problem was production capacity and Ian McDonald had taken some time to address this, as creating new capacity is a long-term process. Ian had eventually solved the problem in Ireland by acquiring three second-hand KBA presses and installing them in a green field site in Kells, County Meath. NI entered into a joint partnership with Smurfit to operate this plant, neatly sidestepping the major problem of trade unions. NI was a non-union operation and to have conceded recognition in the Republic of Ireland would have created a massive problem back home. Ireland was dominated by trade unions and operating there in a non-union environment would have been nigh on impossible, so the joint venture with Smurfit was a very clever solution. As I shall detail later, the dominance of the trade unions in Ireland was one factor which eventually stymied the progress of the Celtic Tiger. Ireland could never quite shake off its old ways and its industrial relations practices diluted many of the initiatives introduced over the years.

The task facing me in Dublin was formidable. NI had been successful in Scotland, particularly in the tabloid market, by rigorously stripping out all 'gratuitously English' content and replacing it with 'pure' Scottish content. In Ireland the task was manifoldly more difficult. It was a separate country with its own political, legal and financial institutions – and it had its own currency. Prior to my arrival, The Irish Sun was more a hybrid than a fully-fledged Irish edition. Some content was created in Dublin but the crucial editorial production process was in London with a team who, frankly, were not particularly good. The rigorous discipline of looking for offending content simply didn't happen. Rebekah Wade knew that things had to change for the paper to be more successful in Ireland and by now she trusted my judgement sufficiently to listen to how I thought it could be done.

What was needed was a major investment in the Dublin editorial team. The most senior journalist was Craig 'Bog Brush' MacKenzie[7], brother of the legendary Kelvin.

---

[6] Ken Hutton, Advertising Manager NI Ireland, now Management Consultant.
[7] Craig MacKenzie b.1948 Editor in Chief, Irish Daily Mirror 1998-2004 Deputy Editor The Irish Sun 2004-2007

He told an excellent story about his brother. A racing freelance once suggested to Kelvin that it would be a great idea for the Sun to buy a racehorse and run it in the Grand National - Sun readers could really get behind this. MacKenzie was eventually persuaded and authorised the purchase of said racehorse. In its first race it won at handsome odds, with many Sun readers having backed it. The horse was to have one more outing before the Grand National but that day the hack phoned looking for MacKenzie urgently. When told he was in conference, he insisted on being put through, "Kelvin, terrible news, the horse has fallen and broken its leg. They're waiting for the vet to arrive and put it down." Kelvin replied, "Then tell the vet to bring two bullets - one for the horse and one for you."

Craig, despite his gruff exterior, had a very soft side. On 1st November 2005 he burst into my office, almost in tears, and sobbed something to the effect that his best mate had just had a heart attack and died. He then mumbled something about the Sports pages and that they would have to be cleared for this. By now I thought that his best friend, a renowned sportsman, had died. As I was consoling him, it emerged that Best Mate was in fact a racehorse which had just collapsed and died. The horse had won the Cheltenham Gold Cup three times and Craig was absolutely correct in his judgment - the story became national news. It was one of the few times that a racehorse made both the front and the back pages of most national newspapers.

For The Sun, what was needed in Ireland was to build a separate editorial base. It took some time and much wrangling in London to achieve this but I got there in the end. Luckily, we had sufficient office space in our premises in Bishop's Square to accommodate it. Mick McNiffe was duly appointed Editor. Looking back, I feel that our Dublin editorial team never quite had the drive and commitment of their Scottish counterparts. To everyone's credit, sales and advertising revenues were increasing but neither by as much as I would have liked. One of the major problems was that, regardless of how we dressed it up, The 'Irish' Sun was still an 'English' paper and no matter how attractive we made it, there remained a sizeable part of the marketplace that wouldn't touch it. In all this, as in Scotland, so-called colleagues in London didn't exactly help. Here, unlike Scotland, one of the biggest issues was advertising content. The decision had already been made to drop all UK advertising from the papers. The plan was eventually to substitute it with paid-for Irish advertising, but in the short-term Ken Hutton and his team had to find alternative copy however they could and all sorts of deals and arrangements were put in place. The longer I was there, the more concerned I became about the specific detail of these arrangements, but Ken assured me that everything was 'above board'.

In my view, if Ken Hutton had one fault it was that he had not fought the Irish cause in London as robustly as I had done for Scotland. In London, Ireland was ultimately the responsibility of Paul Hayes[8]. Ken and Paul had an excellent relationship. They had come through the advertising ranks together but their subsequent relationship was too cosy. I often found myself challenging Paul and demanding action on many issues. I suspect that he would then consult Ken and decide that it wasn't such a big issue after all. A typical example was a UK DIY chain with no stores in the Republic of Ireland but trading in Northern Ireland. The chain had a significant contract with NI and, as a consequence, every week The Irish Sun carried a full-page

---

[8] Paul Hayes,1962-2017, General Manager 2000-04 then Managing Director, Times Newspapers Ltd. 2004-09

advertisement for a range of products priced in sterling and unavailable in the Republic. I demanded that the page be dropped. Paul didn't agree as it would mean raising the issue with the advertiser. Ken, for his part, knew that if the page were dropped, it would mean yet another page to be replaced. The net result was that Paul and Ken (privately of course) decided that it should remain, much to my fury.

As with the rest of NI, the News of the World operated in Ireland in some strange ways. Prior to my arrival, its Irish operation consisted of a few journalists based in Dublin and editorial production based in London. It had a Senior London Editorial Executive in charge of its Dublin operation, one Alex Maranchuk[9]. Like me, Alex was in Dublin a couple of days a week. I was never quite sure what he was doing, but he established a very successful relationship with the 'Taoiseach' (Prime Minister) Bertie Ahern. Ahern regularly appeared at company functions and he duly welcomed me to Ireland at one of these, albeit mispronouncing my name. It was only after I had got The Irish Sun operation off the ground and reasonably well-established that I turned my attention to the News of the World. I already had a good working relationship with its Editor Andy Coulson[10] from my Scotland days and I went to see him in London to test his enthusiasm for creating a full-blown Irish News of the World. As with Rebekah, I felt I was pushing on an open door and Andy suggested that I should deal with his deputy, Neil 'Wolfman' Wallis[11]. During the coming months I got to know Wallis and we formed what I thought was an effective working relationship. Like many journalists, he loved gossip. He provided me with a fascinating insight into the world, as seen through the eyes of the News of the World editorial team. He confirmed many of my earlier prejudices about him and his colleagues. In my view, the News of the World was a nest of vipers, an increasingly tightly controlled fiefdom where management were viewed as the enemy, were not to be trusted and were certainly to be kept in the dark about what was going on. The paper was an accident waiting to happen and its eventual demise and ultimate closure came as no surprise to me.

Wallis and I successfully set up a separate editorial operation in Dublin for the News of the World but, in the end, the project left a sour taste in my mouth. Over many months we had also discussed streamlining the editorial production process across both the Sun and The News of the World. I was keen on this for cost grounds alone, since most of the editorial production, particularly in The News of the World, was undertaken by 'casuals'. There were now established two separate rates for casuals and The News of the World's was 40% higher than that of The Sun's - originally justified because their work was mainly on a Saturday. This was now ridiculous and, while Clive was keen to rationalise the arrangements, he was reluctant to take on the London News of the World team.

I wanted to solve the issue in Dublin mainly because of a shortage of casual staff. I also wanted to be able to rotate them on a flexible shift pattern without worrying whether they worked for The Sun or The News of the World. Wallis recognised the problem and was prepared to recommend it to Andy Coulson. We had even shaken hands on the deal over dinner at Dublin's Michelin 2-star restaurant, Patrick Guibaud (chosen by him but paid for by me). The net result was an incredibly

---

[9] Alex Maranchuk, News International, journalist for 25 years, Irish Editor, News of the World until 2006
[10] Andy Coulson, b. 1948, Editor, News of the World 2003-07, Downing Street Communications Director 2007-11
[11] Neil Wallis, b.1950, Editor, The People 1998-2003, Deputy Editor, News of the World 2003-07

expensive dinner which I felt obliged to highlight to Clive when I next presented my expenses. He asked who my guest had been and when I told him, simply raised his eyebrows and shook his head understandingly. As it turned out, it was also an extremely expensive sham. Wallis consequently arranged a lunch with Andy Coulson to finalise the details of the plan. This time the lunch was at Pont de la Tour in London. As I was introducing the subject of a combined subbing operation over coffee, Coulson hit the roof and started lecturing me on the principles of editorial integrity, and how journalists had a huge allegiance to their own paper. Sadly, he totally missed the point that these were not journalists but mechanics of a production process now so technologically driven that any young person with a modicum of computer literacy could operate it far more effectively than an old-style hack. Getting a lecture about editorial integrity from the Editor of The News of the World also stuck in my craw. Wallis had clearly led me up the garden path and had no intention of delivering on it. The words 'little weasel' always come to mind when I hear his name mentioned.

One of my more interesting experiences in Dublin was my dealings with the publishers' collective trade body in Ireland, NNI (The National Newspapers of Ireland). This was similar to the Newspaper Publishers Association in the UK. It collectively represented the publishers and was a lobby group for the industry. My opinion was that it was a club run by the indigenous publishers to serve their own interests and that the non-indigenous publishers like News International were permitted a seat at the table, but nothing more than that. The Chairman's position rotated between the same indigenous titles and the rest of us were excluded, despite the fact that we all paid the same fees. During my time there, NNI was chaired by Gavin O'Reilly[12] of Independent Newspapers. Gavin was a most agreeable person but as Chairman of NNI his main objective was to thwart the ambitions of 'the enemy' – the English Press. He once described us as, 'the barbarians at the gate'. He clearly had a similar mindset when he castigated Tom Mooney of Smurfit, allegedly telling him that they (Smurfit) had sold their souls to the Devil in agreeing to print NI's titles in Ireland. In some ways, NNI was no more than a talking shop and I was vaguely amused at some of what happened. The other main objective of NNI was to ensure that any proposed government legislation not in their interests should be faced down, or diluted as much as possible. In Ireland there had been discussions on some sort of 'Privacy Bill' but NNI had been so successful in kicking this particular ball into the long grass that it had almost disappeared without trace.

My three years in Dublin were overall extremely happy and worthwhile but I felt I never got the Irish operation to the same level as the Scotland one. There were several reasons for this, but at the heart of it was the paradox of the Celtic Tiger. The economy was booming and everyone wanted to get on the bandwagon. If you were already on it, then you had to move further on as fast as possible. Yet set alongside this apparently miraculous boom, the old Ireland hadn't really changed that much. Trade unions, with their out-dated old practices and labour relations, simply weren't adapting fast enough to fuel the expansion. It was almost as if the economy was built on shifting sands. Trying to move the business as fast and as far as I could, I felt I never could get sufficient traction to make it take off. Our staff in Dublin were

---

[12] Gavin O'Reilly b.1966, former CEO of Independent News and Media, former President of the World Association of Newspapers

willing and were part of an exciting and fast-moving business, but old traditions and practices held them back. A good illustration was our negotiations with our Staff Association, which typically had taken much longer to get off the ground in Dublin than elsewhere in the organisation. The Irish perception was that the Association was somehow anti trade union and therefore couldn't be good. I helped establish it in my final year there and negotiated a three-year wage agreement on an identical basis to the one negotiated in the UK. The formula for calculating the elements of the deal was also identical, yet the final outcome in Dublin was a 4.2% increase compared to 2.8% in the UK. The main reason was that the Irish economy was starting to overheat, particularly in the housing market. Bertie Ahern's explanation for this was slightly worrying, "the reason it's on the rise is probably the boom times are getting even boomer."[13] The rampant inflation drove significantly upwards both the RPI and CPI indices on which our deals were based. I had an extremely difficult conversation with Les Hinton on the subject, and the obvious conclusion was that it was becoming increasingly costly to do business in the Republic of Ireland. We were not the only large organisation to think this. Ireland was in danger of becoming uncompetitive.

There were other factors behind the crash. Immigration in Ireland was increasing extremely quickly to fuel the boom. While there, I rarely encountered any Irish people working in the pub or restaurant sectors. Restaurant prices were also rising steeply and I calculated that eating out in Dublin cost on average around 25% higher than in Glasgow. However, the level of service in the restaurant sector was not always commensurate with the rate of inflation. One weekend Gordon Adams, Tom Mooney and I had dinner in the Unicorn Restaurant in Merrion Row. Gordon was particularly partial to Amarone and ordered a relatively expensive bottle. Our sommelier, a brash Australian, arrived with the wine, opened it, sniffed the cork and poured it into our glasses. Tom said that he would have liked to sample the wine first to which she had curtly replied that she had smelled the cork and that it was fine. As the evening progressed Gordon ordered a second bottle and the same thing happened again. No tasting as had been originally requested, but, worse still, the contents of the second bottle were dispatched into the not yet empty glasses from the first bottle. This time a further, robust conversation ensured. Tom, clearly embarrassed by this, demanded to see the manager and then politely explained that his guests would have liked to have sampled the wine first. Furthermore, they had expected fresh glasses for a second bottle. The manager's response was, "Listen pal, that's our policy and if you don't like it, f**k off."

The crash came less than a year after I left Dublin. The dam finally burst, there was a major banking crisis and Ireland, in danger of defaulting on its loans, had to be bailed out by the EU. It was a sad end to the roaring Celtic Tiger, now reduced to a whimper. Three months earlier, when I cleared out my flat, the agent told me that they were going to sell it and that the asking price would be in the region of €775,000-€800,000. Two years later, it was worth €375,000.

To its credit, Ireland came through the crisis and, like a phoenix, started rising to its former glory again, as I shall describe in Chapter 45.

---

[13] The Irish Times 14th December 1996

Chapter 39   LEAVING NEWS INTERNATIONAL, JANUARY 2007

"I hope that history will record that I appealed to your best hopes, not your worst fears; to your confidence rather than your doubts. My dream is that you will travel the road ahead with liberty's lamp guiding your steps and opportunity's arm steadying your way."   *Ronald Reagan[1]*

When I was appointed to head NI's Irish operation in 2005, I felt that it would probably be the final phase in what had been an exciting, eventful and highly satisfactory career with the company. I was 56 and had a long-term plan to move from Phase 1 to Phase 2 in my life (as described in Chapter 37). Furthermore, there is an inevitable shelf-life for all senior executive positions. About six months later, I attended a personal development course with about 20 of the most senior people in the business. We had to participate in a 360-degree analysis of ourselves and our colleagues, facilitated by external 'experts'. I began to have some doubts about how I now fitted into the organisation and with some of the new people in it. Although not the same as at the end of my time with SDR, I had a strong sense that the time was rapidly approaching when I should move to the next phase of my life.

I calculated that the Irish project would probably take three years maximum and that I should plan for an exit during that time. Furthermore, as Managing Director in Scotland and Ireland, there was unlikely to be anything else for me within the organisation that would be based in Scotland and I definitely wanted the next phase of my life to be there. It was where the majority of my contacts were and, although my daughters were now making their own way in the word, Claire and I had built a wide circle of friends in Scotland. I was not planning to retire, rather I now wanted to pursue what is commonly known as a non-executive career - not 'employed' or solely attached to one company, but free to pursue a range of interests and opportunities. Another factor influencing me was the inevitable decline of the newspaper sector. As I detail in the following chapter, I had seen this coming for some time – one would have needed to be blind not to have noticed what was going on in the marketplace as a whole.

It may sound as if I had a very specific plan to exit full-time employment. The reality was that I had a short to medium term objective, but executing an exit in itself is extremely tricky. In any organisation the last thing one wants to do is overly publicise that you want to leave, but in my case, the concept of early retirement was one that I had carefully floated to some key people in 2006. It was Project Hal that was the catalyst for the change.

I had been closely involved in Project Hal and its planning. In 1999, I had visited a newspaper plant in Finland to see the ultimate in efficiency levels. When I signed the

---

[1] Ronald Reagan 1911-2004, 40th President of the United States

visitors' book, I casually flicked back a few pages to discover the names of R. Murdoch and many senior News Corp figures. As the project unfolded, many of us visited the MAN Roland plant in Augsburg in Germany to see the prototype press operating. I was closely involved in selecting a greenfield site in Scotland where the new presses would be installed. Logistically installing them in Kinning Park alongside the existing presses was never an option. Ian McDonald and I had looked at a number of sites before selecting Eurocentral just off the M8 motorway linking Glasgow and Edinburgh. Purchasing the site had not been easy. It was being developed by Scottish Enterprise and, as I was a non-executive director there, Ian understood my potential conflict of interest. I was therefore never involved in the purchase negotiations. However, he did ask me to unblock an apparent deadlock in the negotiations when it appeared that both parties were unable to conclude the deal. Ian's understanding was that SE's lawyers were being totally unreasonable and our willingness to compromise had reached its limit. As a facilitator, I convened a meeting of the lawyers and technical representatives of both sides and quickly realised that it was our own lawyer who was the source of the problem. I asked for a short adjournment, took the individual into a side room and told her in no uncertain terms that her role was to find the solution to the issue and conclude the negotiations. It was not, as she had been doing, coming up with a never-ending series of reasons that it shouldn't happen. Result - immediate progress, a deal and an extremely grateful Ian McDonald.

Project Hal was a nightmare. With the level of investment required, it needed approval at the most senior level at News Corp and the project itself, however vital to the future of NI, inevitably competed with many other projects within the organisation. Furthermore, there were many within News Corp who viewed newspapers as old technology and not worthy of that level of support. In view of the continuing and accelerating decline of the industry, who is to say that that viewpoint was wrong? It was rumoured that Rupert himself forced through the ultimate decision to proceed and, were it not for his personal support, the project would have floundered.

In 2005, I had become Managing Director of Scotland and Ireland and, two years later, the project in Ireland was almost complete. In mid-January 2007 I met Clive in Wapping and we agreed that the time was right for me to take early retirement and leave the company. There were several other changes taking place at the time and my departure would be part of a long-term restructuring. I was more than happy with the principle of leaving and over the next week, worked on the financial details of my departure. NI, as I have consistently said, was a wonderful organisation to work for and the company provided me with a generous departure package which they stressed recognised my considerable contribution to the company during my 12 years there. They decided to replace me with two General Managers - Steven Walker[2] in Scotland and, eventually, Oliver Keenaghan[3] in Dublin.

I was never one for long drawn out farewells and I completed a brief handover with Steven. Clive hosted an excellent dinner in Glasgow and presented me with the traditional farewell gift for newspaper people – a mock front page of The Scottish Sun. the main headline was 'He's Gone Parking Mad.' This was a reference to the

[2] Steven Walker, former Managing Director The Scotsman Publications Ltd.
[3] Oliver Keenaghan, General Manager, News UK and Ireland 2008-18

last major issue I was dealing with – the move of commercial and editorial staff to new offices in Glasgow City centre. Parking was free around Kinning Park but clearly not so in the city centre! Les also hosted a memorable dinner in Dublin. I left the organisation on excellent terms. I enjoyed each and every day of my 12 years at NI, I worked with a great bunch of people but the time was right for me to move on. Consistent with my philosophy, I never looked back. In fact, it was to be over six years before I set foot in NI's new Glasgow offices. I had known Steven Walker for a long time, both at the Daily Record and then at The Scotsman. I wished him well but my concluding remarks to him were, "Here is my home phone number; please feel free to call me at any time if you need help with anything but, equally, don't feel offended because I will never call you."

Much was made in the media of my departure and they simply couldn't accept the fact that I had taken early retirement. Once again, as they say, never let the facts get in the way of a good story, so in the ensuing weeks several conspiracy theories emerged; a company downsizing, the Scotland operation being 'relegated', a major disagreement between the company and me, and a rather sinister scenario of possible dark events in Dublin. The considerable media coverage greatly enhanced my profile, as commentators debated the various reasons for my departure. The most quoted remarks were from Clive's press release announcing my departure.

"Clive Milner today announced that Colin McClatchie, Managing Director, Scotland & Ireland is retiring and will leave the company on 12 February.

Colin has been with us for almost twelve years and has been instrumental in consolidating our market position in Scotland and latterly in Ireland. His energy, drive and enthusiasm mean that he leaves us with strong and successful management teams in both countries. He moves on with our best wishes in future.

McClatchie said, 'I have been privileged to work, since 1995, in the UK's leading media company and during that time the company has achieved many significant milestones. A matter of particular personal satisfaction is the ascent of The Scottish Sun to market leadership. With the exciting imminent developments for NI, now seems the most appropriate time for my departure. I want now to progress the next stage of my career which will involve my working mainly in non-executive roles.

I wish News International and all my colleagues continued success in the future.'

McClatchie is currently a non-executive director of Scottish Enterprise, Scotland's Economic Development Agency, and Vice Chairman of Scottish Opera."

The bonus of all of this for me was that I was effectively given a huge amount of free publicity announcing that I was about to move on to a non-executive career and therefore open to offers. As they say, there is no such a thing as bad publicity - unless it's your own obituary.

Chapter 40   DECLINE OF THE NEWSPAPER SECTOR

"If the rate of change on the outside exceeds the rate on the inside the end is nigh."
Jack Welch

I left the world of newspapers after more than 35 years. I had worked for three media tycoons - Roy Thomson, Robert Maxwell, and Rupert Murdoch and enjoyed every moment of it - well almost! It is only now that I can reflect on that time, on an industry which had started to decline but, in the last decade, has been in a downward tailspin. This was an industry in which, at its peak, newspapers were the primary source of information, with around 70% of all adults reading a daily newspaper and 80% a Sunday. Fast-forward to a recent US survey[1] in which fewer than 2% of business executives regard print (all print, including newspapers, magazines, books etc.) as their primary source of information. Frighteningly, for those under 30, print doesn't even register on the scale. In the above quote what Jack Welch meant was change before you have to and sadly the newspaper industry didn't do that. Ben Thompson[2] has a further thought, "History shows time and time again, being fabulously profitable with an existing value chain is the best way to fail to recognise a new market opportunity."

The consequences of this were devastating. In the US, over 1800 newspapers have closed since 2014. In 2016 the Newspaper Association of America, founded in 1887, dropped from its name the very word which defined it and is now known as The News Media Alliance. Apart from declining membership, the word 'newspaper' had become meaningless to many of the group's members. The group's Chief Executive[3] recently said "Newspaper is not a big enough word to describe the industry any more. The future of this industry is much broader."

I was extremely fortunate that for most of my time in the industry it was very successful - cash rich and enormously profitable - although that profitability only occurred after the curbing of the destructive power of the print trade unions, which had almost brought the industry to its knees in the early 1980s. After that, the business seemed secure in the long term.

My early years with TRN were when the traditionally strong regional newspaper market dominance was about to be challenged for the first time. Local commercial radio was now providing an alternative source of information – faster, more up to date and continuous, compared to the "static" information flow being provided by newspapers. 24-hour multi-channel news was still to come, but the threat was there for all to see.

---

[1] Quartz Global Executives Survey 2016
[2] Ben Thompson, American business technology and media analyst based in Taiwan. Writes in Stratechery, a subscription based newsletter
[3] David Chavern, Chief Executive News Media Alliance. New York Times 5th September 2016.

There were then 40,000 retailers in the UK offering highly variable standards of service. The "open all hours" corner shops were fast disappearing and it would be some time before the first US style convenience stores (such as 7-Eleven) arrived in the UK.

The other major change taking place was the erosion of the cornerstone of regular readership – the home delivered copy. Today it is much more difficult to have a newspaper delivered. I detailed in Chapter 10 TRN's attempts to introduce the US home delivery model to the UK. It failed partly because of the concept of payment in advance subscription, but also partly because the strong "Little Merchant" home delivery ethic so prevalent in the US just didn't seem to chime here. Getting children up early to do a home delivery round before school proved increasingly difficult. The deregulation of television listings also contributed to the break-up of regular seven-day readership.

Although in a declining market, my SDR years (1984-1994) were as part of a successful team which increased sales of the Daily Record in seven of those ten years to an all-time high of almost 779,000 in 1989. Today that figure is 120,000 copies. Sales of the Sunday Mail increased in eight of my ten years, again with an all-time high of over 900,000 copies in 1991. The current figure is 135,000 copies.

How did we do it? The company had a consistent strategy of behaving as market leader, robustly supporting the brand and marketing it accordingly. The slogan "Your Papers Made in Scotland" played the Scottish card perfectly, not in a nationalistic sense but as a point of difference to the national (UK) press. Moving the Daily Record to full sale or return was enormously beneficial. Our marketing efforts also targeted the ageing readership of the once dominant Scottish Daily Express, replacing them with the next generation of tabloid readers. Likewise, the Sunday Mail vis-a-vis The Sunday Post. Facsimile printing technology assisted our Sunday Mail export drives and its expansion of the English market was a major factor in our success. We also took any potential threats extremely seriously. The Sunday Scot was despatched in a remarkably short time. All in all, it was classic marketing behaviour for a dominant player.

Some say that my legacy was to have built the Daily Record to an all-time high sales figure and that, when I was fired, I proceeded to do the same with The Scottish Sun, terminally injuring the Daily Record in the process. I don't see it like that. Yes, I was successful with both titles, but perhaps a better way of describing the situation is to say that, in the battle for the hearts and minds of the average Scottish tabloid reader, we understood their needs better than our competitors. Throughout it was very much a team effort and I had the benefit of working alongside some great editors who had a strong sense of what their readers wanted. My Daily Record years were characterised by a clear understanding of how a market leader should behave and my Scottish Sun years by how a Number 2 can behave virtually as it likes, in continually attacking the Number 1.

Regardless of all this, the overall market was in decline throughout that entire period, initially slowly, but steadily accelerating during my NI years and now in a rapid tailspin. So where did it all go wrong? By the 90s people were being bombarded from a plethora of sources - terrestrial and satellite television with more than 400 channels and multi BBC and local commercial stations. In spite of these significant challenges, sales of national newspapers held up remarkably well. From 1967 to 1997 sales declined from 15.4 million to 14.3 million copies per day, just over 7%. Cover prices grew at levels significantly higher than the rate of inflation and, next to commercial television, newspapers still represented the greatest mass market opportunities for advertisers, thus making it enormously profitable.

And then came the internet. This was a revolution like no other in that almost overnight it swept all before it. As Rupert Murdoch put it, "the internet has been the most fundamental change in my lifetime and for hundreds of years." The reality was that the newspaper sector simply didn't understand what had happened. Early attempts to counter the threat were to join it and immediately offer content - i.e. intellectual property - free. Before long publishers were enthusing about their new websites. Andrew Neil, never one to hold back, was telling us that Scotsman.com would sweep all before it and how wonderful life was. It hadn't yet occurred to anyone that effectively newspapers were giving away their crown jewels for nothing. The Wall Street Journal was the first to recognise the threat / opportunity and start charging for content.

The other aspect of the arrival of the internet in 1995 was that only a tiny fraction of UK homes had dial-up facilities. This reassured the industry that, at best, the internet's reach might be limited to the top end of the market and never be available to the mass market. Wrong!

In 2005 I hosted a dinner for the Marketing Society's top eight under-26 marketeers in Scotland. During the evening Rob Dalton and I heard with increasing concern about the absence of any daily newspaper in their lives. Information was available from a variety of other sources and time was an increasingly valuable commodity. The early warning signs were certainly there.

In his autobiography Les Hinton eloquently sums up the situation thus: "We still lived in an all paper world and talked with only casual curiosity about the World Wide Web. At News International we were fascinated by the novelty of office-wide e-mail. 20 years later the empires of print were creaking supertankers, left behind in the spray of algorithm-fuelled speedboats. Old media had been like a pyramid with a few at the peak broadcasting to the masses beneath, but technology had turned the pyramid upside down. Now everyone with a 5oz mobile has infinity at their fingertips."

In the years 1997 – 2017 sales of national dailies were decimated. They declined from 14.3 million to 6.2 million copies per day, a decrease of 57%. Suddenly the entire business model was turned on its head. Sales levels supported advertising and, at the same time as they were steeply declining, the internet was hoovering up large amounts of Classified advertising, the other major pillar of the business model. The internet now provided new, convenient vehicles for Classified, particularly jobs, vehicles and property - the three rivers of gold, as they were called. In the US free services like Google and Craigslist grew rapidly whilst the UK equivalents were Google, Rightmove, Autotrader and others. In total, as much as $7bn advertising revenue disappeared from newspapers to these new platforms.

There were other issues on the advertising side. As revenues were flowing from print, publishers were less successful in migrating their existing advertisers across to their online platforms. Furthermore, online purchasing had put enormous pressure on High Street retailers, many of whom went out of business, and who themselves had previously been major sources of newspaper advertising revenue.

Digital proliferation has changed the way we absorb and process information. We are now bombarded with quantity and it has become increasingly difficult to determine quality.

The inevitable conclusion is that the newspaper industry failed to adapt to these challenges. Keach Hagey[4] recently wrote "For as long as I have covered media, I have heard newspaper executives talk about the inevitable transition to digital as an act of faith. But the results are in and it's not working for local papers. Google and Facebook take up much more market share." Another expert said, "It's hard to see a future where newspapers persist and sadly it's a crisis for democracy."

In the UK Johnston Press is a classic example of how quickly the internet crippled a major newspaper group. Writing in its 2006 Annual Report, the Directors believed that the company was internet-proof: "The fundamental requirement for local content and advertising channels will not change. It is well positioned to remain the principal local content provider and thereby to continue to offer advertisers the best possible means available of achieving high reach and response in local communities." Facebook changed that overnight. Everyone now records significant events and posts them to the very audience which would previously have read about them in their local paper. Google's Adwords allows businesses to buy the search rights to some words in key areas. Thus anyone in Falkirk with a faulty boiler could now find a central heating engineer online. That engineer no longer needed to place a Classified ad in the Falkirk Herald to find business. Within a decade the Johnston Press business model had been destroyed. Pre-internet it was operating at margins over 35% but that was nowhere near enough to service debt of over £250 million and in 2018 it was forced into administration.

Two other factors which have contributed to the decline of the press have perhaps been those least acknowledged by the press itself - trust and reputation. As far back as the early 1990s David Mellor[5] warned the press of "drinking in the last chance saloon." This followed the publication of the Calcutt[6] Inquiry which recommended

---

[4] Keach Hagey, reporter The Wall Street Journal
[5] The Rt. Hon. David Mellor QC, b.1949, British broadcaster and journalist. Chief Secretary to the Treasury 1990-2, Secretary of State for National Heritage 1992
[6] Sir David Calcutt QC, 1930-2004, eminent barrister and public servant

the creation of a Press Complaints Commission with an industry Code of Practice. Yet, writing in 1995, Rhys Williams[7] concluded that, far from drinking in the last chance saloon, "newspapers have been enjoying the world's longest after-hours lock-in." At the heart of the matter was the fact that successive governments had not been keen to use statutory powers to regulate the press. The consequence was that the press treated people unfairly and those who were mistreated or misrepresented had no easy access to meaningful redress. An apology for a totally misleading article splashed on a front page might consist of a two-line piece lost at the bottom of page 46. The general public were vaguely aware of what was going on but were reassured by the industry constantly referring to the hoary old chestnuts of free speech, freedom of the press, the public interest and effective self-regulation. My attitude at the time was probably typical. In the early 1990s I sat beside Leslie Grantham[8] at a dinner in London. At the height of his fame, Grantham complained about invasion of his privacy - how the press regularly sifted through the contents of his rubbish bin and stalked him wherever he went. I listened and then asked him if he employed a publicist. He spat out "Of course I do." When I told him that he couldn't have it both ways and that his whingeing was typical of many celebrities, wanting to be always in the public eye, he subjected me to a torrent of abuse. Reflecting afterwards, he was probably right. The press paid lip service, claiming that the sacred cow of press freedom somehow justified their behaviour.

Ironically Mellor himself became a victim, going from "Toe job to no job," as the press gleefully proclaimed in 1992. Mellor had been conducting an affair with an actress, who then sold her kiss and tell story for £35,000 to The Sun through Max Clifford [9]. She later admitted that many of the printed details simply weren't true. Mellor himself in 2011 told The Leveson Inquiry[10] "...the truth was not enough for some of these newspapers. They decided to invent it. I have never owned a Chelsea shirt... that was a total invention...it was a bidding game. If she says this, how much will you pay? If she says that, how much will you pay?"[11]

And so it went on. It took the phone hacking scandal over a decade later for the Government finally to contemplate calling time in the last chance saloon. In some ways, the murder of Milly Dowler[12] was a tipping point. In 2011 media reports suggested that the News of the World had accessed Milly's voicemail after she had been reported missing. The subsequent outcry led to the closure of the News of the World and a series of investigations into phone hacking and media ethics. The Leveson Inquiry was the government's response to the consequences of both the phone hacking scandal and the much more politically sensitive issue of press relations with the police. Originally it was to be in two parts – the first to look at the

---

[7] Rhys Williams, The Independent 18th July 1995
[8] Leslie Grantham, 1947-2018, British actor best known for his role as Dirty Den in Eastenders.
[9] Max Clifford 1943-2017, English publicist specialising in selling kiss and tell stories to tabloid newspapers.
[10] The Leveson Inquiry 2011-12 was a judicial public inquiry into the culture, practices, and ethics of the British Press, headed by Sir Brian Leveson QC, PC, born 1949. English judge, currently President of the Queen's Bench Division and Head of Criminal Justice.
[11] Testimony to The Leveson Inquiry 26th June 2012.
[12] Amanda Jane (Milly) Dowler, 13-year-old schoolgirl reported missing by her parents in 2002 and found dead six months later. A man was subsequently found guilty of her murder.

culture, practices and ethics; the second to look at "unlawful or improper conduct" with media organisations and their relations with the police.

The results of the first part of the Inquiry were published in 2012. The reaction of the press was fascinating. In the lead-up to the Inquiry much was made of press freedom and warnings of the disastrous effects of statutory regulation. Many of the Inquiry witnesses were subsequently discredited. After the Inquiry and the subsequent Not Guilty verdicts of most of those accused of phone hacking there was a collective sense of relief that the matter had somehow been kicked into the long grass. Leveson himself was subsequently pilloried for concentrating solely on the press and skirting around the issue of internet regulation. It was suggested that this made the whole Inquiry redundant - "like issuing a road safety manual for the horse and carriage in the same year that Henry Ford introduced the Model T."

There is a suspicion that the newspaper industry still did not get it. Thousands and thousands of people have had their lives ruined by incorrect reporting but with sometimes only token efforts made to address those issues over the years. The industry denied that the hacking was widespread and that such claims were grossly exaggerated, yet it has provided in excess of £200 million to settle the claims of those whose privacy had been invaded – hardly isolated incidents! Annual losses at News Group Newspapers rose to £91 million in 2018 (£58.8 million the previous year). The accounts included £46.2 million in fees and costs related to legal claims against the company after the voicemail hacking scandal.[13]

An old editor whom I greatly respected once said to me "Never underestimate the intelligence of the reader." I would suggest that over the years the industry did precisely that, ignoring what was a major problem, which eventually severely tarnished the reputation of journalists. They are now, along with politicians, regarded as the least trusted people in our society. The press has recently made much of the issue of fake news online. Were some British newspapers not as guilty of publishing fake news as the very organisations which they now so loudly condemn? Is it not apposite that The Times should now feel obliged to publish above its masthead "Britain's most trusted national newspaper"?

In March 2018 the Culture Secretary Matt Hancock told Parliament that reopening the "costly and time-consuming" Inquiry – which reported on press regulation and ethics in 2012 – was not 'the right way forward'." To MPs' cries of "Shame!" he told them he was formally closing the Inquiry. He said that priority should be given to dealing with the challenges of the modern media. Long grass. Everyone off the hook. Let's have another round in at the Last Chance Saloon!

In reality there are few options left for the industry. There is still a demand for newspapers, albeit severely declining. Newspapers continue to attempt to migrate purchasers of print across to their online editions via subscription. In 2018, Times Newspapers reported that digital subscribers had overtaken print subscribers for the first time. One option therefore would be to increase significantly the cost of the

---

[13] The Times, Business Section, 8th January 2019

printed copy, compared to the online one. Coupled with payment in advance, the route to market could be significantly shortened and simplified. The reality of ten national dailies competing at point of sale, each incurring significant wastage levels, must surely be coming to an end? A firm sale policy must be on the horizon soon. Indeed, for how much longer will there even be ten national newspapers? The Independent no longer has a print version, whilst Mirror Group (Reach) now own The Mirror, The Express and The Star. Further consolidation and fallout is inevitable. One consequence will be the disappearance of one of the original cornerstones of the industry - the CTN (confectioner, tobacconist and newsagent). Confectionery and tobacco are increasingly socially ostracised for health reasons and newspapers are being killed off by the internet.

In summary, the future is dire. In Chapter 33 I predicted that Rupert Murdoch would go down in history as the last of the great press barons. Philip Collins[14] went even further under the headline "The all-powerful press baron is just a myth. For the next generation peer group recommendation is supplementing, not replacing, expert authority. The full panoply of opinion is available within seconds on line... writers are turning on the Twitter machine and talking directly to the public... The serious question for the future will be how to protect serious journalism amid online anarchy." Fittingly, the sub heading of the article was "If the Machiavellian figure (the press baron) being hunted at the Leveson Inquiry ever existed, he belongs to a long-gone era."

Post script: This chapter about the future of a business in which I was involved for most of my working life has been one of the most depressing to write about. I'd therefore like to end on a slightly lighter vein. A friend sent me the following observations about US newspapers by an unknown pundit (with no affirmations of accuracy):

The Wall Street Journal is read by the people who run the country.

The Washington Post is read by people who think they run the country.

The New York Times is read by people who think they should run the country and are very good at crossword puzzles.

USA Today is read by people who think they ought to run the country but don't really understand the New York Times.

The Los Angeles Times is read by people who wouldn't mind running the country, if they could find the time and if they didn't have to leave southern California to do it.

The Boston Globe is read by people whose parents used to run the country.

The New York Daily News is read by people who aren't too sure who's running the country and really don't care as long as they can get a seat on the train.

---

[14] Philip Collins, The Times 2012

The New York Post is read by people who don't care who is running the country as long as they do something really scandalous, preferably while intoxicated.

The Miami Herald is read by people who are running another country, but need the baseball scores.

The San Francisco Chronicle is read by people who aren't sure if there is a country, or that anyone is running it, but, if so, they oppose all that they stand for. There are occasional exceptions if the leaders are not Republicans.

The National Enquirer is read by people who are in line at the grocery store.

The Seattle Times is read by people who have recently caught a fish and need something to wrap it in.

I invite you to ponder what the British equivalents might be!

Early days at News International, October 1996

The Blair Press Fund Lunch April 1998
Discussion on the Northern Ireland problem

With Amanda, London Press Fund Ball 1999

The Branson Press Fund Lunch, November 1998 l-r : Richard Branson,
Doug Riley (BT), my PA Janis Judge, Alex Salmond and CMcC

With Les Hinton, London Press Fund Ball, 28th November 1998

With Joan Collins, 2005

With Anna Netrebko, Mariinsky Theatre, St Petersburg, January 2009

Rupert's Kinning Park Visit 2001
l-r: Lachlan Murdoch, Rupert and Ian McDonald. *Picture: Les Gallagher*

"I insist that I tell them that your train was 20 minutes late !"

With Gordon Brown, Kinning Park 2005. *Picture: John Kirkby*

With Claire, Royal Ascot at York, June 2005

'Parking Mad' - Leaving News International 2007

Chapter 41   PHASE 2 – NON-EXECUTIVE CAREER

"We make a living by what we get but we make a life by what we give." Winston Churchill

In 2007, I set out on the final (non-executive) phase of my career, something that I had been preparing for and thinking about for almost a decade. It would give me complete freedom to determine what I was going to do. By now I had some clear ideas on what I wanted to do but, more importantly, equally clear ideas of what I did not want to do.

I had talked to various people who had gone down the same route. The closest I came to having a mentor was with Sir John Ward. I had closely observed him when he chaired SE and he was always willing to give me time to chat about the role of a non-executive. Eric Hagman[1] was back in Scotland from London and came to see me as he set about rebuilding his network in Scotland. He spent some time detailing his approach to starting a non-executive career and a lot of what he said was particularly helpful. The third person I single out is Lord MacFarlane[2]. Norman and I had got to know each other through the Newspaper Press Fund and he was always interested in what I was doing.

Part of the advice I received was to give careful thought to my overall time commitment. This very much chimed with my thoughts on a work/life balance. I certainly did not want just to substitute the 50-60 hours per week with NI for a similar commitment to other activities. Further useful advice was to be careful about resisting approaches from people solely interested in acquiring my 'contacts book'.

As I left NI, I wrote to everyone I had come across in my time there, thanking them for their support and friendship. Virtually everyone replied wishing me well for the future. Norman's letter was accompanied by a very nice bottle of malt whisky. From Brian Ivory's[3] P.A., I received an entirely different response.

"Dear Mr McClatchie,

This is to advise you that following the announcement of the Queen's 2006 Birthday Honours, Mr and Mrs Brian Ivory will now be known as Sir Brian and Lady Ivory.

I would be grateful if you could amend your records accordingly."

No good wishes there then!

---

[1] Eric Hagman b. 1946, Arthur Anderson 1970-2001, latterly as one of UK's Managing Partners, Director Celtic Football Club 2004-08, Non-Executive Director and Mentor
[2] Lord MacFarlane of Bearsden, Norman, b. 1926, Honorary Life President, MacFarlane Group Plc.
[3] Sir Brian Ivory CBE FRSA FRSE, b. 1949

I had a reasonably clear action plan. I was determined to do a combination of paid-for and pro-bono work. Life had been good to me and I wanted to give something back. Others have expressed this mission statement far more eloquently. Hillary Clinton[4] described it as, "Service is a rent we pay for living." I also knew from the advice that I had received that I would have a lot of approaches for pro-bono work and it was likely that I would have to turn down some. I also wanted to get involved only in sectors where I felt that I could make a meaningful contribution and add value. The first approach occurred as I was leaving NI. I was invited to become Chairman of Scottish Opera. As I describe in Chapter 43, I was already Vice Chairman of the organisation and it was a great honour to become its Chairman. I felt that I could make a positive contribution to the huge task of ensuring that Scottish Opera continued to flourish artistically while staying solvent. I found myself chairing my first board meeting that April and was Chairman for the following seven years.

Around then, I was also invited to become a Governor of St Columba's School in Kilmacolm. Both my daughters had been there and I felt that the school had played a major role in helping them develop into the individuals they now are. I became Chairman in 2011. As I describe in Chapter 44, this turned out to be a very challenging role and I emerged from it somewhat bruised, but feeling that I had made a positive contribution.

Those early months in 2007 were very busy. I was flattered to be approached by a number of organisations in a variety of sectors. I was approached by two business start-ups in the high-tech sector but, after talking to them, I was baffled as to what they were trying to do or create. I therefore came to the inevitable conclusion that if I couldn't understand their modus operandi, it was highly unlikely that I could add value to their business, so I declined both offers.

I took up a number of appointments. I became Non-Executive Director of Dunfermline Press Group. This was a natural fit and I already knew the Chief Executive Deirdre Romanes and her Chairman Donald MacDonald. Deirdre over the years had become a close friend and we eventually bought a home adjoining her property in Cellardyke in 2010. Sadly, we had only a short period of being neighbours before her tragically early death from cancer in 2011. Deirdre was extremely generous and a fun person with a great sense of adventure. Claire and I miss her tremendously.

Shortly after I left NI, Tom Mooney invited me to have dinner with Gary McGann[5]. The result was a consultancy agreement with Smurfit Kappa, the main purpose of which was to plan for the inevitable consolidation of the print sector in Ireland.

As in Ireland, in the UK consolidation is inevitable but the process of getting there is extremely painful. It is unlikely that any major publisher will ever now re-equip, certainly not on the scale of NI's £650 million investment in 2007-09. Sadly, the pre-

---

[4] Hillary Rodham Clinton, b. 1947, American politician and diplomat, First Lady 1993-2001
[5] Gary McGann, b. 1950, Chief Executive, Smurfit Kappa Group 2002-15

consolidation phase is characterised by price cutting and decreasing margins, as existing publishers try to sweat ever increasing capacity on their presses until they fall apart. It will be a bitter struggle, but because of its relatively recent investment, NI is likely to be the last man standing. The downside, as I described in the previous chapter, is how much longer the newspaper print industry will be sustainable in view of the major sales downturn of recent years.

My Smurfit Kappa consultancy lasted three years and was the first of many. For most of them I had to sign a confidentiality agreement, so I am unable to disclose who I worked for but I was involved in a variety of projects. One of the pleasures of no longer being in one-company corporate life was that I could pick and choose who I worked with.

A further opportunity came about directly from one such project. I was asked to mentor someone within it who had just been promoted. Three years later, I'm still performing that role and now have other clients. The mentoring process is light-touch; I am passing on my experience of over 40 years working in a senior role with large organisations. In this case, the chemistry between us is positive and my client benefits from our discussions. For my part, I find it rewarding to be able to pass on my experience and so it is very much a win/win situation. I only ever have a few clients at any one time, but I enjoy it hugely, probably more than any of the other activities I am currently involved in.

In almost all my Non-Executive roles I felt that I was able to make a positive contribution. Early on, I had one experience which didn't work out and from which I learned a lot. I was appointed a Non-Executive Director of a company wholly owned by an extremely successful entrepreneur. I thought the role was to develop company strategy and to help develop a relatively young chief executive. What I subsequently found out was that I was also expected to share my entire contact base and sell the services of the organisation. We parted company amicably after a relatively short time and I still continue to have a high regard for the organisation. Note therefore to potential non-executives - be careful to understand clearly the role you are expected to fulfil and ensure you are comfortable with it before making a commitment. This is called due diligence!

In an ideal world, I would like to have taken additional public sector roles, but the flawed nature of the application process meant that I would never repeat my one experience in this area. I know I am not alone in this. Many highly qualified and extremely capable people simply aren't prepared to go through the archaic and lengthy process that is the basis of the current public appointments system.

One of my proudest achievements was being elected a Fellow of the Royal Society of Edinburgh in 2015. Founded in 1783, the RSE is Scotland's National Academy. I am also currently a Trustee of The Royal Society of Edinburgh Foundation.

CHAPTER 42   MUSIC AND CULTURE

"Ring the bells that still can ring
Forget your perfect offering
There is a crack, a crack in everything
That's how the light gets in." Anthem, Leonard Cohen[1]

Franz Schubert[2] said, "anyone who truly loves music will never be unhappy." Music has been a wonderful part of my life and my enduring love of it fortunately survived Nellie Knox's best attempts to suppress it in my early schooldays. (See Chapter 2). My love of opera is documented in the following chapter, culminating in my 30-year love affair with Scottish Opera.

Claire and I love opera, but our musical tastes are varied. On my childhood visits to the Grand Opera House for the Lyric Opera Company's annual production I saw mainly Gilbert and Sullivan repertoire, but I can also remember productions of The Desert Song, Die Fledermaus and several Oscar and Hammerstein classics. My cousin Diane's mother Belinda and uncles Douglas and Livingstone Armstrong were involved with the Company. My CAI years coincided with the rise of Van Morrison's group Them and I heard them at Sammy Houston's Jazz Studio in Belfast and followed them avidly during their short time together. I was also interested in Bob Dylan's early music.

Shortly after we married in 1975 one of the first things we bought was a high quality hi-fi system and we built up an extensive collection of LPs (vinyl to the modern generation).

The collection is dominated by my favourite artist Frank Sinatra[3]. I cannot remember when I first heard Sinatra, but the man and his music became a passion. I began a collection which eventually encompassed almost all of his recorded music, based on my 'bible'[4] - the definitive listing of all his recording sessions between 1939-82.

I have read most of the literature published about him, including several less than complimentary biographies. There is little to commend Sinatra personally. Most of what he did, to whom and with whom, is well documented and overwhelmingly supports my hypothesis, but as a musician he was in a class of his own.

In his three recording eras the Columbia albums mostly cover his early years. Some of the material is not particularly well-known and, as I found out, very difficult to acquire. In 1953 he left Columbia and signed for Capital and those years (1953-62) are recognised as his finest recordings. His voice was at its peak, he had the best

---

[1] Leonard Cohen 1934-2016, Canadian poet and singer
[2] Franz Schubert, b. 1797 - 1828, Austrian composer
[3] Frank Sinatra 'Ol' Blue Eyes', 1915-1998, singer, Oscar-winning actor, From Here to Eternity, 1954
[4] 'The Frank Sinatra Scrapbook', Richard Peters, 1982, incorporating 'The Sinatra Sessions', a complete listing of his recording sessions between 1939-82 by Ed O'Brien and Scott P Sayers Jr., Pop Universal Souvenir Press

lyricists and arrangers working for him and the very best musicians backed him in the recording studio. His tone and particularly his phrasing, are regarded as the greatest ever. Sinatra then formed his own record company Reprise in 1962 and thereafter all his recordings are on that label. The Capital years include arrangements by Gordon Jenkins, Nelson Riddle, Billy May and Axel Stordohl, and the Reprise Recordings highlight Sy Oliver, Don Costa, Neil Hefti and Quincey Jones.

Sinatra is probably best known now for his recordings from the Reprise years, including 'Strangers in the Night', 'My Way' and 'New York, New York'. In 1980 his PR firm conducted a poll to establish his most popular recordings. Of the top 25, 14 were from the Capital years, with a 1956 recording 'I Got You Under My Skin' the overall favourite (Words and music by Cole Porter, the arrangement by Nelson Riddle).

I commend you to obtain some of the classical Capital albums and sit down with a glass of something, turn up the sound, and experience absolute bliss. I particularly recommend 'Come Fly with Me', 'Come Swing with Me' and 'Come Dance with Me' (all Billy May), 'Where Are You?' (Gordon Jenkins) and 'Songs for Swinging Lovers', 'In the Wee Small Hours', 'Close to You', and my all-time favourite, 'Sinatra's Swinging Session' (all Nelson Riddle).

Like many artists, Sinatra continued to perform beyond his sell-by date. He joined a long list of legends continuing to perform long after their star qualities had diminished, still seeking the applause and adulation of fans.

I first saw Sinatra perform live on 22nd September 1984. Approaching 70, he appeared with the Buddy Rich[5] Band and it is still one of the most memorable evenings of my life. We went with Harry and Irene Scott and the atmosphere was fantastic. The event was sold out. No doubt everyone was there, like me, to see and hear someone they had idolised for so long, while prepared to accept the inevitable shortcomings. Leaving the Albert Hall, Timothy Dalton[6] was directly in front of us and Irene couldn't resist pinching his bottom, to his apparent amusement (I wonder if this would constitute sexual harassment today?)

My second Sinatra performance was on 22nd April 1989, also in the Albert Hall. He appeared with Sammy Davis Jr.[7] and Liza Minnelli[8]. This time we were sitting in the choir stalls, directly behind the stage. The orchestra was conducted by Frank Sinatra Jr.[9] and I was quite shocked by the physical deterioration of his father. One of Sinatra's trademarks was that he always credited the lyricist and arranger of each song before singing and that evening, on several occasions, he simply couldn't remember any names and had to turn around to his son for a prompt. We were less than 20 feet away and it was sad to see such a great artist struggle with his memory.

---

[5] Buddy Rich, 1917- 1997, American jazz drummer and band leader
[6] Timothy Dalton, b. 1946, British actor, with two appearances as James Bond
[7] Sammy Davis Jr., 1925-1990, singer, actor, comedian, dancer
[8] Liza Minnelli, b. 1946, singer, Oscar-winning actress, Cabaret 1972
[9] Frank Sinatra Jr., 1944- 2016, singer, conductor, songwriter, Sinatra's musical director 1988-95

The third and final time we saw Sinatra perform was at Ibrox Stadium in Glasgow on 12th June 1990. Now 74, it was not his finest performance and was not a fitting last view of a great performer, although the Herald's Jack Webster[10] had a totally different view, "Oh yes, it was a major organisational shambles... but without doubt this was also the greatest show business night that I have seen during 30 years in Glasgow. I thought my days of standing and waving were 40 years behind me, but there I was, a sober suited citizen well past that kind of thing, now behaving like a teenage fanatic. On a cold summer night, the stadium became a cauldron of worship to the greatest popular entertainer the world has ever seen. Pundits had said that Sinatra's voice was long-gone so we would be doing no more than fitting a memory to an interior reality. Francis Albert Sinatra gave his own magnificent answer. From the moment he strode onto that massive stage, he transformed that bleak Scottish night into an occasion we quickly sensed was going to live with us forever."

Over the years, I have listened to (and sometimes seen) many singers who were hailed as 'the next Sinatra'. In my view none of them bears comparison with the great man himself. The closest perhaps is Harry Connick Jr.[11], whom I saw in Edinburgh in the early Noughties. Others would argue that Bobby Darin[12], had he lived, might have fitted that mantle.

The Glasgow Sinatra concert was in 1990, when the city was enjoying something of a cultural renaissance and it became the sixth European City of Culture, with Athens the inaugural city in 1985. Not everyone agreed with Glasgow's award. Craig Ferguson,[13] in announcing Glasgow's successful bid with the words "Aw, come on," was saying that, although Glasgow had much to be proud of culturally, it hardly bore comparison with other European capitals. This was not true. Glasgow had established itself in recent decades as a prominent cultural city in the visual arts, literature, popular music, fashion, theatre and films and its club scene was unrivalled. 1990 saw all this cemented, as performers from 23 countries participated in thousands of events, including 40 new commissions and around 60 world premiers. Highlights were the visits of Frank Sinatra, Luciano Pavarotti, the Berlin Philarmonic Orchestra and the Bolshoi Opera, all of which Claire and I were privileged to attend. Being the European City of Culture was a huge success and transformed Glasgow's cultural scene. Glasgow's Concert Hall (Lally's Pally[14]) and the various facilities at the SECC meant that the city could now successfully stage virtually any scale of event.

With Scottish Opera, The Royal Scottish National Orchestra, the BBC Scottish Symphony Orchestra and the National Theatre of Scotland all having headquarters in Glasgow, the city was culturally a fantastic place.

In 2007, while Chairman of Scottish Opera, I attended a meeting to discuss the possibility of Glasgow bidding to become a UNESCO City of Music. The UNESCO

[10] Jack Webster BEM, b. 1931, Herald feature writer and columnist 1986-2000
[11] Harry Connick Jr., b. 1967, American singer, composer, actor, television host
[12] Bobby Darin, 1936-73, American singer/songwriter, multi-instrumentalist, actor
[13] Craig Ferguson b. 1962 Scottish-American television host, comedian, author, actor
[14] Nicknamed after Pat Lally, 1926-2018, Leader of Glasgow City Council and Lord Provost of Glasgow 1995-99

Creative Cities Network was originally set up in 2004. It currently has 180 cities from 72 countries, covering seven creative fields: Craft and Folk Art, Design, Film, Gastronomy, Literature, Music and Media Arts. The UK cities now include Bradford (Film), Dundee (Design), Edinburgh (Literature), Liverpool (Music), Norwich (Literature), Nottingham (Literature), and York (Media Arts).

There were around 30 people at the meeting, most of whom had direct connections with the world of music. There were senior representatives from Glasgow City Council and the four Universities. Perhaps symbolically, the meeting took place in the Principal's office at the Royal Scottish Academy of Music and Drama (now the Royal Conservatoire of Scotland). What followed was a perfect example of how a group of like-minded people can make things happen. The group felt that bidding for the accolade was entirely consistent with the city's massive regeneration since the 1980s, with culture an integral part of its strategy. This was the first of only two meetings and the entire bid process was agreed by the end of the second one. The BBC, the Universities and the City Council put up £50k to finance a full bid and Svend McEwan Brown[15] was commissioned to put the bid together. In just six months he created a hugely impressive bid document which was submitted to UNESCO in June 2008.

The document confirmed Glasgow as the music capital of Scotland and a major player on the world music stage. This was supported by some impressive evidence[16]. "In a typical week, 127 music events are presented in Glasgow.", "Five of the six biggest employers in the music industry are based in Glasgow, with over half of the country's entire music workforce based there.", "Five of Scotland's six National Companies are based in Glasgow." "Glasgow has the highest density of higher education institutions offering courses in music and the largest population of musical students in Scotland." "Music adds £76.4 million worth of output to Glasgow's economy annually."

All in all there are over 800 musical organisations in the City. One example is 'Ye Cronies' which has 200 members and was founded in 1877 with the purpose, "To provide musical entertainment to its members... and provide funds to financially assist artistes during the course of their studies."

In Autumn 2008, UNESCO confirmed that our bid had been successful. I was invited to become Chairman of a new organisation called Glasgow UNESCO City of Music (GUCM).

I quickly set about organising a Board of Trustees comprising the Lord Provost of Glasgow, Bob Winter[17], Bridget McConnell[18], Raymond Williamson[19], Archie

---

[15] Svend McEwan-Brown, b. 1965, m. Roy McEwan, Artistic Director East Neuk Festival, Bid Director 2008 and Director Glasgow UNESCO City of Music 2012-2015
[16] Glasgow City of Music Application Document, June 2008
[17] Bob Winter, b. 1937, Labour Councillor, Lord Provost of Glasgow 2007-2012
[18] Dr Bridget McConnell CBE, b. 1958, Chief Executive, Culture and Sport Glasgow (Glasgow Life)
[19] Raymond Williamson, b. 1942, Employment Judge and former Senior Partner, McRoberts Solicitors

Hunter[20] and Baroness Ramsay[21]. We constituted and registered GUCM as a charitable trust and a limited company.

As the preparatory work was going on, I was able to secure the necessary funding for the enterprise and our first year's budget of £200k was raised from a combination of funding from the Scottish Government, Glasgow City Council, Glasgow, Strathclyde, and Caledonian Universities and the RSAMD. This enabled us to start recruiting a Director for the project and Louise Mitchell[22] started in early 2009.

Despite everything seemingly set fair, GUCM struggled almost from the very start. Glasgow was awarded the designation on the eve of a global financial crisis. Previously the city had been used to "Year of .... Festivals / Events," but this was not a festival, there was no funding stream and a programme of events would take some time to organise. A second issue was where precisely GCUM fitted within the huge bureaucracy which is Glasgow City Council. Some departments thought they should have control of GCUM, particularly the City Marketing Bureau. Furthermore, GCUM's unclear objectives resulted in other departments refusing to help. For example, the Roads Department refused to alter any existing signage to acknowledge the award. The net result was that the City's response was at best lukewarm.

After three years Louise Mitchell departed and Svend McEwan-Brown, now directly working for Glasgow Life, took on responsibility for GCUM. Sadly, by now most of the financial support had been cut back or withdrawn. Svend himself had a major battle with the new Creative Scotland and was unable to secure the regular annual funding which enables any organisation to plan ahead with any degree of certainty. I completed one term as Chairman and was succeeded in 2012 by Peter Lawson.[23] Svend left GCUM in 2015. The company then went into voluntary liquidation, following an HMRC ruling over VAT, but still operates under the wing of Glasgow Life.

Reflecting on his time there, Svend said "The undoubted highlight of the past few years has been the role of GCUM in organising the cultural programme of the 2014 Commonwealth Games in Glasgow."[24] The best example of this was Big Big Sing, at which 40,000 people sang their hearts out all afternoon. Another commission was Kate Molleson's excellent book "Dear Green Sounds"[25].

Svend's final thoughts perhaps sum up best what GCUM achieved "It has been the small things that make a big difference, like creating a truly accurate and up-to-date directory of music in Glasgow, or a website that covers the most comprehensive listings of music events and organisations in Glasgow.

---

[20] Archie Hunter, b. 1943, Senior Partner, KPMG 1992-99, former Chairman, McFarlane Group Plc.
[21] Meta Ramsay, Baroness Ramsay of Cartvale, b. 1936, Labour peer
[22] Louise Mitchell, Director Glasgow Concert Halls 1996-2009, 1st Director GUCM, May 2009 – Feb 2011
[23] Peter Lawson, b. 1958, Partner Miller Samuel Hill Brown, Chairman Tron Theatre 2000-2008 and Chairman Scottish Opera 2014 -
[24] UK National Commission for UNESCO press release UNESCO City of Music changes hands as Glasgow bids farewell to Svend Brown, 2105
[25] Dear Green Sounds : Glasgow's music through time and buildings, Kate Molleson 2015 Waverley Books

These are not sexy and attention-grabbing things, but they did not exist before (very, very few cities have them) and they are very heavily used."

Claire with Luciano Pavarotti, Concert and Gala Dinner, 16th May 1990

Extras in The Prologue. Ariadne auf Naxos, 2018
Back row (l-r):   Trevor Hatton, Peter Sandercock, Anthony Burton
3rd row (l-r):   Sallie Lloyd-Jones, Joseph Kelly, Pat Anderson
2nd row (l-r):   Claire, Janet Sandercock, Catherine Shaw,
Front row (l-r): Jane Ross, Juliet Buchner, Aidan Artymuik
Picture: Richard Campbell.

Chapter 43   SCOTTISH OPERA

"My vision is to lay the treasures of opera at the feet of the people of Scotland."
Sir Alexander Gibson[1]

Opera has played an important part in my life. From early childhood my parents took me once a year to Belfast's Grand Opera House for performances by the Lyric Opera Company and 50 years later I became Chairman of Scottish Opera. For me opera was love at first sight and I have been privileged to hear some of the world's greatest performers, including Anna Netrebko'[2] as Lucia in St Petersburg and Cecilia Bartoli[3] as Norma at the Edinburgh International Festival. Of the original Three Tenors, I have heard Pavarotti[4] (twice), Carreras[5] in Glasgow (where else would an audience member shout, "Gie's Grenada, José!") and watched Domingo[6] conduct Anthony Minghella's[7] memorable production of Madama Butterfly at the Met. I have seen several hundred opera performances, each one unique. I have also seen many different productions of some outstanding operas and I never fail to be inspired by the story telling, the lyrics and the music.

Some of my family were involved with Belfast's Lyric Opera Company in the early 1960s. Opera provision in Northern Ireland has been sporadic since then. During the Troubles, culture in Northern Ireland did not benefit from investment by the UK Government in the same way as many other public realm projects. In the past 40 years many major sports and leisure centres have been built in most towns in Northern Ireland – far more than in any other part of the United Kingdom. I suppose this investment was quite rightly designed to bring the two communities together. Culture is an equally cohesive force, yet does not seem to have benefited to the same extent.

Claire and I gradually developed our interest in opera through the Queen's Festivals and we saw our first Mozart (Cosi) in 1975, Janet Price[8] in Virginia in 1976 and our first Traviata with the Northern Irish Opera Trust in 1978. I am grateful to Stratton Mills[9] for helping me to research the history of opera in Northern Ireland.

Our first Scottish Opera production was in November 1981 in Newcastle-upon-Tyne, where we saw Anthony Besch's[10] memorable Tosca - the first time Scottish Opera had staged Tosca in its 19-year history. There is no logical explanation for this. It can't be said that Sir Alexander Gibson didn't like Puccini – the Company's first ever production in 1962 was Madama Butterfly. The company has staged revivals of the

---

[1] Sir Alexander Gibson, 1926-95, founder and first Musical Director, Scottish Opera
[2] Anna Netrebko, b.1971, Russian operatic soprano
[3] Cecilia Bartoli, b.1966, Cavaliere OMRI, Italian coloratura mezzo-soprano
[4] Luciano Pavarotti, 1935-2007, Cavalieri di Gran Groce OMRI, Italian operatic tenor. The King of the High 'Cs'
[5] José Carreras, b.1946, Spanish tenor, b. Josep Maria Carreras i Coll
[6] Placido Domingo KBE, b.1941, Spanish tenor, conductor and Arts administrator
[7] Sir Anthony Minghella CBE, 1954-2008, British film director, playwright, screenwriter
[8] Janet Price, b.1938, Welsh bel canto soprano
[9] Stratton Mills, b.1932, Member of Parliament 1959-74
[10] Anthony Besch, 1924-2002, opera director

Besch production of Tosca seven times since 1981. It is an extraordinarily high-quality production and aficionados boast about the number of revivals they have seen since then. The latest one in May 2012 was marked by the memorable performance of Robert Poulton[11] as Scarpia, just months before his untimely death. An eighth revival will be staged in October 2019.

We saw our first Wagner, Die Meistersinger at Covent Garden in 1983, its huge cast led by Sir Geraint Evans[12]. When we moved to Glasgow we became regular attendees of Scottish Opera.

Murdoch MacLennan's arrival at SDR in 1993 heralded a refreshing change in the company's involvement in a whole range of areas including culture. I was charged with establishing early communications with a number of organisations and Scottish Opera was by far the most proactive in its ability to understand what the client might want and then deliver it. The first visit from Scottish Opera's Roberta Doyle[13] and Penny Lewis[14] was the start of my relationship with the company that has lasted for almost 30 years. From being a corporate supporter with both SDR and NI, I moved on to become first a Board member, then Vice-Chairman, Chairman for seven years and, finally, my present honorary role as Vice President. It has been a love affair returned in spades by the company. Despite many formidable challenges over the years it has always been a labour of love for me.

The history of Scottish Opera is well documented. Conrad Wilson[15] covered the first ten years, in addition to writing the authorised biography of Sir Alexander Gibson[16]. Cordelia Oliver's[17] book covered the first 25 years[18] and the company itself published a mainly pictorial record of the first 50 years[19]. It describes the start of the Company: "Sir Alexander Gibson and his fellow founders wanted to establish a professional opera company based in Scotland that would be able to draw on the talents of Scottish performers and creatives, as well as attract the highest profile names from the rest of Britain and abroad. With director and designers of the calibre of Peter Ebert[20], Anthony Besch.... and singers of the stature of Dame Janet Baker[21], Helga Dernesch[22], Sir Geraint Evans... all shepherded and cajoled by General Administrator Peter Hemmings[23], Scottish Opera's productions throughout the Sixties gloriously paved the way for half a century of treasured operatic memories."

Almost from the start the company displayed the considerable imagination and innovation which would characterise it for years to come. For example, Thomson

---

[11] Robert Poulton, 1957-2012, baritone
[12] Sir Geraint Evans, 1922-92, Welsh baritone
[13] Roberta Doyle, Scottish Opera Director Marketing and Press 1992-2000, Director of External Affairs 2005-07
[14] Penny Lewis, Scottish Opera Head of Fundraising and Sponsorship 1992-99, Director of Fundraising and Sponsorship 2007-13
[15] Conrad Wilson, 1932-2017, writer and music critic
[16] 'Alex, The Official Biography of Sir Alexander Gibson' Conrad Wilson, 1993, Mainstream Publishing
[17] Cordelia Oliver, 1923-2009, journalist, painter and art critic
[18] 'It Is A Curious Story, The Tale of Scottish Opera 1962-87' Cordelia Oliver, 1987, Mainstream Publishing
[19] '50 Years of Scottish Opera, A Celebration' Scottish Opera, 2013
[20] Peter Ebert, 1918-2012, German opera director, best known for his work with Glyndebourne and Scottish Opera
[21] Dame Janet Baker CH DBE FRSA, b. 1933, opera, concert and Lieder singer
[22] Helga Dernesch, b.1939, Austrian soprano/mezzo-soprano
[23] Peter Hemmings, 1934-2002, opera administrator, impresario, singer, Chief Administrator Scottish Opera 1966-85

Smillie[24] was involved in a marvellous initiative: "Someone came up with the idea of having people queuing overnight for tickets for the opening shows at the Kings' Theatre. There were a couple of flaws in the plan. No one had really heard of Scottish Opera before so it seemed unlikely that there would be a queue. And secondly, we were all students, and there was no way we could afford the ten shillings and sixpence, or whatever it was, for the tickets. But even so, a group of us got together with a Primus stove and some tins of Cream of Asparagus soup and chatted our way through the evening. The only company we had were the local hookers! But it was a great publicity stunt, and was picked up by all the Glasgow morning papers."

During my time with SDR its relationship with Scottish Opera slowly blossomed. It was initially a commercial deal based on trading advertising space for corporate tickets. Roberta had a vision of bringing the world of opera to the much wider audience of tabloid newspaper readers but this took a further five years to come to fruition. The relationship between SDR and Scottish Opera virtually ceased on my departure in 1994 but, when I joined NI in 1995, I re-established my relationship with the company on a much stronger basis. I started organising client opera evenings consisting of a drinks reception, the performance and a dinner afterwards at which one or more members of the cast might join us. I tried to ensure that invitees were an eclectic bunch and I felt that guests enjoyed meeting people from outside their specialised area. Lengthy conversations over dinner often meant us being escorted off the premises very late in the evening or even early morning. I made a point of inviting as many opera 'virgins' as possible. Around 75% of them said they would attend opera again and many went on to become opera converts. It was a win-win situation for everyone and helped build NI's profile within Scotland. The exercise helped us meet and mix with key influencers and decision makers and prepare for our long-term goal of market leadership of all our titles in Scotland. (See Chapter 36).

My relationship with Scottish Opera gradually evolved but always in the role of a corporate supporter, although I did get to meet a number of other people within the organisation over the years, including Duncan McGhie[25], then Chairman. However, it was something of a surprise when in early 2003 he invited me to join the Board. I attended my first board meeting on 16th April 2003.

I didn't know any of the existing board members – David Smith[26] (Vice-Chairman), Dr. Vicki Nash[27], Catriona Rayner[28], Prof. Duncan Rice[29], the two Ian Robertsons (known as Ian James[30] and Dr. Ian[31]), Bill Taylor Q.C[32], Chief Executive Chris

---

[24] Thomson Smillie, Publicity Officer and Development Director, Scottish Opera 1966-78
[25] Duncan McGhie CA, b.1944, Chairman, Scottish Ballet and Opera 1999-2004
[26] David Smith OBE, b.1942, Director and Chief Executive, Dunfermline Building Society 1987-2001, Vice Chairman, Scottish Opera 2001-04
[27] Dr Vicki Nash, b.1967, Director Scotland OFCOM, SO Board member 2001-2005
[28] Catriona Rayner, b.1953, Director Scottish Opera 2000-08, Scottish Ballet 2000-11
[29] Professor Sir C Duncan Rice, b.1942, Principal and Vice Chancellor University of Aberdeen 1996-2010, SO board member 1998-2006
[30] Ian James Robertson, b.1937, Director Scottish Opera 2003-09, Chairman Theatre Royal Board.
[31] Dr J Ian S Robertson FRSE, 1928-2019, Professor of Medicine and SO Board member 1999-2008.
[32] Bill Taylor Q.C., Chairman Scottish Opera 2004-07

Barron[33] and Music Director Richard Armstrong[34]. However, I had done due diligence on the organisation and knew that all was not well. Scottish Opera had, almost throughout its 40-year history, experienced financial crises on a fairly regular basis. Quite recently there had been major discussions about orchestra provision in Scotland, with a recommendation to merge the BBC Scottish Symphony Orchestra and the orchestra of Scottish Opera. The move was vehemently opposed by many and the merger never happened. There were also serious concerns about the relationship between Scottish Opera and Scottish Ballet. Acrimonious discussions on a merger of the two companies resulted in the Boards of both companies resigning en masse in 1999. Duncan McGhie became chairman of the newly merged company shortly afterwards.

I knew I was joining a company in crisis but I was not put off. However, nothing could have prepared me for my first Board meeting. It had scarcely begun when there was a vicious exchange between Duncan McGhie and Nod Knowles[35], the representative of the Scottish Arts Council (SAC). It became clear from the ensuing accusations and counter-accusations that the relationship between the two organisations was toxic to say the least. Within the Board there were also clearly major differences and I witnessed an aggressive exchange between Bill Taylor and Vicki Nash. It was almost as if Q.C Bill was cross-examining a highly dubious witness, with Vicki robustly defending her position. All in all, it was extremely acrimonious and the company clearly had some major issues to deal with.

Over the next few months it became clear that SO was actually fighting for its very survival. The major issues were funding and the increasing deficit that the company was incurring. The problem can be traced back as far as 1991, so it would be inappropriate to place the blame solely on Duncan McGhie, his Board, Chris Barron and Richard Armstrong. To the above cast most certainly should be added previous Chairman Sandy Orr[36] and previous Chief Executive Ruth 'Ka' McKenzie[37] and, indeed, some others from even further back. For example, a production of Macbeth had run massively over budget. My view was that there was an unwillingness throughout the company to accept economic reality when the Scottish Government started to communicate its unhappiness with the situation and also to question the future level of funding being asked for. The situation was further muddied by the SAC commissioning a report from Sir Peter Jonas[38], who concluded that, for a national opera company of Scotland's size, its annual subsidy should be around £9.4 million and not the £7+ million currently being given. The Jonas Report was aptly named. The Scottish Government was never going to raise the level of funding to the Jonas recommendation. On the contrary, it was demanding that the deficit be eradicated and the company put on a more secure long-term financial footing. The Board and Management of Scottish Opera chose to ignore this. This was the scene

---

[33] Chris Barron, Chief Executive Scottish Opera and Scottish Ballet 2000-2005
[34] Sir Richard Armstrong CBE, b.1943, Musical Director, Welsh National Opera 1973-86, Scottish Opera 1993-2005
[35] Nod Knowles, Head of Music, Scottish Arts Council
[36] Sandy Orr OBE, b.1939, co-founder City Inn Ltd. 1995, Chairman Scottish Opera 1992-1999
[37] Ruth McKenzie CBE, b.1957, General Director Scottish Opera 1997-99
[38] Sir Peter Jonas CBE FRCM FRSA, b.1946, British arts administrator and opera company director

when I joined the Board in April 2003 and what followed were some of the most turbulent times that the company has ever experienced.

In no particular order, the following happened over the next three years:

- A direct threat of closure of the entire company
- A major financial and operational restructuring of the company, with significant job losses and reduced output levels for the following two years (the Dark Period)
- The appointment of a new Chairman and Vice-Chairman
- The resignation of the Music Director and the appointment of a successor
- The resignation of the Chief- Executive and appointment of an interim Chief-Executive
- The appointment of a new Chief Executive (now called General Director)
- The disbanding of the full-time chorus
- The establishment of a new funding model for the National Performing Companies in Scotland

This was all achieved against a backdrop of turmoil, ill feeling, interminable feuding and internal division. A number of the Board, including myself, were determined to ensure that the company should never again have to experience a similar situation. Of paramount importance was the need to be financially stable and to establish much better relationships with all our major stakeholders. Central to all of this was the need to agree a funding model going forward whilst at the same time addressing the deficit issue. Matters had reached a head with the publication of the 2003-04 Annual Report suggesting that the accumulated deficit of £3.2 million was a direct consequence of a failure to secure the funding required and a prediction that the situation would continue the following year, 2004-5. This indeed happened, with the deficit eventually exceeding £4 million. The justification was that artistic planning in opera had a much longer timescale than other art forms and it was not unusual for commitments to be made at least three years in advance. Very often the best conductors and singers have commitments up to five years ahead, but the situation is not quite as inflexible as was being suggested. What seems to have happened was that the company made no attempt to rein in its programming, despite many warnings that it was unsustainable. I would even suggest that in some quarters there was an assumption that, since the company had run up deficits before and these had been subsequently written off, there was no reason the same wouldn't happen again. It was a game of poker, with the very future of the company at stake but I saw no mood for compromise from any of the artistic staff, from Richard Armstrong downwards.

The funding model meant that everything was directed through SAC, an organisation responsible for funding everything from the smallest theatre company or musical entity to the National Performing Companies. At the top of the pyramid, with the highest level of funding, was of course Scottish Opera and sadly the perception of it was one of arrogance, unwillingness to face reality, and a perceived profligacy.

In early 2004, I attended a day-long seminar organised by the then Culture Minister Frank McAveety, supposedly to facilitate Scottish Opera's move forward into a new era of austerity. I experienced huge hostility from those SAC members present. That day Chris Barron made the closing speech, in which, despite it now having been clearly established that future funding was to be £7.4 million, he continued to argue that Scottish Opera needed £9.5 million. Everyone went away with the – correct! - impression that Scottish Opera still did not get the message. Sadly, that impression also lingered at the highest levels. At various functions that first year I met the then SAC Chairman James Boyle[39], who conveyed to me his considerable frustration at what was going on and I had a similar conversation with Jack McConnell, then First Minister.

Ultimately there had to be a solution. There would have to be some form of restructuring at Scottish Opera, the deficit would have to be addressed, and a future sustainable level of funding established. There also started to develop within both the SAC and some of the civil servants an alternative scenario, whereby major opera provision in Scotland could be undertaken on an ad hoc basis by visiting touring companies. They believed that this wouldn't be too difficult to achieve. Opera North, Welsh National Opera, English National Opera and Glyndebourne Touring for example could, with adequate funding, be persuaded to come to Scotland on a regular basis and thus audiences would be able to continue to enjoy high levels of artistic performance, but at significantly lower cost - or so the argument ran. Scottish Opera would then only be required to provide small scale touring throughout Scotland and continue with its education programme, but as a fraction of its present size. I believe that this idea gained considerable traction throughout 2004 and, had it happened, it would virtually have spelt the end for Scottish Opera.

What was to follow was a period of intensive negotiations on the future of the company, sometimes via the SAC and sometimes directly with the Scottish Government. Throughout we were fighting a faction which regarded us with contempt and would have been happy to see the company wound up. Most of the negotiations were headed by Duncan McGhie, who performed the Herculean task of finally getting a deal, but he was badly scarred by it all and had already committed to completing his term of office in December 2004. Amongst the Government's negotiators were Sir John Elvidge[40] and Frank McAveety. I liked Frank, having had many dealings with him as leader of Glasgow City Council, but never in a million years was the future cultural landscape of Scotland a brief that he would be comfortable with. Within the mix were also many who would have been happy to sacrifice Scottish Opera on the altar of better harmony within the creative community and who would have relished settling some old scores. The negotiations took a long time, but eventually a deal was done. It enabled the company to survive and continue as the main provider of opera in Scotland, but with a reduced cost base that would be sustainable in the long term.

---

[39] James Boyle FRSE, b.1946, former Controller, BBC Radio 4, Chairman of the Scottish Arts Council 2000-04
[40] Sir John Elvidge KCB FRSE, b.1951, Permanent Secretary of the Scottish Government 2003-10, Director Scottish Opera 2012-16

The torrent of media criticism which then rained down on the company totally ignored the reality that the Scottish Government was no longer willing to tolerate a company not operating within its means. Further it had given a clear signal that it would not only reduce the overall grant, but indicated in the strongest possible terms that the prospects of the grant ever being restored to the previous levels were nil. The settlement we achieved was the price the company had to pay for survival. There was no other way forward and yet this reality was consistently ignored by the press, particularly by Michael Tumelty[41] of The Herald and many of his colleagues. They ignored it not just then but for many years to come. Five years later, Tumelty was still ranting, ".... Scottish Opera didn't know whether it was coming or going. It all led to the company hitting the wall, its full-time chorus disbanded, its house staff decimated, its orchestra kept on but marginalised on Scotland's music scene, and, ultimately the company being shut down as a performing opera company for a year."

In summary, since the early 1990s, Scottish Opera had been an accident waiting to happen. As the top funded organisation within the SAC, it was unsurprisingly regarded with envy, resentment and very often downright hostility. Equally within the company there was an atmosphere of arrogance and denial. The organisation, as part of the denial process, was simply unwilling to listen to what the Scottish Government was saying. The card of supposed inflexibility in long term planning and future commitments was overplayed and used as an excuse for allowing the deficit to continue to increase. The net result was a festering hotpot of ill will between the company, the Government, the SAC and a number of the other arts organisations in Scotland.

In the end common sense and decency prevailed and a negotiated settlement meant the company could carry out a major restructuring exercise, enabling it to plan for a sustainable, long term future. This future would involve inevitably reduced output and some bitter pills to swallow in the 'Dark Period' of 2005-2006 - including tough measures such as the abolition of the full-time chorus (also in 2005-2006) and ultimately a permanent part-time orchestra.

In autumn 2004 the Board decided to advertise for Duncan McGhie's replacement. This was contrary to the previous practice when future chairmen were appointed from within the Board, but with so much else happening it was decided that there should be complete transparency with the appointment. I was part of a subcommittee of the Board, which was tasked with this. From the initial long list, our shortlist produced four candidates, two internal and two external, whom we interviewed before unanimously proposing Bill Taylor Q.C., an existing Board member, as our preferred choice. Bill was appointed in December.

Bill asked me to become his Vice-Chairman and together we tackled many of the issues that the settlement had created. In effect we were almost starting a new

---

[41] Michael Tumelty, b.1946, former teacher. Classical music writer The Herald 1984-2011.

company, with some 90 redundancies and a major reorganisation to be carried out throughout the whole company.

One of the first issues to be tackled was the contract of Richard Armstrong, the Musical Director. The fortuitous and timely award of a knighthood for Richard certainly helped pave the way for his departure. He had led an extremely fruitful era for the company artistically, with many acclaimed productions, including the Ring Cycle. Equally, he had a major responsibility for the company's financially perilous situation and, as I witnessed at first-hand, was totally unsupportive of the changes required to secure the company's future. We wished him well and started the search for a new musical director, which ultimately resulted in the appointment of Francesco Corti[42]. Interestingly Richard's departure was perhaps the first of a series of events that started to re-engineer the fault line between artistic ambition and financial reality. Ironically the major world recession from 2007 onwards helped to reshape further the management of that tension between the costs of artistic expression and those who had to foot the bill for it - usually Government. It was to affect - and indeed still does - many major opera companies around the world (La Scala, The Met, ENO and many others). Financial reality became an increasing fact of life and, although there are many people (and critics!) who don't like it, I make no apologies for being one of the prime instigators of financial prudence as far as Scottish Opera was concerned.

The second issue was the anomalous situation of separate Boards for Scottish Opera and Scottish Ballet. That structure ceased at the end of 2004 on Duncan McGhie's retirement, when the two companies were separated, giving Scottish Opera the chance to reconstitute its Board and make several new appointments. Directors serving on both Boards had to make a choice. For example, Vicki Nash opted to go to Scottish Ballet, telling me that she had no desire to serve under Bill Taylor, perhaps reflecting the major clash I had witnessed at my very first board meeting.

Another major consequence of the restructure was that we had to dispense with the services of the full time 36-strong chorus. This, not surprisingly, was a highly contentious issue and the company had to endure a bad press throughout the affair. The economic reality was that the company was about to go into a dark period, before emerging with an annual output of four or five main scale operas, not all of which would require a chorus. There was therefore no justification for a full-time chorus. However, the members of the chorus did not see it that way and very messy and public discussions ensued. The decision having been made and enacted, some members of the Board were subsequently aghast at Bill's first Chairman's Statement in the annual accounts 2004/05. In it he said, "It is a source of particular regret to me that 2004-05 saw the end of a full-time chorus within the company. I firmly believe that an opera company without a full-time chorus is a contradiction in terms and my personal objective is to return to a situation where the company once again has the work and funding for a full time and first-rate chorus." There was absolutely no possibility of that happening, certainly not during Bill's tenure as Chairman, nor

---

[42] Francesco Corti 4th Musical Director Scottish Opera 2007-13

today some 15 years later. Many of the Board felt that the Chairman should not have been an apologist for his and his Board's collective decision.

Chris Barron left the company shortly afterwards and Bill persuaded Richard Jarman[43] to step in as Interim Chief Executive, providing some breathing space to recruit a suitable replacement. Again, I was part of a selection committee which interviewed a short list of candidates, all face to face with the exception of Alex Reedijk[44], who at the time was General Director of New Zealand Opera. Alex's first interview was conducted via video conference. It was rather frustrating, with the constantly interrupted feed leaving us staring at a blank screen. In later years, I joked to Alex that he must have been in control of the equipment at his end, enabling him to hit the 'Blank Screen' switch every time we asked him an awkward question! Alex came to Glasgow for a second interview, continued to impress us and was offered the job. His track record was impressive on two counts. First, he headed a company only 14.5% of whose funding came from the public sector. Second, he had demonstrated a strong track record of running his operation within budget. Alex brought great experience to the organisation and it is in no small way due to him that the company emerged from its darkest hour to become the highly acclaimed organisation it is today.

Bill Taylor was Chairman for one term only and did not seek a second term. In early 2008 the Nomination Committee met and recommended that I be appointed chairman. I was proud to have been elected to chair a company I loved and which had been through so much and with a considerable amount of work still in progress. It was also my first chairmanship – I had previously sat on a number of boards but always as a Non-Executive Director. I also had to clear my potential appointment with NI – this time through my new boss Clive Milner. Unlike Ian McDonald, Clive didn't quite get the rationale of a high-level public appointment enhancing the company's profile. Incredibly he asked me, "Why on earth would you personally want to do something like that?" The concept of giving something back clearly hadn't occurred to him, but he agreed to my request, albeit reluctantly.

From the onset I initiated a number of changes. I immediately commissioned a major review of corporate governance. We had not yet been formally inspected by the Charity Regulator but I feared that, if we were, we would be found wanting in a number of areas. We were extremely lucky to secure the services of Janet Hamblin[45], an expert in governance within the charitable sector. Janet spent a lot of time with us and produced an excellent report with over 100 recommendations. To the Board's credit, they totally bought into the concept and set about implementing the recommendations at full speed. We formulated policies on many areas and then made sure we complied with them. Anyone reading Scottish Opera's annual reports from 2008 onwards will see a big difference in emphasis, with policies now published in detail.

---

[43] Richard Jarman, General Manager Scottish Opera 1994-1997, Director 2005-06
[44] Alex Reedjik FRC, b.1960 General Director New Zealand Opera 2002-06, General Director Scottish Opera 2006 -
[45] Janet Hamblin, Partner RSM, formerly Scott Moncrieff, specialist in advising charity, social housing, and education sectors. Member of the Scottish Government's Strategic Board.

I gave considerable thought to the style of Chairmanship I would adopt and I was lucky to have served on a number of Boards and observed several people in action. I learned most from Sir John Ward, Chairman of Scottish Enterprise for most of my time there. From John I learned the technique of pacing the meeting, ensuring that everyone contributed, obtaining consensus and then effectively summarising what had been discussed and agreed. This may sound very logical and easy, but in reality can be very difficult to achieve. I also learnt from John how to subdivide the agenda into timed segments, while allowing some flexibility if consensus took longer to achieve. Another of John's great abilities was to ensure his Board made the required decisions, often subtly imposing a tight time deadline. He would also recognise that in any group of individuals some are inevitably more voluble than others and he was adept at making sure everyone had a chance to make a contribution.

The past decade shaped Scottish Opera into a different organisation. The world recession from 2007 did not create a necessarily favourable environment for raising private sector investment, but the company did reasonably well to increase its levels of fundraising. Sadly, public sector funding has now become a real headache. Equally the long-term freeze in council tax put enormous pressure on local authorities and Edinburgh became the first to withdraw its support for Scottish Opera. I found this absolutely shameful, given the huge contribution that the arts make to the economy in Edinburgh.

As far as central government funding is concerned, the long-term prospects are perhaps even bleaker. The previous Labour administration had significantly pegged Scottish Opera's level of support in 2004 and the overall level of support has steadily declined since then.

However, I believe that the SNP administration 'got' and understood culture far better than the previous regime. Cynics would say that it suited them to do so and that anything helping to showcase Scotland would always appeal to them, but they were the first to recognise the significant part that the national companies could play in developing Scotland's cultural landscape. One of the first things the SNP did on achieving a majority in 2007 was to remove the funding of the six national companies from the SAC, with that funding now coming directly from the Scottish Government. Of the six Culture Ministers I dealt with during my time with the company, Fiona Hyslop[46] understood us and our needs better than anyone else. She was also the first minister to recognise that, in return for their funding, the National Companies could also play their part in international relations. Scottish Opera, for example, was able to contribute significant educational projects supporting Scottish Government initiatives in China and India.

As an aside, the Labour party, then in opposition nationally, recognised that its cultural initiatives could perhaps be higher profile. Several of us in the National Companies were invited to meet Harriet Harman[47] just before the 2015 General

---

[46] Fiona Hyslop MSP, b.1964, Cabinet Secretary for Culture and External Affairs 2009-
[47] Rt Hon Harriet Harman MP, QC, b.1959, MP for Peckham 1982- and Camberwell and Peckham 1997- Deputy Leader of the Labour Party

Election. Harriet, accompanied by Margaret Curran[48] and Patricia Ferguson[49], opened the post-lunch discussion with a lengthy statement about being in listening mode and how supportive Labour would be of the cultural sector if elected. The first response came from Vicky Featherstone[50] who complimented the present Scottish administration on their accessibility, saying, "If I have a problem at the National Theatre, I can pick up the phone and get through to Fiona Hyslop almost immediately." Unbelievably Harriet responded by asking, "Who's Fiona Hyslop?" Beside me, Margaret Curran held her head in her hands and whispered, "Colin, please don't tell anyone about what she's just said." Oops!

By the time I became Chairman, we had already sorted out several of the major issues that were a consequence of the new financial settlement put in place at the end of 2004 – the restructuring of the company, the disbandment of a full-time chorus, and the separation of Scottish Opera and Scottish Ballet boards. A new General Director and Music Director were also in place.

There remained much still to be done and major challenges lay ahead. The Board itself was refreshed that first year. I appointed two Vice-Chairs - John McCormick[51] and Lisa Kerr[52] - signifying gender balance at the highest level, and also some regional diversity, as Lisa lived in Elgin. She became my Board champion for diversity and worked extremely diligently. In her six years with Scottish Opera we increased the gender balance to around 75/25% which, at the time was far superior to many of our NDPB counterparts. We were also successful in achieving a geographical balance more accurately reflecting the company's areas of support, but less so in achieving ethnic representation. Apart from John and Lisa, my first Board consisted of Paul Bateman[53], Murray Buchanan[54], Ed Crozier[55], Shields Henderson[56], Richard Jarman, Rona Mackay-Black[57], John Mayne [58], Colin McCallum[59], John Mulgrew[60], Catriona Rayner, Alex Reedijk, Dr Ian, and Ian James Robertson. They were later joined by Dame Elish Angiolini[61], Tony Burton[62], Sir John Elvidge, Dominic Fry[63], Trevor Hatton[64], Peter Lawson, and Dorothy Miell[65]. I list them to demonstrate that they were all highly qualified people who were unpaid yet gave freely of their valuable time to ensure a well-run and dynamic company.

---

[48] Margaret Curran MP Glasgow East 2010-15, Shadow Secretary of State for Scotland 2011-15
[49] Patricia Ferguson b.1958, MSP Glasgow, Maryhill and Springburn 2011-16
[50] Vicky Featherstone b.1967, Founding Artistic Director National Theatre of Scotland 2004-13
[51] John McCormick Controller BBC Scotland 1992-2004, Director Scottish Opera 2005-8, Vice Chairman 2008-
[52] Lisa Kerr, Vice Chair Scottish Opera 2008-14, Principal Gordonstoun School 2016-
[53] Paul Bateman, Boots Retail International, Director Scottish Opera 2007-10
[54] Murray Buchanan, lawyer, Director Scottish Opera 2005-09
[55] Ed Crozier, Promenade Productions, Director Scottish Opera 2006-12, President SRU 2015
[56] Shields Henderson b. 1941, Director Scottish Opera 2008-14, Vice Chairman 2014-16
[57] Professor Rona Mackay-Black, b.1941, Director Scottish Opera 2008-14
[58] John Mayne, Director Scottish Opera 2005-11.
[59] Colin McCallum Director Scottish Opera 2008-14
[60] John Mulgrew OBE, Director Scottish Opera 2008-14
[61] Dame Elish Angiolini, b.1960, Lord Advocate of Scotland 2006-11, Principal St Hugh's College Oxford 2012-
[62] Tony Burton OBE, Director Scottish Opera 2012-18
[63] Dominic Fry, b.1959, Director of Communications and Investor Relations Marks & Spencer PLC, Director Scottish Opera 2011-19
[64] Trevor Hatton former Managing Director Accenture Scotland 2010-16, Scottish Opera Director 2012-18
[65] Professor Dorothy Miell OBE FRSE, Vice Principal University of Edinburgh, Director Scottish Opera and Vice Chair 2017-

Another of the governance recommendations reaffirmed my own view about terms of office. Scottish Opera's constitution specified that trustees (Directors) should be elected for three years and could stand for a second term if agreed. On this I was totally inflexible. Boards need regular refreshment and, if this doesn't happen, the organisation stagnates. The case can always be made for, "Oh, so-and-so has done such a great job, the company will continue to benefit from their great experience and we wouldn't want to lose them." I did not support this argument and best practice dictated fixed terms, and so we bade farewell to many of the capable people listed.

What I also learned from Sir John Ward was that Boards operate best through consensus and the key role of the Chair is to achieve that. In more contentious issues consensus can be difficult to achieve and the Chair's role is to summarise accurately what has been agreed – this also ensures that the dissenters cannot later say later that something was never agreed!

Sometimes there was a far stronger consensus on a contentious issue than might have been expected. This happened with the decision to move the Scottish Opera orchestra to permanent part-time contracts. It came into effect during early 2011 after a protracted negotiation, but there was already a degree of inevitability to it, particularly since circumstances meant that the orchestra were only employed for approximately 30 weeks per year. The 2007- 08 recession was the final straw and Alex Reedijk noted in the 2008/09 Annual Report: "The longer-term future poses a greater challenge as we seek to sustain a vibrant Opera Company for the 21st Century. This will require another robust examination of our operating model along with more imaginative initiatives as we look to absorb our share of the austere times ahead." The concept of a full-time orchestra in our circumstances was unsustainable and would ultimately have pulled the company down, even without the issue of paying people for 52 weeks for just 30 weeks' work.

We wanted to give the members of the orchestra as much notice as possible to enable each of them to make decisions on their own circumstances. Having it in the public domain released a predictable maelstrom from the press.

We also had to test the level of political support. It's helpful to have it although it doesn't actually assist in the process. On 19th April 2010 we briefed Fiona Hyslop, who noted the proposals, saying that if we felt that if that was the right thing to do, we should go ahead. She then added that, with an election coming up, she hoped that there would be no musicians protesting outside the Scottish Parliament. All in all that was as much political support as we were going to get!

The proposal was then put to the Board and they endorsed it unanimously. I should record that despite the considerable flak that erupted throughout what turned out to be a lengthy process, the Board remained resolute and never faltered in their support of the decision. I know that this was a source of particular comfort to Alex, who had to withstand much personal vilification at times.

During the entire process we were aware that at some stage we would have to decide whether or not to include Musical Director Francesco Corti in the discussion. Here we knew that, whichever route we chose, there would be a massive downside. If we were to involve Francesco in the process, his personal loyalty to the orchestra would put him in an extremely difficult position. Equally if he weren't involved in the debate, he was likely to feel excluded. In the end, after much heart-searching, we decided not to involve him.

At the start of the process, I had to make a difficult call to Francesco, then at home in Germany, to explain why we had decided not to involve him. The call went as well as it could. I suspect he came close to resigning, but Francesco was a deeply honourable man who could see the bigger picture and, in my view, secretly probably welcomed not being involved. In late August I was asked to address the orchestra directly along with Alex and spent the best part of three hours at what was, at times, a very stormy meeting. In circumstances like these people are of course very concerned about their future. All the normal human emotions come to the surface – shock, anger, fear - and they have to be dealt with. I stuck to explaining why the company had to do this, that having a full-time orchestra was an unsustainable practice and, most importantly, that we were giving the players as much notice as possible in order to minimise the effects of the outcome. The Minister never did have to endure a protest outside the Scottish Parliament and was generally supportive throughout. Eventually we reached agreement and the new arrangements came into place at the start of the 2011/12 financial year.

My own relationship with Alex over the ten years was an extremely close one. Even though mine was a non-executive role, I possibly spent more time with him than I have with any other colleague. Alex had experienced a rocky start with the previous Chairman, but we forged an effective working relationship based on mutual respect. We had a shared vision of taking a company almost on its knees and with few friends and transforming it into the highly respected and innovative organisation that it is now. Throughout that time, I saw my role being principally to support him, but also to challenge him to deliver his vision in the most effective way possible. Like every relationship, it had its ups and downs. He sometimes didn't like my occasionally brutal style of communication. I have always believed in telling things as they are, with no frills or platitudes. That's my style and Alex grew to understand it. Equally, I never told him how to do his job - he had complete freedom in that area. I also taught him how to manage the Board and we were able to sort out many issues between us, before they could become problems for the Board.

We travelled extensively together throughout the UK to see various productions and in January 2009 we had a fascinating trip to see Lucia di Lammermoor at the Mariinsky in St Petersburg. The circumstances behind the trip were thus: Valery Gergiev[66], the Artistic Director, wanted to give his protégée Anna Netrebko a first run as Lucia very soon after giving birth to her first child and prior to performing

---

[66] Valery Gergiev, b.1953, Russian conductor and opera company Director

the role at the Met later that year. Through Nicholas Payne[67], Gergiev had researched which companies had recently staged Lucia. As a result, the Mariinsky rented Scottish Opera's recent production, including the set. The trip was an eye-opener in many ways. At Schiphol airport KLM announced boarding for the flight to St Petersburg and asked their gold and silver card holders to come forward for priority boarding. Astonishly over 90% of the passengers surged forward, leaving just Alex, me and a handful of other passengers! On landing at Pulkovo airport everyone clapped enthusiastically, something I thought only ever happened with Ryanair.

Russia was incredibly bureaucratic. We stayed at the Ambassador Hotel, aptly in Rimsky-Korsakov Street, where we each were relieved of 150 roubles to 'process' our passports. At dinner I ordered a spicy Bloody Mary, which took some 15 minutes to arrive, having caused some confusion. The end result could have choked a donkey. 'Spicy' had clearly been interpreted as containing as much vodka and as little tomato juice as possible.

We had lunch with the British Consul the following day. I sat beside his gloriously indiscreet wife, who regaled me with tales of modern Russia. The oligarchs were the elite, with a new class - the minigarchs – directly underneath. She told me of meeting one of the latter, who told her that her children were at boarding school in England. When she asked at which school, the lady replied "I don't know, but it's the most expensive one."

The Mariinsky was impressive, the Tsar's box accommodating over 50 people. The performance itself could have been disastrous. Alex had discovered that the Chorus (one of a number at the Mariinsky) were under-rehearsed and Gergiev personally ordered extra rehearsals. Netrebko's Lucia was outstanding and she received a 15 minute ovation. At a reception afterwards both the consul and I spoke, he in Russian, and I in English, assisted by an interpreter. The highlight of the evening for me was meeting Anna Netrebko and I had my photograph taken with her holding my business card!

One of Alex's great strengths is his ability to temper creative desire with financial reality. Unlike some of his predecessors he and his team extracted the absolute maximum out of the finite resources at his disposal. I am extremely proud that, together for ten years, we never ran up a deficit and extracted maximum value from our funding. Alex also used great skill to flex future commitments with budgetary constraints which could suddenly cause us problems - productions were moved from one year to another on a fairly regular basis. The inflexibility of future commitments was overplayed by the previous regime and sometimes used as an excuse to justify a continuing deficit. That didn't happen on our watch and we were very proud of that. No other team in Scottish Opera's history has done that as effectively. Critics, of course, might say that this is not a virtue but, believe me, it ensured Scottish Opera's survival.

---

[67] Nicholas Payne, General Director ENO, 1998-2002, and Director Opera Europa 2003 -

However, operating within budget will be only one part of Alex's legacy. Since he joined the company in 2006, he has also consistently created a balanced repertoire and his legacy is based on his ability to attract both established and up-and-coming directors and their teams to Scottish Opera.

Alex has successfully maintained an on-going collaboration between Scottish Opera and Sir David McVicar[68]. Scottish Opera provided McVicar with the first platform for his talent and he is now one of the greatest opera directors in the world, in demand at all the major opera houses. Alex secured his services for five major productions – revivals of Madama Butterfly and Così fan Tutte and new productions of La Traviata, The Rake's Progress and Pelléas et Mélisande. That McVicar continues to be involved with a relatively small opera company like SO is testament to his gratitude to the company and to his relationship with Alex and his team.

Another significant coup for Alex was securing the services of Sir Thomas Allen[69] when he was taking his first steps in professional directing, after a lifetime as a world-class baritone performing at the world's major opera venues. His Barber of Seville in 2007 was his UK debut as a director and the first of his partnership with designer Simon Higett[70]. Barber was followed by the Mozart trio of The Marriage of Figaro, The Magic Flute and, finally, Don Giovanni in 2013. Tom's four productions for Scottish Opera are particular favourites of mine. His Barber of Seville was acclaimed by the critics and the company has already staged one revival of it. Tom's attention to detail is incredible. I rate his production of The Magic Flute as one of the best I have seen. I had previously seen many productions of the opera and always struggled to understand its complexity. Tom's production was quite superb and on opening night the whole story suddenly became crystal clear to me. For Claire and me Tom's Magic Flute remains one of the highlights of our 30 years' experience of Scottish Opera. I saw the production six times and was as spellbound at the last as I was on the opening night. Tom's Don Giovanni was probably as straightforward an interpretation as possible and I very much hope that there will also be a revival of it, as the original was sadly flawed by some casting issues. Tom also appeared in a 2018 SO production of Ariadne auf Naxos. Claire made her SO debut in this, briefly appearing with 11 other extras in the Prologue as members of an orchestra. They joked afterwards that their curtain call lasted longer than their actual performance. Nevertheless, for Claire, treading the boards on the stages of the Theatre Royal in Glasgow and the Festival Theatre in Edinburgh was a huge thrill.

I was delighted that Tom agreed to join the company in 2014 as Musical Advisor. I can claim some of the credit for this but, as always, it was Alex who made it happen and he and Tom have continued to enjoy an excellent relationship. Tom's wise counsel has benefitted the company many times. He is most charming and I am very proud that he is now firmly part of the Scottish Opera family.

---

[68] Sir David McVicar, b.1956, international opera director
[69] Sir Thomas Allen CBE, b. 1944, English opera baritone and director, Musical Advisor Scottish Opera 2014-
[70] Simon Higett, b.1959, designer, Slade School of Fine Art

Alex and his team also identified the young French-Canadians Renaud Doucet and André Barbe[71] and had faith in them to produce a critically acclaimed production of Manon. This was followed by a highly amusing interpretation of Don Pasquale and an excellent production of La Bohème. The final scene of the latter was particularly memorable and was the best treatment I have ever seen of the final 30 seconds, when directors can struggle with the moments between Rodolfo's anguished cry of "Mimi!" and the climax of the dramatic and moving music.

There are many other parts to Alex's legacy with Scottish Opera. One is his hugely successful effort in commissioning new work from Scottish composers and librettists. The first of the 'Five:15' series was performed in 2008 – five operas each lasting 15 minutes. The first series included debut contributions from Ian Rankin[72], Alexander McCall Smith[73] and Craig Armstrong[74] amongst others. My own particular favourite that year was a young Kate Valentine[75] in The King's Conjecture by Bernard MacLaverty[76] and Gareth Williams[77]. Particularly interesting was the reaction of the critics. 10 musical critics regularly review our work for both national and Scottish newspapers. Interestingly none of them asked for any information about the new works before reviewing them. After the series I constructed a matrix of their collective opinions. Astonishingly their reviews comprised a complete spectrum of opinions. One opera was judged by two critics as the best of the five and as the worst by two others. Quite what that tells us about those critics I'm not sure, but it would appear that they have completely different tastes and opinions and no one should take them too seriously!

Financially Alex's initiative with the Five:15 concept was a huge success. Scottish Opera was able to commission a significant amount of new work with minimal financial risk and the Five:15 series continued for three years. Later Alex was to commission a further series for the Edinburgh International Festival in 2012. Stuart McRae[78] and Louise Welsh's[79] 'Ghost Patrol' won the Sky Arts Southbank Award, but my favourite by far was Craig Armstrong and Zoe Strachan's[80] 'Lady of the Sea'. Its dramatic imagery and imaginative lighting were amongst the best I had ever seen.

Another part of Alex's legacy is the Emerging Artists Programme, which has gone from strength to strength since its launch in 2009. The programme offers graduate singers a wide range of opportunities for one year. Designed to build performance experience, the singers have the chance to perform or understudy principal roles, as well as taking vocal coaching, acting, movement and language sessions and gaining professional guidance in working in the industry. Nadine Livingstone was the first and to date probably the most successful examplar of the programme's potential.

---

[71] Renaud Doucet, stage director and choreographer; André Barbe, costume and set designer
[72] Ian Rankin OBE, FRSE, b.1960, novelist
[73] Professor Alexander McCall Smith CBE, FRSE; b.1948, author, Emeritus Professor Faculty of Law University of Edinburgh
[74] Craig Armstrong OBE, b.1959, Scottish composer of modern orchestral music and film scores
[75] Kate Valentine Scottish soprano
[76] Bernard MacLaverty, b.1942, Irish writer
[77] Gareth Williams, b.1977, Irish composer; first Scottish Opera Composer in Residence
[78] Stuart McRae b.1976, composer opera, orchestral and chamber music
[79] Louise Welsh b.1965, playwright, author of short stories and psychological thrillers
[80] Zoe Strachan b.1975, Scottish novelist and journalist

She starred as Musetta in a main scale production of La Bohème and as Kátya in Kátya Kabanová in the small-scale touring production and as Gilda in Rigoletto. Noteworthy others who have followed Nadine include Marie-Claire Breen, Shuna Scott Sendal, Louise Collet, Andrew McTaggart, Jennifer France and Ben McAtear. Jennifer France returned in 2018, appearing as the Controller in Flight and as Zerbinetta in Ariadne auf Naxos, demonstrating how fantastically talented she is. The Emerging Artist Programme has now expanded to include répétiteurs, directors, costume designers and composers and, to date, over 50 young people have participated in the Programme.

Another successful initiative, the Under 26 £10 ticket scheme, has been running since 2006. Anyone under 26 can buy even the most expensive seat in the house (now around £80) for just £10. Uptake has steadily grown and now almost 10% of Scottish Opera's audience is under 26. I rank this as probably the most successful initiative taken during my time in the company and it augurs well for the future. With the possible exception of the National Theatre of Scotland, Scottish Opera's audience is significantly younger than many of its counterparts.

Of course, being Chairman of Scottish Opera was never completely straightforward and, during my term, there were inevitably a few crises. The appointment of a Musical Director in 2013 to succeed Francesco Corti is one example. Some critics never warmed to Francesco, with a common theme emerging over the years being about his style of conducting and his tendency, on occasions, to drown out the singers. He was particularly savaged for a concert performance of La Fanciulla del West at the Edinburgh International Festival in 2010 when he almost managed to render inaudible a stellar cast of soloists.

Alex and the Board considered a number of candidates. Our first choice was Tobias Ringborg[81], a Swedish conductor who had impressed both the board and the orchestra when he conducted Così fan Tutte in 2009. Sadly, Tobias felt that a permanent role was not for him at this stage of his career. Our second choice was Emmanuel Joel-Hornak[82], who had previously worked for the company, firstly in 1995 and also when he conducted La Traviata in 2008. The orchestra were impressed by him and after an extensive interview process, including meeting the Board, Emmanuel was appointed in 2013.

All I can say on the matter is that the relationship between Emmanuel and the company broke down almost as soon as he started. It was irreparable enough to necessitate a parting of ways. As is perfectly normal in these circumstances, as part of a settlement, both parties signed a confidentiality agreement and moved on. Nothing could have prepared us for the public relations fall-out following Emmanuel's departure. The press simply could not accept a simple parting of the ways and promulgated a series of conspiracy theories behind the departure which went on for several months.

---

[81] Tobias Ringborg, b.1973, Swedish violinist and conductor
[82] Emmanuel Joel-Hornak, French conductor

For the company it was business as usual. Joel-Hornak's departure was a setback and we had to restart the whole selection process. Matters were significantly improved in the interim with the appointment of Sir Thomas Allen as Musical Advisor. The selection process was well underway by the time I completed my second term as Chairman in 2014. Stuart Stratford[83] was appointed Music Director in June 2015, highly commended by both Tom and Wyn Davies.[84] I am enormously impressed by Stuart and his ability to engage with the opera community throughout Scotland.

During my time at Scottish Opera, there is one project on which I have very mixed feelings, the Theatre Royal. On the one hand, I am extremely proud that I was part of the team that ensured the long-term future of the Theatre through the arrangement with Ambassador Theatre Group (ATG) in 2005. I am equally proud that I also headed a major project, (not completed until my tenure as Chairman had ended) that transformed a Victorian theatre to the now modern, shining beacon at the top of Hope Street. What I am not so proud of is its ultimate cost and budget overrun.

The Theatre Royal, a magnificent proscenium arch theatre, is the oldest in Glasgow, having opened on 28th November 1867. Then known as the Royal Coliseum and Opera House, it was soon renamed the Theatre Royal. Not unusual in theatres at that time, the auditorium was destroyed by fire in 1879 and again in 1895, but survived another blaze in 1969. Harry Lauder appeared there in pantomime in 1905 and Stanley Baxter[85] in 1952. The theatre was sold to Scottish Television in 1957 and was used as a venue for live broadcasts. Scottish Opera, under Sir Alexander Gibson, bought it in 1974 and their first production of Die Fledermaus opened on 14th October 1975.

When I joined the Board, there were mixed feelings about the theatre. Many felt that owning and running a theatre was a distraction for an opera company – it was not a core activity and we had limited expertise in the field. We didn't own any of the other theatres in which we performed, so why this one? The other side of the argument was that it was the home of Scottish Opera, where Alexander Gibson and his merry band had created the entity that is now Scottish Opera. There were actually a few holes in this argument. The first performances were in the King's Theatre, not the Theatre Royal, and the company itself was based in Elmbank Crescent. Nevertheless, the argument ran that the Theatre Royal was the spiritual home of Scottish Opera and that it was most appropriate that the company should own the building.

Maintaining the building was both a major headache and a huge cost and it was underutilised. Scottish Opera and Scottish Ballet, its major tenants, between them utilised less than one third of its capacity. Utilisation of the remaining capacity was achieved by renting the theatre to third parties, usually touring productions of musicals, plays, etc., again not a core area of expertise. The lease arrangement with

---

[83] Stuart Stratford b.1973, 6th Music Director Scottish Opera 2015-
[84] Wyn Davies, b.1952. Welsh conductor
[85] Stanley Baxter, b.1926, award-winning Scottish actor, comedian and impressionist

ATG therefore made a lot of sense. ATG became responsible for the upkeep and management of the Theatre, Scottish Opera and Scottish Ballet leased back the number of weeks that they required for their productions and ATG found occupancy for the remaining weeks. As the owner of 26 other theatres around the UK, it was well placed to do this and indeed did it extremely successfully. The arrangement with ATG was thus very much a win-win one for both parties.

Ownership of the Theatre Royal remained a major headache for Scottish Opera for two other reasons. Firstly, the Theatre itself was an ageing Victorian building with an ever-increasing number of issues making it increasingly unfit for purpose. The Board knew it would have to address many of these issues in the short to medium term. The absence of an air conditioning system was a prime example. Regularly patrons fainted from the extreme heat. The second major problem was one of access. Because of the limitations of the site's footprint, the entire audience had to enter the theatre through a relatively tiny space before dispersing to the various levels and concourses, not helped by there being no lifts. This inevitably caused major bottlenecks, both before and after performances. Additional problems were inadequate toilets and a lack of disabled access.

Successive Boards had looked at all these issues over the years, but there was no obvious solution. In late 2008, as a result of STV's departure to Pacific Quay, the site was extensively redeveloped and Tesco Bank built offices on a site adjacent to the theatre on the Cowcaddens Road side. A small parcel of land (360 square metres) remained between their site and the Theatre and Scottish Opera were offered the opportunity to purchase it. It was a once in a lifetime opportunity and the Board decided to take it. Alex more than anyone had the vision to see that not only did this present an opportunity to address the issues but, more importantly, it could potentially transform the Theatre into a 21st century venue offering the very best facilities. The Board appointed the Glasgow based, award-winning architects Page\Park to design the new public spaces and planning permission was obtained in November 2011. Building work commenced in August 2012 to enable completion of the project in time for the Commonwealth Games in 2014. Page\Park were most impressive and the project was personally headed by David Page[86].

I am confident that history will show that the Theatre Royal project spectacularly achieved Page/Park's vision and has provided Glasgow with a landmark building, a 'beacon' at the top of Hope Street. The building itself has won many architectural awards and I continue to meet people who are completely bowled over by it when first visiting it. Working in a very limited space, the project was beset by many technical difficulties, many inherent with the complexities of joining the new to the old. It was something of a miracle that the specially commissioned Commonwealth Games opera 'Anamachara, Songs of Friendship" was performed in the Theatre in July 2014. The new foyers were not open to the public until December and the

---

[86] David Page, b. 1957, founder Page\Park Architects 1981

official opening by the company's patron the Duchess of Gloucester[87] did not take place until the following March.

The Theatre Royal project started out costing £10.8 million and was already well above £14 million by the time I completed my chairmanship in October 2014. It consumed an enormous amount of Board and management time and effort in trying to control costs.

Alex once told me that, on average, public realm capital projects exceed budget by around 40%. I found this staggering and reflected that no other business could survive operating at such a level of cost uncertainty. I concluded that there exists in the construction industry a bubble of deception, obfuscation and misinformation. At the heart of the process is the practice whereby every set of advisers involved usually operates on a fee structure based on the overall cost of the project, meaning there is no incentive to control costs. Unfortunately, in the case of public-realm work, unlike in the private sector, there is always a lender of last resort, i.e. the taxpayer. Examples of major cost overruns are legion in both Scotland and the rest of the United Kingdom. The construction of the Scottish Parliament is probably the best example and to this can be added more recent examples, such as the Glasgow Concert Hall extension. The final cost of the V&A Museum in Dundee, opened in 2018, was more than double the original estimate of £40 million.

Our team struggled manfully to exert control of the costs and, as I said at the onset, I don't feel particularly proud of my role in it. I was certainly not impressed by many of the advisers working on the project and I never felt completely on top of it. I was therefore determined to learn from what was a very painful experience and, as detailed in the following chapter, I ultimately took a very different approach to another capital project shortly afterwards at St Columba's School in Kilmacolm.

History of course takes a very different view, encouraged of course by the construction industry which tends to look at what a fantastic space or building emerges from a project and say that, in the distant future, no one will worry one jot about how much it cost. Needless to say, I remain utterly unconvinced by this argument.

---

[87] HRH the Duchess of Gloucester, Brigitte Eva Van Dews, m. HRH The Duke of Gloucester 1972, Patron of Scottish Opera 1986-

Chapter 44   ST COLUMBA'S SCHOOL 2007-15

"Education is the most important weapon that you can use to change the world."
Nelson Mandela[1]

Both Amanda and Milena attended St Columba's School in Kilmacolm. When we moved there in 1984, Amanda was ten months old and neither Claire nor I had given much thought to future education.

Both girls attended Duchal Nursery School, whose head teacher was Sheena McKerrall.[2] With three helpers, she ran a fabulous little school and both our girls were extremely happy there.

Amanda then went to the local primary. Kilmacolm had no state secondary school, so the nearest were in Port Glasgow and Houston. Kilmacolm did have a highly regarded, independent fee-paying school but at that stage we were not yet thinking of secondary education.

Claire was educated at Sullivan Upper School in Holywood, County Down, one of Northern Ireland's best (non-fee-paying) grammar schools. My experience at Portadown College had been unsatisfactory, but I had been fortunate to be put back on track at CAI, also a non-fee-paying grammar school (See Chapter 2).

We closely monitored Amanda's progress at the local primary school. I often took her to school and in her second year I virtually had to force her to go in. It was a traumatic time for her. By the end of that year there, we decided to send her to St Columba's and, happily, she was accepted. We only learned some time later that she had been bullied and, in the light of her experiences, we decided to send Milena to St Columba's from P1.

Both girls had mostly happy experiences at St Columba's. Under Drew Livingstone[3], St Columba's was a fine school and he operated in what now might be viewed as an autocratic style, but it was entirely appropriate for that time. Both girls flourished and emerged with high academic achievements. St Columba's extra-curricular programmes were outstanding. They were heavily involved with music and regularly performed in the Greenock Festival both individually and in group performances. On the sporting front, like their father perhaps, they excelled slightly less well. Both played hockey - more perhaps because they had to, rather than being particularly keen. Amanda played for the 2nd XI and we spent Saturday mornings on the touchline. Milena did not quite have the same level of enthusiasm. She played at sweeper and when I went to watch her, she seemed to spend most of the time chatting to the goalkeeper, suddenly springing into action when the ball and half the

---

[1] Nelson Mandela 1918-2013, South African anti-apartheid and political leader. President of South Africa 1994-99
[2] Sheena McKerrall b.1945, Headteacher, Duchal Nursery School 1977-2003
[3] Drew Livingstone, b.1944, Rector, St Columba's School 1987-2002

other team were bearing down on them – usually seemingly to her complete surprise.

Both girls had an excellent education there, emerging as stable, well-rounded individuals and well-prepared for the next stages of their lives. Drew Livingstone retired in 2001 and was succeeded by David Girdwood from Stewarts Melville College in Edinburgh.

When I retired from News International in 2007, I was asked by David Ward[4], Chairman of the Board of Governors of St Columba's, to join the Board. David was an impressive character, formerly Rector of Hutchesons' Grammar School in Glasgow. I attended my first Board meeting in September and my fellow Board members were Nichola Anderson[5], Tom Anderson[6], Sara Bishop[7], Russell Crichton[8], Graham Cunning[9], Hugh Currie[10], Aileen Findlay[11], James McAlpine[12], George Morris,[13] Paul Yacoubian[14], and David Girdwood[15]. Despite the absence of any formal governance, the Board had a varied and appropriate skill set and a reasonable gender balance. Nichola, who joined at the same time as me, had left the school relatively recently. Her appointment was an interesting innovation, the Board wanting to create closer links with the younger former pupils.

The key strategic issues were: the future development of the campus to provide more up to date facilities, understanding the requirements of the relatively new body The Office of the Scottish Charity Regulator (OSCR), finance and governance. David Ward was an effective chairman, very much focussed on the agenda, minutes from previous meetings, follow up points etc. I felt however that we spent not enough time on the really substantive strategic issues and too much on day-to-day business.

I had already discovered from previous Board minutes that Nichola's and my appointments had been only briefly discussed by the Board and no other names were put forward. As no one 'black balled' us, we were invited to join - not exactly best governance. To his credit, David Ward had recognised that the issue needed to be addressed, but was cautious. I persuaded him to create a Remuneration and Nominations Committee. He appointed Hugh Currie as its chair along with Paul Yacoubian and me. We investigated remuneration levels in the school, particularly of its senior staff, and created a more transparent process for the appointment of

---

[4] David Ward, Rector Hutchesons' Grammar School 1987-99, Chairman St Columba's School 2007-11, Convenor The Saltire Society 2006-
[5] Nichola Watson (née Anderson) b.1981, physiotherapist, Governor St Columba's 2008-13
[6] Tom Anderson, former partner McGrigor Donald, Governor St Columba's 2002-12
[7] Sara Bishop DL, b.1963, Governor St Columba's 2003-13
[8] Russell Crichton b.1960, Director Spiers and Jeffrey, latterly Director Scotland Rathbone Investment Management, Governor St.Columba's 2005-09
[9] Graham Cunning, b.1965. Head of Corporate Banking, Clydesdale Bank, latterly Corporate Finance Partner, Campbell Dallas. Governor St.Columba's 2003-14
[10] Hugh Currie DL, Board member 2001-, Lithgows Ltd. 1980-2001 latterly as Managing Director, former Chairman CBI Scotland
[11] Dr. Aileen Findlay b.1960, Deputy Chair St Columba's 2012-, GP Bridge of Weir/Houston
[12] James McAlpine b.1961, Managing Director CBC Ltd. Governor St Columba's 2007-13
[13] George Morris b.1964, Chairman Morris and Spottiswood, Governor St Columba's 2005-12
[14] Paul Yacoubian b.1960, Managing Director Craig Corporate Ltd., Governor St Columba's 2007-19
[15] David Girdwood DL b.1957, Rector St. Columba's School 2002-17

governors, with a matrix of skill sets, a proper succession plan, fixed terms of office and, in time, a list of potential future candidates - i.e. a totally open process.

The second major issue was trying to establish the criteria by which OSCR would decide if the school could maintain its charitable status. To succeed, a school had to demonstrate a level of public benefit which could be achieved in a variety of ways, but the main emphasis was on providing financial help in the form of bursaries to help those who could not otherwise afford it. The only problem was that OSCR seemed particularly reluctant to spell out either the exact level of funding required to pass their test, or even the formula on which it was based. Our best estimate was that the school might be required to contribute as much as 5% of total revenue to demonstrate a sufficient level of public benefit. We would not have to find the full level of funding immediately, but it was clear that OSCR wanted to see some statement of intent. It would have been very risky to wait until they came to inspect and then cough up the required figure. After much debate, the Board started to put aside funds immediately.

The final major issue was the need to develop the school's facilities. With over 700 pupils, the facilities, particularly at Senior School, were becoming dated. There had been some attempts to upgrade facilities on an ad hoc basis but what was really required was long-term planning. Because of the lack of space, pupils in Transitus year had to use both Junior and Senior school buildings, half a mile apart, a very unsatisfactory situation. An ambitious plan addressing all the needs had been submitted for planning approval. Although before my time, the various advisors and consultants behind the plan thought that it would be approved, so at my first Board meeting it came as a surprise to all when it was announced that planning permission had been refused. As the new boy I innocently asked a few questions and learned that there had been a vigorous, and clearly highly effective, campaign organised by a group of neighbours of the school. They had garnered considerable local support and a large number of people had written to the local authority opposing the application. I was astonished to find out that the school had taken no steps to get its own side of the argument across. The advisors had told them to say nothing as it would go through anyway. Faced with a public relations disaster, the Board decided to appeal the decision, which would start the whole process again. I found the advice that the Board had been given seriously flawed and told them so. I persuaded them of the need to engage more effectively with the local community. The objectors' group was led by one of the school's neighbours', John Fergus[16]. The outlook from his home, along with that of several other people, would have been severely restricted by the size of the building that the school proposed erecting directly behind them. I and several others were delegated to contact the group. I found them perfectly reasonable people who had become increasingly angry at the lack of contact and consultation with the school. Their campaign was based, not just on the scale of the proposed development, but also on a number of 'soft' issues, such as parking and traffic.

---

[16] John Fergus CA, b.1933, former Chairman Scottish Leather Group, Deacon Convenor Glasgow 1992-93

The outcome of the appeal was that the Reporter upheld the Local Authority decision. His decision was useful in that it dismissed many of the soft arguments and was almost exclusively based on the scale of the development.

It was to be a further eight years before the school was able to fulfil its aspirations, involving two further developments that were to cause considerable dissent and disharmony within the village. It also involved political shenanigans with the majority Labour group in Inverclyde Council, led by Councillor Stephen McCabe, whose ward was in Kilmacolm and who also lived there. As I was to discover, McCabe was 'Old Labour' and his opposition to independent schools was pursued rigorously.

There was no plan B. Over the years there had been informal conversations with Lord Maclay, Laird of the Duchal Estate, which occupied a large part of the footprint of the village. Lord Maclay had been trying to develop parts of the estate for housing and over a decade earlier proposed building a considerable number of houses with Cala Homes. There was huge local opposition to the proposals and the plan failed.

Responsibility for the development was led by James McAlpine and Tom Anderson who reopened discussions with Lord Maclay. This time they were sufficiently positive for them to recommend to the Board that new architects be appointed to work up proposals. The Board accepted their recommendations and appointed Glasgow architects Page\Park. Although not directly involved in the selection process, I was happy to endorse the recommendation, particularly as I had been impressed with their work on the Theatre Royal project. Page\Park now presented an imaginative proposal for a separate campus for Senior School.

In the midst of this, David Ward announced that he intended to complete his term as Chairman at the end of that school year and several of us were flabbergasted when he also announced that he would be succeeded by Hugh Currie. This was not best practice. I believe that David acted in good faith. In his own mind he thought that Hugh was the natural successor; he had 'floated' this to the Board, who seemed quite happy with it. This most definitely was not the case. I spoke to several colleagues who were as shocked as I was. It was agreed that I should contact David and convey our unhappiness, not about Hugh, but about the lack of process in which the matter was being conducted. I also spoke to Hugh and told him the same thing.

I was then phoned by two members of the Board saying that they wished to propose me as Chairman of the Board. Both felt that, even at this late stage, some form of contest would be an obvious way to ensure proper process. I said to both that I would have to think about it. There was merit in the suggestion in that proper governance would be observed and, on that basis, I agreed to stand. The Board of Scottish Opera undertook an almost identical process when I stood down as Chairman. All Board members were given the opportunity to apply and two candidates emerged. Peter Lawson won on a straight vote and the Board unanimously appointed him my successor. Sadly, this was not to happen in this case. Hugh felt that a contest would be in some way divisive and not in the best interests of the school and he withdrew his candidature. I disagreed but respected his opinion. He thought I should not have allowed my name to go forward but, again, I disagreed. To Hugh's great credit, when I was appointed Chairman, he gave me tremendous support and counsel during my four years in office, and remains a friend to this day.

I chaired my first Board meeting in September 2011 and I made one addition to the list of major strategic issues - school numbers. This was perhaps the most concerning of all and it was moved to the top of our risk register. In some ways it should have been no surprise. The world recession was in full swing and it was inevitable that St Columba's would be affected. The first signs were in our recently newly established Bursary Programme. We noticed that more and more applications were not from external candidates, but from existing parents whose financial circumstances had drastically changed because of the recession - the loss of a job or a significant career move. Overall, numbers started to go down at Junior School. Previously they had been stable, with those leaving the area being replaced by new entrants coming to Kilmacolm. This changed as more people were forced to leave the area because of economic circumstances. The pipeline of new people coming into the area simply dried up, particularly from outside Scotland.

On governance, I was able to move very quickly. Helped again by Janet Hamblin, the Board was absolutely on side in instituting many of the best current practices, and also developed new policies on grievance procedure and whistleblowing. George Morris manfully produced our first risk register. I also had to replace David Ward's role as an education specialist. It was essential that, as most of the Board were parents of past or present pupils, there should also be an 'outsider'. In modern corporate parlance, this would be the Senior Independent Director and here we were very fortunate to acquire the services of John Broadfoot[17], the recently retired Rector of Kelvinside Academy.

The Page\Park proposals for a second campus linked by a bridge over the railway line would provide a number of new facilities and classrooms, all urgently required to enable the school to remain competitive and up-to date. Since the new campus would be built on land still designated as greenbelt, the proposals needed to offer a major public benefit. The school proposed to provide a public car park for the entire village, addressing a major, long-term local problem.

I also instituted a major financial review of the project. I assumed that the funding model had been well-developed and I became extremely concerned when Paul Yacoubian told me that this was not the case. Paul's concerns were centred on the major differences between the new and the original developments. The financing of the original development would have been partly funded by the interest on our substantial reserves. With the recession, interest rates had tumbled and our investments were now yielding a fraction of what they had done formerly. There

---

[17] John Broadfoot b.1948, Rector Kelvinside Academy 1998-2009, Governor St Columba's 2012-16

was also the issue of bank borrowing, with a far more restrictive regime now in place. Furthermore, Paul had been unable to start investigating options for this, mainly because he had been unable to get any firm costs from Tom and James, who in turn had still not concluded the deal with Lord Maclay.

All along Maclay had been trying to negotiate a joint project linking the school development with a proposed housing development. Our team was well aware of this and had taken a consistent line: we did not wish to be involved in this and wanted a development for the school only. Maclay was a wily negotiator and had managed to extract one major concession from us. We would, at our cost, provide a major road from Lochwinnoch Road into to our development. Maclay would thus save the cost of providing this should he ever be able to develop any of the rest of his land. The road was to become the most contentious part of our development plan. In the meantime, negotiations were proceeding slowly, but our president Guy Clark[18] was able to intervene. He arranged a meeting between Maclay's team and the school, represented by Guy, David Girdwood and myself. We gave them an ultimatum of concluding the negotiations quickly, or we would abandon the entire project. They changed their position and Tom and James were able to conclude a deal within weeks. After many years, we were at last now able to consider how we would go about securing planning permission for the project and undertake a major communication and consultation exercise with the wider community.

Initially all the residents most affected by the development were invited to a meeting to start the communication process. James McAlpine and Andy Bateman, from Page\ Park, made a short presentation outlining the project. They took questions and the plan was to extend the consultation process to a wider audience so that over time the entire community could see and view our proposals in detail.

Nothing could have prepared us for the wall of hostility we encountered at that first meeting at the school. In hindsight two things contributed to this. Firstly, far more people than expected turned up and had to be shoehorned into the room where the meeting was taking place. Secondly, the room became increasingly hot and, with so many people packed into it, this became a major issue. James and Andy were interrupted several times during the presentation and a very hostile atmosphere developed almost immediately, unfortunately setting the tone that was to continue throughout the entire process. People began making quite outrageous statements on the likely impact of the development. In a series of anecdotal observations, a proposition was swiftly developed that the traffic flow around the existing site would now move en masse onto Lochwinnoch Road (one of the main roads in the village) and cause gridlock in the entire village. It was claimed that we had severely underestimated the impact of traffic on our plans. I visited the area many times over the following weeks and found no evidence of such a situation. It was also suggested that children walking down Lochwinnoch Road to the local primary school might be mown down by the additional traffic turning into our site.

---

[18] Guy Clark FCSI, JP, b.1944, Lord Lieutenant of Renfrewshire 2007-19

This was classic NIMBYism but people are entitled to their opinions. Sadly, the following months were an extremely bitter and fractious period which caused huge friction within the village and polarised opinions. From the school's point of view, their experience during the last planning application had made them understand how important it was to garner maximum support and so it campaigned vigorously, extolling the virtues of the development, not just for the school itself, but for the community as a whole. This included writing to parents, holding public consultation meetings, and talking to the various civic forums such as the Community Council and the Civic Trust.

The initial opposition group of neighbours quickly organised themselves into a 'Save Milton Woods' campaign which quickly turned the issue away from a worthwhile development into something threatening the entire greenbelt of the village. The fact that this was completely untrue was irrelevant. At the centre of the campaign were the immediate neighbours who clearly did not want the development to happen, with the most of their objections based on personal concerns. There is nothing wrong with this. I knew a large number of the group and I absolutely respected their right to object to what we were trying to do. As their campaign unfolded, it grew to include many others who shared their opinions on what was good for the village and again I respected their opinions. However, it also attracted others who behaved quite outrageously. They formented ill-feeling and division within the village for several months and their behaviour stirred up and inflamed passions.

Some of this was played through social media. Social media at the extreme can be a dangerous, almost sinister, and largely uncontrollable medium. On its own it can threaten the very basis and values on which our society is based. It seems to be more about insulting your opponent than about the exchanging of ideas - a shouting match without an umpire. What happened during the St Columba's planning application was appalling and in some ways frightening. The Save Milton Woods campaign had created a website with a chatroom format with an exchange of views that over time became a monstrous distortion of the truth and orchestrated highly personal defamatory attacks on the St Columba's Board. Objective facts were lost in an escalation of division through taunts and slogans. Some of the more extreme views were truly frightening. I fully accept that if you have a public profile, or you represent a lead view on anything, then you have to accept that, in a democracy, people can challenge those views, sometimes in a reasonable way - but nowadays, very often in a totally unreasonable fashion. In such circumstances, one has to be extremely thick-skinned and not overreact to some of the things people say. Nothing could have prepared us for the level of personal abuse and the allegations made against me and some of my colleagues. At its height, a small number of easily identifiable people were commenting on St Columba's plans in an extremely offensive way. We were called liars, accused of misleading people and, at the extreme, somehow being involved for personal gain. There were some absolutely vile comments against James McAlpine and unfounded allegations that James' company would be awarded the construction contract for the project.

Throughout, I had maintained an open line of communication with a member of the Save Milton Woods group. Over time, as some of the comments became increasingly extreme, I contacted him and explained our dilemma. I told him that we simply could not allow some of the comments to go unanswered and the likelihood was that our lawyers would be forced to take action. Although holding opposing views, he was an honourable man. I don't know what he did, but the level of extreme comments significantly reduced. A few people, although they will never know it, were spared being prosecuted for what were absolutely clear cases of defamation.

At a subsequent planning meeting, the council's planning officers supported the application. The level of debate amongst the councillors was quite appalling and reaffirmed my own opinion on the competence levels of a significant number of local councillors. Throughout the meeting, the leader of the council Stephen McCabe sat in the balcony of the hall and one councillor even referred to his presence as 'pulling the strings'. To anyone listening it was blindingly obvious that the Labour group would vote collectively against the application.

The result was that our second planning application was turned down. This time the Board decided not to appeal the decision. The significant economic downturn was continuing to impact on the school roll, with no sign of a change to the trend. At best, in the event of a successful appeal, we might have started construction on a phased basis but, unfortunately, the plan was front-ended in cost terms, effectively preventing this option. Equally, the extent of local feeling against the proposal made us wary of inflaming the situation any further.

It was not a nice time to be living in Kilmacolm. I made a point of continuing to engage with people, whether they supported our case or not. I supported local businesses even if some were against our proposals but I couldn't help but notice that sometimes people would cross to the other side of the street rather than talk to me.

After our application was turned down, we asked Page\Park to look again at the existing site and within a relatively short period of time they developed a very imaginative concept which effectively wrapped a series of low-level classrooms around the two existing detached properties on our site. Page\Park's new plan illustrated a touch of genius in that the elevation of our new proposed campus meant that the views of immediate neighbours would be identical to what currently existed. This was the precursor to a lengthy consultation process but, unlike the last time, John Fergus and other neighbours were involved in the process even before it started, with the result that they had a major input as the proposals developed. They were certainly not pushovers and there were many robust discussions, but they were conducted in an extremely constructive manner and the end result was that the group supported the project. Not everything went smoothly. Early on in the investigative period, a colony of bats was discovered in the existing properties. Bats being a protected species, planning regulations meant that they had to be given the opportunity to migrate to an alternative location before building work could begin. This held the project up for a year and once again reaffirmed my view that modern planning legislation in this country is unnecessarily bureaucratic, inflexible, and only succeeds in blocking proposals, not enabling them to happen. The project now had to be completed in two phases.

By this stage I had almost completed my three-year term as Chairman and intended to step down at the end of it. The Board felt that, as the school was about to embark on a major capital development and was now (because of the bats) faced with having to postpone a major part of that development for a year, it was not the best time to have a new Chairman. They asked me if I would stay on for one more year. I readily agreed to do so, thus giving the Board one year to find a successor.

The relationship between the Board and the parent group is an extremely complex one. When David Girdwood first took over from Drew Livingstone, he brought a totally different style of leadership. Throughout his time at St Columba's he continuously refined that model, in the main to adapt to an ever-changing environment. Parents were now far less deferential than in Drew's time. They increasingly regarded education as a commodity and St Columba's as a quite expensive provider of that. Parents were therefore not slow to challenge the system if they thought it was not providing what they wanted.

Most parents operated on a one-to-one basis in their dealings with the school's representatives and were able to monitor the progress of their offspring effectively. In the world of increasing transparency (and democracy!). David Girdwood and I both worked extremely hard constantly to refine the relationship and the communication process that accompanied it. Through my contact with Scottish Council for Independent Schools (SCIS) I got to know several of my counterparts at other schools and it became apparent that St Columba's had a far more effective and hands on Board structure than most. I regarded this as extremely positive in that our Board, whilst in no way trying to manage the business, had their fingers on the pulse of the school far more effectively than elsewhere. I also learned that in several other schools both Chairman and Board members remained in post for many years. This confirmed my views on the need for defined terms of office and regular rotation to refresh the Board.

In refreshing the Board, I had deliberately asked the Nominations Committee to appoint some people with a strong financial background. To Paul Yacoubian and Graham Cunning we added Kenny Wilson[19] and Calum Paterson[20] and I asked Calum to chair the Development Board, which would oversee the project through to its completion.

My last year as Chairman was mainly taken up with putting the development to bed, securing planning permission, and establishing an ongoing business plan to sustain it. This time, prior to the planning subcommittee meeting, the councillors made a site visit, although I suspect (cynically perhaps) that this was more to be sure that if they turned it down it would be for the right reasons (my personal opinion, I

---

[19] Kenneth Wilson CA b.1969, Senior Partner, Price Waterhouse Cooper, Glasgow, Governor St Columba's 2014-
[20] Calum Paterson CA FRSE b.1963, Managing Partner Scottish Equity Partners, Chair St Columba's School 2016-

hasten to add). On the day, the level of debate was again quite appalling as they muddled their way through the detail of the application. Throughout the process, the political dogma and bias against independent schools shone through in the Labour group but, miraculously, this time the application was passed. We were now able to proceed in modernising the school's facilities, having tried for the best part of ten years to do so. The dogmatism of those Labour councillors on Inverclyde Council astonished me. How could it be that Baroness Liddell, a former Labour Secretary of State for Scotland, happily and graciously accepted our invitation to be Guest of Honour at our annual prize giving, yet Stephen McCabe, our local Kilmacolm councillor, had never set foot in the school building - despite repeated invitations to do so - and distanced himself from us at every stage? New Labour versus Old Labour perhaps?

Inverclyde Council to their credit have spent almost £270 million upgrading their school estate facilities over the past decade or so. A network of schools throughout the region now has the best possible facilities. Councillor McCabe himself was instrumental in creating an imaginative and innovative shared campus for three schools in Port Glasgow. However, he is on record as having wondered on why people in Kilmacolm would want to send their children to St Columba's when they could experience these wonderful facilities in Port Glasgow. In 2013, the last year the Scottish Government published data 76% of St. Columba's pupils achieved grades of C or above compared with the national figure of 12%. More recently the total of St. Columba's pupils achieving 5 As at Higher level regularly exceeds the combined total of all six Inverclyde schools by a factor of 2-1. This might explain why many parents in Kilmacolm make considerable sacrifices to send their children to St. Columba's.

Is it not also ironic that in the same ten years that Inverclyde Council spent £270 million upgrading their school network to the highest standard, they effectively prevented St Columba's from doing the same? Equally ironic is the fact that the standard of academic achievement in Inverclyde schools actually decreased in that period.

I therefore totally agree with Michael Gove, who said when he was Secondary of State for Education 2010-14, "as long as there are people in education making excuses for failure, cursing future generations with a culture of low expectations denying children access to the best that has been thought and written because Nemo and Mister Men are more relevant, the battle needs to be joined."

The new St Columba's campus was financed by a combination of reserves already built up for the project, fundraising, and borrowing. The fundraising process was quite interesting. The school created a short-term contract position for fundraising and recruited Penny Lewis, formerly of Scottish Opera. Fundraising follows a predictable pattern with a pyramid of donors and a small number at the top providing the most support. Around 85% of fundraising comes from 15% of the potential donor list and working with these key people is of paramount importance to the success of any campaign. There is a board at the entrance of the new school building that acknowledges the fundraising efforts of those who supported the campaign. What is fascinating is not the list of names on the board but the names of those who should be there but aren't. People went to quite extraordinary lengths to avoid donating, some coming up with incredible reasons for not doing so. Others donated a lot less than they could have done. They know who they are!

The consultation process was also not without its issues. As already mentioned, the bats resulted in the project being carried out in two phases. Towards the end of my time, as tenders were being submitted for Phase 1 of the project - the refurbishment of the science block - astonishingly they were around 20-25% higher than the advisors had indicated less than two months provisionally. This was a major problem since an independent school has no lender of last resort should the project exceed the expected costs. Calum, to his eternal credit, took an extremely hard line on this. How could we have any confidence in our advisors when, at the first hurdle, costs would end up significantly higher than we were expecting? The situation was so serious that Calum recommended that the Board adopt the almost nuclear option and dispense with the services of our entire team of advisors. He proposed that we manage the project ourselves through our own architect Ian McCrea. The Board unanimously accepted this recommendation. I could see parallels with the Theatre Royal project and St Columba's simply could not afford to have an end position similar to that. It was a bold decision to take but I understand, although I was by then no longer involved, that the entire project ended up within budget.

St Columba's is now firmly established as one of the top independent schools in Scotland. From 2008 onwards it has regularly been in the top 4, with over 60% of pupils achieving A at Higher level peaking at 71.5% in 2015 when it was the top independent school in Scotland. The community in Kilmacolm is extremely fortunate to have such a fine institution in its midst.

I lived and literally slept with the development project from the moment I joined the Board. The project was well on its way to completion as I left, but I was still bowled over by the end result when I attended the opening ceremony some 18 months later. Page/Park, David Page and Andy Bateman particularly deserve tremendous credit for their creative vision and their successful efforts in getting a high level of overall support within the community. Equally enormous credit must go to Calum Paterson and Ian McCrea for ensuring that such a complex project was successfully within budget.

My final words are on David Girdwood. In my four years as Chairman we worked very closely together and I had an excellent relationship with him. David retired two years after I completed my term of office and it was entirely appropriate that the project was named the Girdwood Building in his honour. He served the school incredibly effectively in his years as Rector of St Columba's and I am very proud to have worked alongside him during part of that journey.

Chapter 45   THE GLOBAL IRISH NETWORK

"The 'Celtic Tiger' is a term referring to the economy of the Republic of Ireland from the mid-1990s to the late 2000s, a period of rapid real economic growth fuelled by foreign direct investment. The boom was dampened by a subsequent property bubble which resulted in a severe economic downturn."

I entertained a number of advertisers and contacts at the Rangers versus Celtic, Scottish Cup Final in 1999[1]. Our guests were hugely enjoying the occasion when I heard a strong Irish voice in the adjacent box. This was my first introduction to Dan Mulhall[2], the new, first Irish Consul General in Scotland, and Dan and his Australian wife Greta became close friends. Dan is now Irish Ambassador to the United States of America. As Ambassador in London, he played a major role on the state visit by President Higgins[3] in April 2014. He was also the first ever representative of the Irish Government to lay a wreath at the Cenotaph on Remembrance Day.

I have maintained close links with each of Dan's successors as Irish Consul in Edinburgh - Conor O'Riordan[4], Cliona Manahan[5], Susan Conlon[6], Pat Bourne[7] and Mark Hannify[8]. I do so as someone with an interest in maintaining good relationships between the United Kingdom and the Republic of Ireland but especially between Northern Ireland and the Republic of Ireland. I had also got to know Dan's two predecessors in London, David Cooney[9] and Bobby McDonagh[10], who hosted the visit by Prince Charles to the Irish Embassy in November 2010 (See Chapter 3) and was also heavily involved in the Queen's visit to Ireland.

Being Managing Director of News International in Ireland (2004-07) also provided me with the opportunity to have dialogue with the political establishment there. Just prior to taking up the post, I met Rory O'Hanlon[11] the Ceann Comhairle of Dáil Eireann (The Speaker of the Irish Parliament) in Edinburgh. He invited me for lunch at the Dáil shortly after my arrival in Dublin and was extremely helpful during my time there, facilitating a number of visits for parliamentary debates. As mentioned in Chapter 38, the Celtic Tiger was roaring and the Fianna Fáil Party had been in power for several years, with Bertie Ahern as Taoiseach (Prime Minister). I met a number of government ministers, including Ahern, Dermot Ahern[12] and Conor Lenihan[13] and a

---

[1] 114th Scottish Cup Final, 29th May 1999, Rangers 1 (Rod Wallace), Celtic 0
[2] Dan Mulhall, b. 1955, m. Greta (née Lothian) b.1950, First Irish Consul General, Edinburgh 1998-2001, Irish Ambassador to Malaysia, Director General, Europe, Irish Ambassador, Germany, United Kingdom and United States
[3] President Michael Higgins, b.1941, 9th President of Ireland 2011-
[4] Conor O'Riordan, Consul General 2001-05
[5] Cliona Manahan, Consul General 2005-2010, now Irish Ambassador Denmark and Iceland
[6] Susan Conlon, Consul General 2010-13
[7] Pat Bourne, Consul General 2013-15, now Ambassador to Singapore
[8] Dr Mark Hannify, Consul General 2016-2019
[9] David Cooney, b. 1954, Irish Ambassador to UK 2005-08, Secretary General, Department of Foreign Affairs 2008-12, Vatican 2012-14, Spain 2014-
[10] Bobby McDonagh, b. 1954, Irish Ambassador to UK 2009-13, Ambassador to Italy 2013-2017
[11] Rory O'Hanlon, b.1934, TD for Monaghan / Cavan 1977-2011, Cam Corliagh 2002-07
[12] Dermot Ahern, b.1955, TD, Minister for Foreign Affairs 2004-08, Minister for Justice and Law Reform 2008-11
[13] Conor Lenihan, b. Minister of State 2004-11

number of Teachta Dálas (TDs – Members of the Irish Parliament) but there was no sense of the disaster which was to come. I also lunched with two opposition leaders - Enda Kenny[14] (Fine Gael) and Ruari Quinn (Labour)[15]. Kenny was most impressive. He went on to become Taoiseach in 2011 and was responsible for steering Ireland back from the worst ravages of the Recession and the collapse of the Celtic Tiger.

The 2011 Election resulted in Fianna Fáil losing 51 of its 76 seats and Micheál Martin[16] becoming its new leader. The Celtic Tiger was no longer roaring, but smitten with a lengthy period of laryngitis.

Martin had convened the first Global Irish Economic Forum at Farmleigh in September 2009. He said "The Forum was convened with two broad objectives; to explore how the Irish, at home and abroad, and those with a strong interest in Ireland, could work together and contribute to our overall efforts at economic recovery; and to examine ways in which Ireland and its global community could develop a more strategic relationship with each other, particularly in the economic sector. As indicated in the forum I have also decided to establish a new Global Irish Network (GIN), made up of those invited to Farmleigh and other leading figures in our global community. This network will give greater strategic focus to our economic and cultural promotional efforts abroad."[17]

In December 2009 I was invited to join the newly constituted GIN. I was proud to have been asked and extremely enthusiastic about the task in hand. Ironically, Ireland was replicating the system which Alex Salmond was largely responsible for breaking up in Scotland - the Global Scot Network. I was one of three people from Scotland invited to join GIN, the others being Professor Louise Richardson[18] and Professor Bernard King[19]. As far as I know, I was one of only two Northern Ireland people to be invited, along with Keith Ruddock,[20] who joined in 2013. I also believe we were the only two Protestants in the group.

In Northern Ireland, some people questioned why I should be involved with such a group. Was this not an example of my 'mixed ethnicity'? I had no such doubts. A stable and prosperous Republic of Ireland hand in hand with Northern Ireland was essential for the long-term future of the island, based on mutual co-operation and economic interdependency and absolutely essential to the peace process, to which I have been very committed for the past 40 years.

Some of the 32 UK-based members of the Network met at the Irish Embassy in London on 4th February 2010. The group included several major figures from the Irish community in the UK, including Sir Niall Fitzgerald[21], Sir Bob Geldof[22] , Eddie

---

[14] Enda Kenny, b.1951, Taoiseach 2011-17
[15] Ruari Quinn, Leader Labour Party 1997-2002
[16] Micheál Martin, b.1960, Minister for Foreign Affairs 2008-11, Leader of Fianna Fáil 2011-
[17] Report of the Global Irish Economic Forum, 13th October 2009
[18] Professor Louise Richardson, b. 1958, Vice-Chancellor St Andrew University 2009-16, Vice-Chancellor, University of Oxford 2016-
[19] Professor Bernard King, b.1947, Principal, University of Abertay 1994-2011
[20] Keith Ruddock b.1960, General Counsel, Shell and latterly Weir Group
[21] Sir Niall Fitzgerald, b. 1945, Chairman and CEO, Unilever 1996-2004
[22] Sir Bob Geldof, b. 1951, singer, songwriter, author, political activist

Jordan[23], Sir Terry Leahy[24], Baroness O'Cathain[25], Gerry Robinson[26], and Willie Walsh[27]. Micheál Martin opened proceedings, indicating that he was in 'listening mode' and wanted to hear the group's observations on the current economic situation in Ireland. The discussion was led by Peter Sutherland[28].

What followed was a very unflattering analysis of the Irish economy and the stewardship of the government in managing it. The economy had started to overheat dangerously and was becoming uncompetitive. I cited the example of News International, which in 2006 had concluded a wage settlement which, based on similar indices, meant the Republic of Ireland settlement was a full 50% higher than the UK one (see Chapter 40). The group concluded that much needed to be done in the field of labour relations to drive up productivity and that a number of other measures would be needed.

Micheál Martin deserves great credit for making the first moves to establish a Global Irish Network and the Farmleigh Forum in 2009 made a number of further recommendations to make it happen. The new coalition government between Fine Gael and Labour, led by Enda Kenny as Taoiseach and Eamon Gilmore [29] as Tánaiste (Deputy), moved very quickly to build on it. In June I received a letter[30] from the Taoiseach, inviting me to the second Global Irish Forum to be held in Dublin Castle on the 7th-8th October 2011. He made its purpose abundantly clear: "I look forward to hearing your honest and frank assessment of the challenges facing this country and how we can best overcome them."

The event was one of the most impressive I have ever attended. Every single member of the government was there throughout the two days, along with senior civil servants and the heads of all the government's agencies. Every breakout session was attended by a member of the cabinet and Kenny and Gilmore were also present for the entire event. For the members of the GIN this was certainly no jolly. Apart from the fact that we all paid our own travel costs, we were most definitely singing for our supper. A total of 272 delegates from 37 countries attended, including Chairmen and CEOs of several major international companies, major international figures such as Galen[31] and Hilary Weston, the major Irish-American philanthropist Loretta Glucksman[32], two US ambassadors and most of the major Irish business figures, including Dermot Desmond[33], Denis O'Brien[34], and Martin Naughton[35]. There was also a very strong cultural representation with Dara ó Briain[36], Colm

---

[23] Eddie Jordan, b. 1948, former motorsport team boss, businessman, television personality
[24] Sir Terry Leahy, b. 1956, Chief Executive, Tesco Plc. 1997-2010
[25] Baroness (Detta) O'Cathain, b. 1938, Irish businesswoman, Conservative politician
[26] Gerry Robinson, b. 1948, CEO, Compass Group, CEO and Chairman, Granada Television
[27] Willie Walsh, b. 1961, CEO, International Airlines Group
[28] Peter Sutherland, 1946-2018, Chairman, Goldman Sachs 2006-17
[29] Eamon Gilmore, b. 1955, Tánaiste 2011-14, European Union Special Envoy for the Colombian Peace Process 2015-
[30] Invitation Letter, Enda Kenny, 2nd June 2011
[31] Galen Weston, OC CVO O.ONT b.1940, British Canadian businessman and philanthropist, m.Hilary (née Frayne) 1966
[32] Loretta Brennan Glucksman, Chair American Ireland fund, the largest philanthropic organisation to support Ireland m.1987 Lewis Glucksman 1925-2006
[33] Dermot Desmond b.1950, Irish businessman and financier, 9th richest person in Ireland
[34] Denis O'Brien b.1958, Irish businessman. Irelands richest native-born citizen
[35] Martin Naughton KBE b.1938 Irish businessman and founder of Glen Dimplex
[36] Dara ó Briain b.1977 Irish comedian and television presenter

Tobin[37] and Gabriel Byrne[38]. The final delegate, kept secret until the last minute, was President Bill Clinton, who gave a sparkling 45-minute address and participated in one of the discussions. As a result of the discussion, Clinton agreed to host a function in New York the following year to identify more US investors in Ireland.

The main plenary sessions were structured around Ireland's road to recovery and covered topics including: communicating Ireland's image abroad more effectively; making it more competitive in new and emerging markets; engaging with young leaders of the Global Irish on how to create new employment opportunities; promoting Irish culture; and how to work together to meet the challenges of the future. The real work was done in 16 individual working groups. I participated in two of these, 'Connecting the Irish Diaspora with Ireland and Each Other. How Can We Most Effectively Engage the Next Generation?' and 'Ireland's Reputation Abroad. How Can Ireland and the Global Irish Network Deliver a New Narrative to the International Media?' They were very stimulating discussions with the objectives of coming up with initiatives or recommendations to be presented to the Forum. All in all, the delegates spent 1282 hours in discussion. At the final session, with Kenny and Gilmore on stage, all the ideas were presented. They included ideas for re-envisaging, re-energising and reforming Ireland. Included in the presentation was some criticism of the present system – the need to encourage a more pro-business attitude; to improve the attitude of the Civil Service to this (particularly in the area of visas); more user-friendly procurement processes and less regulation.

Kenny and Gilmore listened carefully to everything and Kenny promised a detailed investigation into all the proposals within 100 days, with many to be implemented within six months, if feasible. That is precisely what happened. The government provided excellent feedback on progress and many of the ideas became a reality within the agreed timeframe.

One of the most impressive outcomes was 'The Gathering,' which took place in 2013. The main objective was to persuade the people of Ireland to invite the diaspora and friends to events in Ireland. Compared to Scotland's relatively mediocre 'Homecoming 2009', the results of The Gathering were staggering. It is estimated that the project delivered 250/270,000 incremental tourists that year and generated €170 million additional revenue from a government investment of €13 million. What it also did was galvanise the entire country, at family, community, and company levels, and help lift the pall of gloom under which the country suffered during the widespread economic austerity.

The Gathering was just one of the initiatives from the 2011 Farmleigh Forum. In my invitation to join the 2013 Forum, Eamon Gilmore wrote[39], "The Global Irish Economic Forum is a success story. Since the first one in 2009, it has helped

---

[37] Colm Tobin b.1955 Irish novelist, writer, playwright and poet
[38] Gabriel Byrne b.1950 Irish actor, film director and producer
[39] Message on 27th September 2013 from the Tánaiste in advance of the 2013 Global Irish Economic Forum

transform the way government does business with leading international figures connected to Ireland.

What started as a single idea when Ireland was at its lowest ebb in 2008 turned into a major driver which helped reset the compass towards economic prosperity. I cannot think of any comparable situation in the UK that could have brought together such a cross-section of government, industry and the diaspora in such a unified fashion and produced such spectacular results.

The focus of the 2013 Forum was on job creation. As Eamon Gilmore wrote, "This year's Forum will build on the achievements of 2009 and 2011 but takes place in a different and more positive economic context to its predecessor. Creating the conditions and policies for significant job creation remains our dominant objective whilst establishing a clear, and positive message for an international audience as we prepare to exit the Troika Programme." The term Troika has been widely used in Greece, Cyprus, Ireland, Portugal, and Spain to refer to the presence of the European Commission, the European Central Bank, and the International Monetary Fund in these countries since 2010 and the financial measures that these institutes have taken.

One new feature in 2013 was the introduction of three regional round tables. I was at the Belfast one as one of five Forum members participating, the others being Anita Sands[40], Gabriel McCaffrey[41], John Spears[42], and Peter Casey[43].

The round table discussion turned out to be four separate events - an 8am breakfast with the Lord Mayor of Belfast, a visit to a training centre for young unemployed people, a round table discussion with entrepreneurs, which included the then Enterprise Minister Arlene Foster and a lunch with members of the local business community. The day ended with a reception in Dublin at 7pm.

The day was extremely interesting for several reasons. At breakfast, we learned that the Lord Mayor of Belfast was a Sinn Féin Councillor and his deputy was from the Democratic Unionist Party. The discussions ranged around the need for more rapid private sector investment in Northern Ireland and the political behaviour mitigating against it. I expressed some fairly strong views on the current situation. I observed that the UK was pouring large sums into Northern Ireland's public sector but what was really needed was the creation of a much stronger private sector. If the level of political debate continued to be about the 'marching season' and on which days the Union Jack could be flown on City Hall, was it really surprising that incoming private sector investment was so low? As one of those paying for all this, the clock was ticking and, if things didn't improve, I would want the tap turned off. The Mayor and his Deputy both agreed that attracting inward private sector investment was crucial and that they were heavily committed to ensuring that this would happen. I was heartened by this.

---

[40] Anita Sands, youngest ever Senior Vice-President, Royal Bank of Canada, COO, UBS Wealth Management
[41] Gabriel McCaffrey, General Manager Canada, Real Decoy
[42] John Spears, MD BMO Capital Markets Montreal
[43] Peter Casey, Founder and Chairman, Claddagh Resources

The visit to the Ashton Centre in the New Lodge area was even more of an eye opener. The Ashton Community Trust, formed in 1993, was engaged in projects aimed at social and economic regeneration of the area. As it was situated in what is now called an 'interface area' (a new expression to me) it had been heavily involved in community relations projects working towards preventing 'interface violence'. We were there to see a Digital Fabrication Laboratory, developed by MIT and the first of its kind in Ireland. We met the participants of a ten-week cross-community programme aimed at 13-24 year olds Not In Education Employment or Training (NEETS) and the programme was intended as an early path into training and employment. The young people we met were effectively at the bottom of the pile, dropouts from the education system with very limited prospects. The fact that they were from both sides of the community and completely united in trying to improve their lot was most heartening. Here were young people mixing naturally side by side. It gave me considerable hope for the future of Northern Ireland.

The round table event with entrepreneurs was equally interesting. Again, they wanted to establish their companies and were thirsty for any knowledge or help that we could give them and, again, couldn't have cared less about the Province's divided history. They wanted to get out there and conquer the world.

Perhaps the most depressing part of the day was the lunch with the local business community. When I again shared my thoughts about flags and marches from the perspective of a UK taxpayer, I detected a certain chill in the air and sensed the response was, "You don't live here, so you don't understand how things are", which of course missed the point entirely. This group had a much higher age profile than the others so perhaps their reaction wasn't really surprising. More importantly, the first two groups represented the future.

The 2013 Forum was impressive. In addition to all 16 members of cabinet being present, there were 12 ministers of state, 32 government officials and the Ambassadors to London, Dan Mulhall, and Washington, Anne Anderson[44]. I participated in the Culture working group, chaired by an old friend Fiach Mac Conghaill[45]. The Culture Minister Jimmy Deenihan[46] sat in on proceedings and, surprisingly, there was a considerable level of tension. At one stage, when Deenihan left the room for a short period, he was roundly condemned by most of those in the room, all senior representatives of the Irish Cultural sector. The perception was that he and the government were doing very little to encourage the sector, either at home or abroad, and we made a number of recommendations in this area.

By the time of the 2015 Forum (entitled '2016 and Beyond, The Vision of a New Ireland'), I sensed there was a mood that the job was now almost completed. My invitation letter, this time from Charles Flanagan[47], dropped a number of hints, "Following an intensive programme of work at home and overseas by government, and by those committed to Ireland, and through the sacrifice of the Irish people,

[44] Anne Anderson, b. 1952, 17th Irish Ambassador to the United States 2013-17
[45] Fiach Mac Conghaill, Director, Abbey Theatre for 12 years, Senator 2011-16
[46] Jimmy Deenihan, b.1952, TD, Minister for Arts, Heritage and the Gaeltacht
[47] Charles Flanagan, b. 1956, TD, Minister for Foreign Affairs and Trade

economic recovery is now beginning to take hold and Ireland's international reputation has been restored.... Our aim is to reach full employment by 2018 and we are on track to achieve this goal, however recovery remains fragile and we want to spread the benefits of a recovering economy across the entire county."

That year there were more regional sessions and I participated in one in Londonderry. It was an excellent example of cross-border cooperation, organised in partnership with the Northern Ireland Science Park, Letterkenny IT, Derry City and Strabane District Council, and Donegal County Council. Much was made of the interdependency of both sides of the border and a major infrastructure project had been announced for the first section of a new dual carriageway on the Derry to Dublin route. The A5 Western Transport Corridor aimed to improve the transport links between the Northwest and Dublin and work eventually started in 2018. At lunch I sat beside Joe McHugh[48] and much of what he said eventually became the Northwest Strategic Growth Partnership in 2017, described as[49], "The first of its kind on the island of Ireland and represents a new approach to joined up government that has the potential to bring about real and positive change for the region." Ironically, it is this type of cooperation that potentially will be threatened by the Brexit deadlock on the Irish backstop.

Not surprisingly, the 2015 Forum turned out to be the last one. After a long period of austerity, the Irish economy had prospered and, although there were challenges ahead, the transformation was well underway and the Celtic Tiger had finally got its voice back.

---

[48] Joe McHugh, b. 1971, TD Donegal, Minister of State for the Gaeltacht 2014-16
[49] Irish Government National Planning Framework 2040

Bells Scottish Open
l-r: Peter Senior, Jim Marshall and CMcC

Chapter 46   GOLF - THE MOST BEAUTIFUL GAME

"Golf is a science, the study of a lifetime, in which you may exhaust yourself, but never your subject. It is a contest, a duel, or a melée, calling for courage, skill, strategy and self control. It is a test of temper, a trial of honour, a revealer of character. It affords a chance to play the man and act the gentleman. It means going into God's out of doors, getting close to nature, fresh air, exercise, a sweeping away of mental cobwebs, genuine recreation of tired tissues. It is a cure for care, an antidote to worry. It includes companionship with friends, social intercourse, opportunities for courtesy, kindliness and generosity to an opponent. It promotes not only physical health but moral force."

David R Forgan[1], 1899

Golf is an individual sport and one of the very few in which the best in the world can play the not so good on a more or less equal basis, because of its unique handicap system. Bobby Jones[2] had an alternative view, expressed thus, "Competitive golf is played mainly on a five-and-a half inch course – the space between the ears."

I have been lucky enough to have played over 350 golf courses throughout the world in ten different countries. I have played some of the world's best golf courses and with some of the best professionals. Playing a round of golf is a truly wonderful experience.

Golf has been the premier sport of at least three generations of McClatchies. My grandfather John was one of the original members of Royal Portrush Golf Club in Northern Ireland. He played off a handicap of four and won many club competitions in the early 1900s.

My father was also a very keen golfer and played at Portadown Golf Club off a handicap of 14. Like me, he was fiercely competitive and putting was by far the best part of his game. He had a very old, rusty hickory-shafted putter, yet he could sink putts from all over the green. We both defied the old maxim, "Half of golf is fun, the other half is putting."

---

[1] David R Forgan, 1856-1931, US banker, 'The Golfer's Creed'
[2] Bobby Jones 1902-71, American amateur golfer, founder and designer of Augusta National Golf Club and co-founder of The Masters Tournament

My mother's brother Stewart was perhaps the most talented. He was a scratch golfer at Belfast's Balmoral Golf Club in Belfast and caddied for the Club's professional Fred Daly[3], when the latter won The Open at Royal Liverpool, Hoylake in 1947.

The Ulster town of Portrush is inextricably linked with golf. The road signs on its outskirts make that abundantly clear:

> Welcome to Portrush
> Major Golf Capital of the World
> Fred Daly: The Open 1947
> Graeme McDowell: US Open 2010
> Darren Clarke: The Open 2011
> Drive Carefully – Putt Well

With a population of just 6,500 for Portrush to have produced three people who have won major Golf Championships is truly remarkable.

Our Royal Portrush family connection started with my grandfather and has continued since. My brother-in-law Sam Moore was Captain of the Club in 2003 and Graeme McDowell[4] used to babysit for his grandchildren, Elle and Stewart. Sam is a real character and his friendship and hospitality at Royal Portrush are legendary. His open golf locker is famous worldwide. Even if you are not playing with Sam, the key to his locker is always on top of it and numerous friends, acquaintances and, in many cases, complete strangers have partaken of what is known as "the Sam Moore Experience." Inside the locker is a bag like those used in hospitals to dispense blood or fluids. Sam's bag is filled with a mixture of Old Bushmills Black Bush Irish Whiskey, Drambuie and Crabbie's Ginger. The 'medicine' is dispensed via a tap into plastic containers, an ample supply of which is always available.

My son-in-law Kumar describes his first visit there – "Going in, I felt I was in an almost sacred place. Sam immediately headed to the Secretary's Office, where I was introduced to everyone including the Secretary Manager Wilma Erskine[5]. I could see that Colin and Wilma had known each other for a long time. Next, we viewed the Captains' Board, where among the many distinguished names is Sam's as Captain in 2003. I saw many of the Club's magnificent trophies, including Fred Daly's and Darren Clarke's[6] Open Championship medals, and Rory McIlroy's scorecard for his Dunluce course record, achieved in 2005. Rory, then 16, shot a 61, playing off a handicap of plus four. We then went to the locker room, where I sampled Sam's excellent elixir. I'm a doctor, but I had never seen a plasma bag used this way. Sam's is no ordinary locker – in addition to the drinks dispenser, it has been adapted to accommodate reserve supplies. Lifting two floorboards revealed a further four

---

[3] Fred Daly, 1911-1990, professional golfer, winner, The Open 1947, Royal Liverpool
[4] Graeme McDowell MBE, b. 1979, US Open Champion 2010, Pebble Beach
[5] Wilma Erskine, b. 1958, Secretary Manager, Royal Portrush Golf Club 1985-2019
[6] Darren Clarke OBE, b. 1960, Open Champion 2011, Royal St George's

bottles of Black Bush and a bottle of Crabbie's. Finally, I couldn't help but notice Sam's neighbours. The adjoining lockers belong to Darren Clarke, and to David Humphreys[7], one of Ireland's most capped rugby players and the eldest son of Claire's cousin Deirdre and her husband George." The Queen visited the Club in 2016 and lunched there, but it is not clear if she visited the locker room to sample Sam's hospitality.

In March 1990, Peter Dobereiner[8] wrote about Sam in Golf World:

"The club rather than the course is the major source of golf's pleasures. And the membership rather than the building and its amenities is what makes the club. The constituents which form the spirit of a golf club are difficult to analyse but an example may help. At Royal Portrush in Northern Ireland a member has converted his locker into a cocktail cabinet generously supplied with a nourishing restorative. He leaves the key on top of the locker and every member is welcome to help himself as and when the spirit moves him.

You may imagine that this would be an expensive gesture. Plenty of members avail themselves of Sam's hospitality when reaching the refuge of the locker room after battling the elements which assail this great Championship links. But this being a good club, the practice quickly grew among the members of topping up the supplies of this welcome free bar. Every so often you quietly slipped a bottle into Sam's locker and this perpetuated a highly civilised tradition.

If you want to test whether you belong to a good golf club, just ask yourself whether the system of Sam's locker would work at your club, or would it be abused. Would it be tolerated by the Board of Management? Would the contents be pilfered by the staff? Would some snake among the membership inform the authorities that intoxicants were being dispensed without the benefit of a licence? Satisfy yourself on these points and you can take pride in belonging to a good club. If you determine that the entire membership is composed of Sams, then you belong to a very good golf club indeed."

Sam caddied for Harry Bradshaw[9] during the Open at Royal Portrush in 1951. Bradshaw was runner up to Bobby Locke at the Open in 1949 and finished 15th at Portrush in 1951. Sam's fee for four days' work was 12 Dunlop 65 golf balls – not a great deal of use to someone who didn't play golf at the time.

In 1988 Royal Portrush celebrated its centenary and among the many clubs participating was a party from Royal Liverpool Golf Club (RLGC) in Hoylake. Some of their comments include:

"We picked up our host Sam Moore at his Ballymoney home and, after suitably laced afternoon tea, we were soon familiarising ourselves with glorious Portrush."

---

[7] David Humphreys MBE, b. 1971, Irish rugby player, 72 international caps, scoring 560 points
[8] Peter Dobereiner, 1908-96, considered to be golf's greatest scribe
[9] Harry Bradshaw, 1913- 1990, professional golfer, Irish Open Champion 1947, 1949, three Ryder Cup appearances, winner, Canada Cup 1958 (with Christy O'Connor Sr.)

"In the evening we learnt with delight that the only other guest in our B&B was Fred Daly. Fred replayed his four rounds at breakfast the following morning."

 "Our first decision was to lock up the rental car, place the keys in the hotel safe and hire a minibus."

"After several pints of stout, back to the Club for the disco. Adrian and Walter were the least bashful and Walter fell deeply in love with the Lord Mayor's wife, to whom he proposed matrimony."

"It was clear the following day that those who had tangled alcoholically ... had come off second best."

"The weather improved again as match number one drove off. For Royal Portrush, their captain Robert Lowry, the Lord Chief Justice, was partnered by Sam Moore. Once we had recovered from the shock of discovering that Robbie's three caddies all carried Uzi submachine guns, we settled down..."

"The achievement of organising 20 RLGC members to arrive in Portrush paled into insignificance beside the fact of getting all 20 back home to their loved ones in one piece – a very happy weekend."

Now in his late-eighties, Sam is still dispensing his medicine from his locker and hopes to continue to do so for many years to come.

I am immensely proud that Royal Portrush again hosted The Open in 2019. Up to then it was the only course outside mainland Britain to have hosted the competition (Max Faulkner[10] won there in 1951). The Club hosted an Amateur Championship and the Irish Open in recent years, but The Open's return to Royal Portrush was long overdue. In 2018 The Club's President Hugh Clark[11] took me round the course to view the changes the R & A made to the course. The adjustments to the existing holes paid respect to the original design philosophy of Harry Colt[12]. Two new holes and several new Championship tees were created, one green moved back significantly, and another reshaped. This stretched the course to 7,337 yards from its previous 7,143, whilst reducing the par from 72 to 71. Harry Colt made very sparing use of bunkers at Portrush and the changes increased the number of bunkers by only three (59 to 62), the lowest by far of any Open venue. Turnberry is next at 81. The majority have around 100, Muirfield has 150, and Royal Lytham St Anne's a staggering 203. Prior to The Open all Portrush members had to clear out and vacate their lockers. In a fitting tribute Sam Moore's was left intact. Shane Lowry[13] proved a worthy and incredibly popular 2019 winner whilst enhancing Ireland's golfing reputation. Irish players have now won The Open five times since 2007.

I played my earliest golf at Portadown Golf Club. I don't remember receiving any formal tuition. Many of my friends would later remark that was pretty obvious. I

---

[10] Max Faulkner OBE, 1916- 2005, professional golfer, winner of The Open 1951, Royal Portrush
[11] Hugh Clark, b. 1946, retired solicitor, President Royal Portrush Golf Club 2014-18
[12] Harry Colt, b. 1869-1951, golf course architect
[13] Shane Lowry b.1987, Irish professional golfer. Winner Irish Open, 2009 (as an amateur) 2015 WGC Bridgestone Invitational

suspect my Father taught me as we went along. When we moved to Killyleagh he played at Downpatrick and Ardglass Golf Clubs before joining Mahee Island Golf Club when he retired. At Ardglass I watched professionals play for the first time. I saw a very young Tony Jacklin[14] and Dave Thomas[15] play an exhibition game and was astonished at how far they could hit the ball. In 1973 I joined Holywood Golf Club, now famous as Rory McIlroy's home course.

At BT I met up with Roy Lyttle, also a very keen golfer, and we played many golf courses throughout Ireland in the six years I was there. Like me, Roy was fiercely competitive and I would best describe our many games together as gladiators locked in combat.

Golf is based on fairness, trust and individual integrity and over the years I have unfortunately witnessed one of the less savoury aspects of the game – cheating. I am not sure if there is a relationship between the value of a prize, or the prestige of a competition, and the ability of some people to cheat. The best-known golf cheat was, of course, Goldfinger in his game against James Bond at Stoke Park. I have seen international football stars, the Chairman of a major plc and many others blatantly cheat in a variety of ways. Cheating is entirely self-delusional. Everyone knows when someone cheats but the offender seems not to realise it.

When Claire and I moved to Newcastle upon Tyne I played several beautiful courses in rural Northumberland and Durham, among them Ponteland, Gossick, Arcot Hall, Wickham, Chester le Street and Beamish Castle. Through my colleague the late Graeme Stanton[16] I became a member of Tyneside at Ryton. We played most Saturdays during my three years there. Graeme was hugely entertaining, an extremely social animal whose Saturday routine consisted of a couple of pints after golf and then a couple more at the Denton Arms on the way home, before heading to St James' Park for the game. Happy days!

The premier club at Newcastle was The Northumberland Golf Club at Gosforth Park, in the middle of the race track - rather like Royal Musselburgh. The European tour held a tournament there in 1980. Claire and I attended on the final day and I recall Greg Norman[17], near the top of the leader board, hitting his opening drive deep into trees at the first hole, a 360-yard dog leg. Forced to play three off the tee, he drove the green and holed a 30-foot putt for a quite remarkable par four. That same summer I also attended my first Open at Muirfield. On a cold and windy Saturday afternoon, I followed one of my heroes Jack Nicklaus[18] for a few holes (it was possible to do that then, but sadly no longer). I also witnessed Arnold Palmer[19] take the longest and most enormous divot I have ever seen and enjoyed watching the constantly wise-cracking Lee Trevino[20] in fine form. Whether today's professionals could cope with partnering a Trevino is questionable. I returned to

---

[14] Tony Jacklin CBE, b. 1944, winner of The Open, Royal Lytham 1969, US Open Champion, Hazeltine 1970
[15] David Thomas, 1934- 2013, Welsh golfer and course architect
[16] Graeme Stanton, Editor of the Evening Chronicle, Newcastle-upon-Tyne
[17] Greg Norman AO, b. 1945, The Open Champion 1986, Turnberry and in 1993 Royal St George's
[18] Jack Nicklaus, b. 1940, The Golden Bear, winner of 18 Major Championships. Regarded as the greatest golfer of all time
[19] Arnold Palmer, b. 1920-2016, winner of seven Major Championships
[20] Lee Trevino, b. 1939, winner of six Major Championships

Muirfield for the last day's play of The Open of 1992 when, on an even wetter afternoon, virtually none of our corporate party moved from the hospitality tent. In a well refreshed room, I pocketed £100, having organised a sweep and drawn Nick Faldo[21], whose 18 pars were enough to win by one shot.

In 1981 we moved to Reading. I had decided at this stage of my career, when I was likely to be moved every three years, I could not afford the often quite substantial joining fees for membership. However, I played many different courses, including the three Berkshire jewels – Wentworth, Sunningdale and The Berkshire. The Old Course at Sunningdale was my favourite, with many happy memories of enjoying a sausage sandwich at the halfway house and watching fascinated as a legendary gentleman with a deformed hand deftly tossed sausages from the grill onto the buns. I cannot think of a better place to be on a summer's evening, sipping a pint of Pimms in the shade of the magnificent tree by the 18th green.

Many years later I was fortunate to play one of the most exclusive courses in the UK, Swinley Forrest, near Ascot. Its list of members starts with HRH Duke of Edinburgh, several other members of the Royal Family and gradually descends to mere Rear Admirals and chiefs of staff of the Armed Forces. The fourball was organised by Alan Chilton, Sales Director of Scottish Television. That day the course was almost deserted (I think there was one other four ball playing), yet when we finished there was a most enormous menu for lunch, including a carvery with magnificent sides of sirloin, leg of lamb and pork. The course exhibited some significant eccentricities. The professional instructed us to play from, as was normal, the yellow (guest) tee boxes. Standing on the first tee, we were somewhat puzzled to find that these were behind the white (members') tees. We subsequently learned that this was because of a stream which wandered across the first fairway, about 170 yards from the tee. The majority of members at Swinley Forrest were relatively elderly and found it increasingly difficult to clear the stream; they therefore came up with a most ingenious solution of moving the white tees 25 yards further forward and putting the guest tees further back (needless to say, I drove into the stream). The other main peculiarity was the stroke indexes. The score card seemed to bear no relation to the holes themselves. For example, stroke index 1 was a par 3 of just over 130 yards. This was as a result of deft footwork by the club. At Swinley Forrest there are no club competitions, but the R&A insisted on the Club supplying stroke indexes. Swinley Forrest simply wrote asking for stroke indexes to The Old Course at St Andrews and adopted these.

I also played at East Berks near Crowthorne with two members - Dave Perry, a TRN trainer, and Adam McKinley, Editor of the Wokingham Times, who would later prove pivotal in my move to Scotland (See Chapter 11). East Berks was a beautiful parkland course, not unlike Sunningdale. One weekday we were joined by Vincent, who, on hearing that we were all newspaper people, told us that he worked for The Sunday Times. During the game I established that Vincent worked in the production area of the newspaper – at the time, one of the most highly unionised parts of the

---

[21] Sir Nick Faldo, b. 1952, winner of six Major Championships

business. Vincent worked one 18-hour shift starting early on Saturday morning and for this he was paid £50,000 a year, which he felt was a perfectly reasonable rate for the job. This was in 1980 and it only increased my contempt for the trade unions in the newspaper sector at that time. At the end of the day Vincent drove off in his large Jaguar.

We moved to Kilmacolm in Scotland in October 1984 and one of the first people I met was John Hunter, who invited me to play golf at the local club. I had played several of the local courses that summer and early autumn – Kilmacolm, Old Ranfurly, Ranfurly Castle, Erskine and Gleddoch – and had discreetly inquired about membership. With the possible exception of Gleddoch, all the others had long waiting lists. Kilmacolm was my first choice and John readily agreed to propose me. Until then, there had been a lengthy waiting list, albeit with village residents given priority. A resolution was passed at the Club's AGM early that December enabling the Club to purchase the course land. In order to finance it, the Club applied a £100 levy on full members for the next five years. The result was the resignation of many elderly members who rarely or ever played. The waiting list was wiped out in one fell swoop and I was in.

Golf was integral to networking at SDR. For example, I joined the company on a Monday and on Friday flew to Majorca for the annual sales conference, which included a round of golf at Son Vida. There were also keenly contested annual matches with our wholesalers John Menzies and the Morgan Group. Menzies always seemed to have the upper hand on these occasions. Each team had two or sometimes three golfers who played regularly and the rest claimed to play only once a year and were thus always allocated the maximum handicap. By some strange coincidence, the Menzies once a year players always seemed to play better than ours. Probably the best example of this was Ian Callaghan[22] playing off 24. He now plays off a handicap of 11 at his home club Pinheiros Altos in Portugal, having done so for many years. The Morgan Group competition was a much more evenly contested affair, with fewer "ringers" on their side. Winning was equally important on these occasions - so much so that I frequently exhorted my usual partner George Gray[23] to hole a putt by giving him the incentive of still having a job the following morning.

Over the years there were other regular golfing occasions. Of course, to the outside world and the non-golfer it seems unlikely that these affairs were for anything other than pleasure but in fact some serious business was transacted. Relationships were built, or maintained, in very much less confrontational and relaxed circumstances and innumerable problems solved. One example was with Scott Stern, SDR's promotional agency. Once or twice a year Harry Scott and his colleague Jim Waterson[24] would golf with George Gray and me. We were all keen golfers. These occasions, particularly the dinners afterwards, were great opportunities for the exchange of ideas and developing new concepts. It became something of a standing

---

[22] Ian Callaghan, b.1947, Wholesale Director 1985-96, Managing Director 1997-2004 John Menzies Distribution
[23] George Gray, Field Sales Manager SDR
[24] Jim Waterson, b. 1956, Associate Director, Scott Stern

joke between Claire and me that, as I would be polishing my clubs and packing my bags, she would ask, "and which annual match are you playing today?"

Another regular golf occasion grew from adversity and is a very good example of how an excellent working relationship was created on the golf course. Scottish Television (STV) was SDR's major advertising outlet and over the years the vigorous (some would say vicious) competition between newspapers meant that STV enjoyed a lucrative slice of advertising revenue from print media. SDR's media buying agency at the time was Shaw Advertising, presided over by David Shaw. David and I had got to know each other when I assumed responsibility for the marketing function at SDR. He was a hugely expansive man with a warm and deeply generous heart. He was also one of the most successful producers of amateur drama in Scotland. Larger than life, he hated the word 'amateur' and would say, "The Pantheon Theatre Company is the best non-professional troupe in Scotland." David was also one of the funniest men I have ever met. The critics savaged a Pantheon production of Cabaret, suggesting that a number of the male chorus were wooden. David's response was that it was extremely difficult to recruit Nazis in Newton Mearns (Glasgow's predominantly Jewish area).

My first formal negotiation between SDR and STV had resulted in Alan Chilton[25] threatening to walk out and my telling him that if he did so I would withdraw all our television advertising there and then. This major confrontation was indicative of the fractious relationship between our two companies and clearly was one that required nurturing. In an effort to address it, Andy Crummey[26] from STV invited David and me to Gleneagles for a round of golf and dinner with Alan. As an ice-breaker it worked incredibly well and established a format which was repeated many times over the years. It certainly benefited both companies. We all became close friends and, although that never compromised our business relationship, it enabled us to negotiate from a position of mutual respect. The other advantage was that it enabled David to, time and time again, take advantage of short-term market opportunities, due to his relationship with Andy.

The following year I teamed up with a group for the first of many foreign tours, initially in Northern Ireland (springtime) and Spain (autumn). Amongst the party were Harry Scott, Jim Oliver[27], Gordon Adams, Bill MacNaught and Chris Marshall[28]. In those days we shared rooms and my snoring became legendary. Sharing with Gordon at El Parisol, I woke one morning to realise that Gordon's bed was a bare frame. I discovered him sleeping in the bath, having deposited his mattress and bedding there. Once, when Claire came to the airport to meet me after a trip, a stranger asked her if she was Mrs McClatchie. When she replied that she was, he said "You have my deepest sympathy." It was Chris Marshall, who had shared a room with me. In Orlando I shared with Harry, who never really adjusted

---

[25] Alan Chilton, Sales Director Scottish Television
[26] Andy Crummey, b.1955, Scottish Television 1982-86, latterly as Sales Director, Scotland
[27] Jim Oliver b.1942 founder Windex. Chairman Partick Thistle FC 1990-97
[28] Chris Marshall b.1958 Director of Sales Scottish and Newcastle. Chief Executive Edgecumbe Consulting

to the time lag (my theory) or my snoring (his theory). As a consequence, Harry often went shopping in the middle of the night.

The first trips to Northern Ireland were at a time when the province was struggling to maintain tourism during "The Troubles". We stayed in Portrush at O'Neill's Causeway Coast Hotel, where the owner often insisted on ferrying us to restaurants in his Jaguar, rather than have us take taxis. My friends were greatly impressed with Northern Ireland's friendship and hospitality.

Spain in mid-November was succeeded by Florida. The schedule was brutal but somehow achievable as we were all a lot younger in those days - 36 holes per day, with 18 on the last day - 13 rounds in all. We played in fourballs with the exception of one game with a five-ball format (four balls and Gordon's provisional). At that time of the year daylight was at a premium, so we often set off in darkness at 6.30am to find a golf course (no Sat Nav in those days). The day would consist of a quick breakfast, morning round, half hour lunch and straight out again for the afternoon round. If play was at all slow, our last group often finished in the dark, aptly illustrating Ben Hogan's[29] remark, "The only thing a golfer needs is more daylight". A quick beer followed, then back to the hotel, a 15-minute turnaround and out to dinner. It is little wonder that we arrived back home completely exhausted but, as those of you who have done this will know, no signs of tiredness could be shown. Consequently, the recovery period for these trips took a long time. On our final American trip, we hired a 12-seater mini bus, which was driven by Harry. The last night had been particularly late and we were all feeling rather jaded as we assembled at 6.15am with our luggage and clubs. The lift arrived, the luggage was hurled in, but unfortunately someone jostled Harry just as he was getting in and the coach keys tumbled down the lift shaft. Chaos! The lift was taken out of service and an engineer was soon crawling around the basement looking for the keys. They were eventually found, but not before a number of American guests started complaining about being late for breakfast. Harry, in terse Glaswegian vernacular, told them he couldn't care less and did they realise we were due on the first tee in less than half an hour? Sadly, this was to be the last trip for that group. Harry moved to Thailand, where he lived until his death in 2016. I hadn't seen him for many years, but we kept in touch and he kindly looked after Amanda, Milena and Kumar during their various trips to Bangkok over the years.

SDR became the official media sponsor of The Bell's Scottish Open at Gleneagles, which gave us a team place in the Pro Am. The first year our team consisted of Endell Laird, Jim Marshall[30] (a client) and me. We played with Peter Senior[31]. Peter was most engaging, chatting and giving advice freely, unlike Nick Faldo. One of the latter's teammates that year told me that Faldo shook his hand on the first tee and didn't say another word until they walked off the 18th green. For an amateur, particularly a high handicapper like me, these were nail-biting occasions, with the

---

[29] Ben Hogan, 1912-97, winner of nine Majors
[30] Jim Marshall b.1948, Co-founder Baillie Marshall Group 1980, latterly Royal Bank of Scotland Brand Advertiser and Marketing Director 2003-10
[31] Peter Senior b.1959, Australian professional golfer. Winner of over 20 tournaments worldwide.

event played in front of up to a few thousand spectators. Standing on the first tee, being introduced to the crowd and then desperately hoping to dispatch a decent drive was pretty daunting. Surprisingly, Jim Marshall, who then played off a handicap of two, was the most nervous of all and topped his first drive no more than 100 yards. After losing balls at the second and third holes he became a jibbering wreck. Despite advice from Peter, Jim continued to spray the ball all over the course. At the seventh, a blind drive, Peter played the furthest ball in the middle of the fairway. It was only after we had all holed out that it was discovered that Peter had inadvertently played Jim's ball. He said, "Jim, I'm so sorry for playing your ball. Because the ball was in the middle of the fairway, I never dreamed it was yours." The round continued, albeit with Endell insisting on holing out at every hole. Having taken an eternity to hole a short putt for an eight at a par three, I had to remind him that only two scores counted, and his eight was not one of them!

The wind was now starting to get up. I was the only one to drive the short 254-yard par four 14th hole and as we approached the green the spectators applauded my shot, assuming I was the professional. They quickly realised I wasn't after I three putted. By the time we reached the 18th hole the wind was really howling but fortunately we were down-wind. I hit what turned out to be the longest drive of my life – just over 300 yards. I hit a 6 iron into the heart of the green, much to the applause of the hundred-odd people huddling in the stand behind the green, and two putted. After we shook hands and walked off, three or four young boys approached me and asked, "Mr Senior could we please have your autograph?" I'm ashamed to say I hastily scribbled "Peter Senior" on their programmes, before scuttling off, hugely exhilarated. Peter Senior was great company and helped us all to relax - even Jim. The next morning, he sent each of us a dozen golf balls and a lovely note saying how much he had enjoyed the day - a true gentleman.

I played in four more Scottish Open Pro Ams – with Brian Marchbank[32], Barry Lane[33], Steven Richardson[34] and Andrew Sherbourne,[35] but the most enjoyable experience was undoubtedly with Peter Senior.

At NI I had formed an excellent working relationship with Tom Mooney of Smurfit Kappa. Smurfit was NI's printing partner in Ireland and Ian McDonald, my boss at NI, had introduced us. Tom and I got on really well from the onset and he and his wife Brenda became close friends. At that time Smurfit, were the main sponsors of the European Open, one of the principal events of the European Tour. I was in the right place at the right time when, in 2001, Ian McDonald had to pull out of Tom's team in the Pro-Am and nominated me to take his place. Claire and I spent two days at the K Club in Kildare with Tom and Brenda, and Andy and Diane Kemp.

The next morning, we teamed up with Massimo Scarpa[36] whose main claim to fame was that he played both right and left handed. That day he played right handed,

---

[32] Brian Marchbank, b.1958, Scottish professional golfer, son of Bill, the then professional at Gleneagles Hotel
[33] Barry Lane, b.1960, English professional golfer, 17 professional wins
[34] Steven Richardson, b.1966, English professional golfer, 3 professional wins
[35] Andrew Sherbourne, b.1961, English professional golfer, 3 professional wins
[36] Massimo Scarpa b.1970, Italian professional golfer, 1 European Tour win

except when chipping and putting. He explained that he had much more feel for the shot when he was playing around the green left handed. Although relatively short, he drove the ball impressively, but his putting was off that day. Tom, Andy and I produced net birdies on each of the first three holes and, on the fourth tee, Andy suggested to Massimo that he might up his game and contribute to the score.

Over the following six years I was lucky to play with Adam Scott[37], Paul Casey[38], Ricardo Gonzalez[39], Colin Montgomerie[40], Tonchai Jaidee[41] and Paul McGinley[42]. With the exception of Monty, all their careers significantly improved after playing with us, a fact which we usually relayed to our professional partner on the first tee. It was always a great ice breaker.

Adam Scott was only 22 when he played with us and went on to become a major champion. Our coaching obviously worked! Adam generated the fastest club head speed of any golfer I've ever played with and was already showing the fantastic talent which would lead to an outstanding career. We also had great fun that day with Alistair Mclean[43], Adam's caddy, who has been with Colin Montgomerie for most of his professional career. A soft-spoken Glaswegian, Alastair, when prompted, revealed a fund of great stories.

Paul Casey was 25 when we played with him in 2003. It was also the first occasion that I played with anyone whose caddy used a rangefinder, which enabled us to understand better the debate on club selection. At the 13th they had a lengthy discussion on the carry required to clear the water down the right-hand side of the fairway; they determined it was 270 yards and successfully took it on. At the 18th the carry over the water at the apex of the dogleg was 295 yards and Paul decided to have a go. The ball almost carried the hazard, landing on the bank and falling back into the water. This was on the limit of his range and that shot was not repeated during the four rounds of the tournament. 15 years later, both these club selections and results would be considered fairly modest. Nevertheless, Paul Casey was the finest ball striker I ever played with and the only weakness in his game then was his putting.

Like Paul, Colin Montgomerie was most entertaining and we were thrilled to learn that we had drawn him in the 2005 Pro Am. That year we played the Ryder Cup course and, in a shotgun start, the 9th was our first hole. Caddied by Alistair, Colin got off to a bad start; a pulled drive ended up in deep rough after hitting a tree and he eventually finished with a 6. Although my partners had both holed out for 5 net 4, which I couldn't better, I insisted on holing out. Walking over to the 10th tee I said to Colin, "Thanks for being so patient. I did that because when I eventually write my

---

[37] Adam Scott b.1980, Australian professional golfer. Rank World number 1 2014, 29 professional wins. Winner US Masters 2013
[38] Paul Casey b.1977, English professional golfer, Rank World number 3 2009, 19 professional wins
[39] Ricardo Gonzalez b.1969, Argentinian professional golfer, 4 European Tour wins
[40] Colin Montgomerie OBE b.1963, Scottish professional golfer, winner of a record 8 European Tour Order of Merit titles, winner of 3 Senior PDA titles
[41] Tonchai Jaidee b.1969, Thai professional golfer, record career earner on the Asian Tour. 8 European Tour wins
[42] Paul McGinley b.1966, Irish professional golfer. Winner of 4 events in the European Tour. Ryder Cup Captain 2014 at Gleneagles
[43] Alistair McLean, Colin Montgomerie's caddie for over 10 years

memoirs, I want to be able to say that at the 9th at the K Club, I had a 5 and you had a 6." Thankfully Colin appeared to see the funny side of this. He was going through a very messy separation and eventual divorce from his first wife Eimear[44]. He asked me which newspaper group I worked for. Telling him I was with News International, I said I thought they had been giving him a pretty reasonable time in terms of reporting, but that the Daily Mail seemed to be giving him a particularly rough ride. This clearly struck a nerve and he uttered a string of expletives against his wife, claiming that she was leaking all sorts of things to Richard Kay[45] of the Daily Mail. I innocently asked him if Brian MacLaurin[46] (one of the UK's leading PR executives) had played any part in all this. "No, no," said Colin, "He works for me." Much relieved, I was able to tell him that Brian's father Peter[47] was my next-door neighbour. This seemed to put Colin at ease and he went on to be gloriously indiscreet throughout the rest of the round – indeed, had I been a journalist, I would probably have had at least five major exclusives that day. He and Alastair had a long debate on his second shot to a Par 5 and at 250 yards to the pin, they concluded that, even with a 3-wood, it was on the limit of his range. It's interesting to note how much golf technology has changed in the intervening 10 years, with professionals now regularly hitting the same club over 280 yards and, as we saw at Royal Troon in 2017, Henrik Stenson[48] hitting more than 300 yards.

Monty also reflected on his career and the pain of never having won a Major. At that stage he thought he would play on for no more than two or three years and had no plans to play Senior Golf. Happily, he changed his mind and we were delighted when he went on to win three major Senior titles. As well as being a really interesting golfing companion, Monty joined enthusiastically in every bit of banter and gossip and shared all our jokes. He was also free with advice, something I rarely found playing with top professionals. He took me aside at one stage to show me that I was holding the club too firmly (the truth is I was probably white-knuckled due to the pressure of the occasion). Monty talked to me about the principles of soft hands, which helped me greatly throughout the rest of the round.

The other professional I hugely enjoyed playing with was Paul McGinley, like Colin later to be a Ryder Cup captain. He was the most meticulous golfer I've ever played with, constantly analysing his game. Like Monty he was quite happy to give advice and taught me one shot, the hooded sand wedge, which I have used frequently ever since.

I was also very fortunate to attend four Ryder Cups, two at the Belfry, one at the K Club and the last one at Gleneagles. Even more enjoyable was the fact that the European team won on all four occasions. The Belfry occasions were particularly memorable, with Concorde flying overhead after the European victory and Christy O'Connor Jnr's[49] fantastic 2-iron to the 18th in 1988. Socially it was also a great

---

[44] Eimear Montgomerie, b. 1969, wife of Colin 1993-2006
[45] Richard Kay, b. 1962, Daily Mail gossip correspondent
[46] Brian MacLaurin, b.1949 PR Supremo, Crown Communications, The Hatch Group and Brian MacLaurin associates
[47] Peter MacLaurin 1919-2010, Smith and MacLaurin Paper
[48] Henrik Stenson, 1976, Winner, The Open, Royal Troon 2017
[49] Christy O'Connor Jr. 1948-2016, Irish professional golfer with 4 wins on the European Tour

occasion as I stayed at Jim Black's[50] beautiful, thatched Tudor house in the picturesque village at Barton-under-Needwood, along with a colleague Graham Bird[51] from Johannesburg. By far the most memorable Ryder Cup experience was the 2006 event at the K Club, where Claire and I were guests of Tom and Brenda Mooney. Tom had rented a cottage just 100 yards from the entrance to the K Club and we stayed there for four days. Despite appalling weather which turned some of the spectator areas into mud baths, the atmosphere was fantastic. Finally, Claire and I were at the Gleneagles event in 2014 where Paul McGinlay's superb captaincy ensured a fantastic European victory. The logistics at that event were quite superb, the best I have ever encountered at a major sporting event, and Scotland should be very proud of what it achieved.

The group that I have toured with for the longest time started in 2001, when Charlie Murray[52] of Sun Chemical invited me for a weekend's golf at La Manga. The original four members were Charlie, Peter Hepworth[53], and Alan Burton[54], all of Sun Chemical, and David Crow[55] of Johnston Press. Alan Burton subsequently had hip surgery, hence my addition to the group. Sixteen years later, the group is still going strong, now expanded to eight. It is no longer a corporate event, as most of us have retired and Charlie lives in the US. In the group are Peter Hepworth, Tom Mooney, Brett Lawrence[56], and me (all retirees), Colin Colverd[57] (Sun Chemical) and the two Davids - Crow and Smith[58] (Johnston Press). Allan Wain[59] joined us in 2019. Long may it continue! The group is now organised by Peter Hepworth, who also handles logistics and the kitty - an essential role in any tour. I am the handicap secretary but I am also 'Paddy Power', bookmaker and creator of a wide variety of betting opportunities. I have yet to meet a more enthusiastic band of punters and 'Paddy Power' certainly needs to keep his concentration at all times, especially after dinner each evening, when bets are laid for the following day's game. Craig Patterson on another tour best summed up my dual persona "a friend – richer for knowing you as a golfing buddy – poorer for knowing you as 'Paddy Power'."

On trips organised by Mike Graham, I golfed in either Tenerife and Turkey each year from 2009 to 2013. The first year I joined I only knew Mike and Eddie McKechnie. I first met Eddie when he was a partner at McGrigor Donald. He is one of life's great characters, suave, urbane and a great raconteur with a deep booming voice. Also, like Mike, Eddie had the reputation of being a hypochondriac and had that year contracted some form of virus during a trip to Australia. On our flight to Turkey we sat together and he told me about his experiences with this mystery virus. He was still talking about it when we landed at Antalya some five hours later. His final remark was priceless, "You know, in all of this Mike (Graham) has been fantastic.

---

[50] Jim Black b.1946, Managing Director, The Burton Mail 1988-2007
[51] Graham Bird b.1946, Johannesburg, newspaper manager
[52] Charlie Murray, Sun Chemical latterly as President, North American Inks 2010-18
[53] Peter Hepworth b.1951 Managing Director Sun Chemical Publications UK
[54] Alan Burton 1946-2016, Sales Director, Sun Chemical
[55] David Crow b.1954, Managing Director Print and Logistics, Johnston Press 1998-
[56] Brett Lawrence b.1961, Management Consultant JPI Media, Director of Production, Guardian News and Media 2006-17
[57] Colin Colverd b.1966, Sales Director Sun Chemical
[58] David Smith b.1964, Financial Director, Johnston Press 2004-
[59] Allan Wain b.1959 NI Operations Director (North) 2007-15

When I was having tests to determine if I could have been suffering from a range of conditions, Mike had had all of these himself and was of enormous help." Hypochondriacs Inc!

Mike's wife is Christina, a keen golfer and curler. They are a hugely entertaining couple, well-illustrated by their comments about their creating a basement study to accommodate Mike's retirement. Out of Christina's earshot, Mike told everyone that the main feature of said study would be an internal door lock, "to keep her out." Meantime Christina was regaling everyone on how the study would have an external door lock, "to keep him in there."

Another good friend Steve Sampson organised an annual golf day at Prestwick, usually between Christmas and New Year. It was loosely called a golf day but in fact was more an excuse for a good lunch (for which Prestwick is famed). The occasion was aptly named the Kummel Cup and necessitated me leaving home at an early hour, never quite knowing when I'd return. Steve always had an eclectic bunch of guests, who reflected his various interests and background – a few 'toffs' from his old school Loretto, some from what could be termed his drinking club The Jeroboams, some newspaper and media people, a few footballers, and the odd politician. I recently came across the joining instructions of the 2006 event, "Some Housekeeping. The list is now closed and your dietary requirements have been noted – Port, Kummel or Gin.... Be there at 8:15 sharp, golf must not be allowed to interfere with lunch.... Mrs Bennett (the club steward) is alert for any lunch only guests. Please come any time you like, don't be too concerned about being too early whilst the athletes golf, this is not a shopkeepers' club." That day I met David Livingstone[60] whom I had not seen since our Daily Record days - when he claimed I used to sign his expenses. It was a marvellous day's entertainment, and the Kummel Cup continued for several years until Steve left First Press Publishing and the Daily Record – a very sad loss to the golfing calendar.

Now I am also part of another event organised by Fred Hallsworth, who was one of my fellow non-execs at Scottish Enterprise and a member of one Scotland's most exclusive golf clubs, the Carnegie Club at Skibo Castle. In 2010, Fred organised our first Highland Golf Tour, a three-day event consisting of a local course on Day 1, the showcase event on the second day with 36 holes at Skibo, 18 holes Stableford, a 15-hole Texas Scramble, completed by a ferociously contested One-Club competition over the final three holes. The day concludes with a most impressive barbeque at the Clubhouse and on the third day we play a course on the route home. The original invitees were all non-execs with SE: Fred, Charlie Morrison, Sir Jim McDonald, Iain McLaren, Iain MacDonald and Ian Crawford[61] - plus Jack Perry, the former Chief Executive. The group has subsequently been joined at times by Steve Boyle[62] and Craig Paterson[63]. Over the years, we have played some absolute jewels – Tain, Brora, Markinch and Fortrose, Golspie, Lossiemouth, Nairn, Royal Dornoch and Castle

[60] David Livingstone b.1953, presenter of Sky TV's golf coverage 1995-2018
[61] Ian Crawford b.1954, Vice President, Global Services IBM 2001-07
[62] Steve Boyle b.1963, technology entrepreneur
[63] Craig Paterson b.1955, Chairman and CEO, Melville Craig Group 1985-2001, Founder Footballaid 2002-

Stuart. The day at Skibo is the highlight of the tour, always culminating in the famous One-Club competition. A lot of thought goes into selecting the club to be used. Before the first tour Ian Crawford is alleged to have spent almost six months researching the matter before concluding that a 3-Iron was the ultimate club of choice. He then proceeded to hack his way up the rough on the first hole for a 10. A 3-wood seems to be the most popular choice and it is extraordinary that with a combined par of 13 for the three holes, the competition has been regularly won with a score of 17.

In 2009 Claire and I bought a holiday home in the village of Cellardyke in Fife. We had gradually fallen in love with the East Neuk of Fife, having become regular attendees at the annual East Neuk Festival, a series of chamber music concerts established through the generous patronage of Donald MacDonald[64] and run by Svend Brown. Deirdre Romanes was one of the original patrons and had invited us to the first festival. In the following two years, we stayed during the festival with our friends Shields and Carol Henderson. The second year I had played golf at Crail and Elie and thoroughly enjoyed both courses. When I retired from NI, Claire and I had debated about buying a holiday home but had been unable to agree where. My preference was for France and Claire's for the East Neuk. My enthusiasm for a base in France was sharply reduced during a trip to Glyndebourne in 2008, when we had nightmare experiences at Gatwick Airport. On Tuesday 7th April 2009, lunching in Glasgow with Deirdre and Shields, Deirdre casually mentioned that she was thinking of selling one of her houses in Cellardyke and wondered whether Claire and I would be interested in purchasing it. I duly reported this to Claire. Result - we viewed the house that Friday and concluded the deal over an excellent lunch at The Cellar in Anstruther. We love the house.

I decided to join a golf club in Fife and applied to Elie. On discovering that there was a waiting list of around five years, I decided also to apply to Crail, where I was admitted almost immediately. Crail is a tremendous club, with two courses in quite outstanding scenery at the corner of the East Neuk of Fife. The Balcomie is the seventh oldest golf club in the world, having been established in 1786, and the second course, the Craighead, was designed in 1999 by Gil Hanse[65]. It is a formidable test of golf. I was able to join Elie within two years, much earlier than I anticipated - and perhaps not surprising, given the regular receipt of emails from the secretary recording the demise of members. Elie is also an outstanding links course, particularly well-suited for holiday golf.

As a senior, what does the wonderful game of golf hold for me in the future? I hope to play the game for many more years and the handicap system is a great facilitator. Physical strength and the length of the shots may decline, but the rest of the faculties tend to remain much the same. People often remark, when referring to older members: "His short game is fantastic, better than ever." Our short game remains the way it was for most of us; it's the rest of our game which slowly declines.

---

[64] Donald MacDonald CBE b. 1939, Co-founder MacDonald Orr, Chairman Scottish Chamber Orchestra 1985-2014
[65] Gil Hanse b. 1963, American golf course architect, designer of Castle Stuart and the Rio 2016 Olympic golf course

In the 60+ years I have been playing golf, I have had an average handicap of around 18, the lowest being 14 which gradually increased to 25. In 2018, I made a major effort and reduced it to its current 24, but I feel that there is still room for improvement. I am continually striving to play better. However, as I stand on the first tee, I am never quite sure which swing is going to appear that day. I wish I could follow Ben Hogan's advice, "Reverse every natural instinct and do the opposite of what you're inclined to do, and you will probably come close to having a perfect golf swing." Sadly, I have never enjoyed the luxury of a trusted and consistent swing and it seems that more often than not I play coarse golf rather than the other way around. Michael Green[66] once famously described the coarse golfer as, "One who shouts, 'Fore!' when he putts."

And yet perhaps more than any other sport, golf is a game in which temporary flights of fancy are possible. Over the years, when my score was normally in the 90s and frequently even more, I have managed to break 80 three times. I can still remember the courses - the Glasgow Club, Royal Burgess, and Crail's Balcomie. These were rare days when I was relieved of my neurological limitations for a few hours and was able to play better than I have ever done before. To those three occasions I add two others – level par over nine holes at Royal Burgess and five holes in succession with a score of 1 under par at Luffness. For me this was Nirvana, but sadly this state of grace is always temporary, although it sets a benchmark to aspire to in future rounds. As Bobby Jones said, "golf is the closest game to the game we call life. You get bad breaks from good shots. You get good breaks from bad shots – but you have to play the ball where it lies."

Regardless of all this, golf remains a wonderful game. Keep swinging!

---

[66] Michael Green, 1927- 2018, author, 'The Art of Coarse Golf' 1996, Robson Books Ltd.

Chapter 47   THE FUTURE OF GOLF

"People still want private golf clubs; they just don't want to pay a lot of money for
a product that hasn't innovated since the days of Sam Snead."
Anonymous US golf commentator

Golf faces a bleak future. Ironically, professionally the game is in great shape. Golf is no longer the sole preserve of the American and European Tours because both Tours now visit parts of the world which are neither American nor European. The explosive growth of golf in both the Far East and China has created vast new markets for what is now a truly international game. However, the quite disgraceful attitude of those top professionals who boycotted the 2016 Olympics in Rio de Janeiro tarnished the game's reputation. They were the only absentees from the entire range of sports represented at the Games. What was a massive opportunity to introduce golf to a vast new audience was negated in the early stages by the perception that some of the world's highest paid athletes couldn't be bothered to participate.

Within the amateur game there are three main issues which need addressing: equality, ageing membership and the recruitment of new (particularly younger) members. The consequences of these issues are that membership of golf clubs in Scotland has fallen by 25% in the last ten years, whilst subscriptions have increased by 40%. The nomadic vast battalion of pay-as-you-go golfers now makes up 80% of Scotland's golfing population.

Golf started as a predominately male game and although the division between the sexes has slowly narrowed, the administrators of the game have consistently lagged one or two paces behind the direction of travel. Unfortunately, many people still feel that sexism is alive and well in golf clubs the length and breadth of the land. In a society where men and women are by law completely equal, step forward any golf club in Scotland where the male/female ratio is anywhere near equal. I use Kilmacolm Golf Club in Renfrewshire as an example. When I joined Kilmacolm in 1985 male membership was 71% of the total and women could only play at specified times. There were four areas of the clubhouse - a tiny one designated for women only, a 'mixed' lounge, a male-only lounge, and another tiny area for Juniors. Only the two lounges had bar facilities. The mixed lounge (about 80% of the footprint) was off limits for women on Saturdays, unless they were dining at the club with their partner in the evening, but there was an unwritten rule that they could not enter until after 7pm. Women were not allowed to use the main entrance, meaning that when couples arrived, they would have to enter through different doors and meet inside. Many years passed before the committee sanctioned a change to this antiquated custom.

As recently as 1991, writing in the club's centenary book[1], the late Ian Archer[2], looking forward to the next 100 years wrote, "There may even be grudging realisation that when the world was invented, the Almighty had intended that men and women were or should be equal." That Archer should be writing this in 1991, looking forward to the next 100 years, speaks volumes about the attitudes towards women in most golf clubs at that time. A lot of this has now changed and some would say that Kilmacolm has achieved full equality. Although the 2000 AGM actually voted down equality proposals, Kilmacolm became an equal status club in 2003 and there is now one committee running the club, drawn from both male and female members. Competitions are still run separately although in 2016, the Club's 125th Anniversary, there were two mixed competitions to celebrate the occasion. In 2018 Jane McDonald[3] became the first and very successful female Captain of the club.

All this sounds wonderful and seems to point to a totally integrated golf club. The reality is somewhat different. The consequence of becoming an equal status club was that ladies were then required to pay the full subscription. They got nothing in return for this. The club's excellent 125th Anniversary Book[4] notes, "During the three years from 2000 the club committees carefully and transparently examined with the membership, men and ladies, what the issues were. We heard differing attitudes, opinions, and concerns expressed by the membership before proposals from the committee were approved. In retrospect the theme of 'let's approve the principle, keep it simple and let it evolve' reassured the membership and we became an equal a status club in 2003". Cynics could rewrite that statement of intent as 'We don't like it, we are only approving it through gritted teeth, and having done so let's kick it into the long grass and do nothing'. Result: lady membership was 29% of the total before the change and had dropped to 19% by 2015, a decrease of 49%. It is still falling. Male membership declined by 12% in the same period. The 1918 Representation of the People Act granted the vote to women over the age of 30. Nick Rodger wrote in The Herald recently that, although it is now over 100 years since the Suffragette movement won this right, Emmeline Pankhurst would still have difficulty in getting a Saturday morning tee off time in most of Scotland's golf clubs. On this the authors comment, "Clearly it is important that all the clubs' playing times and the opportunities of the whole membership to participate are regularly reviewed and are allowed to evolve, and any perceived unfairness should be considered on its merits as part of the ongoing evolutionary process of Equal Opportunities." – not exactly a call to action. However, there is a positive note. "It is interesting that some of our best girl golfers have played for our Junior Newton Shield League team – previously for boys only – and do rather well off the white tees!"

---

[1] 'A Very Pleasant Golfing Place. A Centenary History of the Kilmacolm Golf Club', Gray Laidlaw and David Mason, 1991, Kilmacolm Golf Club, Beith Printing Co. Ltd.
[2] Ian Archer (Dan) 1943-2002. Sports journalist and author
[3] Jane McDonald
[4] 'The Kilmacolm Golf Club, A Celebration of 125 Years', Sir David Mason and Vic Weldon, 2017, Rannoch Press

Perversely, at the heart of the equality issue is an argument that, since men and women differ in physical capacity, they should not be treated equally in the world of golf. Lord Wellwood[5] stated in1880, "We would venture to suggest 70 or 80 yards as the average length of a ladies drive advisedly – not because we doubt a lady's power to make a longer drive – but because that cannot be done without raising the club over the shoulder. Nor do we presume to dictate but we must observe that the postures and gestures required for a full swing are not particularly graceful when a player is clad in female dress." Clearly ladies' golfing attire has changed during the past century and, as golf historians have observed, as their skirts have got shorter, their drives have got longer. Billie Jean King[6] famously tested the issue of the physical capacity proposition by beating Bobby Riggs[7] in September 1973 at tennis. The US golfing authorities later invited a female professional to play on a men's PGA tour event in 2004. One would have assumed that they would have invited the best female player to participate but no, they invited a 15-year-old novice, Michelle Wie[8], not once but twice. Needless to say, she failed to make the cut on both occasions.

The stance of The Royal and Ancient Golf Club of St Andrews (The R&A) on this is interesting. For years, The R&A had been fighting what many simply regarded as a rearguard action against admitting female members. The arguments were well documented - perfectly reasonable to want to have their own club; our ladies already have their own club and wouldn't want to join ours; ladies wouldn't want to pay the full fee anyway etc. Anyone watching the excruciating interview with The R&A secretary Peter Dawson[9] on the steps of Muirfield during the 2013 Open must have cringed at his attempts to justify The R&A's position. In 2009 another example of that position was the issue of honorary membership for the Principal of St Andrew's University. Traditionally the R&A granted honorary membership to the Principal, but in 2009 they refused to grant this to Dr Louise Richardson, the incoming Principal. It was both shameful and a public relations disaster. How can The R&A claim to be the sole governing body of golf, male and female, when it excludes women from its own 'private' club? In the end, as in Augusta before it, change was coming. After a major consultation The R&A, albeit somewhat reluctantly, moved on and admitted female members.

If the actions of The R&A were a public relations disaster, then Muirfield finessed them many times over. Founded in 1744, The Honourable Company of Edinburgh Golfers is one of the oldest in golf. It nestles on the southern shores of the Firth of Forth, alongside the village of Gullane. Like The R&A, Muirfield has taken its reputation as one of the most exclusive golf clubs very seriously. The Club has been aptly described: "Muirfield remains one of the most scenic courses in the country, with views dating back to Victorian times." Alasdair Reed recently wrote in The Times: "It would be harsh and inaccurate to describe Muirfield as golf's last bastion

---

[5] Lord Wellwood, 2nd Baron Moncrieff, 1840-1939, Scottish judge
[6] Billie Jean King, b.1943, tennis player and winner of 39 Grand Slam Titles
[7] Bobby Riggs, 1918-95, World's No.1 tennis player 1946-47
[8] Michelle Wie, b.1989, winner, 2014 US Open, Pinehurst No. 2
[9] Peter Dawson OBE, b.1948, Chief Executive, The R&A (1999-2015)

of misogyny – a number of other single sex clubs still exist, but it has long been viewed as the most prominent and entrenched. In recent years the gender barriers have come tumbling down at Augusta, Royal St George's, Royal Troon and The R&A, but Muirfield continued on ploughing its own increasingly lonely furrow. There was a kind of wilful perversity about the proudly pachydermous men of Muirfield. Their stance was less aligned to the great and noble institution of golf than to Millwall supporters' defiant chant: 'Nobody loves us and we don't care.'"

Muirfield is a magnificent links course and the Clubhouse and dining facilities are superb, but, as a visitor, there is a lingering feeling of not being welcome, with the Club bestowing a massive favour in letting one play there. Payne Stewart's[10] experience was an example. When US Open champion, he asked to play a round at Muirfield and was refused on the grounds that the course was full on that day. Instead he played nearby Gullane and, during his round, looked over to see a deserted Muirfield.

The issue of female membership came to a head during the 2013 Open, which was staged at Muirfield. Peter Dawson, then Secretary of The R&A, incensed many in his justification of Muirfield's stance on women. In response, Scotland's First Minister Alex Salmond made it clear that the Scottish Government would in future not support the event if it were played on a course which barred female members. The reaction of Muirfield members was indignity and outrage. "We are not going to be told by anyone what we can do" and "Over our dead bodies" were typical comments. Their reaction was metaphorically to stick two fingers in the air to anyone who dared to criticise them - despite this now including Alex Salmond and most of the general public.

The Muirfield Committee, in an effort to rein in some of the most vocal dissenters, persuaded them that holding a ballot on the issue might be the most sensible way forward. In the lead-up to the ballot in 2016 there was a lot of public interest in the outcome. In a last-ditch effort to influence the vote, the most strident dissenters sent a letter to all members. Details of its content inevitably ended up in the press. In it they expressed almost comical concerns about what would be endangered by the admission of female members. In response to the media coverage, the dissenters turned their attention to the media itself, accusing it of trying to influence public opinion on the issue.

In the event, The Honourable Company of Edinburgh Golfers was not for listening and, despite the proposal to admit female members being recommended by the Committee, the ballot did not garner the two thirds majority necessary to pass it. Fairly soon afterwards, perhaps in an effort to restore its own reputation, The R&A removed Muirfield from the roster of Open venues. The result of the ballot was predictable - a public relations disaster whereby the reputation of Scotland and golf as a whole was severely damaged and mocked globally. Muirfield members had earned their club pariah status the world over. Even the Club Captain somewhat

---

[10] Payne Stewart, 1957-99, US Open Champion 1991 (Hazeltine), PGA Champion 1989 (Kemper Lakes), 1991 (Pinehurst No.2)

understatedly admitted "I don't think we can ignore the fact that what happened did some damage to the Club's reputation."

Muirfield did acknowledge relatively quickly the maelstrom of negative opinion which the ballot had created and shortly afterwards - perhaps with a little prodding from the R&A - they organised a second ballot. This time they got the result the Committee wanted – 82% in favour of admitting female members.

Less than 15 minutes after Muirfield announced its decision, The R&A confirmed that the Club was back on The Open roster. The net result was that the whole exercise was seen as nothing more than a pragmatic attempt to reinstate The Open at Muirfield. A plethora of further negative publicity followed the announcement.

Unlike The R&A, which quickly admitted several honorary female members when it ended its men only policy in 2014, Muirfield admitted that it had no plans to do so and the Captain had to acknowledge that it might be 2024 before there could be women members. His choice of language is fascinating; "Our members have been very clear that they don't want an artificial female presence. They want them to become members of the Club and to be treated equally. We are not after a token woman." Astonishingly he then admitted: "But it can be quicker. The membership process is deliberately designed to allow people to be accelerated or slowed down, depending on the calibre of the application." In some ways, this typifies the sort of regime which everyone suspected, but couldn't quite believe, existed at Muirfield. This type of governance would be judged utterly unacceptable and thrown out of the Boardroom of any other major company in the land, but here was the Captain of Muirfield extolling it as a virtue.

Reaction to the announcements was overwhelmingly negative. An editorial in The Herald stated, "The Pragmatic Company of Edinburgh Golfers does not have much of a ring to it...however, yesterday's decision might be seen as more pragmatic than principled." The *Daily Mail* was much more critical: "It (the R&A announcement) was an interesting decision. If The R&A were really dead set on advancing the cause of women's golf, wouldn't it have been better to wait five years, rather than 15 minutes to see if attitudes have really changed at Muirfield and then, if they have, allow the Club back on the rota. Instead, the governing body left themselves wide open to the accusation that what they are most interested in is appearances. Have the members really come round to thinking women are no longer second class citizens and they'd like to play their part in ending decades of shameless discrimination, or do we think they might have been persuaded to hold their noses out of vanity, knowing that if they did, they'd get The Open back. The juxtaposition of the two announcements means precious few will be convinced it is the former."

The most scathing criticism from a female perspective came from Alyson Rudd, writing in The Times under the headline "Muirfield's reinstatement is like rewarding a brat with Disneyland." "I am not assuming that sexism exists in this part of East Lothian. It does. They (the members of Muirfield) voted against women members as recently as last year and then spent the ensuing months weighing up the terrible choice in front of them. Women or The Open? What a terrible dilemma. Even worse though is that this blatant compromise is being hailed as a triumph for both golf and equality. Is it really worth celebrating when men do the right thing for self-aggrandisement?

In the event, Muirfield moved relatively quickly and in June 2019 formally invited 12 female members to join, although the Captains statement in announcing that the club had finally joined the 21st century with regard to women's rights clearly was oblivious of its past. "This marks a milestone in the club's illustrious history and we look forward to welcoming all our new members to share in the great values and traditions of our club"

At a time when the beleaguered sport is facing its greatest crisis, where does all this leave golf? The long-term solution for most clubs is total integration, which should result in them attracting more female members and attracting, nurturing and retaining more young people to become the next generation of members. Unfortunately, the current fiasco may only accelerate the present trend. When Augusta National first admitted female members in 2012 in a wave of publicity, Condoleeza Rice and Darla Moore[11] were admitted as its first two women members. Today there are just three. The R&A quickly announced a series of honorary members when it ended its Men Only policy in 2014, but there have been few similar announcements since then. The scale of the problem was revealed at Scottish Golf's National Conference in 2018. Over 83% of golf clubs in Scotland still have a Saturday reserved for the main men's competition, thus continuing to stifle gender balance.

For the second issue of ageing membership I use evidence from the Glasgow Golf Club. In his excellent centenary book[12], Nevin McGhee[13] sums up the issue very clearly, writing in 2003, "Like many other golf clubs we have an ageing membership. The average age is now around 58 and this will rise. In turn, it means that the number of members who will complete 40 years and so qualify for life membership will also increase... there are 882 members of the club and over 23% are not paying the full subscription, with 8% (Life Members) paying no subscription. (Note 15 years later they are now required to pay one quarter of the annual subscription). The ageing membership also means that more members have retired and are not therefore out and about making business contact with people they might wish to propose for membership. The combination of these factors taken with the significant entry costs involved for a young man with a growing family, plus the fact that not as many sons of members [personal note; no daughters here!] are joining these days means that demand for membership was not as great as it once was."

In that last sentence McGhee is talking about the second reason for falling membership - the success, or lack of it, in clubs recruiting young people, who should go on to be the lifeblood of the club. In this area golf clubs in general have also been behind the pace. The terms 'Juvenile' and 'Junior' particularly are rather derogatory

---

[11] Darla Moore b.1954, American investor and philanthropist
[12] 'Killermont; The Home of Glasgow Golf Club', Nevin McGhee 2003, Glasgow Golf Club
[13] Nevin McGhee b.1944, BBC Northern Ireland and Scotland, latterly founder McGhee PR 2002-

and yet that is how most golf clubs refer to their young members. The treatment of Juniors varies from club to club and has centred around rules and regulations which tend to have more Don'ts than Do's. In other words, the regulations tend to be less enabling and more restrictive. On how many occasions have we witnessed adult members approaching the first tee and automatically assuming that any juniors already on the tee should instantly give way. Happily, Kilmacolm Golf Club is in the vanguard of encouraging young people to take up the game and be part of the club. The professional Ian Nicholson[14] performs a significant amount of missionary work, regularly visiting both schools in Kilmacolm in an effort to encourage participation in the game from an early age. He holds regular coaching sessions. For example 25 boys and girls attended his recent Easter coaching academy. Equally significantly, all 25 enjoyed lunch in the main lounge of the club, but sadly the present male/female ratio for this year's Academy was 80/20 – a similar ratio to our overall membership. This inability to attract young female members is particularly depressing since we have within the club two of the best female golfers in Scotland, Megan and Eilidh Briggs. Even having two of the finest female exemplars in the sport still does not appear to motivate young girls to join Kilmacolm.

The third major issue that clubs are wrestling with is the 'external' factors affecting membership. A significant threat is posed by the continuing development of 'Pay as you Play' courses, which require no entrance fee or annual subscription. It caters well for golfers who want to play on only a few occasions per year and are encouraged to go to a 'Trophy Course' rather than the traditional club. The 2008 recession also contributed to this with a reduction in 'corporate golf', causing visitor numbers to decrease at most golf clubs. Finally, changing social attitudes means that the 5/6 hours for the weekend four-ball does not fit well in today's world. Golf clubs need to recognise these trends and adapt. They must embrace them through a variable suite of memberships, shorter competition formats and more flexibility with visitor requirements.

Golf Clubs are fighting for their very existence and there will be more casualties in the foreseeable future. If the issue of integration is sensitively handled, female membership could well turn out to be the saviour of many golf clubs, but many will have to change their ways even further before they can attract significant numbers of women across the threshold. Ditto with the treatment of young members.

Ten years ago, The Herald's golf correspondent, the late Douglas Lowe[15], wrote about what he called 'Scottish golf's time bombs'. He summarised the issues as, "An increasingly elderly membership, a lack of women and girls, the need to engage with the young, and attract families, a requirement for more flexible memberships, particularly in that squeezed middle age range and the rise of the nomadic golfer." It would seem that in the intervening decade not much has changed, but to Lowe's list should be added the need to join the vast online community and also adopt social media. The Herald's current correspondent Nick Rodger[16] recently summed up the

---

[14] Ian Nicholson, b.1972, Professional, Kilmacolm Golf Club since 1999
[15] Douglas Lowe 1952-2011, golf correspondent The Herald 2003-10
[16] Nick Rodger golf correspondent, The Herald 2011-

situation as follows, "Golf in this country has never moved quickly. A sense of complacency, apathy, and an element of taking the eye off the ball, both from those running the game and from some of the member clubs themselves, hasn't helped. Deeply entrenched sneering, pompous attitudes and a bitter resistance to change continue to come home to roost. There is no doubt that closures of golf clubs will continue and a natural, if brutal, cull will unravel. It's not golf's fault that society has become so clamorous. Those attributes of patience, self-discipline, dedication, and respect which are at this game's bedrock are qualities which are not necessarily defining traits of a modern world which demands instant gratification."

The key to the future of golf is not just the direction of travel; far more important will be its pace. Golf clubs must identify and react to changing trends far more quickly than they have done in the past. I leave the last words to Nevin McGhee, "I believe we should aim collectively to lift our eyes from the immediate horizon, beyond our own time as members. We should not automatically reject change because of a spurious claim that 'that's the way things have always been done'."

Chapter 48   FOOTBALL

"The secret of being a good manager is to keep the six players that hate you away from the five who are undecided." Jock Stein[1]

Football has been described as a game for gentlemen, played by hooligans. For some strange reason it is known as The Beautiful Game. It is also a sport where increasingly people behave quite appallingly.

Andy Crummey invited me to the 1987 Rangers versus Aberdeen League Cup Final at Hampden Park. At lunch I met for the first time Alan Montgomery[2], whom I found knowledgeable and hugely entertaining. Lunch was a relatively modest affair in terms of alcohol consumption, in contrast to many subsequent football matches I attended, where alcohol was consumed on an almost industrial scale.

The game kicked off, Rangers moved the ball up the park and, in the penalty area, an Aberdeen player cleanly tackled and dispossessed a Rangers player. Barely 20 seconds into the game, Alan Montgomery leapt to his feet and at the top of his voice shouted, "F**king penalty, referee!" He then sat down as if this was a perfectly normal thing to do. Two minutes later there was a similar incident, Alan was again on his feet, "Are you f**king blind referee?" This time there were menacing murmurs from adjourning Aberdeen supporters and two stewards approached Alan and told him that if he repeated this behaviour he would instantly be ejected. I was to see this type of behaviour many times, when high profile, well-respected figures behaved like hooligans when supporting their football team.

Although not my favourite sport, I have followed football all my life. Aged ten, I attended my first game at Shamrock Park, Portadown and saw the home team provide some pretty modest fare in the Irish League. This was in the early Sixties and I remember being thrilled to get the autograph of the team's veteran centre forward Jimmy Jones[3]. I stress the term veteran, because Jones at this stage was almost bald with an enormous girth, and moved at an extremely modest pace, but nevertheless had the knack of scoring regularly.

I arrived at Newcastle-upon-Tyne in 1972 and became a lifelong fan of Newcastle United. Newcastle reached the finals of the FA Cup in 1973 and the League Cup in 1976. In the 1973 Final, they were comprehensively outplayed by Liverpool. My abiding memory was the complete contrast in emotions after the final whistle, half of the stadium ecstatic and the other half (us) utterly dejected. For the 1976 Final, I met up with David Todd[4], an advertising colleague at NC&J. David's white Ford Escort company car now neatly matched the team colours of black and white stripes, much to the consternation of the company's Transport Manager, who went completely

---

[1] Jock Stein CBE 1922-85, Manager Celtic FC 1965-78
[2] Alan Montgomery Deputy Chief Executive and Financial Director, Scottish Television
[3] Jimmy Jones 1928-2014. Irish League footballer; 3 Northern Ireland caps
[4] David Todd, Founder, David Todd Associates London

berserk when he saw it. To a great fanfare, we were cheered off on Friday lunchtime from the front entrance of the Newcastle Chronicle and Journal offices in the Groat Market. We drove around the corner, parked, and had several pints in the Printer's Pie (excluding David of course). Needless to say, the long journey to London included many pit stops. This time the opposition was Manchester City but it ended in a 2-1 defeat for Newcastle. I also attended the 1999 FA Cup final with Gordon Adams, but sadly the result was a 2-0 defeat by Manchester United.

The next time I watched Newcastle was in November 2002 at Old Trafford in a Premier League match. Our seats were at the Stretford end and my host had warned me not to wear any Newcastle memorabilia, as that part of the ground was extremely hostile to away supporters. This was a gross understatement. I have never been in a more hate-filled environment. This atmosphere perpetuates itself to this day in just about every football club in the land. In Scotland it exhibits itself as naked sectarianism, particularly at Rangers and Celtic games. Elsewhere, more worryingly, racism is prevalent and the footballing authorities struggle to find any solution to the problem. Such behaviour has no place in modern society, yet apart from barring the odd errant spectator, the lack of action by the football authorities exhibits a form of collective myopia. At Old Trafford that day, I had no doubt that the slightest acknowledgement of good play by Newcastle on my part would have led to physical aggression from those around me. The game itself was a fantastic example of Premier League football at its very best. It ebbed and flowed from end to end before Manchester United won 5-3. My other memory was the quite extraordinary hostility of the 60,000 Manchester fans towards Alan Shearer[5]. Shearer had turned down an offer from Manchester United before signing for his home club. As a consequence, he was vilified, abused, and booed throughout the game. It certainly made me appreciate for the first time the level of restraint that players have to exhibit. Shearer scored twice in the game and, had I been in the same position, the temptation to run to the Stretford end and stick two fingers up at the crowd would have been huge - as no doubt would have been the ensuing riot.

After leaving Newcastle in 1981, it would be 35 years before I saw Newcastle win. In September 2016 my brother-in-law Mick Goodwin[6] took me to Derby County where I savoured a 0-2 win. Well worth the wait!

When I arrived in Scotland in 1984 my introduction to football in Glasgow was not at the cauldrons of Ibrox or Parkhead, but at Partick Thistle F.C. Claire and I had established a close friendship with Harry Scott and his wife Irene. I had never known Harry to have any great interest in football but out of the blue he phoned to tell me that he and his friends, Jim Oliver, Brown McMaster[7] and Angus McSween[8] had bought the club. They set about transforming what was then an old and run-down football club. Harry significantly improved corporate hospitality. I was invited on several occasions and the pre-game lunch was followed by a preview of the

---

[5] Alan Shearer CBE, DL b.1970. Southampton, Blackburn and Newcastle United (206 goals), England (30 goals)
[6] Mick Goodwin b.1953. Managing Director Goodwin Building Contractors Ltd.
[7] Brown McMaster, 1949-2015, Chairman, Partick Thistle FC
[8] Angus McSween, b.1956, founder, CEO, Iomart Plc.

match by the club's official historian Robert Reid[9], a teacher and lifelong fan with an encyclopaedic memory of all matters Thistle. Reid had apparently attended every Thistle game for over 50 years.

What amazed me during Harry's period with Thistle was how someone with no apparent previous interest in the game could become so immersed in it. There is a famous line in The Little Orange Book (see chapter 13) where Harry's optimism ran riot, "don't worry, the Jags will be in Europe next year." Over the years it became clear to me that he wasn't the only person that this happened to.

During my period with SDR, Robert Maxwell was involved with football through his ownership of Derby County and, subsequently, Oxford United. The latter was interesting, as Maxwell - true to form - had some radical thoughts, not only on ground sharing, but also on merging two clubs, Oxford United and Reading. There seems to be little evidence of successful UK business people making the same impact on football clubs as on their original businesses. I remember at the time of the Mirror Group flotation in 1988 one very senior merchant banker telling me, "You know, Colin, we generally have a rule of thumb that says; if a successful business man takes over a football club, we consider they're starting to lose their marbles." This proved extremely prescient.

Once, at an SDR board meeting in London, Maxwell opened proceedings by announcing, "Gentleman, I am thinking of buying you a football club." Shock, horror around the table. Endell Laird quickly interrupted - in my view unwisely - without establishing the club in question and made a long, rambling argument about the inadvisability of Scotland's leading newspaper becoming involved with a football club. Maxwell quickly swatted that one away. His ownership of Derby County didn't seem to have had a negative effect on the sales of the Daily Mirror - an interesting and highly challengeable proposition. Having established the club in question was Dumbarton F.C., I pointed out that, as they were in the 2nd Division, they were not exactly a club of much consequence. Maxwell was furious and said that I clearly knew nothing about football. Did I not realise that Derby County also played in the 2nd Division and they were a very major club? Unusually, the day was saved by Joe Haines, "Bob, for God's sake, Dumbarton's average gate is just over 500." End of story – the matter was never discussed again. Subsequently Maxwell was offered several other basket cases in Scottish Football, but fortunately was never tempted again.

At SDR, I was now increasingly involved in the marketing of our papers and soon was to have my first experience of the Scottish Football Association, described at the time as, "The organisation in charge of the professional game, but run by a bunch of amateurs". They had contacted David Shaw, offering sponsorship of The Scottish Cup and requesting a meeting to discuss it. Although I suspected that it would be a high-ticket item and unlikely to fit within our portfolio of activities, I thought it was worth investigating. The SFA was to be represented by Bill Wilson[10]. Only one

[9] Robert Reid, b. Honorary Vice President and historian, Partick Thistle FC
[10] Bill Wilson, Commercial Director SFA

person? I queried, thinking it unusual that the SFA would have only one representative at such a high-level negotiation. The day before the meeting I contacted David again to enquire what facilities Bill would require. "None," was the answer.

The meeting turned out to be relatively short. After introductions and coffee, Bill removed from his jacket pocket two sheets of A4 paper and handed one over to me. He then read out verbatim from his sheet a short list of benefits that the sponsor of the Scottish Cup would get. As he was going through the list, he frowned, reached over the table and took back my sheet of paper. He then took out his pen, crossed out one item and handed the sheet of paper back, muttering, "That's no longer available." So far, the meeting had lasted less than two minutes. Bill indicated that he had concluded his presentation and I had to ask, as he had made no mention of it, how much it would cost. "£1 million per year for three years," was Bill's sole response. I asked how the SFA had arrived at the valuation for the package, naively expecting that we would be given a detailed value proposition. Bill's response was, "Because Tennents were paying £750,000 a year, and it's worth more than that." End of meeting!

After the meeting we did a detailed evaluation of the proposition, but it could never stack up against the main argument of why anyone would want to invest £1 million a year with such a bunch of clowns. In fairness, the proposition did offer some huge commercial and sponsorship opportunities but as Endell had first clumsily articulated at the meeting with Maxwell, such opportunities had to be evaluated with great care. Football was a mass audience sport, supported by a level of fanaticism not seen in most other sports. As Bill Shankly famously said, "some people think football is a matter of life and death. I don't like that attitude. I can assure you it is much more than that." Football is tribal, partisan, parochial, local and extremely sensitive. No two fans ever see a game in the same light and so reporting a football match requires great skill on the part of the sports journalist to ensure a lack of bias. These differences of perception are best illustrated by two of my drivers at News International. Walter was an ardent Rangers fan and Steven a Celtic fan. One Monday, after an Old Firm game, Walter gave me his views on the game. Later that day Steven gave me his opinion, which seemed to be about a totally different game. Endell's observation was extremely valid, particularly as in some quarters there was a perception that the Daily Record was the 'Daily Ranger'. Impartial coverage was vital. Needless to say, when I joined News International, I actively encouraged my colleagues in The Scottish Sun to perpetuate the 'Daily Ranger' perception as much as possible, as detailed in Chapter 30.

I have attended many Rangers and Celtic games during my more than 30 years in Scotland, often as a corporate guest of the club, or one of their supporters. My first visit to Ibrox came during David Murray's period at Rangers. Murray and I had already locked horns over the ill-fated Sunday Scot and, as I got to know him better, I never ceased to remind him that he'd thrown in the towel too early. That evening my first impression, sitting in the directors' box, was of being surrounded by many people, all identically dressed - club blazer, club tie, grey trousers and, somewhat bizarrely, tan shoes. I couldn't help but be amazed that when people became involved with Rangers, they all immediately adopted this dress code.

My first trip to the modern Celtic Park was to an Old Firm game as a guest of Peter McLean[11], who handled News International's PR and had previously done the same at Celtic. One of the most interesting aspects of going to occasions like these is meeting a fascinating cross-section of people and this one was to prove no exception. In the Boardroom Peter introduced me to Allan MacDonald[12], the new Chief Executive of Celtic. As I have often noted, coming into the world of football seems to instil a completely different (and somewhat puzzling) thought process. MacDonald was holding court and talking about Raphael Scheidt, a recent Brazilian signing. I am told that the first reaction to this of many canny Glaswegians within the Club was "My God, with a name like that, he'd better be good." MacDonald waxed lyrical about Scheidt's abilities and about how he would transform the team. No expert on football, I was more than a little puzzled at some of MacDonald's theories. As it turned out, Raphael was Scheidt by name and sh*** by nature, as indeed was a lot of what Alan MacDonald told us that afternoon.

Over the years I also got to know several members of the Celtic Board, including Tom Allison[13], Eric Hagman[14] and their Chairman Brian Quinn[15]. Brian invited me to join the Board for what turned out to be an extraordinary lunch. I suspect the real reason I was invited was because of News Corp's part ownership of Sky television. For some time, Celtic (and Rangers) had recognised that Scottish football was becoming something of a backwater and that there was no great prospect of this changing. This was reflected in the significant difference in television revenues from both the Scottish and English games. Both clubs realised that the only way that they could ever break away from this depressing future was by finding a way to join the Premier League in England. There was already a precedent for such a move - Welsh clubs Swansea and Cardiff City periodically competed in the English Premier League, so why not Rangers and Celtic? Despite both teams having a worldwide fan base and significant home support, the Premier League was showing no enthusiasm for letting Rangers and Celtic join the bonanza - turkeys voting for Christmas comes to mind. Both Rangers and Celtic had figured that the influence of Sky television could be a key factor. Both clubs had calculated (correctly in my view) that they had considerable leverage through their huge worldwide fan bases. Each was a far more attractive proposition than many of the clubs languishing in the lower half of the English Premier League. Accordingly, the race was on to lobby the senior people at Sky to get them to exert their considerable influence and financial muscle on the Premier League and ensure places for Rangers and Celtic.

We had a most enjoyable lunch and discussed the battle for market leadership taking place between The Scottish Sun and the Daily Record. Needless to say, I provided an extremely biased version of events, sticking the knife into the Daily Record at every

---

[11] Peter McLean b.1964, Founder and Managing Director PMPR 2000-
[12] Allan MacDonald OBE b.1952, Chief Executive Celtic FC 1999-2000
[13] Tom Allison b.1948, Director Celtic FC 2001-2011. Chairman Peel Ports Group
[14] Eric Hagman b.1946, Arthur Andersen 1970-2001, latterly Senior Partner. Director Celtic FC 2004-08, mentor
[15] Brian Quinn CBE b.1936, Deputy Governor Bank of England, Chairman Celtic FC 2000-07

available opportunity, much to everyone's amusement. There was of course also a lengthy discussion on Celtic's desire to join the English Premier League.

About half way through we were joined by Martin O'Neill[16], the Celtic manager. We were told that Martin was not feeling very well and suffering from a heavy cold. In the event, Martin turned up in his tracksuit and a heavy quilted coat which he kept on during the lunch. For most of the time he said absolutely nothing, but I became increasingly aware that he was constantly staring at me. Brian Quinn had also noticed that Martin was not contributing, so when the first opportunity presented itself he said, "And what do you think about that one, Martin?" To everyone's surprise, he opened with a vicious attack on the Scottish Press in general and The Scottish Sun in particular, citing one by one a long list of occasions when The Scottish Sun had either attacked, criticised, or commented unfairly on him personally. Having frequently heard such complaints over the years, I tried to be conciliatory. I said that I was very sorry he felt like that but, given his very high profile, surely he must recognise the huge level of public interest in him, his team, and the club. Glasgow being a football mad city, people like him were inevitably always in the public spotlight. What I didn't say - but certainly felt - was that since he was being handsomely rewarded for managing one of the biggest football clubs in Scotland, this sort of attention came with the job. I finished by saying that none of this was personal and he should rise above it or, better still, just ignore it.

Rather than calming the situation, this seemed to put him into orbit and he launched into another diatribe, the gist of which was that The Scottish Sun was totally biased against Celtic. I told him I strongly disagreed and suggested that no two people saw a game in exactly the same way. I told him about Walter and Steven's views of an Old Firm game. Listening to their views on the game, I suggested that any reasonable person would conclude that they could not both have watched the same match. I also asked Martin why, as he clearly felt aggrieved by this, he had not contacted the Editor to complain. All in all, it was extremely embarrassing and throughout both rants there was complete silence around the table. Brian Quinn brought matters to a perhaps premature end; he thanked me for coming, said what a productive conversation we had had and escorted me out of the room. As I left, I glanced round and saw Martin continuing to stare at me, as he had done for the entire period. Brian apologised for Martin's outburst, saying that he had never seen him behave like this. I reassured him that I had seen and heard a lot worse. For the record, after discussing all of this with Bruce Waddell, I wrote to Martin to say that I was sorry about the way that he felt and invited him to meet Bruce to discuss his grievances. I never received a reply.

Another interesting experience was attending a Champions League game between Borussia Dortmund and Rangers in December 1999. I was invited by Frank Cullen[17] of NTL, which was then the principal sponsor of both Rangers and Celtic. Frank had

---

[16] Martin O'Neill OBE, b.1952. Player and football manager Wickham, Norwich City, Leicester City, Celtic, Aston Villa and Republic of Ireland.
[17] Frank Cullen b.1950. Managing Director NTL 1998-2001

recently arrived in Glasgow and I had introduced him to several people and we had struck up a friendship.

I had always wanted to go on one of these trips, mainly to see at first-hand how our sports writers managed to rack up such enormous expenses on such occasions. The first person I bumped into in the Departure Lounge was Rodger Baillie, the Scottish Sun's Senior Football Reporter, whose astonishment at seeing me was something to behold. With Rodger was my next-door neighbour, the Daily Mail's Ian Archer, now sadly deceased. I had known Ian for almost 25 years and met him often at the golf club. I had a high regard for him as a journalist. He was a fantastic wordsmith and his copy was always interesting and extremely readable. Like many sports journalists, his alcohol consumption was also legendary. In my early years in Kilmacolm I golfed early on Sundays, usually around an hour behind Ian's fourball. By the time we adjourned to the bar after a round, Ian would be on his fourth or fifth vodka before driving to STV's studios, just in time to present Scotsport at 5pm. Often those of us watching would remark on the poor colour quality of the television as Ian's face frequently looked a brightish pink!

On boarding the aircraft, the group was divided into three. The club officials, management and the team (under the watchful eye of Dick Advocaat[18]) all sat at the front of the aircraft, the sponsors and supporters in the middle, and the 'hacks' occupied the rear. It was fascinating to watch the drinks trolley progressing down the plane. At the front everyone had soft drinks and wine was seemingly the main choice of the sponsors, but at the rear of the plane the hacks consumed anything they could get their hands on.

Frank and I spent a very pleasant two days in Cologne, although it was absolutely freezing. On Tuesday evening we travelled back to Dortmund for the game and witnessed a wretched performance by Rangers. At the airport, we were reunited with the team and the sports journalists. The only item of note was the extremely late arrival of Ian Archer and his friend Alan Davidson[19], who almost missed the flight and looked as if they had been dragged through a hedge backwards, clearly having been 'on the lash' - confirming my original suspicions as to why journalists' expenses were so high on such occasions.

So, what is the future of football? It is an appallingly run business, with practices which would not be tolerated elsewhere and where the overall standard of governance is virtually non-existent. The game awash with cash from television revenue. Even the smallest clubs in the Premier League are guaranteed around £100 million a year, but is this sustainable? It can continue only as long as the level of audience is maintained, as that is the only currency that broadcasters are interested in. Even that is an oversimplification of the issue. In its early years, Sky's prime objective was to build subscribers and sport, particularly football, was an extremely effective weapon in doing so. Securing broadcasting rights to a whole range of events meant enthusiasts were forced to become subscribers. As with the marketing

---

[18] Dick Advocaat b.1947. Dutch footballer and manager Rangers FC 1998-2000
[19] Alan Davidson 1950-2007. Chief sports writer Evening Times

of other commodities, the hardware required was relatively inexpensive and, in those early days, the free provision of satellite dishes and boxes was commonplace. As for audience, football delivered the biggest numbers by far, hence the value of broadcasting rights soared. Sky was happy, as it was building market share and all the costs were directly passed on to the subscriber. Recent European competition regulation has resulted in the emergence of BT Sport and others as major competitors to Sky, which has proved to be a bonanza for the Premier League, particularly as they can now leverage up to five separate broadcasting packages. I still have doubts as to whether this is sustainable in the long term. The first issue is availability. In order to sustain separate packages for Sky, BT and the others, broadcasters have had to schedule games seven days a week, with the consumer now getting almost saturation coverage. Sustaining viewing audiences will therefore become increasingly difficult. Another issue is attendance figures, which may be by no means as important now as they were in the past, but the big clubs still play to capacity audiences. Arsenal generate £1 million from every home game and Manchester United the same, with regular gates of 75,000. Elsewhere average attendances have declined in recent years but broadcasters do not want to televise games played in half-empty stadia. Another dynamic is ticket prices. If the fans' perception is that clubs are awash with broadcasting cash, the ability to increase ticket prices may become limited. In the 2016/17 Season, there was a revolt from Liverpool fans after the club tried to increase season ticket prices substantially. A much more interesting point was the club's instant climb-down in the face of this revolt. It may well be that football clubs are creating a long-term problem for themselves by being unable to raise gate receipts, even in line with inflation, because fans think they don't need to.

My final thoughts on the beautiful game are about its morality. The spectre of match fixing has been in the game ever since the 1960s. The exponential rise in betting, particularly the advent of spread betting, provides many opportunities for corruption. Italian football in particular has gone through several major crises, with officials fired, clubs relegated, and so on. The biggest challenge the game has faced is the perception that the corruption exists at the very highest level. Recent purges at FIFA and UEFA, including Messrs. Blatter[20] and Platini[21], would appear to some to be no more than putting a finger in the dyke.

All in all, I remain unconvinced about the ability of football either to effectively regulate itself or to stamp out corruption. Tom Bower[22] in his 2003 book[23] laid bare many of the most questionable practices within the game. I think Bower is probably the best investigative journalist of his era. He has carried out forensic investigations into many prominent people - Richard Branson, Robert Maxwell and Mohamed Al-Fayed[24] to name but a few. His publication won the William Hill Sports Book of the

---

[20] Sepp Blatter b.1936. President FIFA 1998-2015
[21] Michel Platini b.1955. President EUFA 2007-15
[22] Tom Bower b.1946. British investigative journalist
[23] 'Broken Dreams: Vanity, Greed and the Souring of British Football', Tom Bower, 2003, Simon and Schuster UK Ltd.
[24] Mohamed Al-Fayed b.1929. Egyptian business magnate

Year, is a fascinating read and illustrates extremely effectively what a thoroughly immoral business football is. It seems little has changed since then.

Finally, there are many other factors contributing to the overall mix. With the Bosnan Ruling and the subsequent extraordinary rise in the number of football agents, it is astonishing that the English Premier League clubs have been unable to exert any control over agent fees. Transfer costs of players joining English clubs from Europe are around 20-25% higher than those between the European clubs, reflecting not only the vast sums of money available to the Premier League clubs, but also the apparent poor negotiating ability and financial management of the English clubs themselves. The latest statistics show Manchester United paying an average salary of £6.5 million to each member of their squad.

Peter McLean recently published some fascinating data[25] about the most influential people on social media in Scottish Football. Celtic F.C. have 3 million followers across all social media platforms but staggeringly Rangers Manager Steven Gerrard has over 8 million followers on Instagram.

The overall conclusion is, not surprisingly the game of football is hugely popular but vastly corrupt. Perhaps it should be rechristened 'The Mad Game' rather than 'The Beautiful Game'?

---

[25] Peter McLean publisher "The Scottish Football Social Media Influencers Tables" PMPR Excellence Limited, 29th July 2019

Part VI: Sport

Chapter 49   RUGBY AND PIERS

"Football is ninety minutes of pretending you're hurt. Rugby is eighty minutes of pretending you're not."

It was once argued that rugby was a game for hooligans played by gentlemen, but some recent off-field controversies have tarnished the game's reputation. Dwarf throwing, high jinks, bar-room brawls and even players fighting amongst themselves have periodically hogged the headlines, whilst a much more serious issue is the long-term well-being of players in an increasingly physical sport. A recent report[1] revealed that the average weight of a Five/Six Nations player has gone from 13st 5lbs in 1995 to 16st 7lbs today, an increase of almost 25%. Another report[2] revealed that for the average severity of match injuries - the time taken for a player to recover was 37 days (2016-17) compared to 16 days (2002-03).

I became a major rugby fan only after moving to Scotland in 1984. As a young man my interest level was relatively minor – neither my brother nor I had distinguished ourselves on the rugby fields of Portadown or Coleraine. I don't remember my parents being particularly interested in the game, although I do remember going to the old Lansdowne Road in Dublin on a few occasions in the 1950s.

It was almost 30 years before I attended another international game, but once I moved to Scotland I attended Murrayfield fairly regularly to witness Scotland's extremely variable performances there. Sadly, I was not there to witness either of their two Grand Slams in 1984 or 1990, although I did see some of their games when they won the final Five Nations Championship in 1999.

When the Six Nations was created in 2000, I attended the first Scotland game at the Stadio Flaminio in Rome and I have also been at many of the great matches at Twickenham, the Millennium Stadium, The Aviva and Stade de France, usually as an Ireland supporter. Although we have lived in Scotland for over 30 years, and we support Scotland in almost everything, Ireland is the 'home team' in rugby for Claire and me.

Murrayfield has not been a happy hunting ground for us. I was not present when Ireland won there in 1985, but attended the fixture regularly thereafter. I bought a very smart, emerald green jacket specially to wear to these fixtures. It was 14 years old, and looking distinctly shabby before I first witnessed an Ireland victory wearing it in 2003.

I wasn't born when Ireland won their first Grand Slam in 1948, but I was at the Scotland game with Charlie Murray at Twickenham in 2009 and our group had to scurry to a nearby pub to witness Ireland beating Wales 15-17 to achieve Ireland's

---

[1] BMJ Open Sport and Exercise Medical Journal November 2018
[2] England Professional Rugby Injury Surveillance Report December 2018

second Grand Slam. That resulted in an extremely lively evening, of which I remember absolutely nothing. Claire and I watched Ireland win a third Grand Slam at home on St Patrick's Day in 2018 with great excitement and a realisation that we were witnessing a golden era of Irish rugby.

Our interest in rugby increased when Amanda met Piers Francis[3] in Edinburgh in March 2014. Their relationship blossomed sufficiently to survive a five-month separation when he went to New Zealand having secured a two season contract with Counties Manukau, starting in April 2015. He returned to the UK in November 2014 to play fly-half for Doncaster Knights in the second tier of English rugby. This gave him some valuable competitive game time and enabled him and Amanda to meet up again. Claire and I met Piers for the first time that December and, with our friends Stephen, Sue and Laura Warwick[4], went to Doncaster in March 2015 to see him play against Bristol. Doncaster were beaten by Bristol that day, but we all saw enough in Piers to know that he had talent. We also met Piers' parents David and Heather for the first time.

Piers returned to New Zealand in April 2015 to start training with Bombay Rugby Club, a premier club in the County's Manukau province, in the lead up to the start of the Mitre Cup. The competition is the premier one in New Zealand provincial Rugby and sits in the tier just below Super 15 rugby, so it was a significant move for him. He and Amanda had decided they wanted to be together, so she went to Auckland with him. It was a huge wrench seeing our daughter move to the other side of the world, but we knew that Piers' driving ambition was to play for England and that New Zealand rugby was a stepping stone to realising that.

Piers' move to Counties Manukau meant he was coached by Tana Umaga[5], who had played more than 70 times for the All Blacks, and Tana became Piers' mentor. Later that season it was announced that Umaga was moving to coach the Auckland Blues, one of the five New Zealand Super 15 rugby franchises, and he clearly had seen enough potential in Piers to sign him for the Blues squad for the 2016 Super Rugby season. This operates in the first half of the year whilst the Mitre 10 Cup is played in the second half, thus players can play for two teams. For us it was the start of a whole new experience in Southern Hemisphere rugby, of which we became avid and enthusiastic fans.

Piers was now part of a squad which included seven current or former All Blacks and was involved in an intensive training regime on which he absolutely thrived. Although his weight increased by only 2-3kg from his Doncaster days, there was a huge difference in his physique. I once said to Claire, after looking at some of Piers' personal data, that he was exactly the same weight as me, which brought the response, "Yes, but his is distributed differently." Pre-season training went well, but he sustained an ankle injury in the final warm-up game, which was to keep him out

---

[3] Piers Francis b.1990, English professional rugby player. Clubs include Edinburgh, Waikato, Doncaster, Counties Manukau, Auckland Blues and Northampton Saints. Capped five times for England.
[4] Stephen Warwick b.1951 m. Sue (née Peirse-Duncombe) 1d. Laura 1s. David, formally MD Ashworth (part of Saint Gobain Group)
[5] Tana Umaga, b.1973, 77 caps for the All Blacks, 22 as Captain. Head Coach Auckland Blues 2015 – 18

for six weeks. This sadly coincided with our first visit to New Zealand and although, we saw the Blues play both the Hurricanes at Eden Park and the Crusaders in Christchurch, Piers was not in the squad.

While we were there, we met Tana Umaga and many of his team mates. Piers eventually played his first game for the Blues and Umaga himself presented him with his club tie. I became a huge fan of the Blues and watched every one of their games in those two seasons, courtesy of some very early morning starts. Astonishingly, although not an early morning person, Claire also watched almost every game and knew all of the Blue's players by sight. As Piers recovered from injury, Tana told him that he was considering playing him at number 12. Prior to playing for the Blues, all Piers' rugby had been played at number 10, so this was a significant development. Equally significant was that the established Number 12 in the squad was George Moala[6], a current All Black.

Piers played nine times for the Blues that season, all at number 12. For the last few games he also took over goal kicking duties from Ihaia West[7]. During that season he was taken off with a numb arm (a stinger), stretchered off in a neck brace with concussion, suffered a broken finger and a bruised shoulder and on several occasions had stitches in his head and ears – all part of playing professional rugby today.

In his second season Piers scored over 100 points for Counties Manukau. Remarkably, apart from a few stitches, he stayed injury free until the final game of the season, when he dislocated his thumb. He and Amanda then came home for a short break in October 2016, travelling via the US, where Piers paid a return visit to Arizona for a session with his NFL kicking coach Gary Zauner[8]. He stayed with Ted and Adeline in California during Thanksgiving. Their three granddaughters were present at dinner when he was describing his experiences in Arizona. One innocently asked, "Why does it take you three days to learn to kick a ball?" In Scotland in November we had an early Christmas with all the family, including David and Heather, before Piers and Amanda returned to New Zealand in time for his pre-season training.

Although he was very much looking forward to his second season, there was a level of uncertainty for Piers, as the Blues had signed the legendary Sonny Bill Williams[9]. With Williams having been injured at the Olympics, Piers started the first two games of the season at number 12, with Ihaia being the main place kicker. From the fourth game Piers played the rest of the season at Number 10, with Sonny Bill at number 12. He was now also the main place kicker. That season he played every game and kicked over 100 points at an average of over 75%. Early on he realised that he might now also be part of a little bit of history. On 7th June the Blues were due to play the British and Irish Lions at Eden Park and, provided he stayed injury free, he might

---

[6] George Moala, b.1990, Auckland Blues 2012 –. Four All Blacks caps.
[7] Ihaia West b.1992, Auckland Blues, Hurricanes; currently with La Rochelle
[8] Gary Zauner b.1950, American football coach (NFL League) of the Minnesota Vikings, Baltimore Ravens and Arizona Cardinals
[9] Sonny Bill Williams b.1985, played Rugby Union (50 caps) and League for the All Blacks. Auckland Blues 2017-

become one of very few Englishmen ever to play against the Lions. In anticipation, David and Heather had booked their flights to New Zealand months before.

At this time, he was approached by two English premiership clubs and, unlike the previous year, he felt that the time was now right to come back to the UK. He knew that he could never be considered for England while playing in New Zealand and so signed a three-year contract with Northampton Saints.

Three weeks before the Lions game, he appeared to be badly concussed playing against the Stormers in South Africa. However, he came through all the concussion protocols and played the following week. All was set for the historic game against the Lions on 7th June. However, at 5am one morning as he was driving Amanda to Auckland airport, he took a call from Eddie Jones[10], the England rugby head coach asking him if he would like to play for England on their upcoming summer tour to Argentina in June. He had watched some of Piers' games, and was impressed enough to ask him how he felt about playing for England. Piers initially thought it was a hoax call from one of his friends, but wasted no time in telling Jones that he would love to have the opportunity to play for England. I have observed Jones closely ever since. A brash, in-your-face Australian, he mostly endeared himself to the British public with a series of off the cuff remarks, often politically incorrect, but highly amusing. I especially liked his response when asked to apologise for describing New Zealand as "a sh***y little island off the coast of Australia." He said: "Sorry, I meant two sh***y little islands." Two days after Eddie's phone call the squad was announced, with Piers one of 12 uncapped players. His only problem was that he was contracted to play for the Blues in Samoa the weekend before the Lions game. At this stage the England squad had assembled for a match against the Barbarians, before travelling to Argentina. It was agreed that Piers would fly back from Samoa after the Blues game and then fly directly from Auckland to Argentina to link up with the squad, albeit ten days after everyone else. He believed his prospects of playing were doubtful, especially as the first game was taking place only four days after his arrival.

David and Heather were now in New Zealand. Along with their daughter Lucy and Amanda they flew to Samoa to see the Blues game and then returned to Auckland for the Lions game, in which the Blues memorably beat the Lions 21-18, with a fantastic final try by Ihaia West set up by Sonny Bill Williams. Amanda, David, Heather and Lucy then made the trip to Argentina in the hope that Piers might play. At the end of his first training session Eddie Jones told him he was unlikely to be in the squad for the first game, as he had arrived so late. After two further training sessions the squad was announced, with Piers among the finishers.

On Saturday 10th June 2017 Piers realised his life-long ambition, when he came off the bench to play for 20 minutes in an England jersey. He played at number 12 and set up two tries, one a layoff for George Ford[11] and the other for Denny Solomona[12].

---

[10] Eddie Jones b.1960, Australian Rugby Union player and coach. England Head Coach 2015 -
[11] George Ford b.1993, Leicester Tigers and England (45 caps, 232 points)
[12] Denny Solomona b.1993, New Zealand born England rugby player, Sale Sharks and England (5 caps)

England, 7 points down with 25 minutes to go, triumphed 38-34. That evening Amanda, David, Heather and Lucy were there to see him presented with his first England cap. Even more was to come the following Saturday, when he was selected in the starting line up at number 12 for the second test. Again, England won, this time by 35-25. When Piers went over to score his first try for England, Claire and I were watching at home, clapping and cheering with enormous pride.

Piers and Amanda returned to New Zealand in June. Piers went to Japan for the final Blues game and Amanda spent a long weekend in Queenstown with Tana's wife Rochelle, who had become a very dear friend. Piers and Amanda had two and a half fantastic years in New Zealand, travelling extensively and making many new friends. In Amanda's case it started with a tearful farewell on platform 1 of Glasgow's Central Station but ended with us being closer than ever to her. She and Piers make a great team. She realised very early on that if she were to support Piers fully, it would be difficult to have a 9-5 job, so she carved out a role contracting in PR.

They moved back to the UK in August and Piers' first season at Northampton was a varied one. He had a disastrous start, breaking his jaw in the team's final warm-up game. Having recovered from that, a leg injury prevented him from linking up with the England squad for the Autumn Internationals until the very final game. However, he came off the bench to win his third cap and his first at Twickenham for the 48-12 defeat of Samoa. I was extremely proud to be there to see it with Heather, David and Amanda. Thereafter his season stalled. Two concussions and the team going through a wretched period meant he was not in the squad for the home internationals. Northampton eventually finished ninth in the Premiership, well below their potential. Replacing their Director of Rugby Jim Mallinder[13] in mid-season was hardly ideal but essential.

Nevertheless, luck was on Piers' side when he was then included in the final England training squad for the Barbarians' game. He was selected and scored two tries in the game and, although England were defeated 45-63, he went on to be part of the squad which toured South Africa in summer 2018, when he received his fourth England cap in the first Test at Ellis Park, Johannesburg. We went to South Africa to support him and saw the third Test in Cape Town.

Our family's connections with rugby have increased, with my nephew Sammy Moore's son Stewart[14] joining the Ulster Academy at the age of 19. Like Piers, Stewart is a number 12. He played in the Ulster Under 16, Under 17 and Under 19 squads. During his final year at school he scored 21 tries in 13 games and played twice for Ireland's Under 19s, before making his Senior debut in Ulster's pre-season games against Gloucester, Wasps and Uruguay. He was capped twice for Ireland at the Under 20 World Cup in Argentina in 2019 and scored a memorable try against Australia which quickly had more than 100,000 views on YouTube.

---

[13] Jim Mallinder b.1966. Rugby Union coach Northampton Saints 2007-2017
[14] Stewart Moore, b.1999 Ulster Academy. Part of Ireland's Under 20s World Cup Squad, Argentina 2019

Rugby also features prominently on Claire's side of the family. Her father was president of the Queen's University Rugby Association. Of her cousin Deirdre Humphreys' sons, David was capped 72 times for Ireland, scoring 560 points, and is currently Director of Rugby at Gloucester whilst Ian[15] played for Leicester Tigers, Ulster and London Irish.

Piers has completed his second season with Northampton, now coached by Kiwi Chris Boyd. It was a much better season and the team finished in fourth place in the Premiership and made the end of season playoffs. Piers himself scored eight tries, the second highest in the team.

Internationally he made the final England training squad for the last Autumn International against Australia, but not the match day squad.

Prior to the World Cup in Japan in the Autumn of 2019, Piers was part of the 38 man final England training squad and won his fifth cap in the warm-up game against Wales at Twickenham. In August 2019 he was confirmed as one of the 31 players in England's World Cup squad. We are all understandably very proud of his achievements.

---

[15] Ian Humphreys b.1982, Leicester Tigers, London Irish and Fly Half for Ulster

Chapter 50   FAMILY LIFE

"As you walk down the fairway of life, you must smell the roses for you only get to play one round." **Ben Hogan**

Like every father, I am extremely proud of my daughters. Claire and I have been extremely fortunate that Amanda and Milena have successfully navigated their way through the many hazards that young people encounter nowadays. I regard them as best friends and we speak almost every day, wherever they are. The arrival of Milena's daughter Tarryn in 2016 has enriched our lives even further and we are besotted grandparents. Amanda is expecting our first grandson in December 2019.

Amanda and Milena grew up in Kilmacolm and both graduated with law degrees from Edinburgh University, but there the similarity ends. They are now in settled relationships but got there by entirely different routes.

After graduation Amanda announced that she would like to spend a gap year travelling. A fairly robust conversation while walking the dog the following day helped clarify her thoughts. My position was simple – there would be no financing of such an expedition unless there was a clear career plan and a job awaiting her on her return. Shortly afterwards she enrolled for a one-year postgrad Diploma in Broadcast Journalism. This ultimately led to a career in media, which included news reading and reporting on local radio, some television and a brief spell in PR in London and, later, Auckland, New Zealand. She also completed her Diploma in Legal Practice and was offered a traineeship with Pinsent Masons in Edinburgh starting in September 2012. In February that year, prior to commencing her traineeship, she set off on her own to spend five months backpacking in South America, Australia, Thailand, Malaysia and Bali.

For a family as close as ours her trip, particularly her time in South America, was nail biting. Early on Claire joined her for three weeks in Venezuela and Peru. As she then backpacked alone in some lawless parts of South America, we were hugely relieved when she was finally airborne from Santiago en route to Australia. Naively we thought this might be the end of her travel bug, but it turned out not to be so.

18 months into her traineeship Amanda met Piers who was then playing for Edinburgh. They met on 19th March and hit it off very quickly. Claire and I sensed from the start that it might develop into a serious relationship and we were keen to learn more about him.

From an early age Piers had one interest – rugby. He was brought up in Gravesend in Kent and played mini rugby between the ages of five and 12. He played at Old Gravesendians, eventually representing Kent at various age levels, but he encountered several major setbacks. At 14 he became part of the Saracens Academy, which involved travelling twice a week with a group on a four-hour round trip to Barnet. His first setback was at 17 when Saracens informed him that they considered him too slight to make the grade. This was on the train back from school, on a phone call which cut out mid-way through. He was told a letter would be sent to him outlining everything but he never received it. Shortly afterwards the family decided that Piers would spend a year in New Zealand to concentrate on rugby and David[1] took him there in January 2009. He started playing at Auckland Marist, one of Auckland's club sides, his rugby progressed and one year turned into four, as he went through the Auckland Academy, the Auckland Squad and the Chief's wider training squad, eventually playing in the Waikato ATM Cup squad in 2012. He was far away from home, rooming with teammates and initially knew only his parents' close friends Martin and Debbie Ballard. However, his dedication and determination paid off and he was signed in November 2012 by Edinburgh, then coached by Michael Bradley[2]. Due to a groin injury he made only a handful of appearances for the team. Bradley departed at the end of the season, replaced by Alan Solomans[3]. Piers started the first game of the 2013-14 season, broke his foot and was out for the entire season. For him, Edinburgh was a very unhappy experience in a team riven with division and, having had very limited playing time, his contract was not renewed.

Piers' subsequent rugby experiences were described in the previous chapter. Claire, Amanda and I went to Cape Town in June 2018 to watch the Third Test between South Africa and England at Newlands Stadium. Although Piers was not in the squad that day, we witnessed an English victory on an extremely wet day. We thoroughly enjoyed a 10 day visit to the Western Cape, joining David, Heather and Lucy for part of the time. Towards the end of the trip, Piers announced his passport had been found in his room in the hotel in Durban in which the England squad had stayed. He would have to fly there to collect it – and received much ribbing about his carelessness. We met up with Amanda and Piers again in Northamptonshire after our trip and just before we left Piers casually asked for my advice about something in the garage. I said I'd be delighted to, as very few people now asked my advice about anything. He then confessed that the Durban trip was a cover: in Johannesburg he had bought diamonds for an engagement ring which he had designed and he had had to go there to collect it. He then asked for my permission to propose to Amanda. I wholeheartedly gave it, and assumed that the engagement would happen very soon but, great romantic that he is, he planned to propose to her in Paris some ten days later. During the subsequent Paris trip, I anxiously waited for news, and as time went on I began to wonder if he had changed his mind or if Amanda had turned him down. Neither was the case – that weekend France won the World Cup; Paris was mobbed for 48 hours and Piers could not find a quiet moment to propose. In the end he proposed at a chateau in the Burgundy region, very appropriate I thought, as there are two great loves in Amanda's life – Piers and champagne. Fittingly their wedding will be in France in August 2020.

---

[1] David Francis, b. 1958, West Malling, Kent, m. Heather (née Gardner b.1969) 1984.
[2] Michael Bradley, b.1962 Edinburgh coach 2011-13.
[3] Alan Solomans b.1950, Edinburgh coach 2013-16

Milena followed a totally different path. Like Amanda she is extremely bright. At Junior School one teacher told us that she was a dreamy child, frequently gazing out of the window. The teacher was determined to catch her out and one day asked "What did I just say, Milena?" Quick as a flash, Milena gave the correct answer. After this happened several times, the teacher admitted defeat. At her wedding, I mentioned another of Milena's characteristics. She could walk into a room notice and instantly identify one thing which was different or new since the last time she had been there. As we used to say, "The only flies on Milena are paying ground rent." She studied law at Edinburgh University, completed her Diploma and joined MacRoberts LLP as a trainee solicitor. She became a fully qualified solicitor and, just before she married Kumar in September 2014, became Legal Counsel at the Glasgow office of Renewable Energy Systems Ltd, a renewables developer.

Claire and I included both girls in many of our social activities from an early age. As a consequence, their social skills developed enormously as they grew up. I was extremely proud when these were called into effect during my time as chairman of the Newspaper Press Fund in Scotland. In 2003 Chris Oakley[4] the national chairman invited Claire and me to the National Press Fund Ball in London. Claire was unable to attend through illness and Amanda was drafted in, then aged 16. At the dinner Amanda was seated between Chris Oakley and Norman Fowler[5], now Speaker of The House of Lords. To my delight she acquitted herself extremely well. Sometime later Milena was to have a similar experience, this time at the Press Fund Ball in Glasgow where she found herself seated between John Swinney and Bob Bird – equally challenging but in different ways!

Milena met Kumar Chetty soon after she moved to Edinburgh. Kumar lived in Edinburgh but was a medical student at Glasgow University, so their long courtship was initially conducted via the M8 motorway.

The Chetty family history is fascinating. Kumar's family can trace their origins back many generations to Madras, now Chenai. Two or three generations back some of the family moved to South Africa and settled in Pietermaritzburg and Durban, which both had large Indian communities. Pietermaritzburg was where Gandhi was famously ejected from the first-class compartment of a train. Later the Chettys found themselves under the apartheid regime. A recent television documentary described how two of the Chetty family had a close connection with Nelson Mandela. Mandela, when in hiding, had stayed at one of the family's farms in Pietermaritzburg and Kumar can vividly remember visiting the farm as a child. During their terrible experiences under the apartheid regime, the family, all highly educated, realised that their only salvation was to get out of South Africa. Kumar has established that nine of his great aunts and uncles were educated at Scottish

---

[4] Chris Oakley CBE b.1943 CEO Regional Independent Media. Chief Executive Midland Independent Newspapers 1991-97
[5] Peter Norman Fowler, Baron Fowler, Kt, PC. b.1938. British politician in Margaret Thatcher's cabinet. Lord Speaker since 2016

universities and all 27 of his father's generation who came to the UK are highly qualified professionals.

Kumar was born in London. His father Sathia[6] had originally studied medicine, before deciding to teach physics and eventually moving to Edinburgh. His mother Marie is from Ayr and attended the RSAMD before becoming a drama teacher. Kumar's first days were spent in hospital with assumed severe jaundice until his mother said to the consultant "You do realise he's mixed race?" "Aaah," was the reply.

Kumar was educated at James Gillespie's High School in Edinburgh. He then studied medicine and is now a partner in a GP practice in Maryhill in Glasgow. At their wedding I related an incident from when he and Milena were staying at our house in Cellardyke. I had asked him to cut the grass. After some time pushing the lawnmower up and down with little success, he asked my neighbour Eddie Allan if there was anything wrong with it. Eddie advised him to try plugging it in! Telling me the story afterwards, Eddie paused and then said "So, Kumar's a doctor then?" The Fife sense of humour and timing is wonderful and Eddie and Ann have often had us in stitches with their observations of life.

Just over three years ago Kumar and Milena presented us with our first grandchild Tarryn[7]. I had a degree of apprehension – after all, I was the father who told Amanda and Milena that they only became really interesting once they were over five. Milena, when she announced her pregnancy said "And of course, Dad, you'll not be interested in the child until it's at least five years old." However never was there a truer saying "I may not be rich and famous, but I do have a priceless grandchild." I was instantly smitten with Tarryn. Claire and I are extremely fortunate that, since Milena returned to work, Tarryn often spends one day a week with us. It's a joy to watch her grow up.

When I was in corporate life, my spare time was taken up with family, music and golf so I had little time to develop other interests and hobbies. However, I did dream of many things that I would like to do when time became available.

One was my ever-increasing interest in food and wine and several strands to this developed over the years. First, Claire and I were fortunate to have dined at some very good restaurants. Second, around 1990, Janis's then husband Jim Judge[8] proposed me for membership of the Scottish Society of Epicureans (more on them later). Our regular family get togethers with Ted and Adeline also increased my desire to produce top quality food – they both cooked to professional standards and I wanted to do the same. This also naturally involved building a wine collection to accompany the great food! To facilitate all this, I needed an array of cookery books and subsequently created my own series of them. Finally, at one stage I invested

---

[6] Sathia Chetty b.1948, Pietermaritzburg, m. Marie (née Devine) b.1954, 2s. Kumar and Devin, 1d. Hannah.
[7] Tarryn Olivia Chetty b.2016
[8] Jim Judge b.1956, retired dentist

with three others in a restaurant start-up which eventually comprised three restaurants in Glasgow, Edinburgh and Manchester.

Let me now look at each of these strands. First the restaurants. In corporate life I could often choose the restaurant and over a lengthy period I sampled many Michelin star establishments (including several with two stars) throughout the UK - and indeed a few further afield. Two in particular stand out – first the Auberge de Soleil, St. Helena in the Napa Valley, California. Ted, Adeline and I had a fabulous meal there. It included a sensational starter called 'The Seven Deadly Sins'. My other memory there was Ted pointing out to the sommelier that Gevrey Chambertin was misspelt in the wine menu – information that he did not appear particularly grateful to receive. My particular favourite is the late Andrew Fairlie's[9] restaurant at the Gleneagles Hotel. I had experienced his cooking at One Devonshire Gardens where he won his first Michelin star and was privileged to have met him on a few occasions. He struck me as one of life's gentlemen and enormously committed to what he did. His restaurant at Gleneagles was almost immediately awarded a Michelin star and four years later it became Scotland's first and only two-star establishment – a thoroughly deserved accolade. Everyone hopes that Andrew's tragically early death will not diminish his legacy there.

My ever-increasing interest in food (and wine) was further enhanced when I became a member of the Scottish Society of Epicureans. This grand organisation was founded over 60 years ago and its members visit dining establishments and give a critique of the menu. It is always a fine dining experience – the menu and wine list are agreed in advance with the chef and sommelier and, on many occasions, we have the exclusive use of the restaurant. The chef joins us after the meal, when the courses are dissected, occasionally in great detail. For example, at Nick Nairn's[10] new Glasgow restaurant the expression on Nick's face was a joy to behold as one elderly member suggested that one of the wines was "perhaps six months too young." At the New Club in Edinburgh a guest sommelier was extolling the virtues of the Chablis when one member said, "Listen, I wouldn't wash my car with Chablis." I was Chairman of the society in 2002-04 and I'm extremely honoured to have been asked to write its history now that I have completed this tome.

Without doubt the greatest influence in developing my culinary skills has been Ted and Adeline. From my earliest visits to California they presented some incredible dishes which over the years I've tried to reproduce. Incidentally they have been greatly assisted by the range of fresh fruit and vegetables there. On my last visit they took me to their local fruit and veg 'shop' - The Berkeley Bowl which is almost the same size as a UK supermarket. For example, around 30 different types of mushrooms are displayed in a unit over 5 yards in length.

Needless to say, when Ted and Adeline visit, we all combine to produce a significant culinary experience. Our last one in Kilmacolm was a seven-course epic with matching wines. The three of us spent an entire morning sourcing ingredients and

---

[9] Andrew Fairlie 1963-2019 chef and restaurateur
[10] Nick Nairn b.1959, Scottish celebrity chef and youngest Scottish chef to win a Michelin star

the afternoon assembling them prior to cooking. The highlight on the occasion was 'The Seven Deadly Sins' course which in fact was seven mini starters combined on one plate. Claire's memory is of the kitchen being completely awash afterwards.

Ted and Adeline continue to produce astonishing creations. Since his cancer diagnosis they entertain his surgeon and oncologist and their wives regularly. For his last effort he reproduced the menu from the first-class section of the Titanic's maiden voyage. His research indicated it consisted of 14 courses but he settled for eight! Ted and I are already planning a menu for his next visit in 2020. This will be the 27 bite dinner in the style of Ferran Adrià's celebrated El Bulli.

The production of cookery books has become an increasingly lucrative field with even minor 'celebrities' penning their own personal recipe book. I have avoided these for the last decade by putting together my own collection of recipes which I have simply cut out from newspapers, colour supplements and magazines and sellotape these onto A4 paper inside a polypocket. I now have 16 volumes with over 12,000 individual recipes.

Fish alone accounts for four volumes. As I write, English asparagus has just come into season and it is one of the highlights of my culinary year to sample the first produce. The season lasts less than two months but I can savour this fabulous vegetable in any of my 90 different recipes for asparagus. I realise that my reader may think I am obsessed with all this. Claire certainly does! With this book nearing completion, I am eagerly looking forward to indexing my entire recipe collection.

I have to confess to another abiding passion – collecting malt whisky. The origins of this go back to 1973 when my first Christmas stocking from Claire contained a miniature bottle. I eventually assembled a miniature collection which was displayed in Tandlehill on a shelf above the panelling in our dining room. Over the years I attended dinners and often was given a miniature of whisky as a gift. Over time whisky dominated the miniature collection. When we left Tandlehill its dominance increased even further when we discovered that, at some stage, one of Claire's cleaning ladies had significantly changed the make-up. The vodka miniatures now contained water only! Currently I only have whisky miniatures and the collection now includes over 100 blends and over 150 malts.

I suppose it is also no surprise that the collection should eventually move from miniatures to the real thing. This started mainly because of Harry Scott who had designed packaging for a number of clients in the whisky industry. When Harry left for Bangkok in 1999, I purchased his small collection of the one-off bottles he had produced for various clients. Little did I realise what this would lead to. I have now extended the collection to over 160 different whiskies, mostly malts, from which I derive enormous pleasure.

I took my interests in food and wine to the ultimate level when I invested in a restaurant business. I had met Liz McAreavey[11] through the Entrepreneurial

---

[11] Liz McAreavey b.1962 Chief Executive at Edinburgh Chamber of Commerce October 2016 -

Exchange. She had just sold a successful catering business and was looking for a further investment opportunity. With Sean Spillane she had decided to create a restaurant business. Her first venture, called 'Tempus', was in the newly opened Centre of Contemporary Arts in Glasgow. Liz had appointed a chairman, Arthur Watt, and also wanted to appoint a non-executive director. My NI contract prevented me from doing this but I made a small investment in the business and so was able to be involved. I was interested in learning how to create a new business. Over time the experience improved my skillset in the areas in raising and managing cash, systems and marketing. I also learned a lot about how not to run a business. Liz was hungry for expansion. Tempus was still experiencing many start up issues when she opened a second restaurant 'Hurricane' in Edinburgh. The same pattern was repeated when she opened another branch of Hurricane in Manchester. In some ways it was unsurprising that the business eventually crashed. Excessive overheads, poor decision making on location, over rapid expansion and cashflow were the main reasons for its demise. I emerged minus my investment, but older and wiser from the experience.

Part VII: Family

Chapter 51   CHARITY

"If you haven't got charity in your heart, you have the worst kind of heart trouble."
Bob Hope[1]

I have been involved in a number of charities and have a number of observations about the sector. First, the level of good in our society, the desire of people to help others, is huge. Second in a supposedly caring society, there is a huge need for more effort. Too often there is a disconnect between how the public purse is spent and the many gaps where there is no public support. The National Lottery was designed to address this in part, but has not totally succeeded. The Grenfell Tower disaster is a prime example of the contrast between the inability of the collective civic body to address even the most basic needs of those affected and the huge groundswell of practical help offered by that same society. My third observation is that charitable effort inevitably involves raising money and whilst a huge number of people unite to do this, a few take it as an opportunity to get their hands on these funds through criminal activity. It is a sad reflection on our society that we now have to regulate such activities extensively. In Scotland we have the Office of the Scottish Charity Regulator (OSCR). My final observation is that whilst there are huge numbers who willingly support the concept of charity, it is surprising that there are equally large numbers who will go to extraordinary lengths to avoid doing so - more of this later. J.K. Rowling[2] through 'Harry Potter' neatly summed up the situation, "It is our choices, Harry, that show what we truly are, far more than our abilities."[3]

I have been directly involved in three charities and also support a number of others. I became involved in Childline in the mid-1980s and sat on its Scotland Committee. Esther Rantzen,[4] the founder of Childline, is an excellent example of someone who has devoted a huge amount of time to a very worthy cause and she uses her high profile to reveal the extent of child abuse in our society. Esther was one of the first people of our generation to take a taboo subject and force society to confront it.

Harry Scott chaired the Scottish Committee of Childline and its main objective was to raise funds to finance a call centre and offices in Glasgow to assist and provide support for children being mentally or physically abused at home but with no one to share their problem with. Harry was a man of considerable ambition and through him the Committee had the vision to organise a number of lavish, high profile events, always premium priced, which raised considerable sums for the charity. Harry's mission statement was typical of the man, "I haven't got time to piss around organising a load of mince." The Childline Balls and Dinners became some of the

---

[1] Bob Hope KBE KC*SG KSS 1903-2003, British-born American stand-up comedian and actor
[2] J.K. Rowling CH OBE FRSL FRCPE FRSE, b.1965, British novelist, philanthropist and screenwriter
[3] 'Harry Potter and the Chamber of Secrets' Copyright © J.K. Rowling 1998
[4] Dame Esther Rantzen DBE, b. 1940, journalist, TV presenter, campaigner

biggest social events in Glasgow, attended by hundreds of people, with each event raising around £40,000 in the 1980s.

A major source of funds in events like these is the auction. One thing we learned was the need to secure a signature of intent to purchase after accepting a final auction bid. Many people wake up the morning after an auction horrified to be told (usually by their spouse) that they had successfully acquired something at a charity dinner, usually at an outrageous price. However they honour their commitment, but at one Charity Ball we had someone who successfully bid £3,000 for a painting in front of 500 people and tried to deny all knowledge of having done so the next day. Childline eventually got its money!

Those years on the Childline Committee were great fun. The hard work involved in running a successful event was made the more worthwhile by not just supporting a cause but also hugely enjoying the process. As a new arrival in Glasgow I also learned the great value of auctioning signed Rangers and Celtic footballs. Any half decent auctioneer could raise large sums of money from them and provide the audience with huge entertainment at the same time. Prior to one event, we were assembling all the items for the auction when someone idly picked up the Celtic match ball and examined it in some detail. As Scott Stern had provided both balls, Harry was asked whether this might be an old Celtic ball, as Celtic's current star Paulo Di Canio's signature was missing. Harry demanded to see the ball, examined it and, quick as a flash, took out his black pen and scrawled 'P Di Canio' onto the ball. End of problem!

I also had the privilege of chairing Saints and Sinners from 2009-11. Ironically, as with the Press Fund, I ended up being Chairman without ever having sat on the committee. I succeeded Fred MacAuley[5], who vaguely explained that the incoming Chairman wanted to postpone his term of office temporarily because of business commitments. I was parachuted in to fill the gap.

The Saints and Sinners Club of Scotland was established in 1964 and the inaugural lunch was held in Edinburgh on 8th January 1965, with Lord Rosebery[6] as its first Chairman. Until his death in 2018, Sir Eric Yarrow[7] was its oldest surviving member. The concept originated in the United States, where Bing Crosby[8] was a founding member, before a London branch was created, followed by one in Scotland. In 2017 the Club raised £120,000, which was distributed to 135 small Scottish charities. Membership is limited to 100 and over the years the club has raised over £2 million for worthy causes. It was recently aptly described thus, "They function as a stock exchange of good companionship, where the shares are always good value.

As with all charity committees, the key tasks facing a new chair are to ensure that the organisation is fit for purpose, that there is a proper succession plan in place, that the key office holders (usually Treasurer and Secretary) are effective and that there is a

---

[5] Fred MacAuley, b.1956, Scottish comedian and presenter
[6] Neil Primrose, 7th Earl of Rosebery, 3rd Earl of Midlothian, b. 1929
[7] Sir Eric Yarrow, 1920-2018, third Baronet MBE DL FRSE, Chairman, Yarrows of Scotstoun, President (1987-2018)
[8] Bing Crosby, 1903-1977, American singer and actor

system in place to ensure regular turnover of members to avoid the committee becoming static. Another important task is to look at how the programme generates the desired funds. Saints and Sinners had a well-established programme - Glasgow and Edinburgh lunches, a golf day (alternately at Prestwick and Muirfield), a clay pigeon shoot at Dunkeld and a race meeting (usually at Hamilton). These events worked extremely effectively but attendance at the lunch meetings was declining and, in terms of fundraising, had fallen well behind the other events. The root cause of this was, sadly, an ageing membership who no longer wanted to host a table of guests at lunch but still wanted to contribute to and be part of the club. As membership was limited to 100, it required some innovation to solve the issue and I eventually persuaded the Committee to introduce a new category of membership - Life Membership for those over 65 who, for a reduced subscription, could enjoy membership in perpetuity. This enabled the club to recruit new members who could play a more active role on the fundraising front. I also persuaded the Committee to take a hard look at the rest of the membership and their contributions and purged a few 'inactive' members from the ranks, thus releasing a few more places.

The second area that I tackled, somewhat controversially, was fundraising at the actual lunches. Unlike some other charities, Saints and Sinners had a tradition whereby there would be only one 'hit' for donations at the lunch. This was in the form of 'Heads or Tails,' decided on the spin of a coin, with a single winner eventually emerging. For this a donation of £10, later rising to £20, was requested, but the Treasurer Graham Simmers[9] told me that by no means everyone took part. I persuaded the committee, not without some serious objections, to raise the amount to £40. My argument was that if you wanted to attend such a major social occasion and enjoy the kudos of being a member of Saints and Sinners, you simply had to stick your hand in your pocket a little deeper for the privilege. Under the stewardship of David MacRobert[10] and latterly Alan Thornton[11] the method of securing the £40 was refined. Members were asked to stand, "We're now going to play a game of heads or tails. If you wish to participate you are required to donate £40 to the worthy cause of Saints and Sinners. If you don't wish to do so, you may sit down." After some grumbling from the members, this format is now well established and the lunches now make a sensible contribution to the overall fundraising target.

I have huge admiration for high profile individuals like Esther Rantzen who donate their time to charitable causes. During my time in Reading I organised a large-scale promotion in association with a major car dealership. They hosted a reception to launch the promotion and Ernie Wise[12] attended the function. To secure his services, we made a reasonably substantial donation to a charity. A most unassuming man, Wise told me that he donated around 20 days per year to such charitable causes – quite something considering he was at the height of his fame.

---

[9] Graham Simmers CBE, b. 1935, CA, S&S Treasurer, Captain, The R&A 2001-02

[10] David MacRobert, b. 1953, former Partner, MacRoberts Solicitors

[11] Alan Thornton, b. 1956, owner, Caledonian Industries Ltd.

[12] Ernie Wise OBE 1925-99, English comedian and one half of the comedy duo Morecambe and Wise, a national institution on British television

I had the privilege of meeting Joan Collins[13] at a gala performance of Follies in 2005. She attended the function as a supporter of the NSPCC, and, with auctioneer Christopher Biggins posed wearing a high-quality faux diamond bracelet. This was put up for auction with the highest bidder securing not just the bracelet but also meeting and having a picture with Collins herself. I ended up as the highest bidder in a keenly contested auction. Immediately afterwards Collins rolled up her other sleeve to reveal a second bracelet which Biggins then persuaded the second highest bidder to purchase. Further raising of both sleeves revealed several more bracelets on each which Biggins again skilfully persuaded the next highest bidders to purchase – quite the cleverest and most successful piece of auctioneering I have ever witnessed. Collins herself has worked with the NSPCC, Breast Cancer Research and is a patron of the children's hospice charity, Shooting Star Chase.

[13] Dame Joan Collins DBE b.1933, English actress, author and columnist

Chapter 52   ROYALTY AND THE REPTILES

"I would like to go to Russia very much, although the bastards murdered half my family." HRH Prince Philip, Duke of Edinburgh[1]

The relationship between the Royal Family and the Press has not always been an easy one. It is a marriage of convenience dependent on a mutual understanding of each other's roles and needs. It was the Duke of Edinburgh who first christened the Press 'the Reptiles'. I was first introduced to Prince Philip at a Newspaper Society Lunch in London with the words "And this is Colin McClatchie, who heads Rupert Murdoch's newspaper empire in Scotland." Philip looked me straight in the eye, said, "Hard luck" and moved swiftly on. Such brevity is apparently commonplace with the Royals. Ben Fogle[2], knowing for several months that he was to meet the Queen[3], deliberated on what he would say, narrowing it down to four possible topics. To his opening line, "Terribly cold ma'am," HM replied, "Warmer than last year, though we could do with a little rain," and moved on.

As a small boy I waved to the Queen Mother[4] passing through Portadown in the mid-1950s and was thrilled when she waved back! Since then I confess that I have been an unashamedly avid monarchist. Regardless of the individual members' personal idiosyncrasies, collectively the institution is admired throughout the world and delivers fantastic value to the country at a relatively small cost.

Contrast my viewpoint with that of Liz Lochhead[5]. Sitting beside her at the Chancellor's Dinner at Glasgow University recently, we had a most agreeable conversation. Prior to the speeches, we were asked to stand for the Loyal Toast. She pointedly refused to stand, muttering about her opposition to the Royal Family. Although I respected her opinion, I considered her actions to be an appalling display of bad manners, not only for the occasion but also to the host. When I questioned her about her position afterwards, she used words like "privilege, waste of money, class." From an SNP perspective it is interesting that Alex Salmond, when First Minister, went out of his way to reassure Scots that the monarchy would be safe in an independent Scotland.

The longevity of the the Royal Family is impressive. There cannot be too many like the Duke of Edinburgh, who decided to 'retire' at the age of 96. When the announcement was made, the Press went into overdrive about Philip's long history of 'foot-in-mouth disease'. Some feel that he has elevated tactlessness to an art form. Philip himself describes it as, "Dontopedalogy. It is the science of opening your mouth and putting your foot in it, a science which I have practised for many years."

---

[1] HRH Prince Philip, Duke of Edinburgh b. 1921. Born in Greece, Consort of Queen Elizabeth II
[2] Ben Fogle, b.1973, English writer, broadcaster and adventurer
[3] HM Queen Elizabeth II b.1926, first child of HM King George VI and HM Queen Elizabeth
[4] HM Queen Elizabeth, the Queen Mother 1900-2002
[5] Liz Lochhead, b.1947, Scottish poet, playwright and broadcaster. Makar 2011-16.

Usually people don't stay offended too long about Philip's statements. Amongst the classics are:

"The Philippines must be half empty- you're all here running the NHS."

"If you stay here much longer, you'll be slitty eyed." (To a British student in China)

"There are a lot of your family in tonight." (To Mr Atul Patel at a Buckingham Palace reception for British Indians)

"You are a woman, aren't you? (to a Kenyan woman)

"I declare this thing open, whatever it is." (Annex to City Hall in Vancouver)

"How do you keep the natives off the booze long enough to get them through the test?" (Oban driving instructor)

"You managed not to get eaten then." (To a British student in Papua New Guinea)

"If it's got four legs, and it's not a chair, if it's got two wings and flies, and is not an aeroplane, and if it swims and is not a submarine, the Cantonese will eat it."

"How many of the buggers did you have to shoot for lunch then?" (eating venison at a lunch in Oxford and noticing deer outside)

"What do you gargle with – pebbles?" (to Tom Jones)

Philip's utterances over the years filled the pages of a highly amusing book published in 2002[6].

My favourite Philip anecdote concerns two meetings 16 years apart with players from the Scottish Rugby team. During both the Rugby World Cups in Wales in 1999 and England in 2015 a reception was held for the players. In 1999 Philip approached a group of Scottish players and during the conversation they told him how proud they were that the SRU Patron was the Princess Royal[7]. "Alas," said Philip, "If it doesn't fart or eat hay, she's not interested." Fast forward, same reception 16 years later, with a different group of Scotland players. Philip asked if Anne was still Patron of the SRU. "Indeed, she is, sir, but alas we don't eat hay." Quick as a flash Philip responded "You must fart a lot then."

I have been privileged to have been presented to several members of the Royal Family over the years. Firstly, Princess Anne, who opened the new Daily Record Building at Anderson Quay in 1971, long before my time there. As the final arrangements for the visit were being made, protocol required that a lavatory be available for Princess Anne at a certain point in her tour through the building. Unfortunately, there was only a Gents' there and Vic Horwood refused to remodel it for the occasion. As a compromise the urinals were removed. Some years later

---

[6] 'Prince Philip: Wise Words and Golden Gaffs' Phil Dampier, Ashley Walton, 2012, Barzipan Publishing
[7] HRH Princess Anne the Princess Royal, KG, KT, GCVO, QSO, CD, b.1950, second child and only daughter of HM Queen Elizabeth II

Princess Anne attended a performance of Bill Bryden's[8] 'The Ship', sponsored by The Daily Record. The Board were presented to her and, just before my turn, Kevin McMahon whispered to me "Ask her about the urinals and whether she noticed that they had been removed." I also hosted Princess Anne at the International Show Jumping Masters in 1994 which was sponsored by the Daily Record.

I met Prince Charles[9] on a number of occasions at Holyrood, at the Irish Embassy and, on a particularly enjoyable occasion, at Clarence House, when he presented the Prince of Wales Medal for Arts Philanthropy to several recipients, one of whom was Carol Grigor[10], a particularly generous benefactor of Scottish Opera. The event was hosted by Joanna Lumley[11] and, like many others in the room, I made a beeline for her afterwards and, having elbowed several people out of the way, I was chatting to her along with another man. We were both charmed in spades by Ms. Lumley and when she left we both confessed what big fans we were. It was only then that I realised that my fellow admirer was George Osborne[12], then Shadow Chancellor of the Exchequer.

As Chairman of Scottish Opera, I met our patron the Duchess of Gloucester many times. She took a great interest in the company and, during my seven years as Chairman, was a frequent visitor to Scotland and to our productions. I was particularly impressed by her in 2014 at a reception in Buckingham Palace, hosted by the Queen and Prince Philip for the Irish Community in the UK, shortly before President Higgins' state visit to the UK. During the reception I felt a tap on my shoulder and was asked to come to meet the Duchess, who had found out that I was attending the event. Being presented to the Queen that evening was one of the highlights of my life. I was introduced as Chairman of Scottish Opera and, being an Irish evening, she was momentarily startled and looked at me, "Scottish Opera?" "Yes ma'am," I said, "The Chairman of Scottish Opera is an Irishman" Beaming smile from Her Majesty as I passed on. Ditto with Prince Philip – no mention of Rupert this time.

The proudest moment of all, not just for me but for my family, was my award of a CBE in the Birthday Honours List 2017. The award was for services to music and to the community in the West of Scotland. We all looked forward to the investiture which took place in February 2018 at Buckingham Palace. Claire, Amanda and Milena attended the ceremony and saw me presented with my CBE by Prince Charles. One could not fail to be impressed by the whole affair, an example of British ceremony at its very best in pomp, tradition and perfect organisation. The Prince of Wales was most impressive. With more than 80 honours to award and clearly well-briefed, he spoke to every recipient, in my case for two and a half minutes. We talked about Scottish Opera, funding for the Arts, the long-term trend of reduced

---

[8] Bill Bryden CBE, b.1942, British stage and film director and screenwriter.
[9] HRH Prince Charles, Prince of Wales, b. 1948, heir apparent to the British throne as the eldest child of HM Queen Elizabeth II. Longest serving heir apparent in British history.
[10] Carol Grigor (formerly Hogel) CBE, FRSE, b.1945, American philanthropist and concert pianist
[11] Joanna Lumley OBE, FRGS, b.1946, model, actress and activist
[12] The Rt. Hon. George Osborne CH, PC, b.1971, Chancellor of the Exchequer 2010-16, Editor London Evening Standard 2017-

public funding and philanthropy. He also mentioned Carol Grigor, even though it was over five years since he had presented her with her award. All in all, it was a fantastic occasion followed by an excellent lunch at the Goring Hotel, at which Kumar and Tarryn joined us. By the end, all of us agreed that it had been one of the best days of our lives.

God save the Queen!

Buckingham Palace Reception with Her Majesty The Queen, March 2014
Picture: British Ceremonial Arts

European Open Pro-Am, K Club, 2007 with l-r: CMcC, Oliver Keenaghan, Paul McGinley and Tom Mooney.

'The Magnificent Seven' Algarve 2018 l-r: Colin Colverd, Tom Mooney, David Crow, CMcC, Brett Lawrence, David Smith and Peter Hepworth

Close Family, l-r: Sam and Niki (Moore), Ted and Adeline, CMcC and Claire

Milena and Kumar, Wedding Day, 20th September 2014

Amanda and Piers - Engagement July 2018

Piers - First England try, Argentina vs England, Second Test 17th June 2017,
and inset with Eddie Jones

Stewart Moore celebrates his famous try. Australia vs Ireland Under 20s World Cup
Argentina June 2019

Tarryn, Kumar and Milena 2019

Tarryn acquiring early information on 'The Troubles'

Investiture by Prince Charles, February 2018
Picture: British Ceremonial Arts

Outside Buckingham Palace with Amanda, Claire and Milena, February 2018

Picture: Palace Photos

Chapter 53   REFLECTIONS ON THE FUTURE

"A week is a long time in politics." *Attributed to Harold Wilson c.1964*
"The weak are a long time in politics." *In the spirit of Theresa May[1] c.2019*

Well, that's it! A lifetime condensed into 417 pages. Have I covered everything? Not quite. Got to keep something back for the second edition. Is it completely accurate? I think so, although I have occasionally worried about my memory and so I have tried to validate everything. Fortunately, in the words of a famous agony aunt[2], I've had very few CRAFT moments ("Can't Remember A F***ing Thing!"), although I'm not sure that I necessarily agree with her definition of the five stages of adulthood "Lager, Aga, Saga, Viagra and Gaga" – not yet anyway.

So what of the future? Average life expectancy for men and women is now 79.2 and 82.9 years respectively[3]. These figures had been steadily growing for a number of years, until they peaked in 2016 in two countries. One was the opioid-ridden USA and the other was the UK. I can't say that I lose any sleep over this, but as I get older the often taboo subjects of death and how we die are inevitably of much greater interest.

The statistics themselves are the consequence of significant advances in medical science, with more effective drugs and much more education about health and lifestyle. The downside is that they now have created an increasingly ageing population. There is now major debate on care, on death and, in particular, how to ease pain in the lead-up to death. In his recent book[4] Richard Holloway[5], who has previously backed attempts to legalise assisted suicide, advances the proposition that increasing longevity is having "a profoundly distorting effect on the balance of society as a whole." A tendency to overtreat patients leaves some in a "marginalized existence, whose sole purpose is staying alive and keeps too many people alive long after any pleasure or meaning has gone from their lives." He concludes "Care of the elderly is close to swamping the resources of the NHS, turning it into an agency for the postponement of death, rather than the enhancement of life."

Many doctors are now questioning existing protocols, whereby elderly patients are taken into hospital for often futile and invasive emergency treatment, rather than allowed to die peacefully in their own homes. Recent Marie Curie research shows that the average person spends 23 days in an emergency hospital bed during the last year of their life and is taken to hospital on more than one occasion. I recently analysed a series of newspaper death notices and noted that the vast majority of people are listed as having "died peacefully". This may well be the case at the point of death, but most evidence suggests quite the opposite in the lead-up to it. A widow recently wrote[6], "Craig was only 45 when cancer took over his entire body. It was horrific to watch him suffer. No amount of palliative care could help him. He begged to go to Switzerland but sadly it was too late. I don't believe anyone should have to go through what Craig did." In some areas the medical profession is suggesting that a better outcome would be for patients to be allowed to die at home, with nature taking its course

---

[1] The Rt Hon Theresa May b.1956 Prime Minister 2016-19
[2] Virginia Ironside b.1945, British journalist, agony aunt and author
[3] Office of National Statistics
[4] Waiting for the Last Bus, Reflections on Life and Death, Richard Holloway 2018 Canongate Press.
[5] Richard Holloway FRSE, b.1933. Scottish writer, broadcaster and cleric, Bishop of Edinburgh 1986-2000
[6] Lisa Wilson, Cumbernauld, The Herald 3rd April 2019

and palliative care improving those final days, rather than being over-treated in hospital. However, there is an increasing desire to be released as quickly and as painlessly as possible, with little point in prolonging terminal and, in many cases, extremely painful illnesses. A recent poll[7] found that nine out of 10 people in Scotland support legalising assisted dying. Campaigners want Scotland to adopt legislation based on the Oregon model in the United States, where patients with six months to live can ask their doctor to prescribe a lethal dose of medication. It is then up to the patient to administer it to end their life early. Yet all this is a subject on which the government, the legal system and the medical profession have maintained entrenched positions. As I write, a newspaper[8] carries a highly predictable headline "Terminally ill man loses court bid for assisted death." Supreme Court justices rejected his bid to appeal against an earlier ruling in his fight over current legislation, which prevents him from being helped to die. The court declined permission for an appeal, saying that only Parliament can change the law. All this surely points to having more joined-up thinking to find a better outcome. I make no apologies for raising what some may consider a morbid subject. I intend to live the rest of my life to the full and I have no fear of death but, when the time comes, I would prefer it to be truly peaceful. As Spike Milligan[9] put it, "I'm not afraid of dying – I just don't want to be there when it happens."

I now reflect on what I have to look forward to. With knowledge expanding exponentially, we increasingly know less – a rather depressing thought. The impact of this on the younger generations might be that historical perspective will become less important. This might, for example, explain some of the voting patterns in recent elections throughout the world, which have greatly puzzled political analysts – it might even explain the election of Donald Trump!

In the late 1990s I attended a series of newspaper conferences in America. At each one there was a Futurist, who would predict what was going to happen in 20 – 25 years time. When I look back at my notes, a common theme was predictions about the new world of information technology, computers and software. Much of this came to pass and at times massively disrupted traditional industries. The first digital camera was invented in 1975. Some 20 years later, Kodak still employed 175,000 people and sold 85% of the world's photo paper, yet within a few years their business model disappeared and they went bankrupt. The world of software also resulted in massive changes. Uber - just a software tool - doesn't own any cars, but is now the world's biggest taxi company. Similarly, Airbnb is now the world's biggest hotel company without owning any property.

The pace of change can be variable, but even in the 1970s a Futurist at Stanford University was establishing Amara's[10] Law, which applied to the development of technology. It stated that we tend to overestimate the effect of a technology at the start and underestimate its effect in the long term. The best example of Amara's Law occurred when Paul Krugman[11] wrote in 1998 "By 2005 or so, it will become clear that the internet's impact on the economy has been no greater than the fax machine. As the rate of technological change in computing slows, the number of jobs for IT specialists will decelerate and then actually turn down. Ten years from now the phrase 'information technology will sound silly." I heard Krugman

---

[7] Populus poll 2019, commissioned by Dignity in Dying Scotland
[8] The Herald, 26th November 2018
[9] Spike Milligan KBE 1918-2002, British-Irish comedian, writer, playwright and actor
[10] Roy Amara 1925-2007, American researcher, scientist and futurist
[11] Paul Krugman b.1953, distinguished Professor of Economics, Graduate Centre of the City University of New York. Winner of Nobel Prize for Economics 2008

speak in Glasgow[12] in 2003 and his thoughts on the Scottish economy were fascinating. Conversely his thoughts on the internet were somewhat wide of the mark.

So, what does the future hold? Undoubtedly it will be challenging – a world with more people but decreasing resources. The world's population today is 7.6 billion, but is expected to rise to 10 billion by 2052[13]. Oil, gas, water, fish, trees – even healthy air – are already in short supply in some parts of the world. The lesson in all this is that many of our resources are finite, the price we pay for them is increasing and ultimately we may have to restrict their consumption.

Yet the future is also tremendously exciting. We live in a world with the potential of driverless cars, drones and flying taxis. This is the world of algorithms, artificial intelligence, autonomy, Big Data, Deepmind, Machine-Learning, Neural network, Natural language, Robotics and Watson – and that's just for starters.

The potential of driverless cars is enormous. In 2017 Singapore started trialling driverless taxis, while Scotland plans to offer the first driverless bus services between Fife and Edinburgh by 2021. Car ownership will eventually become unnecessary. Instead we will summon a driverless car to take us to our destination, without needing to park it. Significantly fewer cars will mean fewer parking spaces needed, particularly in cities. There are many social benefits. By taking humans out of the equation, with no excessive speed, or the influence of alcohol, texting and the other risks, it is estimated that road deaths could reduce by 1 million per year. Sweden is already targeting zero road deaths by 2025.

Is all this necessarily going to make the world a better place? I have major concerns on several aspects of our society. One of them is government, which has become pervasive and tries increasingly to regulate more areas of our lives - and at enormous cost. My view is that government is rapidly approaching the point at which its costs are too great. In 1776 Adam Smith in "The Wealth of Nations[14]" reasoned that governments "are themselves always and without any exception the greatest spendthrifts in the society." As well as central government, in post devolution Scotland we have a separate Parliament, 32 local authorities, 23 NHS bodies, 10 universities, 48 colleges and more than 100 other bodies and quangos. We have become a society with more takers than givers, with a government which blindly promotes even greater spending. This is despite the fact that we have an extremely narrow tax base, with only 17,500 top bracket tax payers, higher rates of taxation than the rest of the UK and – what a surprise – decreasing inward investment. Oh, yes, and we also want to become independent! As Adam Smith warned, the money is in danger of running out and the cupboard is bare.

Circa 1790 Alexander Fraser Tytler[15] is credited with the prediction that democracies are destined to fail, with a life of 200 years at most. Failure occurs when a majority of voters support the candidate who promises them the greatest benefit from the public treasury. Without exception, the promised benefits reach an unsustainable level, the democracy collapses and is replaced with a dictatorship. How apt is this today? Well, here are three recent headlines from The Times: 'PM woos voters with high-speed railway to Sydney and tax cuts.' The first paragraph reads, "Australia's struggling centre right government has unveiled a free-spending budget before next months election that offers tax cuts to more

---

[12] Fraser of Allander Series 2003.
[13] United Nations Population Fund
[14] Adam Smith, 1723-1790, Scottish economist, philosopher and author.
[15] Alexander Fraser Tytler FRSE 1747-1813, Lord Woodhouselee. Scottish advocate, judge, writer and historian. Professor of Universal History and Greek and Roman Antiquities, University of Edinburgh.

than half the population." (3rd April 2019). The second headline is 'Modi promises £230 billion to poor farmers days before poll opens,' with the first paragraph, "India's Prime Minister has promised a £230 billion package to debt-ridden farmers in a late appeal for their support in the world's biggest election." (9th April 2019). The third headline, "Pressure grows on Macron to cut tax," with the first paragraph, "President Macron is poised to give a second wave of reforms after voters demanded honesty and lower taxes in an un-precedented consultation." (9th April 2019). Perish the thought, but could the actions of Jeremy Corbyn[16] and Nicola Sturgeon bring Tytler's predictions even nearer?

And yet I have some nagging doubts about those with the greatest wealth. Sadly, there seems to be an increasing reluctance to pay in full the taxes that the state levies. It seems that the more people earn, the more they try to shield their wealth from the tax authorities. Within the accounting profession there is an industry whose specific objective is to minimize tax. At its heart this sometimes means little more than coming up with ingenious ways of avoiding the taxes that our system deems fair. This exists at both corperate and individual level. Some years ago, the Republic of Ireland came up with a novel scheme to tackle this by publicly naming and shaming those caught deliberately avoiding their tax liabilities. In the UK there is a suggestion that the Honours system now looks for evidence of tax evasion. If found, the honour is blocked. My suspicions are perhaps most raised by the recent release of the 'Panama' papers suggesting widespread tax avoidance.

Another thread in the argument is executive pay. A recent article in The Guardian[17] highlights the issue of ballooning executive pay and increasing inequality. In the UK the average pay ratio between FTSE100 Chief Executives and their staff has gone from 20:1 in the 1980s to 129:1 in 2016. In the US the situation is even more extreme with the equivalent ratios being 50:1 in the 1980s and 312:1 in 2017.

Equally depressing is the fact that the culture of philanthropy appears to have failed to take root in the UK. The most recent Sunday Times Giving List[18] revealed that only one in 14 donated more than the previous year, despite their wealth growing by £113 billion. The number donating more than 1% has reduced by one quarter in the past two years. Contrast the US experience where Mackenzie Bezos pledged to donate half of her $37 billion divorce settlement to charity.

Perhaps we need to encourage those who have benefitted from successfully creating wealth to accept as a civic duty the responsibility of giving back – this might be a way of reducing the costs of providing local services. The Prince of Wales recently suggested that we pick up litter in a new National Day devoted to cleaning up Britain. The principle of community spirit and self-help could become a model for the future, with applications in many other areas. The Daily Mail was convinced of the merits of this and within three months signed up almost 550,000 volunteers to the cause. The scale of this remarkable achievement may help reduce the costs of our increasingly expensive public services.

And then there is Brexit, which was supposed to be about sense and sensibility but in reality has been all about pride and prejudice. In my view David Cameron was guilty of terrible political judgement when, panicked at the rise of UKIP, he abrogated Parliament's responsibility and allowed a referendum on the subject. After such a narrow Leave majority in the referendum (52:48%) it was always going to be difficult to achieve any form of

---

[16] Jeremy Corbyn b.1949, Leader of the Labour Party since 2015
[17] Richard Partington, 'Ballooning Executive Pay Is At Last Coming Under Scrutiny' The Guardian 24th April 2019
[18] Andrew Ellison, 'Charity Begins And Ends At Home For Richest One Thousand' The Times 13th May 2019

consensus. It therefore seems incredulous that Theresa May's government only turned at the very last moment to cross party talks to try to achieve this consensus. It certainly demonstrated poor leadership and judgement so it is unsurprising that May eventually had to fall on her sword. MPs themselves also emerge with little credit, unable to agree on anything amongst themselves. Humility is such a rare quality in politicians. On the Tory side many of the MPs, particularly those in the cabinet, were also jostling for the leadership of the party itself. Does this not amply demonstrate Rochefoucauld's[19] famous maxim, "the name and pretense of virtue is as serviceable to self-interest as our real vices." Is it little wonder that Members of Parliament are now among the least trusted of all people in public life. I chaired three organizations, between them for a total of fourteen years, and never once required a vote to agree a decision – it was always achieved through consensus. Oh, that our politicians might behave the same way! MPs must surely seriously look at their behaviour post Brexit yet I fear that Parliamentary democracy might be the biggest loser in all this.

It will be interesting to hear Cameron's views on all this when his memoirs are published at the end of 2019. One comedian has suggested it will be entitled 'Swineshead Revisited'. For my part, I was a reluctant Remainer. The day after the referendum I woke up to discover that I shared my country with a huge number of simply awful people who have become even worse ever since. I often wonder if our second referendum should be about these people leaving instead?

Finally, I turn to social media. This is one of the greatest transformational phenomena and one that has radically changed our lives in the past 20 years. Facebook alone has 2.2 billion people clicking, sharing and commenting every month. In the UK, a recent OFCOM survey suggests that children have become such screen addicts, they are abandoning their friends and hobbies. Researchers found, "under-fives spend an hour and 16 minutes a day online.

Social media now presents unheard of opportunities for interaction and communication. With innovation, however, comes responsibility and there is increasing concern about its activities on two fronts – competition and reputation. First, competition. In the US Elizabeth Warren[20], a potential Democrat candidate for President demanded the break up of Amazon, Apple, Google and Facebook. "We need to stop this generation of big tech companies from throwing around their political power to shape the rules in their favour, and their economic power to snuff out or buy every potential predator."[21] "They have too much power over our society. They have bulldozed competition, used our private information for profit and tilted the playing field against everyone else."[22]

Second, the problem facing Facebook, Instagram and WhatsApp is perhaps the biggest hurdle of all – reputation. The main charge is that the fundamental right of privacy is not being protected. The UK Government is currently preparing a White Paper that is expected to put pressure on social media companies to take responsibility for extremist content. That might also make them liable for defamatory comment, just as for print media.

The other major charge against social media is that it has encouraged and facilitated high levels of personal abuse. Many in public life now have to endure continuous hateful commentary and threats. Many have sought help as a result and some have withdrawn from

---

[19] Francois de La Rochefoucauld 1613-80, French author of maxims and memoirs
[20] Elizabeth Warren b.1949, American politician and academic, Senior Senator, Massachusetts 2013 -
[21] Sunday Times 17th January 2019
[22] Sunday Times 10th March 2019

Twitter because of it. Twitter was recently described as "the equivalent of dipping your private parts in honey and exposing them to angry bees."[23]

I cite the recent experience of a friend, an owner of a small business for over 30 years. The business has been exemplary in motivating and looking after its staff and recently it introduced smart staff uniforms. A new 17-year-old member of staff refused to comply with this and resigned. She was not required to work her two-week notice period but paid in full. What followed was a series of inaccurate and vitriolic attacks online from both her and her mother. Rather frighteningly, over a three-week period over 4,000 others joined in, physically threatening the owner and his family and in some cases suggesting that people firebomb his premises. The police were actively involved and offered considerable physical and emotional support, but admitted that they were powerless to prevent the social media commentary. The owner described it as the most frightening three weeks of his entire life. We have a society in which people can behave in this fashion yet many find it acceptable.

The last words on the subject come from one of Mark Zuckerberg's[24] original mentors. In a recent book[25] Roger McNamee writes, "Internet platforms insinuated themselves into our lives through a combination of compelling value and clever appeals to the weakest element of user psychology. In less than a generation, these platforms have made themselves indispensable. We put tech on a pedestal. That was a mistake. We let the industry make and enforce its own rules. That was also a mistake. We trusted them not to hurt users or democracy. That was a disastrous mistake which we have not yet corrected."

However, I wonder if poor behaviour by individuals is any different to that of large organisations. Take the banks as an example. They lend us funds at substantial interest rates whilst giving almost no return on the funds we give them (deposits). Service is provided through a network of high street branches, now closing down rapidly, particularly in rural communities and small towns. Instead they provide a cash machine to enable us to access our own money. Now the long-term plans are to charge us for even this service. At least they are consistent in their avarice and lack of service. In days gone by the formula was much simpler but essentially the same, "Open at nine, borrow at three, lend at nine and close at three." Isn't life grand?

Enough of my musings - I hope some of them have given you food for thought. I also hope that you have found my story interesting and, more importantly, amusing. I have had a great life with, I hope, much more to come, but as with everyone there have been ups and downs, sadness, challenges and setbacks. The latter do not in any way negate the joy and fulfilment that I have experienced. Paul Anka[26] wrote a wonderful song, 'My Way'. Amanda was going to use it as part of the soundtrack on a video she made to celebrate my 70th birthday but decided the first two lines were perhaps not the most appropriate, referring, as they did, to the end being near and facing the final curtain. The song nevertheless beautifully illustrates my wonderful life – a full life that I did my way.

---

[23] Parliamentary Health and Wellbeing Service 2018
[24] Mark Zuckerberg b.1984, American technology entrepreneur. Co-founder, Chairman and CEO, Facebook
[25] Zucked; Waking Up to the Facebook Catastrophe, Roger McNamee, HarperCollins 2019
[26] Paul Anka b.1941, Canadian singer, songwriter and actor. Anka wrote the lyrics for this song based on a French song called 'Comme d'habitude' recorded by Claude Francois. Anka heard it in France and wrote 'My Way' when he returned to New York. He gave it to Frank Sinatra who recorded it on the 30th December 1968 – just over 50 years ago. Claude Francois, Giles Thibout, Jacques Revaux and Anka are all credited as the songwriters and the lyrics are by Warner Chappell Music, France.

Finally, thank you for buying my book. Please also tell your friends about it!

I leave you with the words of a traditional Irish blessing.

May the road rise to meet you,
May the wind be ever at your back,
May the sun shine warm upon your face,
May the rains fall soft upon your fields
And until we meet again

May God hold you in the palm of his hand.

Colin.

ACKNOWLEDGEMENTS

No endeavour can ever succeed without a tremendous team effort from people who are expert at what they do and this memoir is no exception. A large number of people have helped me in both researching and writing this book and I sincerely thank them all.

Derek Currie, David Girdwood, Michael Graham, Tom Mooney, Kevin McMahon, Jack Perry, Alex Reedijk, the late Dr. Ian Robertson and Sir John Ward read parts of the various drafts and made many helpful comments and corrections.

My brother Ted and particularly my sister Niki were extremely helpful in putting together both sides of the family history. Niki has shown great forbearance in dealing with my frequent phone calls over three years, diligently providing the answer to each query. I am also grateful for contributions from Diane and David Stockholm, Norah and John Crowe and John Sheehan.

The greatest contribution came from my wife and editor Claire and Amanda. Claire has manfully tackled many, many drafts and interpreted what I've been trying to say. My most sincere thanks for this Herculean task.

Thanks also to my two other helpers, Jamie Eatock and latterly Nina Mackie. They typed up and shaped a never-ending flow of thoughts – most of them written but sometimes delivered on 'the hoof'. A special word of thanks to Colin Fyfe from Colcom, my I.T. specialist, who kept my computer systems functioning through sometimes testing times.

Major appreciation to all those who in their own way contributed to my research. They are: Iain Callaghan, Joe Cassells, Colin Crosby, Hugh Clark, Margaret Clarke, Ed Curran, Fred Hallsworth, the late Liam Kane, Baroness Helen Liddell, Roy Lyttle, Scott McCulloch, Gerry Power, Ian Steele, Malcolm Speed, Gordon Terris, Bruce Waddell and Ann Wood.

I am also grateful to Mark Sweeney, Picture Editor, The Scottish Sun for his help with many of the pictures from my News International Period.

Finally, a special thanks to David Willis and Andy Mushet of William Anderson and Sons Ltd. Printers, for all the help and advice provided to turn this from a manuscript into the finished article.

APPENDIX 1

MCCLATCHIE, Colin James Stewart, CBE, FRSE. Chairman, Prescient, since 2007; Trustee, RSE Scotland Foundation, since 2017; Public Interest Member, Council, Institute of Chartered Accountants Scotland, since 2017; Vice-President, Scottish Opera, since 2015; Member, Global Irish Network, since 2010; b. 1.1.49, Belfast; m., Claire McConaghy; 2 d. Educ. Coleraine Academical Institution; Queen's University, Belfast. Senior Management Positions, Thomson Regional Newspapers, Belfast, Newcastle, Reading, Edinburgh, 1971-84; Circulation/Marketing Director, Scottish Daily Record and Sunday Mail Limited, 1984-94 (and Managing Director, Maxwell Free Newspapers Ltd, 1990-93); Marketing Consultant 1995; General Manager, News International Newspapers (Scotland) Ltd, 1995-2004; Managing Director (Scotland & Ireland), News International Newspapers, 2004-07; Chairman, St Columba's School, Kilmacolm, 2011-15; Chairman, Scottish Opera, 2008-14 (Vice-Chairman, 2004-07, Director, 2003-14); Chairman, Saints and Sinners, 2009-11; Chairman, Glasgow, UNESCO City of Music, 2008-12; Non-Executive Director, Scottish Enterprise, 2004-09 (Chairman, Nomination and Remuneration Committees), Beattie Communications, 2007-08, Dunfermline Press Group, 2007-08; Chairman, The Kemsley Agency, 2008-10; Life Vice President, Newspaper Press Fund (Chairman West of Scotland District, 1998-2000); Chairman, Institute of Directors, Scotland, 2002-04 (Chairman West of Scotland Branch, 2001-02); Director, Scottish Networks International, 2001-03; Director, Scottish Enterprise Glasgow, 2002-04; Chairman Scottish Society of Epicureans, 2002-04; President, Queens University Association Scotland, 2003-05. Clubs: Saints and Sinners, since 2001; Founder Member, Edinburgh Oyster Club, 2003. Recreations: family; golf; cooking; opera; theatre.

Source: Who's Who in Scotland 2018

APPENDIX 2 - GLOSSARY OF ACCRONYMS

ACSEF	Aberdeen City and Shires Economic Future
BNPC	British Newspaper Printing Corporation
BT	Belfast Telegraph Newspapers Ltd.
CAI	Coleraine Academical Institution
EG	Evening Gazette, Teesside
GAEA	Glasgow Association of Estate Agents
IAB	Scottish Enterprise International Advisory Board
IoD	Institute of Directors
ICAS	Institute of Chartered Accountants Scotland
INSEAD	European Institute of Business Administration
JPL	Johnston Press Limited
MCC	Maxwell Communications Corporation
MGN	Mirror Group Newspapers Ltd.
NCJ	Newcastle Chronicle & Journal Ltd.
News Corp.	News Corporation, parent group of News International
NI	News International Newspapers Ltd., part of News Corp.
NGN	News Group Newspapers
	(The Sun and The News of the World)
NINS	News International Newspapers (Scotland) Ltd.
NNI	National Newspapers of Ireland
NPF	The Newspaper Press Fund
OSCR	Office of the Scottish Charity Regulator
QUB	The Queen's University of Belfast
SAC	Scottish Arts Council
SDR	Scottish Daily Record and Sunday Mail Ltd.
SE	Scottish Enterprise
SEG	Scottish Enterprise Glasgow
SO	Scottish Opera
SRC	Student Representative Council QUB
SRS	Scottish Road Services
St. C	St. Columba's School, Kilmacolm
STV	Scottish Television
TNL	Times Newspapers Ltd. (The Times and The Sunday Times)
TRN	Thomson Regional Newspapers Ltd.
TVN	Thames Valley Newspapers Ltd, Reading

Further copies of this book can be ordered through visiting **www.colinmcclatchie.com**
or **William Anderson & Sons Ltd** on **0044+ 141 440 2881**